eKNOW 2016

The Eighth International Conference on Information, Process, and Knowledge Management

April 24 - 28, 2016

Venice, Italy

eKNOW 2016 Editors

Conceição Granja, Norwegian Centre for Integrated Care and Telemedicine, University Hospital of North Norway, Norway

Roy Oberhauser, Aalen University, Germany

Lubomir Stanchev, Cal Poly/Computer Science, USA

Dirk Malzahn, Dirk Malzahn Ltd. / HfH University, Germany

Printed from e-media with permission by:

Curran Associates, Inc.
57 Morehouse Lane
Red Hook, NY 12571

proceedings.com

Some format issues inherent in the e-media version may also appear in this print version.

Printed by Curran Associates, Inc. (2016)

International Academy, Research, and Industry Association (IARIA)
412 Derby Way
Wilmington, DE 19810

Phone: (408) 893-6407
Fax: (408) 527-6351

petre@iaria.org

Additional copies of this publication are available from:

Curran Associates, Inc.
57 Morehouse Lane
Red Hook, NY 12571 USA
Phone: 845-758-0400
Fax: 845-758-2633
Email: curran@proceedings.com
Web: www.proceedings.com

TABLE OF CONTENTS

EKNOW 6: KNOWLEDGE IDENTIFICATION AND DISCOVERY

eKNOW 2016

Forward

The Eighth International Conference on Information, Process, and Knowledge Management (eKNOW 2016) was held between April 24 and April 28, 2016 in Venice, Italy. The event was driven by the variety of the systems and applications and the heterogeneous nature of information and knowledge representation, requiring special technologies to capture, manage, store, preserve, interpret and deliver the content and documents related to a particular target.

Progress in cognitive science, knowledge acquisition, representation, and processing helped to deal with imprecise, uncertain or incomplete information. Management of geographical and temporal information became a challenge, in terms of volume, speed, semantic, decision, and delivery.

Information technologies allow optimization in searching and interpreting data, yet special constraints imposed by the digital society require on-demand, ethics, and legal aspects, as well as user privacy and safety.

Nowadays, there is notable progress in designing and deploying information and organizational management systems, experts systems, tutoring systems, decision support systems, and in general, industrial systems.

Capturing, representing, and manipulating knowledge was and still is a fascinating and extremely useful challenge from both the theoretical and the practical perspective. Using validated knowledge for information and process management, as well as for decision support mechanisms, raises a series of questions the conference was aimed at.

The conference had the following tracks:

- Decision support systems
- Knowledge fundamentals
- Information and process management
- Knowledge semantics processing and ontology
- Knowledge management systems
- Knowledge identification and discovery

We take here the opportunity to warmly thank all the members of the eKNOW 2016 technical program committee, as well as the numerous reviewers. The creation of such a high quality conference program would not have been possible without their involvement. We also kindly thank all the authors that dedicated much of their time and effort to contribute to eKNOW 2016. We truly believe that, thanks to all these efforts, the final conference program consisted of top quality contributions.

Also, this event could not have been a reality without the support of many individuals, organizations and sponsors. We also gratefully thank the members of the eKNOW 2016 organizing committee for their help in handling the logistics and for their work that made this professional meeting a success.

We hope eKNOW 2016 was a successful international forum for the exchange of ideas and results between academia and industry and to promote further progress in the field of information, process and knowledge management. We also hope that Venice, Italy, provided a pleasant environment during the conference and everyone saved some time to enjoy the unique charm of the city.

eKNOW Advisory Committee

Dirk Malzahn, Dirk Malzahn Ltd. / HfH University, Germany
Roy Oberhauser, Aalen University, Germany
Conceição Granja, Norwegian Centre for Integrated Care and Telemedicine, University Hospital of North Norway, Norway

eKNOW Special Area Chairs

Technological foresight and socio-economic evolution modelling

Andrzej M.J. Skulimowski, AGH University of Science and Technology - Krakow, Poland

eKNOW 2016

Committee

eKNOW Advisory Committee

Dirk Malzahn, Dirk Malzahn Ltd. / HfH University, Germany
Roy Oberhauser, Aalen University, Germany
Conceição Granja, Norwegian Centre for Integrated Care and Telemedicine, University Hospital of North Norway, Norway

eKNOW Special Area Chairs

Technological foresight and socio-economic evolution modelling
Andrzej M.J. Skulimowski, AGH University of Science and Technology - Krakow, Poland

eKNOW 2016 Technical Program Committee

Gil Ad Ariely, Interdisciplinary Center Herzliya (IDC), Israel
Panos Alexopoulos, iSOCO, Spain
Jesus Manuel Almendros Jimenez, Universidad de Almería, Spain
Amin Anjomshoaa, Vienna University of Technology, Austria
Annalisa Appice, University of Bari Aldo Moro, Italy
Zbigniew Banaszak, Warsaw University of Technology, Poland
Ladjel Bellatreche, LISI- ENSMA/ Poitiers University, France
Peter Bellström, Karlstad University, Sweden
Jorge Bernardino, Polytechnic Institute of Coimbra, Portugal
Yaxin Bi, University of Ulster - Jordanstown, UK
Marco Bianchi, Fondazione Ugo Bordoni, Italy
Grzegorz Bocewicz, Koszalin University of Technology, Poland
Khalil Bouzekri, MIMOS Berhad, Malaysia
Martine Cadot, University of Nancy1, France
Massimiliano Caramia, University of Rome "Tor Vergata", Italy
Salem Chakhar, PBS - University of Portsmouth, UK
Yu Cheng, IBM TJ Watston Research Center, USA
Chi-Hung Chi, CSIRO, Australia
Dickson K.W. Chiu, Dickson Computer Systems, Hong Kong
Paolo Cintia, University of Pisa, Italy
Marco Cococcioni, University of Pisa, Italy
Ting Deng, Beihang University, China
Ioan Despi, University of New England, Australia
Chiara Di Francescomarino, Fondazione Bruno Kessler (FBK), Italy

Ali Eydgahi, Eastern Michigan University, USA
Francesca Fallucchi, Guglielmo Marconi University, Italy
Abed Alhakim Freihat, University of Trento, Italy
Elvis Fusco, Centro Universitário Eurípides de Marília – UNIVEM, Brazil
Susan Gauch, University of Arkansas, USA
Lorraine Goeuriot, LIG - Université Grenoble Alpes, France
Conceição Granja, Norwegian Centre for Integrated Care and Telemedicine, University Hospital of North Norway, Norway
Gregory Grefenstette, Exalead, France
Pierre Hadaya, ESG UQAM, Canada
Preben Hansen, University of Illinois, Urbana-Champaign, USA / Stockholm University, Sweden
Georges Hebrail, Electricité De France (EDF) R&D, France
Daniela Hossu, University 'Politehnica' of Bucharest, Romania
Lili Jiang, NEC Laboratories Europe, Heidelberg, Germany
Vana Kalogeraki, Athens University of Economics and Business, Greece
Khaled Khelif, EADS- Val de Reuil, France
Daniel Kimmig, Landesanstalt für Umwelt, Messungen und Naturschutz Baden-Württemberg (LUBW), Germany
Marite Kirikova, Riga Technical University, Latvia
Frank Klawonn, Ostfalia University of Applied Sciences, Germany
Tomomi Kobayashi, Waseda University, Japan
Andrew Kusiak, The University of Iowa, USA
Franz Lehner, University of Passau, Germany
Johannes Leveling, CNGL, Ireland
Elżbieta Lewanska, Poznan University of Economics, Poland
Chee-Peng Lim, Deakin University, Australia
Dickson Lukose, MIMOS-Berhad, Malaysia
Dirk Malzahn, Dirk Malzahn Ltd. / HfH University, Germany
Philippe Marchildon, Université du Québec, Montreal, Canada
Mohammed Ameen Marghlani, King Abdulaziz University, Saudi Arabia
Luis Martínez López, University of Jaén, Spain
Bruno Martins, University of Lisbon | IST & INESC-ID, Portugal
Marco Mevius, HTWG Konstanz, Germany
Toshiro Minami, Kyushu Institute of Information Sciences, Japan
Anirban Mondal, University of Tokyo, Japan
Yasuhiko Morimoto, Hiroshima University, Japan
Mirco Nanni, ISTI-CNR, Italy
Roy Oberhauser, Aalen University, Germany
Olasunkanmi Olajide, Federal University of Agriculture, Nigeria
Daniel O'Leary, University of Southern California, USA
Jonice Oliveira, Federal University of Rio de Janeiro (UFRJ), Brazil
Joanna Isabelle Olszewska, University of Gloucestershire, United Kingdom
Sethuraman Panchanathan, Arizona State University, USA
Andreas Papasalouros, University of the Aegean - Samos, Greece

Ludmila Penicina, Riga Technical University, Latvia
Tuan D. Pham, The University of Aizu - Aizu-Wakamatsu, Japan
Lukas Pichl, International Christian University, Japan
Edy Portmann, Institute of Information Systems - University of Bern, Switzerland
Przemysław Pukocz, P&B Foundation / AGH University of Science and Technology, Poland
Lukasz Radlinski, West Pomeranian University of Technology, Poland
P.Krishna Reddy, International Institute of Information Technology Hyderabad (IIITH), India
Ulrich Reimer, University of Applied Sciences St. Gallen, Switzerland
Pierre N. Robillard, Polytechnique Montréal, Canada
Fariba Sadri, Imperial College of Science, Technology and Medicine, UK
Aitouche Samia, University Hadj Lakhdar Batna, Algeria
Jagannathan Sarangapani, Missouri University of Science and Technology, USA
Dobrica Savic, International Atomic Energy Agency, Austria
Erwin Schaumlechner, Tiscover GmbH - Hagenberg, Austria
Giovanni Semeraro, University of Bari "Aldo Moro", Italy
Jungpil Shin, University of Aizu, Japan
Andrzej M. Skulimowski, AGH University of Science and Technology, Poland
Lubomir Stanchev, California Polytechnic State University (Cal Poly), USA
Ryszard Tadeusiewicz, AGH University of Science and Technology, Poland
Masakazu Takahashi, Yamaguchi University, Japan
Carlo Tasso, Università di Udine, Italy
Takao Terano, Tokyo Institute of Technology, Japan
I-Hsien Ting, National University of Kaohsiung, Taiwan
Jan Martijn van der Werf, Utrecht University, Netherlands
Robert van Doesburg, Immigration and Naturalization Service of the Netherlands (IND), Netherlands
Stefanos Vrochidis, Information Technologies Institute, Greece
Da-Wei Wang, Institute of Information Science - Academia Sinica, Taiwan
Haibo Wang, Texas A&M International University, USA
Hongzhi Wang, Harbin Institute of Technology, China
Hans Weigand, Tilburg University, Netherlands
Peter Wiedmann, HTWG Konstanz, Germany
Shengli Wu, University of Ulster - Newtownabbey, Northern Ireland, UK
Takahira Yamaguchi, Keio University, Japan
Dayu Yuan, Google Machine Intelligence, USA
Mansour Esmaeil Zaei, Panjab University, India

Copyright Information

Performance Indicators for Business Rule Management

Martijn Zoet
Optimizing Knowledge-Intensive Business Processes
Zuyd University of Applied Sciences
Sittard, the Netherlands
martijn.zoet@zuyd.nl

Koen Smit
Digital Smart Services
HU University of Applied Sciences Utrecht
Utrecht, the Netherlands
koen.smit@hu.nl

Eline de Haan
Centre for Application Development
Dutch Tax and Customs Administration
Utrecht, the Netherlands
ey.de.haan@belastingdienst.nl

***Abstract*— With increasing investments in business rules management (BRM), organizations are searching for ways to value and benchmark their processes to elicitate, design, accept, deploy and execute business rules. To realize valuation and benchmarking of previously mentioned processes, organizations must be aware that performance measurement is essential, and of equal importance, which performance indicators to apply to the performance measurement processes. However, scientific research on BRM, in general, is limited and research that focuses on BRM in combination with performance indicators is nascent. The purpose of this paper is to define performance indicators for previously mentioned BRM processes. We conducted a three round focus group and three round Delphi Study which led to the identification of 14 performance indicators. Presented results provide a grounded basis from which further, empirical, research on performance indicators for BRM can be explored.**

Keywords-Business Rules Management; Business Rules; Performance Measurement; Performance Indicator.

I. INTRODUCTION

Business rules are an important part of an organization's daily activities. Many business services nowadays rely heavily on business rules to express assessments, predictions and decisions [2][15]. A business rule is [11] "*a statement that defines or constrains some aspect of the business intending to assert business structure or to control the behavior of the business.*" Most organizations experience three challenges when dealing with business rules management: 1) consistency challenges, 2) impact analysis challenges, and 3) transparency of business rule execution. A consistent interpretation of business rules ensures that different actors apply the same business rules, and apply them consistently. This is a challenge since business rules are often not centralized, but they are embedded in various elements of an organization's information system instead. For example, business rules are embedded in minds of employees, part of textual procedures, manuals, tables, schemes, business process models, and hard-coded as software applications. Impact assessment determines the impact of changes made to business rules and the effect on an existing implementation. Currently, impact assessments can take significant time which results in situations where the business rules already have changed again while the impact assessment is still ongoing [1]. Transparency, or business rules transparency, indicates that organizations should establish a system to prove which business rules are applied at a specific moment in time. To tackle the previously mentioned challenges and to improve grip on business rules, organizations search for a systematic and controlled approach to support the discovery, design, validation and deployment of business rules [2][21]. To be able to manage or even address these challenges, insight has to be created concerning business rule management processes at organizations. This can be achieved using performance management, which can provide insight into an organization's current situation, but can also point towards where and how to improve. However, research on performance management concerning BRM is nascent.

The measurement of performance has always been important in the field of enterprise management and, therefore, has been of interest for both practitioners and researchers. Performance systems are applied to provide useful information to manage, control and improve business processes. One of the most important tasks of a performance management system is to identify (and properly) evaluate suitable Performance Indicators (PI's). The increase of interest and research towards identifying the right set of indicators has led to 'standard' frameworks and PI's tailored to industry or purpose. Examples of such frameworks are the balanced scorecard, total quality management framework, and seven-S model [9][18]. Moreover, research on standard indicators is increasingly performed for the sales and manufacturing processes. To the knowledge of the authors, research which focuses on performance measures for BRM is absent. This article extends the understanding of performance measurement with regard to the BRM processes. To be able to do so, the following research question is addressed: "*Which performance indicators are useful to measure the BRM processes?*"

This paper is organized as follows: In section two we provide insights into PI's and BRM. This is followed by a description of the research method used to construct our artifact in section three. Furthermore, the analysis of our research results is described in section four. Subsequently, our results which led to our Performance Indicators for BRM are presented section five. Finally, in section six we discuss which conclusions can be drawn from our results, followed by a critical view of the research method and results of our study.

II. Related Work and Background

The aim of using a performance measurement system is to provide a closed loop control system in line with predefined business objectives. In scientific literature and industry, an abundance of performance management systems exists [6]. Although a lot of performance systems exist, in general, they can be grouped into four base types [9]: 1) consolidate and simulate, 2) consolidate and manage, 3) innovate and stimulate, and 4) innovate and manage. The predefined business objectives, and, therefore, the creation of the closed loop control system, differ per base-type. In the remainder of this section, first the four performance measurement system base-types will be discussed after which the registration of a single performance measure will be presented. Subsequently, the processes will be discussed for which the performance management system is created. The last paragraph will focus on bringing all elements together.

Performance measurement systems of the first base-type, *consolidate and stimulate,* are utilized to measure and stimulate the current system performance. The formulation process of PI's is usually performed with employees that work with the system, possibly in combination with direct management, and is, therefore, a bottom-up approach. Examples of this type of performance measurement system are the "control loop system" or "business process management system". Performance measurement systems, that focus purely on measuring and maintaining the current performance level, are classified as the second base-type *consolidate and manage.* Consolidate and manage is a purely top-down approach in which PI's are formulated by top management based on the current strategy. Each PI defined by the top-management is translated into multiple different underlying PI's by each lower management level. Two examples of performance measurement systems of this type are "management by objectives" and "quality policy development".

The third base-type, *innovate and stimulate*, focuses on the customer and the product or service delivered to the customer by the organization. To define the PI's, first the quality attributes of the product or service delivered to the customer need to be defined. Based on these quality attributes, PI's for each business process that contributes to the product or service is defined. An example of a performance measurement system of this type is Quality Function Deployment (QFD). The fourth base-type, *innovate and manage*, focuses on the future of the organization while managing the present. It is a top-down approach in which PI's are formulated, based on the strategy of the organization. Furthermore, these PI's are then translated to the lower echelons of the organization. Furthermore, PI's that are used to manage the current state of the organization are specified. The combination of both measures is used to make sure that the company is performing well while at the same time steering it into the future. An example of this performance measurement system type is the Balanced Score Card.

In addition to choosing the (combination of) performance measurement system(s), the individual performance indicators (PI's) of which the performance measurement system is composed have to be defined. A PI is defined as: "*an authoritative measure, often in quantitative form, of one or multiple aspects of the organizational system.*" Scholars as well as practitioners debate on which characteristics must be registered with respect to PI's [8][14]. Comparative research executed by [14] identified a set of five characteristics each scholar applies: 1) the PI must be derived from objectives, 2) the PI must be clearly defined with an explicit purpose, 3) the PI must be relevant and easy to maintain, 4) the PI must be simple to understand, and 5) the PI provide fast and accurate feedback.

The performance measurement system in this paper is developed for the elicitation, design, acceptation, deployment, and execution process of BRM. A detailed explanation of the BRM processes can be found in [23]. However, to ground our research a summary is provided here. The value proposition (end result) of a business rule set is delivered when the business rule set is executed. Business rule sets can provide the following value propositions: classification, assessments, diagnosis, monitoring, prediction, configuration design, modelling, planning, scheduling, and assignment [3]. Before the business rule set can be executed, it first needs to be elicitated, designed, accepted, and deployed. The elicitation process exists out of two main tasks: determining the scope and identifying sources. In the task *determining scope*, the value proposition of the business rule set is determined. After the scope has been determined, the data sources that influence the business rule set have to be identified. Data sources can be sources such as human experts, documentation, laws, and regulation. After the data sources have been determined the design process starts which consists of five phases. First, the scope is decomposed by means of a business rules architecture. The business rules architecture is a structure which decomposes scope in multiple fine-grained modular business rule sets that adhere to the single responsibility principle [11]. The purpose of the context architecture is to create a normalized business rule set in which individual business rule set can be changed without affecting other parts. For example, the scope is "determine candidate profile" which can be composed into multiple business rule sets: "determine candidate personality rating", "determine candidate cognitive rating", and "candidate maturity rating." After the business rule architecture is created it is verified (to check for semantic / syntax errors) and validated (to check for errors in its intended behavior). After the validation of the business rules architecture, a fact model and the business rules are defined for each individual business rule set. Furthermore, the verification and validation of the fact model and business rules take place per business rule set. After each individual business rule set has been validated, also, the scope (the combination of business rule sets) as a whole is validated. Until this moment, the scope, business rule sets, business rules and fact models have been modelled in an implementation-independent language. An implementation-independent language is considered as: "*a language that is not tailored to be applicable to a specific information system*" [23]. An implementation dependent language, on the other hand, is defined as: "*a language that is tailored to be applicable to a specific information system*" [23]. Implementation dependent business rule languages have a specific grammar which can only be interpreted by a specific system. Examples of such systems are [19] and [20]. The translation from an implementation-independent language to an implementation dependent language is the goal of the deployment process. The last BRM process is the execution process which transforms a platform specific rule model into the value proposition it must deliver.

BRM is a process that deals with the elicitation, design, acceptation, deployment, and execution process of business rules within an organization to support and improve its business performance. Organizations are realizing that business rules are crucial resources that should be managed to stay competitive and innovative. Since no absolute measurement exists to measure the success of BRM as whole as well as individual BRM processes in an organization, this research will focus on identifying PI's from the perspective of the first base-type, *consolidate and stimulate*. This implies that we will apply a bottom-up approach and will involve employees working on business rules and their direct management. Our focus per PI will be on the characteristics as defined by [8]: 1) derived from objectives, 2) clearly defined with an explicit purpose, 3) relevant and easy to maintain, 4) simple to understand, and 5) provide fast and accurate feedback.

III. RESEARCH METHOD

The goal of this research is to identify performance measurements that provide relevant insight into the performance of the elicitation, design, acceptation, deployment, and execution process of business rules. In addition to the goal of the research, also, the maturity of the research field is a factor in determining the appropriate research method and technique. The maturity of the BRM research field, with regard to none-technological research, is nascent [10][15][23]. Focus of research in nascent research fields should lie on identifying new constructs and establishing relationships between identified constructs [5]. Summarized, to accomplish our research goal, a research approach is needed in which a broad range of possible performance measurements are explored and combined into one view in order to contribute to an incomplete state of knowledge.

Adequate research methods to explore a broad range of possible ideas / solutions to a complex issue and combine them into one view when a lack of empirical evidence exists consist of group-based research techniques [4][13][16][17]. Examples of group based techniques are Focus Groups, Delphi Studies, Brainstorming and the Nominal Group Technique. The main characteristic that differentiates these types of group-based research techniques from each other is the use of face-to-face versus non-face-to-face approaches. Both approaches have advantages and disadvantages, for example, in face-to-face meetings, provision of immediate feedback is possible. However, face-to-face meetings have restrictions with regard to the number of participants and the possible existence of group or peer pressure. To eliminate the disadvantages, we combined the face-to-face and non-face-to-face technique by means of applying the following two group based research approaches: the Focus Group and Delphi Study.

IV. DATA COLLECTION AND ANALYSIS

Data for this study is collected over a period of six months, through three rounds of focus groups (round 1, 2 and 3: experts focus group) and a three-round Delphi study (round 4, 5 and 6 Delphi study), see Figure 1. Between each individual round of focus group and Delphi Study, the researchers consolidated the

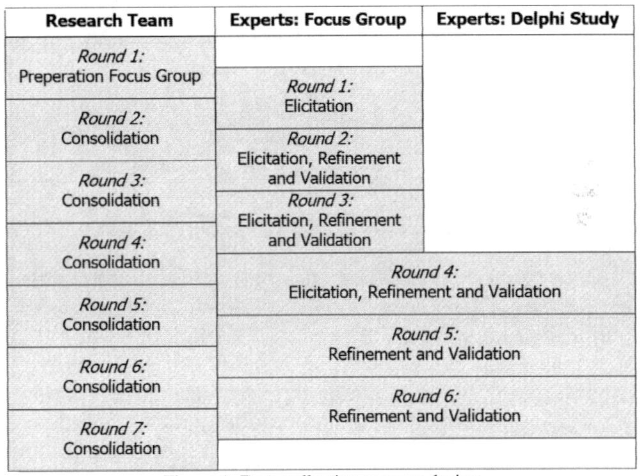

Figure 1. Data collection process design

results (round 1, 2, 3, 4, 5, 6 and 7: research team). Both methods of data collection are further discussed in the remainder of this section.

A. Focus Groups

Before a focus group is conducted, a number of key issues need to be considered: 1) the goal of the focus group, 2) the selection of participants, 3) the number of participants, 4) the selection of the facilitator, 5) the information recording facilities, and 6) the protocol of the focus group. The goal of the focus group was to identify performance measurements for the performance of the elicitation, design, acceptation, deployment, and execution process of business rules. The selection of the participants should be based on the group of individuals, organizations, information technology, or community that best represents the phenomenon studied [22]. In this study, organizations and individuals that deal with a large amount of business rules represent the phenomenon studied. Such organisations are often financial and government institutions. During this research, which was conducted from September 2014 to November 2014, five large Dutch government institutions participated. Based on the written description of the goal and consultation with employees of each government institution, participants were selected to take part in the three focus group meetings. In total, ten participants took part who fulfilled the following positions: two enterprise architects, two business rules architects, three business rules analysts, one project manager, and two policy advisors. Each of the participants had, at least, five years of experience with business rules. Delbecq and van de Ven [4] and Glaser [7] state that the facilitator should be an expert on the topic and familiar with group meeting processes. The selected facilitator has a Ph.D. in BRM, has conducted 7 years of research on the topic, and has facilitated many (similar) focus group meetings before. Besides the facilitator, five additional researchers were present during the focus group meetings. One researcher participated as 'back-up' facilitator, who monitored if each participant provided equal input, and if necessary, involved specific participants by asking for more in-depth elaboration on the subject. The remaining four researchers acted as a minute's secretary taking field notes. They did not intervene in the process; they operated from the sideline. All focus groups were video and audio recorded. A focus group meeting took on average three and a half hour. Each focus group meeting followed the same overall protocol, each starting with an introduction and explanation of the purpose and procedures of the meeting, after which ideas were generated, shared, discussed and/or refined.

Prior to the first round, participants were informed about the purpose of the focus group meeting and were invited to submit their current PI's applied in the BRM process. When participants had submitted PI's, they had the opportunity to elaborate upon their PI's during the first focus group meeting. During this meeting, also, additional PI's were proposed. For each proposed PI, the name, goal, specification and measurements were discussed and noted. For some PI's, the participants did not know which specifications or measurements to use. These elements were left blank and agreed to deal with during the second focus group meeting. After the first focus group, the researchers consolidated the results. Consolidation comprised the detection of double PI's, incomplete PI's, conflicting goals and measurements. Double PI's exist in two forms: 1) identical PI's and 2) PI's which are textually different, but similar on the conceptual level. The results of the consolidation were sent to the participants of the focus group two weeks in advance for the second focus group meeting. During these two weeks, the participants assessed the consolidated results in relationship to four questions: 1) "Are all PI's described correctly?", "2) Do I want to remove a PI?" 3) "Do we need additional PI's?", and 4) "How do the PI's affect the design of a business rule management solution?". This process of conducting focus group meetings, consolidation by the researchers and assessment by the participants of the focus group was repeated two more times (round 2 and round 3). After the third focus group meeting (round 3), saturation within the group occurred leading to a consolidated set of PI's.

B. Delphi Study

Before a Delphi study is conducted, also a number of key issues need to be considered: 1) the goal of the Delphi study, 2) the selection of participants, 3) the number of participants, and 4) the protocol of the Delphi study. The goal of the Delphi study was twofold. The first goal was to validate and refine existing PI's identified in the focus group meetings, and the second goal was to identify new PI's. Based on the written description of the goal and consultation with employees of each organization, participants were selected to take part in the Delphi study. In total, 36 participants took part. Twenty-six experts, in addition to the ten experts that participated in the focus group meetings, of the large Dutch government institutions were involved in the Delphi Study, which was conducted from November 2014 to December 2014. The reason for involving the ten experts from the focus groups was to decrease the likelihood of peer-pressure amongst group members. This is achieved by exploiting the advantage of a Delphi Study which is characterized by a non-face-to-face approach. The twenty-six additional participants involved in the Delphi Study had the following positions: three project managers, four enterprise architects, ten business rules analyst, five policy advisors, two IT-architects, six business rules architects, two business consultants, one functional designer, one tax advisor, one legal advisor, and one legislative author. Each of the participants had, at least, two years of experience with business rules. Each round (4, 5, and 6) of the Delphi Study followed the same overall protocol, whereby each participant was asked to assess the PI's in relationship to four questions: 1) "Are all PI's described correctly?", "2) Do I want to remove a PI?" 3) "Do we need additional PI's?", and 4) "How do the PI's affect the design of a BRM solution?"

V. RESULTS

In this section, the overall results of this study are presented. Furthermore, the final PI's are listed. Each PI is specified using a specific format to convey their characteristics in a unified way.

TABLE I. EXAMPLE OF PI RESULT: TIME MEASUREMENT TO DEFINE, VERIFY, AND VALIDATE A BUSINESS RULE.

PI 09: The amount of time units needed to define, verify, and validate a single business rule. **Goal**: Shortening the time needed to deliver defined, verified, and validated business rules.	
S	The number of time units per selected single business rule: • Measured over the entire collection of context designs; • During the design process; • (Sorted by selected context design); • (Sorted by selected complexity level of a business rule); • (Sorted by selected scope design); • (Sorted by selected time unit).
M	• Context design • Business rule • Complexity level of a business rule • Scope design • Time unit

Before the first focus group was conducted, participants were invited to submit the PI's they currently use. This resulted in the submission of zero PI's. Since this result can imply a multitude of things (e.g. total absence of the phenomena researched or unmotivated participants), further inquiry was conducted. The reason that no participants submitted PI's was because none of the participants had a formal performance measurement system in place. Some measured BRM processes but did so in an ad-hoc and unstructured manner. The first focus group meeting resulted in 24 PI's. This first focus group meeting also had one interesting side-discussion: can a PI be configured to monitor specific individuals? For example, "*the number of incorrectly written business rules per business rule analyst.*" Since the discussion became quite heated during the meeting, it was decided that each expert would think about and reflect on this question outside the group and that this discussion would be continued in the next focus group meeting.

After analyzing the results of the first focus group the 24 PI's were sent to the participants of the second focus group. During the second focus group, the participants started to discuss the usefulness of the PI's and the fact that too many PI's is also not a good thing. This resulted in the removal of ten conceptual PI's. Ten PI's were discarded because they did not add value to the performance measurement process concerning BRM. This resulted into 14 remaining PI's, which had to be further analyzed by the researchers. Also, the discussion about the PI's formulated to measure specific individuals was continued. At the end, only three experts thought this was reasonable and useful. The other seven disagreed and found it not useful which has led to the exclusion of PI's targeted at a specific individual.

During the third focus group, the participants discussed the remaining 14 final PI's which led to the further refinement of goals, specifications, and measurements. Additionally, the subject-matter experts expressed a certain need to categorize PI's into well-known phases within the development process of business rules at the case companies. From the 14 remaining PI's, nine PI's were categorized as business rule design PI's, two PI's were categorized as business rule deployment PI's, and three PI's were categorized as business rules execution PI's.

After the third focus group, the 14 PI's were subjected to the Delphi Study participants. In each of the three rounds, no additional PI's were formulated by the 26 experts. However, during the first two rounds, the specification and measurement elements of multiple PI's were refined. During the third round, which was also the last round, no further refinements were proposed and participants all agreed to the 14 formulated PI's which are presented in table 2.

TABLE II. PI'S DERIVED FOR BRM.

PI 01: The frequency of corrections per selected context design emerging from the verification process.

> **Goal:** Improve upon the design process of business rules.

PI 02: The frequency of corrections per selected context design, emerging from the verification process, per business analyst and per type of verification error.

> **Goal**: Improving the context design.

PI 03: The frequency of corrections per selected context design emerging from the validation process per complexity level of a business rule.

> **Goal**: Improve upon the design process of business rules.

PI 04: The frequency of corrections per selected context design emerging from the validation process per type of validation error.

> **Goal**: Improve upon the validation process for the benefit of improving the context design.

PI 05: The frequency of corrections per selected context architecture emerging from the design process per scope design.

> **Goal**: Improve upon the design process for the benefit of improving the context architecture.

PI 06: The frequency of instantiations per selected context design

> **Goal**: Provide insight into the possible instances of a context design.

PI 07: The frequency per selected type of validation error.

> **Goal**: Improve upon the design process for the benefit of improving the context design.

PI 08: The frequency per selected type of verification error

> **Goal**: Improve upon the design process for the benefit of improving the context design.

PI 09: The number of time units required to define, verify, and validate a single business rule.

> **Goal**: Shortening the lead time of a business rule with regard to the design process.

PI 10: The frequency of deviations between an implementation dependent context design and an implementation independent context design.

> **Goal**: Improve upon the deployment process.

PI 11: The frequency of executions of an implementation dependent business rule.

> **Goal**: Gaining insight into which business rules are executed.

PI 12: The frequency of execution variants of a scope design.

> **Goal**: Gaining insight into which decision paths are traversed to establish different decisions.

PI 13: The number of time units required for the execution per execution variant.

> **Goal**: Shortening the lead time of an execution process with regard to enhancing an execution variant.

PI 14: The amount of business rules that cannot be automated.

> **Goal**: Provide insight into which business rules cannot be automated.

Analyzing the defined PI's showed that three out of fourteen (PI 11, 12, and 14) are PI's that can be classified as *'innovate and manage'* PI's. PI eleven and twelve focus on the number of times a business rule is executed. Thereby providing insight in which business rules are most applied. PI twelve goes beyond that and shows which variants of business rules are executed. In other words, it shows the characteristics of the decision based on which citizens get services. This insight can be used to determine how many and which citizens are affected by changing specific laws (and, therefore, business rules). In other words, this can be used to further support the development of law. PI fourteen indicated the amount of business rules that cannot be automated and that needs to be executed manually. This can also provide an indication of the amount of workload that organisations encounter due to the manual execution of these specific business rules. This PI can be used to decide if these business rules should be executed manually or that they should be reformulated in such a manner that they can be executed mechanically.

VI. DISCUSSION, CONCLUSION, AND FUTURE WORK

From a research perspective, our study provides a fundament for PI measurement and benchmarking of the elicitation, design, acceptance, deployment, and execution processes of BRM. Several limitations may affect our results. The first limitation is the sampling and sample size. The sample group of participants is solely drawn from government institutions in the Netherlands. While we believe that government institutions are representative for organisations implementing business rules, further generalization towards non-governmental organizations amongst others is a recommended direction for future research. Taken the sample size of 36 participants into account, this number needs to be increased in future research as well. This research focused on identifying new constructs and establishing relationships given the current maturity of the BRM research field. Although the research approach chosen for this research type is appropriate given the present maturity of the research domain, research focusing on further generalization must apply different research methods such as qualitative research methods which also allow incorporating a larger sample size in future research regarding PI's for BRM.

This research investigated PI's for the elicitation, design, acceptance, deployment and execution of business rules with the purpose of answering the following research question: "*Which performance measurements are useful to measure the BRM processes?*" To accomplish this goal, we conducted a study combining a three round focus group and three round Delphi Study. Both were applied to retrieve PI's from participants, 36 in total, employed by governmental institutions. This analysis revealed fourteen PI's. We believe that this work represents a further step in research on PI's for BRM and maturing the BRM field as a whole.

REFERENCES

[1] M. Alles, G. Brennan, A. Kogan, M. Vasarhelyi, "Continuous monitoring of business process controls: A pilot implementation of a continuous auditing system at Siemens," International Journal of Accounting Information Systems, 7, 2006, 137-161. doi: 10.1016/j.accinf.2005.10.004

[2] J. Boyer, H. Mili, "Agile Business Rules Development: Process, Architecture and JRules Examples," Heidelberg: Springer, 2011.

[3] J. Breuker, W. Van De Velde, "CommonKADS Library for Expertise Modelling: reusable problem-solving components," Amsterdam: IOS Press/Ohmsha, 1994.

[4] A. L. Delbecq, A. H. Van de Ven, "A group process model for problem identification and program planning," The Journal of Applied Behavioral Science, 7(4), 1971, 466-492.

[5] A. Edmondson, S. McManus, "Methodological Fit in Management Field Research," Academy of Management Review, 32(4), 2007, 1155-1179.

[6] M. Franco-Santos, L. Lucianetti, M. Bourne, "Contemporary performance measurement systems: A review of their consequences and a framework for research," Management Accounting Research, 23(2), 2012, 79-119.

[7] B. Glaser, "Theoretical Sensitivity: Advances in the Methodology of Grounded Theory," Mill Valley, CA: Sociology Press, 1978.

[8] M. Hudson, A. Smart, M. Bourne, "Theory and practice in SME performance measurement systems," International Journal of Operations & Production Management, 21(8), 2001, 1096-1115.

[9] L. Kerklaan, "The cockpit of the organization: performance management with scorecards," Deventer: Kluwer, 2007.

[10] A. Kovacic, "Business renovation: business rules (still) the missing link," Business Process Management Journal, 10(2), 2004, 158-170.

[11] R. Martin, "Agile Software Development: Principles, Patterns and Practices," New York, 2003.

[12] T. Morgan, "Business rules and information systems: aligning IT with business goals," London: Addison-Wesley, 2002.

[13] M. K. Murphy, N. Black, D. L. Lamping, C. M. McKee, C. F. B. Sanderson, J. Askham, "Consensus development methods and their use in clinical guideline development," Health Technology Assessment, 2(3), 1998, 31-38.

[14] A. Neely, H. Richards, H. Mills, K. Platts, M. Bourne, "Designing performance measures: a structured approach," International Journal of Operations and Production, 17(11), 1997, 1131-1152.

[15] M. L. Nelson, J. Peterson, R. L. Rariden, R. Sen, "Transitioning to a business rule management service model: Case studies from the property and casualty insurance industry," Information & Management, 47(1), 2010, 30-41.

[16] C. Okoli, S. D. Pawlowski, "The Delphi method as a research tool: an example, design considerations and applications," Information & Management, 42(1), 2004, 15-29.

[17] R. Ono, D. J. Wedemeyer, "Assessing the validity of the Delphi technique," Futures, 26(3), 1994, 289-304.

[18] V. Owhoso, S. Vasudevan, "A balanced scorecard based framework for assessing the strategic impacts of ERP systems," Computers in Industry, 56, 2005, 558-572.

[19] Pegasystems, "Pega Decision Management Optimize Your Business Processes with Real-Time Decisioning," Retrieved March, 2016, from https://www.pega.com/products/pega-7-platform/decision-hub

[20] Progress Software, "Progress Software – Corticon," Retrieved March, 2016, from https://www.progress.nl/corticon.

[21] R. Ross, "Business Rule Concepts," Houston: Business Rule Solutions, LLC, 2009.

[22] A. Strauss, J. Corbin, "Basics of qualitative research: Grounded theory procedures and techniques," Newbury Park: Sage Publication, INC, 1990.

[23] M. M. Zoet, "Methods and Concepts for Business Rules Management," Utrecht: Hogeschool Utrecht, 2014.

A Literature Review of Methods for Dengue Outbreak Prediction

Duc Nghia Pham*, Syahrul Nellis†, Arun Anand Sadanand*, Juraina binti Abd. Jamil†, Jing Jing Khoo†, Tarique Aziz*, l Dickson Lukose*, Sazaly bin Abu Bakar† and Abdul Sattar‡
*MIMOS Berhad, Malaysia
†TIDREC, University of Malaya, Malaysia
‡IIIS, Griffith University, Australia
Email: nghia.pham@mimos.my, syahrul.nellis@mimos.my, arun.anand@mimos.my, juraina@um.edu.my, jing.khoo@um.edu.my, tarique.aziz@mimos.my, dickson.lukose@mimos.my, sazaly@um.edu.my, a.sattar@griffith.edu.au

***Abstract*—This review provides the current dengue surveillance situation including (i) the factors that contribute to dengue transmission and (ii) the method to combat the disease. Dengue fever now is the most common mosquito-borne disease that infected around 100 billion population, mostly from Asia Pacific. This alboviral disease not only worsens people's health, but also has a great social and economic impact in areas where these endemics arise. Currently, the transmission of this disease is influenced not only by the climatic factors (e.g., rainfall, temperature, wind speed and humidity) but also by non-climatic factors like socio-environmental factors (e.g., population density, land use activity, vector control and transportation). Previously, prevention methods such as vector control, were used by public health agencies in combating the transmission of dengue outbreak. Recently, with the improvement of knowledge and technology, new methods and models are developed, not only for detection but also for prediction of dengue trends and outbreaks. An effective prediction model would be particularly helpful to detect unusual occurrences of disease and to allow for targeted surveillance and control efforts of the disease. In this paper, we review and summarize the development of dengue outbreak tools by researchers in the Asia Pacific region.**

Keywords–Dengue Outbreak Prediction, Statistical Analysis, Spatial Analysis, Machine Learning

I. Introduction

Dengue is a mosquito-borne viral disease that has rapidly spread in all regions of the world in recent years. This arboviral disease is transmitted by two main vectors, which are Aedes Aegypti and Ae. Albopictus [1]. Both mosquitoes have adjusted to human neighborhood with larval habitats and ovipositor in natural and artificial (e.g., rock pools, tree holes, blocked drains, pot plants and food and beverage containers, and leaf axis) collections in the urban and peri-urban environment [2].

Dengue can be brought on by any of four viral serotypes (Dengue Virus (DENV) 14), and is transmitted by day-biting urban-adapted Aedes mosquito species [3]. After an incubation period ranging from 4 to 14 days, patients normally can encounter a range of symptoms, from a sub-clinical disease to debilitating but transient Dengue Fever (DF) to life-threatening Dengue Hemorrhagic Fever (DHF) or Dengue Shock Syndrome (DSS) [4] [5]. The most severe forms of dengue disease are DHF and DSS. They are life debilitating, and youngsters with DENV disease are especially at danger of advancing to severe DHF/DSS [6]. Until now there is no specific treatment or vaccine for dengue.

DF is a major public health concern and also re-emerging infectious disease that affects millions of people worldwide. It is also a major public health concern for over half of the world's population and is a main source of hospitalization and death especially for youngsters in endemic nations. The majority of the poor nations are particularly vulnerable to the transmission of dengue infection [6]. This vector borne disease always can be found in urban and suburban areas of regions such as Africa, South-East Asia, Americas, Eastern Mediterranean and Western Pacific [7]. It is assessed that consistently, there are 70500 million dengue infections, 36 million cases of DF and 21 million cases of DHF and DSS, with more than 20000 deaths per year [7].

An expected 50 million cases of dengue diseases occur annually and approximately 2.5 billion people live in dengue endemic countries [8]. Other than that, DF inflicts a significant health, economic, and social burden on the populations of these endemic areas. A scientific working group report on dengue published by the World Health Organization (WHO) shows that nearly 75% of the global disease burden is due to dengue [9]. Demographic change, urbanization, deficient local water supplies, relocation led to an increase in the global incidence of dengue and about 3.6 billion people are currently at risk [10]. These parameters can also be defined as non-climatic parameters that have an impact on the dengue outbreak. But other researches also found that the spread and establishment of dengue is also mainly facilitated by a changing climate around the world [11].

The rest of this paper is organized as follow: Section II provides an overview of different types of dengue data that were used in previous studies. Section III outlines several climatic and non-climatic factors that were commonly used in previous studies for dengue outbreak prediction. Section IV then summarizes and describes different techniques for dengue outbreak prediction from the three main streams: (i) spatial analysis, (ii) statistical and mathematical analysis, and (iii) machine learning. Finally, the paper discusses potential directions for future work in Section V and summarizes the conclusion in Section VI.

II. Dengue Data

Dengue data is very important to dengue surveillance study since it can trace and identify the dengue incident from the dengue data results. For this review, we considered the data for both DF and DHF cases as 'dengue incident'. In many dengue epidemiology studies, the dengue incident data that was collected either in hospitals or medical centers can be classified into 3 groups, namely suspected, probable and confirmed cases [4]. A suspected case is a clinically compatible case of dengue-like illness, dengue, or severe dengue with an epidemiological linkage. A probable case is a clinically compatible case of dengue-like illness, dengue, or severe dengue with laboratory results indicative of probable infection. Lastly, a confirmed case was a clinically compatible case of dengue-like illness, dengue, or severe dengue with confirmatory laboratory results. A confirmed case refers to a dengue case that was confirmed by the serological tests IgM capture enzyme-linked immunosorbent assay (ELISA) with single positive IgM in the lab [12]. Most research reviewed in this paper used the suspected and confirmed cases.

III. Dengue Factors

Identifying key factors that contribute to dengue infection is very valuable in controlling and predicting dengue outbreaks. In this section, we review and summarize the key climatic and non-climatic factors that were found to have an impact on the spread of dengue.

A. Climatic Factor

Over the last decade, the climatic changes around the globe have had a major impact on the transmission of dengue. Climate change happens when there is an increase in greenhouse gases that make the air and Earth's surface warmer. This actually happens when there is a high concentration of greenhouse gases in the atmosphere, including carbon dioxide, methane, and nitrous oxide. This is due mainly to human factors, for example, the utilization of fossil fuel, changes in the use of an area, and agriculture [13]–[15]. These changes will have an influence on the dynamic pattern of climate variables around the world, especially the temperature, rainfall, precipitation and humidity, and extreme weather occurrences such as El Nino Southern Oscillation (ENSO) [16]–[18].

Studies have demonstrated that a change in these factors can influence various aspects of the arthropod vector's life cycle and survival, the arthropod population, vector pathogen interactions, pathogen replication, vector behavior and, of course, vector distribution [19] [20]. For example, temperature increases not only effect the reproduction and mosquito activity, but also decrease the incubation time of larvae [16]–[19]. Various studies recorded different lag times for the larva incubation period ranging from 4 to 16 weeks [17] [21]–[24]. The increase in the larva incubation period will exacerbate the rate at which mosquito vectors transmit the disease.

Extremely hot temperatures also impact the DF expansion by extending the season in which transmission occurs [25] [26]. This occurs when lengthy drought conditions exist in endemic areas without a stable drinking water supply. The storage of drinking water increase the number of breeding sites for the mosquito vector [27] [28]. These extremely high temperatures are also a result of the climate change phenomena and ENSO cycles. Among the studies reviewed, the ENSO phenomena were associated with local temperature and precipitation changes. It was showed that a decrease in ENSO could result in an increased temperature and decreased rainfall leading to increased water stockpiling. This favors mosquito reproducing places and, in this way, increases dengue transmission [16] [29] [30].

The changes in the world climate have also impacted rainfall trends, and, in combination with the temperature increase, it becomes the main regulator of evaporation that directly affects the availability of water habitats [31]. Rainfall itself, can influence the conditions in the case of both high and low precipitation. In the high precipitation conditions, it can flush away eggs, hatchlings, and pupae from compartments in the short term [32] [33]. In the longer term situation, residual water can create breeding habitats, thereby expanding the adult mosquito population [34]. For the low rainfall condition, together with dry temperature it can lead to human behavior of saving water in water storage containers, which may become breeding sites for Ae. Aegypti [35] [36]. In the end, climatic conditions can be seen affecting the virus, the vector and human behavior both directly and indirectly.

Looking into the previous research from years before, especially the association between climatic factors and the transmission of dengue, we can see that there is a link between them either in a positive or negative correlation [37]–[44]. However, the connection between dengue and the climatic factors still remains debatable because of the potential influence of other socio-demographic factors that can have an impact on dengue transmission [13] [45]–[47].

B. Non-Climatic Factor

In recent years, a few authors have begun looking at several non-climatic factors, such as, human growth, human movement, and socioeconomic constraints as effect to dengue transmission [20] [45] [48] [49]. A recent study done by Gubler [50] shows that the growing population in developing countries became a contributing factor to the increase of dengue transmission and expansion. This unprecedented population growth, mostly in high density population area may provide new man-made breeding sites through discarded automobile tires, non-biodegradable plastics, cell phones, and tin [51] [52]. These consumer products will become ideal breeding sites for the most potent dengue vector, A. aegypti. Finally the increasing density of A. aegypti mosquito population combined with increased human populations contributed to the transmission of dengue in urban area. The effect of human growth factor can also be dangerous when it is combined with the rapid urbanization process that actively happens in the urban areas, especially in low and middle income countries [20] [53].

Rapid urbanization not only contributes to the population explosion but also has an impact on people's socioeconomic behavior in urban and suburban areas. Recent studies found that non-climatic factors, such as housing types, poor garbage disposal, poor water storage, and cross-border travel, strongly correlate to the number of dengue cases [12] [54]–[56]. It was also showed that other socioeconomic factors, such as low level of education and low coverage of infrastructure, can contribute to the number of dengue cases in urban areas [57]–[59]. People who live in high population density areas are highly vulnerable to dengue infection because of poor housing conditions and/or the lack of public services, such as inadequate drainage or improper sanitation system [60]–[62]. Indeed, several residual water containers, which are key mosquito breeding sites, are naturally or artificially created in these areas. Thus, poor living conditions play an important role in the spread of dengue [46] [63] [64].

In addition, it was showed that the geographical distribution of dengue is potentially influenced by travel and trade factors [7] [54] [65]. Urbanization has increased the population mobility and consequently contributes to the spread of dengue between urban and rural areas [25] [66]. Globally, increases in international passengers were identified as the main cause for dengue transmission between countries and continents [67]. This is very dangerous because an infected immigrant or visitor from a dengue-endemic country can carry a new virus strain into another country and causes a dengue spread [47] [68]. Global trade was also identified as one main driver in the global transmission of dengue [66] [69]. Indeed, the higher the number of cargo and goods are transported around the world, the higher the chance mosquitoes carrying the virus arrive in a new place that has suitable environmental conditions for their survival and breeding.

IV. Research Method

As discussed in the previous section, there are several factors that have an impact on a dengue outbreak. Several methods have been developed and studied to comprehend the complex relationship between these factors and dengue in order to accurately predict the number of dengue cases for better prevention and/or proactive mitigation. In general, the existing methods for dengue outbreak prediction that we reviewed can be classified into three groups: (i) spatial analysis, (ii) statistical and mathematical analysis, and (iii) machine learning system.

A. Spatial Analysis

Kernel density is the most popular method that is used in dengue transmission studies in the geographical epidemiology field [70]–[73]. This method was applied to identify and map out hotspots with a high concentration of reported dengue cases [74]. It can detect dengue clusters and generate risk maps based on the correlation with climatic and non-climatic factors. Another popular method is Geographically Weighted Regression (GWR) [75]. It can predict the risk levels of a dengue outbreak and identify the spatial dependency between DF cases and the factors involved [76] [77]. In addition, Local Indicators of Spatial Autocorrelation (LISA) has been used to study the impact of climatic and non-climatic factors on dengue transmission [78] [79]. LISA can be regarded as a spatial risk index to identify both significant spatial clusters and outliers [80]. Thus, it is often used to examine the spatial temporal patterns of the spread of dengue.

Recently, the integration of spatial statistics and non-spatial statistics has become more prominent. Although spatial statistics can improve the comprehension of dengue surveillance by enhancing the detection of patterns , users can potentially misinterpret the results. Integration of both statistical approaches not only maintains the visualization advantage of spatial statistics but also enables the testing of statistical significance of relationships between dengue parameters and the number of dengue incidents. In our review, spatial statistical analysis was mostly integrated with linear regression techniques, such as logistic regression and Poisson regression [81]–[84].

B. Statistical and Mathematical Analysis

Infectious dengue surveillance and control efforts encompass a wide variety of fields and require integration, synthesis, and analysis of information. This requirement can be met by the application of quantitative analysis, especially the combination of different analytical models. The past decade has witnessed a large increase in dengue research activities on statistical and mathematical methods. Following an apparent trend in surveillance research, statistical methods have become popular in dengue outbreak detection and control, especially in generating early warning of dengue outbreaks. A statistical model can be defined as an empirical relationship between the location of known virus occurrences and a set of underlying parameters, such as climatic and non-climatic variables [85] [86].

The two most popular statistical approaches that are used in the dengue studies are regression and time series techniques. The regression technique is a method that has two functions, one for detecting outbreaks in surveillance process that support the basis of laboratory reports, and second is for syndrome surveillance. The regression technique commonly used by the clinical and epidemiological researchers is Poisson regression [18] [87]–[90]. It is normally used to analyze the correlation between the number of dengue cases and one or more dengue factors in order to predict the number of future dengue cases [91]. Poisson regression, using a Generalized Additive Model (GAM), was often used when dealing with nonlinear data as it can improve the prediction accuracy by automatically calculating the optimal degree of nonlinearity of the model directly from the data [92]–[94].

A part from that, time series methods were also commonly used by the researchers to find the variable that have an impact on dengue incidents. This approach has been widely used in the early detection of infectious disease outbreaks, especially focusing on the emerging or re-emerging infections. Unlike other statistical approaches, this type of analysis was chosen based on the assumption that the incidence of infectious diseases is related to the previous incidence and the population at risk [95]. One of the most popular time series methods for studying the correlation between dengue and its variables is the Autoregressive Integrated Moving Average (ARIMA) method [96]–[99]. The advantage of this method is that it can provide a comprehensive set of tools for arrangement model distinguishing proof, parameter estimation, and gauging. In addition, it offers incredible adaptability in investigation, which is added to its prevalence in a few dengue research.

The ARIMA model can be extended to handle occasional parts of an information arrangement. The seasonal ARIMA (SARIMA) model is an extension of ARIMA to an arrangement in which a pattern repeats seasonally over time. This statistical model is particularly interesting when there are time conditions between observations [100]. The assumption that each observation is associated to past ones makes it possible to model a temporal structure, with more dependable expectations, particularly for regular diseases [101] [102]. The example research that used this model can be seen in the study done in Thailand and India [49] [103] [104].

Recently, numerical procedure has been progressively used as an alternative to statistical models to interpret and anticipate the number of future infectious diseases. Many complex mathematical models have been developed to predict the occurrence, dynamics and magnitude of dengue outbreaks using a combined environmental and biological approach. These models have the capability to produce an useful approximation and thus enable the conduction of conceptual experiments that would otherwise be difficult or impossible. Mathematical models allow precise, rigorous analysis and quantitative prediction of dengue transmission and outbreak [105] [106]. Examples of mathematical models that were applied in the dengue surveillance research are the Susceptible-Infected-Recovered (SIR) model and its extensions [107]–[109].

C. Machine learning system

Technology improvement, in the computer science field, already gives a new hope in the dengue surveillance research and study. As mentioned in the previous section, statistical methods have been widely used in dengue outbreak prediction. Given a specific theory, statistical tests can be applied to epidemiological data to check whether any correlations can be found between different parameters. However, machine learning systems can do much more. A machine learning system can automatically hypothesize and derive the associations of dengue factors directly from the raw data. The advantage of this approach is that it can be used to develop the knowledge bases used by expert systems. Given a set of clinical cases, a machine learning system can produce a systematic description of those clinical features that uniquely characterize the clinical conditions. Several machine learning approaches have been used to predict dengue outbreaks, such as Artificial Neural Network (ANN), Alternating Decision Tree Method (ADT), Support Vector Machine (SVM), Fuzzy Inference System (FIS) and its hybrid model called Adaptive Neuro-Fuzzy Inference System (ANFIS) [110]–[116]. This new approach has a potential role to play in the development of dengue prediction and it will be great importance to the relevant decision makers who are typically responsible for budgets and manpower in the public health sector.

V. Future Work

Research into dengue surveillance methods has increased dramatically over the last two decades. Many new methods are designed for specific monitoring systems or still in experimental and developmental stages and not used in real practical surveillance. From the past research, this review has noted that there's need to an advancement of tools to assist dengue prevention and control. Tools like [117] allow scientists to easily model data and apply different spatio-temporal kriging techniques. The combination between spatial, statistical and mathematical analysis together with machine learning system can become a holistic solution to this problem. This hybrid application has the potential to understand the complex relationship between climatic factors, non-climatic factors and dengue, and thereby can obtain better prediction. As information sorts and sources turn out to be progressively vast and complex, there's need to procedures to coordinate dissimilar and frequently inadequate information into fitting tools. This obstacle can be solved by using Big Data Analytic (BDA). Big Data is a term used to portray data arrays that make customary information, or database, preparing risky due to any combination of their size, frequency of updated, or diversity [118]. The research team of IBM, teamed up with the university researchers, used BDA to predict the outbreak of deadly diseases such as dengue fever and malaria [119]. Another research on the application of BDA in dengue study was carried out by the Telenor group in collaboration with Oxford University, the U.S. Center for Disease Control, and the University of Peshawar [120]. Looking to the sources of data collection, there's need to a new platform for catering the information with current vast technology. The online data sources such as social media networking like Twitter and Facebook can become new valuable data sources and can assist the epidemiologist on real-time dengue scenario. With this new technology, dengue cases mostly the under reported cases can be captured and it can overcome the problem such as the accessibility to public health center.

VI. Conclusion

The improvement of dengue prediction frameworks holds incredible potential for enhancing general well-being through right on time cautioning and checking of infection. There are numerous perspectives to consider when pondering techniques for dengue observation. A hefty portion of the routines depicted in this survey are dynamic zones of exploration and new strategies are continually being produced. As more information sources get to be accessible, this pattern is relied upon to proceed, and the systems depicted here give a preview of alternatives accessible to general well-being investigators and specialists. We trust that it is essential to create, utilize and coordinate spatial, factual and scientific examination together with machine learning framework approaches for dengue transmission perfect with long haul information on atmosphere and non-climatic changes and this would propel projections of the effect of both components on dengue transmission. With progressing upgrades in the information and philosophies, these studies will assume an inexorably essential part in our comprehension of the perplexing connections in the middle of environment and well-being.

Acknowledgment

This research was supported by the Science Fund Grant 01-03-04-SF0061 by the Ministry of Science, Technology & Innovation Malaysia (MOSTI).

References

[1] V. R. Louis, R. Phalkey, O. Horstick, P. Ratanawong, A. Wilder-Smith, Y. Tozan, and P. Dambach, "Modeling tools for dengue risk mapping - a systematic review," International journal of health geographics, vol. 13, no. 1, 2014, p. 50.

[2] P. Cattand, P. Desjeux, M. Guzmán, J. Jannin, A. Kroeger, A. Médici, P. Musgrove, M. B. Nathan, A. Shaw, and C. Schofield, "Tropical diseases lacking adequate control measures: dengue, leishmaniasis, and African trypanosomiasis," in Disease Control Priorities in Developing Countries, 2nd ed., D. Jamison, J. Breman, A. Measham, G. Alleyne, M. Claeson, D. Evans, P. Jha, A. Mills, and P. Musgrove, Eds. Washington (DC): World Bank, 2006.

[3] S. Karl, N. Halder, J. K. Kelso, S. A. Ritchie, and G. J. Milne, "A spatial simulation model for dengue virus infection in urban areas," BMC infectious diseases, vol. 14, no. 1, 2014, p. 447.

[4] World Health Organization and the Special Programme for Research and Training in Tropical Diseases, Dengue: guidelines for diagnosis, treatment, prevention and control. World Health Organization, 2009.

[5] World Health Organization, Dengue haemorrhagic fever: diagnosis, treatment and control. World Health Organization, 1986.

[6] S. Bhatt, P. W. Gething, O. J. Brady, J. P. Messina, A. W. Farlow, C. L. Moyes, J. M. Drake, J. S. Brownstein, A. G. Hoen, and O. Sankoh, "The global distribution and burden of dengue," Nature, vol. 496, no. 7446, 2013, pp. 504–507.

[7] D. J. Gubler, P. Reiter, K. L. Ebi, W. Yap, R. Nasci, and J. A. Patz, "Climate variability and change in the United States: potential impacts on vector-and rodent-borne diseases," Environmental health perspectives, vol. 109, no. Suppl 2, 2001, p. 223.

[8] D. S. Shepard, E. A. Undurraga, R. S. Lees, Y. Halasa, L. C. S. Lum, and C. W. Ng, "Use of multiple data sources to estimate the economic cost of dengue illness in Malaysia," The American journal of tropical medicine and hygiene, vol. 87, no. 5, 2012, pp. 796–805.

[9] Special Programme for Research & Training in Tropical Diseases (TDR), "Scientific working group report on dengue," Geneva, Switzerland: World Health Organization, 2007.

[10] D. S. Shepard, R. Lees, C. W. Ng, E. A. Undurraga, Y. Halasa, and L. Lum, "Burden of Dengue in Malaysia. Report from a Collaboration between Universities and the Ministry of Health of Malaysia," Unpublished report, 2013.

[11] J. A. Patz, W. Martens, D. A. Focks, and T. H. Jetten, "Dengue fever epidemic potential as projected by general circulation models of global climate change," Environmental Health Perspectives, vol. 106, no. 3, 1998, p. 147.

[12] S. Thammapalo, V. Chongsuvivatwong, A. Geater, and M. Dueravee, "Environmental factors and incidence of dengue fever and dengue haemorrhagic fever in an urban area, Southern Thailand," Epidemiology and Infection, vol. 136, no. 01, 2008, pp. 135–143.

[13] S. Hales, N. De Wet, J. Maindonald, and A. Woodward, "Potential effect of population and climate changes on global distribution of dengue fever: an empirical model," The Lancet, vol. 360, no. 9336, 2002, pp. 830–834.

[14] K. Nakhapakorn and N. K. Tripathi, "An information value based analysis of physical and climatic factors affecting dengue fever and dengue haemorrhagic fever incidence," International Journal of Health Geographics, vol. 4, no. 1, 2005, p. 13.

[15] M. L. Parry, Climate Change 2007: impacts, adaptation and vulnerability: contribution of Working Group II to the fourth assessment report of the Intergovernmental Panel on Climate Change. Cambridge University Press, 2007, vol. 4.

[16] B. Cazelles, M. Chavez, A. J. McMichael, and S. Hales, "Nonstationary influence of El Nino on the synchronous dengue epidemics in Thailand," PLoS Med, vol. 2, no. 4, 2005, p. e106.

[17] Y. Hsieh and C. Chen, "Turning points, reproduction number, and impact of climatological events for multiwave dengue outbreaks," Tropical Medicine & International Health, vol. 14, no. 6, 2009, pp. 628–638.

[18] Y. L. Hii, H. Zhu, N. Ng, L. C. Ng, and J. Rocklöv, "Forecast of dengue incidence using temperature and rainfall," PLoS Negl Trop Dis, vol. 6, no. 11, 2012, p. e1908.

[19] G. Kuno, "Review of the factors modulating dengue transmission," Epidemiologic reviews, vol. 17, no. 2, 1995, pp. 321–335.

[20] D. J. Gubler, "Epidemic dengue/dengue hemorrhagic fever as a public health, social and economic problem in the 21st century," Trends in microbiology, vol. 10, no. 2, 2002, pp. 100–103.

[21] J. A. Patz, P. R. Epstein, T. A. Burke, and J. M. Balbus, "Global climate change and emerging infectious diseases," Jama, vol. 275, no. 3, 1996, pp. 217–223.

[22] P. Arcari, N. Tapper, and S. Pfueller, "Regional variability in relationships between climate and dengue/DHF in Indonesia," Singapore Journal of Tropical Geography, vol. 28, no. 3, 2007, pp. 251–272.

[23] M. Karim, S. U. Munshi, N. Anwar, and M. Alam, "Climatic factors influencing dengue cases in Dhaka city: a model for dengue prediction," The Indian journal of medical research, vol. 136, no. 1, 2012, p. 32.

[24] A. L. Buczak, B. Baugher, S. M. Babin, L. C. Ramac-Thomas, E. Guven, Y. Elbert, P. T. Koshute, J. M. S. Velasco, V. G. Roque Jr, and E. A. Tayag, "Prediction of high incidence of dengue in the Philippines," PLoS Negl Trop Dis, vol. 8, no. 4, 2014, p. e2771.

[25] A. K. Githeko, S. W. Lindsay, U. E. Confalonieri, and J. A. Patz, "Climate change and vector-borne diseases: a regional analysis," Bulletin of the World Health Organization, vol. 78, no. 9, 2000, pp. 1136–1147.

[26] J. A. Patz and W. K. Reisen, "Immunology, climate change and vector-borne diseases," Trends in immunology, vol. 22, no. 4, 2001, pp. 171–172.

[27] O. Caldern-Arguedas, A. Troyo, M. E. Solano, A. Avendao, and J. C. Beier, "Urban mosquito species (Diptera: Culicidae) of dengue endemic communities in the Greater Puntarenas area, Costa Rica," Revista de biologia tropical, vol. 57, no. 4, 2009, p. 1223.

[28] O. Wan-Norafikah, W. Nazni, S. Noramiza, S. Shafaar-KoOhar, S. Heah, A. Nor-Azlina, M. Khairuh-Asuad, and H. Lee, "Distribution of aedes mosquitoes in three selected localities in Malaysia," Sains Malays, vol. 41, 2012, pp. 1309–1313.

[29] S. Hales, P. Weinstein, Y. Souares, and A. Woodward, "El Nino and the dynamics of vectorborne disease transmission," Environmental Health Perspectives, vol. 107, no. 2, 1999, p. 99.

[30] M. Tipayamongkholgul, C.-T. Fang, S. Klinchan, C.-M. Liu, and C.-C. King, "Effects of the El Nio-Southern Oscillation on dengue epidemics in Thailand, 1996-2005," BMC Public Health, vol. 9, no. 1, 2009, p. 422.

[31] J. Chompoosri, U. Thavara, A. Tawatsin, S. Anantapreecha, and P. Siriyasatien, "Seasonal monitoring of dengue infection in Aedes aegypti and serological feature of patients with suspected dengue in 4 central provinces of Thailand," Thai J Vet Med, vol. 42, no. 2, 2012, pp. 185–193.

[32] K. N. Kolivras, "Changes in dengue risk potential in Hawaii, USA, due to climate variability and change," Climate Research, vol. 42, no. 1, 2010, pp. 1–11.

[33] L. K. Wee, S. N. Weng, N. Raduan, S. K. Wah, W. H. Ming, C. H. Shi, F. Rambli, C. J. Ahok, S. Marlina, and N. W. Ahmad, "Relationship between rainfall and Aedes larval population at two insular sites in Pulau Ketam, Selangor, Malaysia," Southeast Asian J Trop Med Public Health, vol. 44, 2013, pp. 157–166.

[34] A. Troyo, D. O. Fuller, O. CaldernArguedas, M. E. Solano, and J. C. Beier, "Urban structure and dengue incidence in Puntarenas, Costa Rica," Singapore journal of tropical geography, vol. 30, no. 2, 2009, pp. 265–282.

[35] S. Thammapalo, V. Chongsuwiwatwong, A. Geater, A. Lim, and K. Choomalee, "Socio-demographic and environmental factors associated with Aedes breeding places in Phuket, Thailand," Southeast Asian Journal of Tropical Medicine and Public Health, vol. 36, no. 2, 2005, p. 426.

[36] Y. L. Cheong, K. Burkart, P. J. Leito, and T. Lakes, "Assessing weather effects on dengue disease in Malaysia," International journal of environmental research and public health, vol. 10, no. 12, 2013, pp. 6319–6334.

[37] Y. Nagao, U. Thavara, P. Chitnumsup, A. Tawatsin, C. Chansang, and D. CampbellLendrum, "Climatic and social risk factors for Aedes infestation in rural Thailand," Tropical Medicine & International Health, vol. 8, no. 7, 2003, pp. 650–659.

[38] A. Chakravarti and R. Kumaria, "Eco-epidemiological analysis of dengue infection during an outbreak of dengue fever, India," Virol J, vol. 2, no. 1, 2005.

[39] V. Wiwanitkit, "An observation on correlation between rainfall and the prevalence of clinical cases of dengue in Thailand," Journal of vector borne diseases, vol. 43, no. 2, 2006, p. 73.

[40] P.-C. Wu, H.-R. Guo, S.-C. Lung, C.-Y. Lin, and H.-J. Su, "Weather as an effective predictor for occurrence of dengue fever in Taiwan," Acta tropica, vol. 103, no. 1, 2007, pp. 50–57.

[41] J. C. Semenza and B. Menne, "Climate change and infectious diseases in europe," The Lancet infectious diseases, vol. 9, no. 6, 2009, pp. 365–375.

[42] R. C. Dhiman, S. Pahwa, G. Dhillon, and A. P. Dash, "Climate change and threat of vector-borne diseases in India: are we prepared?" Parasitology Research, vol. 106, no. 4, 2010, pp. 763–773.

[43] H.-L. Yu, S.-J. Yang, H.-J. Yen, and G. Christakos, "A spatio-temporal climate-based model of early dengue fever warning in southern Taiwan," Stochastic Environmental Research and Risk Assessment, vol. 25, no. 4, 2011, pp. 485–494.

[44] C.-M. Liao, T.-L. Huang, Y.-J. Lin, S.-H. You, Y.-H. Cheng, N.-H. Hsieh, and W.-Y. Chen, "Regional response of dengue fever epidemics to interannual variation and related climate variability," Stochastic Environmental Research and Risk Assessment, vol. 29, no. 3, 2015, pp. 947–958.

[45] W. J. H. McBride, H. Mullner, R. Muller, J. Labrooy, and I. Wronski, "Determinants of dengue 2 infection among residents of Charters

Towers, Queensland, Australia," American journal of epidemiology, vol. 148, no. 11, 1998, pp. 1111–1116.

[46] D. Vlahov, N. Freudenberg, F. Proietti, D. Ompad, A. Quinn, V. Nandi, and S. Galea, "Urban as a determinant of health," Journal of Urban Health, vol. 84, no. 1, 2007, pp. 16–26.

[47] J. O'Shea and M. R. Niekus, "Potential social, economic, and health impacts of dengue on Florida," Advance Tropical Medicine and Public Health International, vol. 3, no. 2, 2013, pp. 32–64.

[48] M. Coosemans and J. Mouchet, "Consequences of rural development on vectors and their control," in Annales de la Société Belge de Médecine Tropicale, vol. 70, no. 1, 1990, Conference Proceedings, pp. 5–23.

[49] M. S. Sitepu, J. Kaewkungwal, N. Luplerdlop, N. Soonthornworasiri, T. Silawan, S. Poungsombat, and S. Lawpoolsri, "Temporal patterns and a disease forecasting model of dengue hemorrhagic fever in Jakarta based on 10 years of surveillance data," The Southeast Asian journal of tropical medicine and public health, vol. 44, no. 2, 2013, pp. 206–217.

[50] D. J. Gubler, "Dengue, urbanization and globalization: the unholy trinity of the 21st century," Tropical medicine and health, vol. 39, no. 4 Suppl, 2011, p. 3.

[51] J. M. Hayes, E. Garca-Rivera, R. Flores-Reyna, G. Surez-Rangel, T. Rodrguez-Mata, R. Coto-Portillo, R. Baltrons-Orellana, E. Mendoza-Rodriguez, B. F. DE GARAY, and J. Jubis-Estrada, "Risk factors for infection during a severe dengue outbreak in El Salvador in 2000," The American journal of tropical medicine and hygiene, vol. 69, no. 6, 2003, pp. 629–633.

[52] S. Ma, E. E. Ooi, and K. T. Goh, "Socioeconomic determinants of dengue incidence in Singapore," Dengue Bulletin, vol. 32, 2008, pp. 17–28.

[53] A. Mondini and F. Chiaravalloti Neto, "Socioeconomic variables and dengue transmission," Revista de Sade Pblica, vol. 41, no. 6, 2007, pp. 923–930.

[54] A. Wilder-Smith and D. J. Gubler, "Geographic expansion of dengue: the impact of international travel," Medical Clinics of North America, vol. 92, no. 6, 2008, pp. 1377–1390.

[55] M. M. Ramos, H. Mohammed, E. Zielinski-Gutierrez, M. H. Hayden, J. L. R. Lopez, M. Fournier, A. R. Trujillo, R. Burton, J. M. Brunkard, and L. Anaya-Lopez, "Epidemic dengue and dengue hemorrhagic fever at the TexasMexico border: results of a household-based seroepidemiologic survey, December 2005," The American journal of tropical medicine and hygiene, vol. 78, no. 3, 2008, pp. 364–369.

[56] H. Padmanabha, D. Durham, F. Correa, M. Diuk-Wasser, and A. Galvani, "The interactive roles of Aedes aegypti super-production and human density in dengue transmission," PLoS Negl Trop Dis, vol. 6, no. 8, 2012, p. e1799.

[57] A. J. McMichael, "The urban environment and health in a world of increasing globalization: issues for developing countries," Bulletin of the World Health Organization, vol. 78, no. 9, 2000, pp. 1117–1126.

[58] T. Kjellstrom, S. Friel, J. Dixon, C. Corvalan, E. Rehfuess, D. Campbell-Lendrum, F. Gore, and J. Bartram, "Urban environmental health hazards and health equity," Journal of urban health, vol. 84, no. 1, 2007, pp. 86–97.

[59] M. Hagenlocher, E. Delmelle, I. Casas, and S. Kienberger, "Assessing socioeconomic vulnerability to dengue fever in Cali, Colombia: statistical vs expert-based modeling," Int J Health Geogr, vol. 12, no. 36, 2013, p. 10.1186.

[60] J. B. Siqueira, C. M. Martelli, I. J. Maciel, R. M. Oliveira, M. G. Ribeiro, F. P. Amorim, B. C. Moreira, D. D. Cardoso, W. V. Souza, and A. L. S. Andrade, "Household survey of dengue infection in central Brazil: spatial point pattern analysis and risk factors assessment," The American journal of tropical medicine and hygiene, vol. 71, no. 5, 2004, pp. 646–651.

[61] R. F. Flauzino, R. Souza-Santos, C. Barcelllos, R. Gracie, M. d. A. F. M. Magalhes, and R. M. d. Oliveira, "Spatial heterogeneity of dengue fever in local studies, City of Niteri, Southeastern Brazil," Revista de Sade Pblica, vol. 43, no. 6, 2009, pp. 1035–1043.

[62] N. E. A. Murray, M. B. Quam, and A. Wilder-Smith, "Epidemiology of dengue: past, present and future prospects," Clinical epidemiology, vol. 5, 2013, p. 299.

[63] M. E. Wilson, "Infectious diseases: an ecological perspective," BMJ: British Medical Journal, vol. 311, no. 7021, 1995, p. 1681.

[64] R. Bhatia, A. P. Dash, and T. Sunyoto, "Changing epidemiology of dengue in South-East Asia," WHO South-East Asia Journal of Public Health, vol. 2, no. 1, 2013, p. 23.

[65] P. Reiter, "Climate change and mosquito-borne disease," Environmental health perspectives, vol. 109, no. Suppl 1, 2001, p. 141.

[66] L. M. Gardner, D. Fajardo, S. T. Waller, O. Wang, and S. Sarkar, "A predictive spatial model to quantify the risk of air-travel-associated dengue importation into the United States and Europe," Journal of tropical medicine, vol. 2012, 2012.

[67] D. A. Cummings, R. A. Irizarry, N. E. Huang, T. P. Endy, A. Nisalak, K. Ungchusak, and D. S. Burke, "Travelling waves in the occurrence of dengue haemorrhagic fever in Thailand," Nature, vol. 427, no. 6972, 2004, pp. 344–347.

[68] N. W. Beebe, R. D. Cooper, P. Mottram, and A. W. Sweeney, "Australias dengue risk driven by human adaptation to climate change," PLoS Negl Trop Dis, vol. 3, no. 5, 2009, p. e429.

[69] R. Romi, G. Sabatinelli, L. G. Savelli, M. Raris, M. Zago, and R. Malatesta, "Identification of a North American mosquito species, Aedes atropalpus (Diptera: Culicidae), in Italy," Journal of the American Mosquito Control Association, vol. 13, no. 3, 1997, pp. 245–246.

[70] N. C. Dom, A. H. Ahmad, Z. A. Latif, and R. Ismail, "Measurement of dengue epidemic spreading pattern using density analysis method: retrospective spatial statistical study of dengue in Subang Jaya, Malaysia, 20062010," Transactions of The Royal Society of Tropical Medicine and Hygiene, 2013, p. trt073.

[71] S. Aziz, R. Aidil, M. Nisfariza, R. Ngui, Y. Lim, W. W. Yusoff, and R. Ruslan, "Spatial density of Aedes distribution in urban areas: A case study of breteau index in Kuala Lumpur, Malaysia," J Vector Borne Dis, vol. 51, 2014, pp. 91–96.

[72] F. R. Barreto, M. G. Teixeira, M. C. Costa, M. S. Carvalho, and M. L. Barreto, "Spread pattern of the first dengue epidemic in the city of Salvador, Brazil," BMC Public Health, vol. 8, no. 1, 2008, p. 51.

[73] R. V. Araujo, M. R. Albertini, A. L. Costa-da Silva, L. Suesdek, N. C. S. Franceschi, N. M. Bastos, G. Katz, V. A. Cardoso, B. C. Castro, and M. L. Capurro, "So Paulo urban heat islands have a higher incidence of dengue than other urban areas," Brazilian Journal of Infectious Diseases, vol. 19, no. 2, 2015, pp. 146–155.

[74] A. C. Gatrell, T. C. Bailey, P. J. Diggle, and B. S. Rowlingson, "Spatial point pattern analysis and its application in geographical epidemiology," Transactions of the Institute of British geographers, 1996, pp. 256–274.

[75] C. Brunsdon, A. S. Fotheringham, and M. Charlton, "Geographically weighted regression: a method for exploring spatial nonstationarity," Encyclopedia of Geographic Information Science, 2008, p. 558.

[76] H. M. Khormi and L. Kumar, "Modeling dengue fever risk based on socioeconomic parameters, nationality and age groups: GIS and remote sensing based case study," Science of the Total Environment, vol. 409, no. 22, 2011, pp. 4713–4719.

[77] B. Baharuddin, S. Suhariningsih, and B. S. S. Ulama, "Geographically weighted regression modeling for analyzing spatial heterogeneity on relationship between dengue hemorrhagic fever incidence and rainfall in Surabaya, Indonesia," Modern Applied Science, vol. 8, no. 3, 2014, p. p85.

[78] M. Naim, "Spatial-temporal analysis for identification of vulnerability to dengue in Seremban District, Malaysia," International Journal of Geoinformatics, vol. 10, no. 1, 2014.

[79] S. Naish and S. Tong, "Hot spot detection and spatio-temporal dynamics of dengue in Queensland, Australia," ISPRS-International Archives of the Photogrammetry, Remote Sensing and Spatial Information Sciences, vol. 1, 2014, pp. 197–204.

[80] L. Anselin, "Local indicators of spatial association-LISA," Geographical analysis, vol. 27, no. 2, 1995, pp. 93–115.

[81] P. Jeefoo, N. K. Tripathi, and M. Souris, "Spatio-temporal diffusion pattern and hotspot detection of dengue in Chachoengsao Province, Thailand," International journal of environmental research and public health, vol. 8, no. 1, 2010, pp. 51–74.

[82] P.-C. Wu, J.-G. Lay, H.-R. Guo, C.-Y. Lin, S.-C. Lung, and H.-J. Su, "Higher temperature and urbanization affect the spatial patterns of

dengue fever transmission in subtropical Taiwan," Science of the total Environment, vol. 407, no. 7, 2009, pp. 2224–2233.

[83] R. Lowe, T. C. Bailey, D. B. Stephenson, R. J. Graham, C. A. Coelho, M. S. Carvalho, and C. Barcellos, "Spatio-temporal modelling of climate-sensitive disease risk: Towards an early warning system for dengue in Brazil," Computers & Geosciences, vol. 37, no. 3, 2011, pp. 371–381.

[84] A. M. Stewart-Ibarra, n. G. Muoz, S. J. Ryan, E. B. Ayala, M. J. Borbor-Cordova, J. L. Finkelstein, R. Meja, T. Ordoez, G. C. Recalde-Coronel, and K. Rivero, "Spatiotemporal clustering, climate periodicity, and social-ecological risk factors for dengue during an outbreak in Machala, Ecuador, in 2010," BMC infectious diseases, vol. 14, no. 1, 2014, p. 610.

[85] J. P. Messina, O. J. Brady, D. M. Pigott, N. Golding, M. U. Kraemer, T. W. Scott, G. W. Wint, D. L. Smith, and S. I. Hay, "The many projected futures of dengue," Nature Reviews Microbiology, 2015.

[86] N. R. Council, Under the weather: climate, ecosystems, and infectious disease. National Academies Press, 2001.

[87] E. Pinto, M. Coelho, L. Oliver, and E. Massad, "The influence of climate variables on dengue in Singapore," International journal of environmental health research, vol. 21, no. 6, 2011, pp. 415–426.

[88] A. Earnest, S. Tan, and A. Wilder-Smith, "Meteorological factors and El Nino Southern Oscillation are independently associated with dengue infections," Epidemiology and infection, vol. 140, no. 7, 2012, pp. 1244–1251.

[89] W. Hu, A. Clements, G. Williams, S. Tong, and K. Mengersen, "Spatial patterns and socioecological drivers of dengue fever transmission in Queensland, Australia," Environmental health perspectives, vol. 120, no. 2, 2012, p. 260.

[90] W. W. Fairos, W. W. Azaki, L. M. Alias, and Y. B. Wah, "Modelling dengue fever (DF) and dengue haemorrhagic fever (DHF) outbreak using poisson and negative binomial model," Int J Math Comput Sci Eng, vol. 4, 2010, pp. 809–814.

[91] C. Wang, B. Jiang, J. Fan, F. Wang, and Q. Liu, "A study of the dengue epidemic and meteorological factors in Guangzhou, China, by using a zero-inflated poisson regression model," Asia-Pacific Journal of Public Health, 2013, p. 1010539513490195.

[92] M. Bouzid, F. J. Coln-Gonzlez, T. Lung, I. R. Lake, and P. R. Hunter, "Climate change and the emergence of vector-borne diseases in Europe: case study of dengue fever," BMC public health, vol. 14, no. 1, 2014, p. 781.

[93] F. J. Colón-González, C. Fezzi, I. R. Lake, and P. R. Hunter, "The effects of weather and climate change on dengue," PLoS Negl Trop Dis, vol. 7, no. 11, 2013, p. e2503.

[94] M.-J. Chen, C.-Y. Lin, Y.-T. Wu, P.-C. Wu, S.-C. Lung, and H.-J. Su, "Effects of extreme precipitation to the distribution of infectious diseases in Taiwan, 19942008," PLoS One, vol. 7, no. 6, 2012, p. e34651.

[95] U. Helfenstein, "Boxjenkins modelling of some viral infectious diseases," Statistics in medicine, vol. 5, no. 1, 1986, pp. 37–47.

[96] M. D. Eastin, E. Delmelle, I. Casas, J. Wexler, and C. Self, "Intra-and interseasonal autoregressive prediction of dengue outbreaks using local weather and regional climate for a tropical environment in Colombia," The American journal of tropical medicine and hygiene, vol. 91, no. 3, 2014, pp. 598–610.

[97] N. C. Dom, A. A. Hassan, Z. A. Latif, and R. Ismail, "Generating temporal model using climate variables for the prediction of dengue cases in Subang Jaya, Malaysia," Asian Pacific Journal of Tropical Disease, vol. 3, no. 5, 2013, pp. 352–361.

[98] A. Earnest, S. B. Tan, A. Wilder-Smith, and D. Machin, "Comparing statistical models to predict dengue fever notifications," Computational and mathematical methods in medicine, vol. 2012, 2012.

[99] S. Promprou, M. Jaroensutasinee, and K. Jaroensutasinee, "Forecasting dengue haemorrhagic fever cases in Southern Thailand using ARIMA models," Dengue Bulletin, vol. 30, 2006, p. 99.

[100] U. Helfenstein, "The use of transfer function models, intervention analysis and related time series methods in epidemiology," International journal of epidemiology, vol. 20, no. 3, 1991, pp. 808–815.

[101] F. F. Nobre, A. B. S. Monteiro, P. R. Telles, and G. D. Williamson, "Dynamic linear model and SARIMA: a comparison of their forecasting performance in epidemiology," Statistics in medicine, vol. 20, no. 20, 2001, pp. 3051–3069.

[102] H. Trottier, P. Philippe, and R. Roy, "Stochastic modeling of empirical time series of childhood infectious diseases data before and after mass vaccination," Emerging themes in epidemiology, vol. 3, no. 1, 2006, p. 9.

[103] S. Bhatnagar, V. Lal, S. D. Gupta, and O. P. Gupta, "Forecasting incidence of dengue in Rajasthan, using time series analyses," Indian journal of public health, vol. 56, no. 4, 2012, p. 281.

[104] S. Wongkoon, M. Jaroensutasinee, and K. Jaroensutasinee, "Assessing the temporal modelling for prediction of dengue infection in northern and northeastern, Thailand," Tropical biomedicine, vol. 29, no. 3, 2012, pp. 339–348.

[105] J. E. Mazur, "Mathematical models and the experimental analysis of behavior," Journal of the Experimental Analysis of Behavior, vol. 85, no. 2, 2006, pp. 275–291.

[106] M. Choisy, J.-F. Gugan, and P. Rohani, "Mathematical modeling of infectious diseases dynamics," M Tibayrene, Encyclopedia of infectious diseases: modern methodologies, John Wiley and Sons Inc, Hoboken, 2007, pp. 379–404.

[107] M. Aguiar, R. Paul, A. Sakuntabhai, and N. Stollenwerk, "Are we modelling the correct dataset? Minimizing false predictions for dengue fever in Thailand," Epidemiology and infection, vol. 142, no. 11, 2014, pp. 2447–2459.

[108] S. Polwiang, "The seasonal reproduction number of dengue fever impacts of climate on transmission," PeerJ PrePrints, vol. 2, 2014, p. e756v1.

[109] M. Derouich and A. Boutayeb, "Dengue fever: Mathematical modelling and computer simulation," Applied Mathematics and Computation, vol. 177, no. 2, 2006, pp. 528–544.

[110] H. M. Aburas, B. G. Cetiner, and M. Sari, "Dengue confirmed-cases prediction: A neural network model," Expert Systems with Applications, vol. 37, no. 6, 2010, pp. 4256–4260.

[111] T. Faisal, M. N. Taib, and F. Ibrahim, "Neural network diagnostic system for dengue patients risk classification," Journal of medical systems, vol. 36, no. 2, 2012, pp. 661–676.

[112] V. S. H. Rao and M. N. Kumar, "A new intelligence-based approach for computer-aided diagnosis of dengue fever," Information Technology in Biomedicine, IEEE Transactions on, vol. 16, no. 1, 2012, pp. 112–118.

[113] S. A. Fathima and N. Hundewale, "Comparitive analysis of machine learning techniques for classification of arbovirus," in Biomedical and Health Informatics (BHI), 2012 IEEE-EMBS International Conference on. IEEE, 2012, pp. 376–379.

[114] A. Munasinghe, H. Premaratne, and M. Fernando, "Towards an early warning system to combat dengue," International Journal of Computer Science and Electronics Engineering, vol. 1, no. 2, 2013, pp. 252–256.

[115] A. L. Buczak, P. T. Koshute, S. M. Babin, B. H. Feighner, and S. H. Lewis, "A data-driven epidemiological prediction method for dengue outbreaks using local and remote sensing data," BMC medical informatics and decision making, vol. 12, no. 1, 2012, p. 124.

[116] T. Faisal, M. N. Taib, and F. Ibrahim, "Adaptive neuro-fuzzy inference system for diagnosis risk in dengue patients," Expert Systems with Applications, vol. 39, no. 4, 2012, pp. 4483–4495.

[117] E. Pebesma, "spacetime: Spatio-Temporal Data in R," Journal of Statistical Software, vol. 51, no. 7, 2012.

[118] J. K. Najjar, Planning for Big Data: A CIO's Handbook to the Changing Data Landscape. CreateSpace Independent Publishing Platform, 2014.

[119] IBM uses big data to predict outbreaks of dengue fever and malaria. [retrieved: September, 2015]. [Online]. Available: http://venturebeat.com/2013/09/29/ibm-uses-big-data-to-predict-outbreaks-of-dengue-fever-and-malaria/

[120] Telenor research deploys big data against dengue. [retrieved: September, 2015]. [Online]. Available: http://www.telenor.com/media/press-releases/2015/telenor-research-deploys-big-data-against-dengue/

fNIRS Neural Signal Classification of Four Finger Tasks using Ensemble Multitree Genetic Programming

Jinung An*, Jong-Hyun Lee†, Sang Hyeon Jin* and Chang Wook Ahn†

*IoT-Robot Convergence Research Division
Daegu Gyeongbuk Institute of Science & Technology (DGIST), Daegu 711-873, Republic of Korea
Email: robot@dgist.ac.kr and jinjinsh@dgist.ac.kr

†Department of Computer Engineering
Sungkyunkwan University (SKKU), Suwon 440-746, Republic of Korea
Email: ljh08375@skku.edu and cwan@skku.edu

***Abstract*—Accuracy of classification and recognition in neural signal is the most important issue to evaluate the clinical assessment or extraction of features in brain computer interface. Especially, classification of multitasks by measuring functional Near-Infrared Spectroscopy (fNIRS) is a challenging due to its low spatiotemporal resolution. To improve the classification accuracy of fNIRS neural signals for multitasks, an evolutionary computing method was proposed. Four healthy participants performed four finger tasks which are digit-active, digit-passive, thumb-active and thumb-passive. To classify the four tasks, a multitask classifier was devised by the ensemble multitree genetic programming (EMGP). The experimental results validate the performance of the proposed classifier. The comparison of the conventional and proposed classifiers at the real classification experiment shows the higher accuracy of the proposed method. Moreover, it reveals the improvement of classification accuracy when compared with conventional classifiers in the additional experiment of fifteen dataset in University of California Irvine machine learning repository. The proposed classifier can be effective to classify and recognize the fNIRS neural signals during multitasks. Moreover, the subject dependent learning can be designed for the local brain activation training based on neuro-feedback. After data learning for all classes, the subject tries to make their brain activation of an active task as similar with a passive task by the online motor-imagery with action observation. As a result, the subject is trained to concentrate his brain activation for the essential area of brain. The proposed classifier can be applied well because high classification accuracy is essential to the neuro-training system. Finally, the classification accuracy of the proposed EMGP is 5.48% higher than the average of conventional classifiers.**

Keywords–fNIRS; Classification; Finger Tasks; Neural Signal; Emsemble Learning; Mutitree Genetic Programming

I. Introduction

Paralysis from a stroke or nerve injury has a terrible effect on patients' daily life. Especially, upper limb disorders greatly affect their routine with great inconveniences. Over 30 percent of stroke survivors suffer because their hand motor ability is increasingly turning into disability, even after rehabilitation for a year [1]. The conventional rehabilitation programs only provide passive approaches to patients, but it has limited effect [2]. Currently, there are many researches for promoting the neuroplasticity by brain monitoring or neurofeedback [3]. The patients can perform the interventions more actively by neurofeedback from a brain computer interface (BCI). The first step for the neurofeedback is the neural signal classification and recognition of patients.

Many techniques allow for real-time monitoring of brain activity. Invasive approaches have been successfully employed in human primates. Although such invasive methods have a high performance, non-invasive sensors to monitor brain activity are preferred in order to widely adapt to most of clinical environments, including rehabilitation medicine. Conventional non-invasive brain recording techniques are mainly electroencephalography (EEG), functional magnetic resonance imaging (fMRI) and functional near-infrared spectroscopy (fNIRS).

EEG is the most widely used technique adopted in BCI [3]. EEG provides good time and space resolution, but it has too high sensitivity so that the noisy data requires additional pre-processing for training [4]. fMRI has also been used to interface with the human brain [3]. Although it has advantages such as high temporal and spatial resolution and whole brain coverage including the central, electro-magnetic compatibility constraints, high sensitivity to movement and high costs make it unsuitable in a common therapeutic environment. fNIRS is an optical approach that locally observes cortical activity based on the neurovascular coupling [4]. It is easy to use, safe, affordable, and relatively tolerant to movements. So it can be mobile and operated wirelessly [5]. Compared to EEG, fNIRS allows for the classification of more stable cortical activity and requires less additional processing [4]. There have been many researches of neurofeedback based on fNIRS for various types of classifiers and applications. Classification of hand motor imagery with support vector machines (SVM) and hidden Markov models (HMM) were implemented [6]. An online classification system for BCI was researched in [7]. The classifier was based on a real time difference calculation for both side hand motor imagery. In these studies, the brain activation was induced by motor tasks.

Although many researches have been studied, it is still difficult to design an effective classification system for neuro-monitoring and neurofeedback because the kinds of data have some problems such as vast volume and noises from the human body. For grasping tasks recognition with considerable accuracy, the high-density observation that uses a lot of sensors and frequent measurement is required but it dramatically increases the size of data. To overcome these problems effectively, this study approaches the system with a perspective on machine learning by means of evolutionary computation (EC) inspired by biology that shows outstanding performance to find global optimum model. In this paper, we proposed a classification method based on the ensemble multitree genetic programming (EMGP) for the neural signal recognition for multiple tasks with higher accuracy. The main advantage of the proposed learning algorithm is that the search algorithm based on EC looks for global optimum model in very wide search space effectively, and the sensitivity feature of genetic programming (GP) helps the multi classifiers to ensure their diversity. Consequently, the low spatial resolution problems of fNIRS measurement can be relieved.

The rest of the paper is organized as follows: Section 2 describes the proposed neural signal classification method in detail and in Section 3, the experimental results are depicted. Conclusion is presented in Section 4.

II. Proposed Classification Method

The proposed classification method consists of the data modeling and the EMGP classifier. The neural signal data are collected by fNIRS, noise is reduced by preprocessing, and a data model is built to make the data easier to be handled by the multi-tasks classifier. The proposed EMGP has the major distinction of the multiple classifiers with parallel learning in contrast with [8]. This difference gives the outstanding robustness and search capability to the proposed method. Of course, some modifications are required to compose the effective algorithm with consideration for the structural aspect, characteristics of the data, and medical domain knowledge. All mentioned methods are summarized in the subsections below.

A. fNIRS data modeling for multitask classifier

The fNIRS neural signals are acquired by 24-channels optical brain-function imaging system (FOIRE-3000, Shimadzu Co) at a sampling rate of 7.7 Hz. It uses safe near-infrared light to assess the concentrations of oxygenated hemoglobin (Oxy-Hb) and deoxygenated hemoglobin (Deoxy-Hb) in the cerebral blood at wavelengths of 780 nm, 805 nm, and 830 nm. This study uses Oxy-Hb for analysis and classification, which is found to be more correlated with the regional cerebral blood flow (rCBF) than deoxy-Hb [9]. An increase in rCBF reflects an increase in neural activity [10]. The optical probes are placed on the fronto-parietal regions of the brain cortex to cover an area of 21×12cm. The subjects performed five types of tasks denoted by T_{DA}, T_{DP}, T_{TA}, T_{TP}, and $Rest$ as follows:

- $\{T_{DA}\}$ - Actively grasping four digits except thumb
- $\{T_{DP}\}$ - Passively grasping four digits except thumb by functional electrical stimulation (FES)
- $\{T_{TA}\}$ - Actively grasping thumb except the remains
- $\{T_{TP}\}$ - Passively grasping thumb by FES
- $\{Rest\}$ - Rest without performing any tasks

Each subject performed four types of tasks for three times for a total of 48 sessions for 4 subjects. The task signs are sent to subject at regular intervals like [Rest → Task → Rest] as shown in Figure 1. The signals were collected via 24 optical fibers attached to the pre-frontal cortex for 40 seconds in each session. The dataset contained 14,784 samples and 24 features

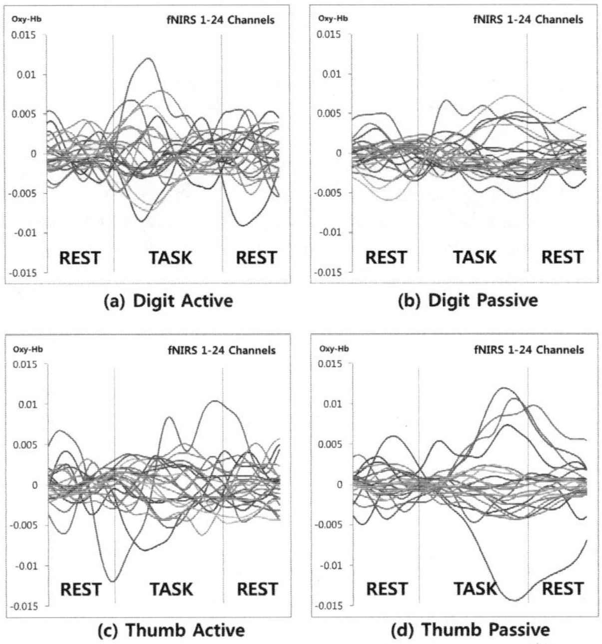

Figure 1. fNIRS data model of four finger tasks.

as described in Figure 1. Noise interference in hemodynamic signals may arise from instrumental, experimental, or physiological sources. Particularly, physiological noises often overlap in frequency with the expected neural signals [11]. In this study, we employ wavelets [12] for noise reduction.

B. Multitree Genetic Programming (MGP)

In the proposed classifier the fitness function, selection strategy, crossover, and mutation of conventional MGP have been modified. The major point is the ensemble in the parallel operation of multiple classifiers. It is robust from noises and can improve the accuracy by the concept of swarm intelligence [13]. If the swarm who has a number of individuals has diversity and active cooperation amongst individuals, the swarm is more intelligent than any individual in the swarm. The system is designed to induce this swarm intelligence. Sufficient numbers of multitrees satisfy the first condition. In addition, the sensitivity of GP and mutation operator help the swarm keep the diversity. Finally, the crossover in parallelized learning of evolutionary groups leads to the cooperation of individuals.

1) Problem formulation: Given a set of pre-processed training data $X := \{x_1, x_2, \ldots, x_m\}$ with corresponding labels $Y := \{y_1, y_2, \ldots, y_m\}$, where $y_i \in \{\pm 1\}$ for $i = 1, i = 2, \ldots, m$, our next goal is to estimate a function $f : X \to \{\pm 1\}$ to predict whether a new signal observation $z \in X^*$ will belong to class $+1$ or -1. We define classes for the tasks $\{T_{DA}\}$, $\{T_{DP}\}$, $\{T_{TA}\}$, $\{T_{TP}\}$, and $\{Rest\}$.

2) The structure of an individual: An MGP individual consists of independent n trees. The best fitness trees in each group at the final stage of MGP learning become n classifiers. In this study, the internal nodes of tree consist of math operators, i.e. $\{+, -, *, /, exp, log, root\}$. The leaf nodes are selected among R and features. R is random variable from 0 to 1. The decision of each tree is determined by the result of the formula calculation. In other words, if the result is negative, the decision is class A.

3) Ensemble technique for MGP: We utilized and modified the Bagging and Boosting [14] ensemble methods for MGP. At the bagging, different sampled feature sets are allocated to MGP evolving group. Although the different feature sets lead to additional tree validation after the external crossover, it is valuable to reserve the diversity of classifiers. Boosting technique is performed to ensure the diversity between trees in a classifier during the learning time. The details of ensemble for MGP are treated as follows.

Upper nodes of GP individual are decided from early generations as the learning directivity can be kept in the state with a high probability. Therefore, the initial weighting significantly influences the diversity of the ensemble classifiers. To obtain the diversity, each of n groups has different weighting values toward the samples that are separated in n groups by a random sampling algorithm. The detailed process of the ensemble is shown in Figure 2.

The variation of fitness in a group decreases as passing generations. The proposed system sets a new weighting criterion when the fitness variation is less than a lower threshold for the verification of convergence. The weighting criteria for each sample set the number of misclassifications for the individuals in the top k percent. The k is empirically decided as 10 in this paper. The lower threshold is 50 percent of the variation when the weighting criteria are changed.

Algorithm 1 Discrete AdaBoost for EMGP

Samples $x_1, x_2 \dots, x_n$
Desired outputs $y_1, y_2, \dots, y_n, y \in \{-1, 1\}$
Initial weight $w_{1,1}, w_{2,1}, \dots, w_{n,1}$ set to $\frac{1}{n}$
Separate the samples to k groups by random sampling
ith evolving group weight update $w = w \times \alpha$ in ith sample group
Error function $E(f(x), y, i) = e^{-y_i f(x_i)}$
Weak learners $h : x \rightarrow [-1, 1]$
for t in $1, 2, \dots, T$ **do**
  Choose $f_t(x)$:
  Find weak learner $h_t(x)$ that minimizes ϵ_t, the weighted sum error for misclassified points $\epsilon_t = \sum_i w_{i,t} E(h_t(x), y, i)$
  Choose $\alpha_t = \frac{1}{2} \ln \left(\frac{1-\epsilon_t}{\epsilon_t} \right)$
  Add to ensemble:
  $F_t(x) = F_{t-1}(x) + \alpha_t h_t(x)$
  Update weights:
  $w_{i,t+1} = w_{i,t} e^{-y_i \alpha_t h_t(x_i)}$ for all i
  Renormalize $w_{i,t+1}$ such that $\sum_i w_{i,t+1} = 1$
end for

Figure 2. The Algorithm Specification of Discrete AdaBoost for EMGP

4) Final decision: Instead of training a single classifier, we train multiple GP groups which mean the number of tree in each individual for the purpose of further improvment in the overall accuracy as described in Figure 1. We consider a multiple n - classifier functions $\{f_1, f_2, \dots, f_n\}$ and a data set $\{(x_i, y_i)_{i=1}^{m}\}, x_i \in X, y \in Y$. The tree groups are trained in parallel to predict $f_{i=1}^{n} : x \rightarrow \{\pm 1\}^n$. The outputs from all classifier functions are then defined as an m-dimensional binary vector $y = [y_{1,i}, y_{2,i}, \dots, y_{m,i}]$, such that $y_{j,i} = 1$ if f_i recognizes x_j and 0 otherwise for $i = 1, 2, \dots, n$. The number of correct assignments is $N_1(f_i) = \sum_{j=1}^{m} y_{j,i}$ and the number of mistakes is $N_0(f_i) = m - \sum_{j=1}^{m} y_{j,i}$. In order to make the final decision from the set of functions $\{f_i, \dots, f_n\}$, we define the following majority voting rule:

$$\begin{cases} +1 & if \quad \sum_i^n f_i(z) \geq k \\ -1 & else \quad \sum_i^n f_i(z) \leq n - k \end{cases} \tag{1}$$

where $k < n$ and $i = 1, 2, \dots, k$ making similar predictions defined by the $k - of - n$ majority classifier for $k \geq \frac{n}{2}$. Thus, we have two possible outcomes from all classifiers $F : X \rightarrow \{+1, -1\}$. Machine learning consists of training and testing phases. In both phases, we train and test five different groups of multiple classifiers $E_1, E_2, \dots, E_5$.

Group E_1 is trained by taking samples from the digit-active task $\{T_{DA}\}$ as positive and samples from the remaining tasks as negative. Likewise, group E_2 is trained by taking samples from digit-passive task $\{T_{DP}\}$ as positive and samples from the remaining tasks as negative.

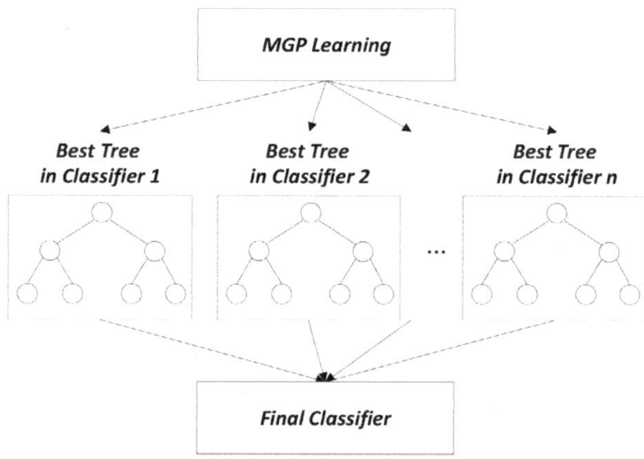

Figure 3. Combining decisions from the best tree in each classifier

In the training phase, each individual base MGP is separately trained using the same input data from the 10-fold cross validation. During the testing phase, unseen examples are applied to all base functions simultaneously in real time. Further, a collective decision is obtained on the basis of the majority voting scheme using Equation (1). In other words, once each of the n base classifiers from the MGP evolving group has cast its vote as shown in Figure 3. The majority voting strategy assigns the test patterns to the class with the largest number of votes and outputs are provided as the final prediction.

III. EXPERIMENTAL RESULTS

The simulation environment of the proposed EMGP is constructed in C++. Parameters such as population size, depth limitation, iteration number, probability of internal crossover, external crossover, and mutation are set 10000 individuals, 10 depths, 1000 generation, 0.7, 0.05, and 0.1, respectively. The parameters of the conventional classifiers are set as default value of WEKA [15]. All accuracy results in this paper were obtained by 10-fold cross validation.

TABLE I. ACCURACIES AND ROOT RELATIVE SQUARED ERROR (RRSE) (%) OF THE CONVENTIONS AND PROPOSED EMGP FOR OVERALL BRAIN DATA

Classifier	Accuracies	RRSE
PART	97.78	25.20
Jrip	96.59	31.27
Naive Bayes	57.01	96.98
Bayes Net	74.20	75.36
J48	98.13	22.83
BFTree	97.44	26.73
FT	97.88	24.24
NBTree	97.59	25.77
RBFNetwork	62.48	86.47
Max. of Conv.	98.13	22.83
Proposed GP	99.39	15.03

TABLE II. CLASSIFICATION ACCURACIES (%) OF CONVENTIONAL CLASSIFIERS AND PROPOSED EMGP FOR SUBJECT DEPENDENT LEARNING

Classifier	S_1	S_2	S_3	S_4
PART	98.64	98.53	98.26	98.97
Jrip	98.32	97.51	96.78	97.83
Naive Bayes	76.81	72.67	73.05	71.42
Bayes Net	92.47	95.34	90.71	88.90
J48	98.43	98.62	98.34	98.91
BFTree	97.94	97.47	98.13	98.45
FT	98.56	98.86	98.86	98.62
NBTree	97.59	98.02	97.72	98.29
RBFNetwork	83.90	84.03	85.44	80.76
Max. of Conv.	98.64	98.86	98.86	98.97
Proposed GP	99.43	99.10	99.02	99.24

Table 1 shows the classification results for conventional classifiers which are implemented in WEKA and the proposed EMGP. The conventional algorithms used in the experiment are Pruning rule based classification tree (PART), Jrip, naive Bayesian, Bayesian Network, J48, Best First Decision Tree (BFTree), Functional trees (FT), Naive-Bayes tree (NBTree), and radial basisbasis function network (RBFNetwork). In consideration of the structure of the tree based GP, the tree-based learning algorithms such as PART, Jrip, J48, BFTree, FT, and NBTree were selected as the target of comparison tests. Probability based algorithms such as naive Bayesian and Bayesian Network; and RBFNetwrok that is a universal learning technique are used. In this experiment, the full data obtained by the previous description is compared based on the accuracy. By referring to the results of Table 1, it can be seen that the proposed classification method has the best accuracy with the minimum RRSE when compared with conventional classifiers.

In the subject dependent test as shown in Table 2, EMGP classified the four finger-grasping tasks with the best accuracy. Here we compared the performance of the training and testing for single subject data. Other signal patterns may come on the same motion according to individual differences. Thus, this experiment was performed to exclude the uncertainty. As expected, it was able to confirm that the learning accuracy is improved overall.

To show the appropriateness of the proposed method, fifteen UCI datasets [16] are used as benchmark dataset. Table 3 shows specifications of each dataset. The data set for the biological signals were chosen as a test candidate. If the learning ability is good in this result, the proposed algorithm is to be used universally in bio-signal data. Table 3 shows the classification results for conventional classifiers and the proposed EMGP. The classification accuracy of EMGP is 5.48% higher than the average of conventional classifiers.

TABLE III. NUMBER OF SAMPLES (S) AND FEATURES (F) ALONG WITH MODEL SIZE FOR UCI DATASET, AND CLASSIFICATION ACCURACIES (%)

	Specifications			Results	
Dataset	S	F	ModelSize	Conv.	EMGP
Blood Transfusion	748	4	2992	77.20	79.54
Breast Cancer	683	9	6147	96.18	97.21
Breast Tissue	106	9	954	66.46	68.87
Cleveland	297	13	3861	50.13	44.78
Glass	214	9	1926	61.89	69.62
Heart	270	13	3510	79.55	78.51
Ionosphere	351	33	11583	89.68	95.15
Lung Cancer	27	56	1512	55.56	59.25
Olitos	120	25	3000	69.81	84.16
Parkinson	195	22	4290	82.34	90.76
Pima Indian Diabetes	768	8	6144	75.00	76.56
Sonar	208	60	12480	67.47	88.46
Soybean	47	35	1645	98.58	100.00
SPECTF Heart	80	44	3520	73.06	80.00
Wine	178	13	2314	85.52	97.75
Mean	286.13	23.53	4391.86	75.22	80.70

IV. CONCLUSION

The classification of four finger-grasping tasks, based on neural signal data, isf challenging task in non-invasive neuro-monitoring due to the difficulty of recognition for activation near different cortical areas. Many machine-learning techniques have been developed to obtain highly accurate classification performance. This paper also targets the improvement of the neural signal recognition and proposes a new classification method for neural signal recognition during multitasks which is based on EMGP with considerations of the signal characteristics. The high sensitivity of GP is known as a disadvantage to handle signal data. The proposed GP tried to solve the problem by using multiple classifiers consisting of several trained GP trees with majority voting. Also, the system performs the parallel learning with several evolutionary groups. According to the experimental results, we validated the relevance of the proposed method.

In the future work, approaches based on probability theory regarding the margin to solve such problems would develop GP classifiers. The current decision which combines method with the majority voting can be improved by theoretical approaches or advanced ensemble combiners such as weighted voting and stacking. This study can be applied to activate the brain training for enhancing brain plasticity. For the applications, the subject dependent learning in this paper can be designed for the local brain activation training based on neuro-feedback. In other words, the learning models] collected through a pre-experiment can systematically help the user in a specific area immersion. Future research will continue to focus on the application of EMGP.

ACKNOWLEDGMENT

Dr. Ahn is the corresponding author. Dr. An and Mr. Lee contributed equally to this work. This work was supported by the DGIST R&D Program of the Ministry of Science, ICT and Future Planning (15-RS-02).

REFERENCES

[1] E. Buch, et al., "Think to move: a neuromagnetic brain-computer interface system for chronic stroke." Stroke, vol. 39, no. 3, 2008, pp. 910-917.

[2] N. Hogan, H. I. Krebs, B. Rohrer and J. J. Palazzolo, "Motions or muscles? Some behavioral factors underlying robotic assistance of motor recovery." Journal of rehabilitation research and development, vol. 43, no. 5, 2006, pp. 605.

[3] W. Wang, et al., "Neural interface technology for rehabilitation: exploiting and promoting neuroplasticity." Physical medicine and rehabilitation clinics of North America, vol. 21 no. 1, 2010, pp. 157-178.

[4] N. Birbaumer, "Breaking the silence: brain-computer interfaces (BCI) for communication and motor control." Psychophysiology, vol. 43, no. 6, 2006, pp. 517-532.

[5] M. Ferrari and Q. Valentina, "A brief review on the history of human functional near-infrared spectroscopy (fNIRS) development and fields of application." Neuroimage, vol. 63, no. 2, 2012, pp. 921-935.

[6] N. Birbaumer and G. C. Leonardo, "Brain-computer interfaces: communication and restoration of movement in paralysis." The Journal of physiology, vol. 579, no. 3, 2007, pp. 621-636.

[7] G. Pfurtscheller, et al., "The hybrid BCI." Frontiers in neuroscience, vol. 4, 2010.

[8] D. P. Muni, R. P. Nikhil and D. Jyotirmoy, "A novel approach to design classifiers using genetic programming." Evolutionary Computation, IEEE Transactions on, vol. 8, no. 2, 2004, pp. 183-196.

[9] E. Gratton, et al., "Measurement of brain activity by near-infrared light." Journal of Biomedical Optics, vol. 10, no. 1, 2005, pp. 011008-01100813.

[10] M. Jueptner and C. Weiller, "Review: does measurement of regional cerebral blood flow reflect synaptic activity?-Implications for PET and fMRI." Neuroimage, vol. 2, no. 2PA, 1995, pp. 148-156.

[11] S. Coyle, et al., "On the suitability of near-infrared (NIR) systems for next-generation brain-computer interfaces." Physiological measurement, vol. 25, no. 4, 2004, pp. 815.

[12] B. Abibullaev and J. An, "Classification of frontal cortex haemodynamic responses during cognitive tasks using wavelet transforms and machine learning algorithms." Medical engineering & physics, vol. 34, no. 10, 2012, pp. 1394-1410.

[13] E. Bonabeau and M. Christopher, "Swarm intelligence: A whole new way to think about business." Harvard business review, vol. 79, no. 5, 2001, pp. 106-115.

[14] T. G. Dietterich, "Ensemble methods in machine learning." Multiple classifier systems, Springer Berlin Heidelberg, 2000, pp. 1-15.

[15] M. Hall, et al., "The WEKA data mining software: an update." ACM SIGKDD explorations newsletter, vol. 11, no. 1, 2009, pp. 10-18.

[16] A. Asuncion and N. David, "UCI machine learning repository." [http://archive. ics. uci. edu/ml] (2007).

Technology Foresight of Remote Sensing Based on Patent Analysis

Haibin Liu
China Academy of
Aerospace Systems Science and Engineering
University of South Australia
Beijing, P.R.China
e-mail: liuhb@spacechina.com

Chao Song
China Academy of
Aerospace Systems Science and Engineering
Beijing, P.R.China
e-mail:1142184538@qq.com

***Abstract*—In this paper, we propose a new method of patent analysis for technology foresight by using patent co-citation clustering, technology life cycle theory, and Logistic model and apply it in the field of remote sensing. Firstly, the co-citation clustering method is used to analyze patents about remote sensing, which can visually show the distribution of patents and select the core patents groups with strong co-citation relationship that represents the technical groups in this field. Through the analysis of the clusters, 8 main technical directions are obtained. Then, we search patents again for the main technical directions, and use the technology life cycle theory and Logistic model to analyze and forecast the future development trend of technology. According to the analysis, the remote sensing technologies are found that have passed through a long period of germination. Among them, "remote sensing image processing technology in later period" is in the growing stage, which is being developed rapidly. The technologies related to "remote sensing imaging equipment" and "remote sensing image initial processing" are becoming mature. Based on these analyses, some suggestions on the future development, application direction and industrial prospects of remote sensing technologies are advocated.**

***Keywords*—Remote sensing; Patent co-citation analysis; Technology life cycle; Logistic model; Technology Foresight.**

I. INTRODUCTION

Remote sensing technology is a comprehensive detecting technology, which uses modern optics and electronics detection apparatus to detect and record the characteristics of the electromagnetic wave of the remote target without contacting. By analyzing and interpreting the characteristics, properties and changing pattern of the target are revealed. The basic principle is that the characteristics of electromagnetic wave of different objects are different, and by detecting the reflection of electromagnetic wave and the electromagnetic wave emitted by the object, the information of the object is extracted, which can help to identify the remote objects [1].

Remote sensing technology has the characteristics of large detection range, high speed of data acquisition, short cycle and is rarely subject to ground conditions, which can be widely used in military and civilian areas, such as military reconnaissance, military mapping, marine monitoring, meteorological observation, vegetation classification, land utilization planning, etc. The application of remote sensing technology to a certain field can improve the information decision support ability and the competitiveness to get more benefits [2]. At present, with the rapid development of aviation, space and unmanned aerial vehicle (UAV) technology, remote sensing technology has entered the commercial application stage, and has great potentials for development and application. Therefore, it is very important to carry out the remote sensing technology foresight to make clear the technology development trend. It will be helpful to realize the new breakthrough of remote sensing technology, and gradually take the advantageous position in the development of industrial technology. It will have a profound impact on improving the level of social information, promoting sustainable economic development, improving people's living quality, and enhancing public safety and national defense [3].

The importance of technology foresight is gradually realized, but it's a very difficult work because that technological development is a complicated process, which is influenced by many factors, such as science, economy, society and so on. Technology foresight requires a comprehensive set of methods. At present, the activities of technology foresight around the world mainly adopts the methods based on experts' opinions such as Delphi and workshops. Some other methods are Scenario analysis and Technology Roadmap. The objective and quantitative research methods for technology foresight are quite few. In some studies, the literature bibliometrics is introduced, which is a quantitative tool of technology foresight [4]. In this paper, we propose a method of patent analysis to make technology foresight of remote sensing. This method is based on the patent data and can use them for efficient clustering and intuitive display. It can be used as a new quantitative tool in the specific aspects of technology foresight. It can play the role of reference, support and verification in technology foresight, and improve the scientificalness and objectivity of the research.

In this paper, a study on the patents of remote sensing field is carried out, in which the main technical directions and the patent life cycle in the remote sensing field are analyzed by the method of co-citation clustering and Logistic model. In Section 2, we present the research methods in the study, including patent co-citation analysis, LinLog visualization clustering method, and S-curve Technology Life Cycle Forecasting method, and introduce the database we use. In the Section 3, we carry out an empirical study in the field of remote sensing, which prove the validity of the method. In the Section 4, we draw some conclusions and look forward to the future works.

II. RESEARCH METHODS & DATA SOURCE

A. Patent Co-citation Clustering Analysis

Co-citation is that two or more patents are all cited by the same patent. Generally, patents with co-citation relationship have certain correlation in content. The more frequently patents are co-cited; the more similar they are [5]. However, it is not comprehensive to measure the related strength only with the total number of co-citations. When basic patents both have large number of citations, they are more likely to be co-cited, which can't mean they're more similar. In this paper, (1) is adopted[6] to express the related strength of patent I and patent J—Cij:

$$Cij = \frac{Nij}{\sqrt{Ni} \cdot \sqrt{Nj}} . \qquad (1)$$

In (1), N_{ij} represents the number of co-citations of patent I and patent J; N_i and N_j respectively represent the number of citations of patent I and patent J.

After the calculation of the relationship between patents, we cluster patents according to their related strength. Some scholars have taken some research on document co-citation clustering. Reference [7] introduced the citation contexts in document clustering, which can increase the effectiveness of the bag-of-words representation. Reference [8] used co-citation cluster analysis to propose a knowledge-transfer analysis model. Reference [9] used Girvan-Newman algorithm in the patent co-citation clustering to identify the main technologies of Apple Corp.

This paper uses the LinLog visualization clustering method to cluster the patents, and explore the main technical directions of the remote sensing field. LinLog model, which is proposed by Noack Andreas in 2007, is a kind of force-directed algorithm based on the energy function, which can show a good clustering effect to a large number of nodes [10]. This algorithm applies the idea of mechanics to the layout of the graph, which assumes that a repulsion force exists between any two nodes, and a pulling force exists between the nodes which are related. The starting positions of nodes are random, and then each node can adjust its position according to the repulsion force and pulling force from the other nodes, until the pulling force and the repulsion force reach equilibrium [11]. Obviously, any two nodes will not overlap due to the existing repulsion forces, and the related nodes will be close to each other under the pulling force. Each cluster represents a group of patents with strong co-citation relationships, which have strong correlation and represent a technical direction in this field.

B. S-curve Technology Forecasting and Logistic Model

Verhulst proposed the growth model in 1938[12]. According to this model(Figure1), the growth process of the technology is similar to that of human, and it can be experienced in the germination stage, growing stage, mature stage and decline stage. In the germination stage, the growth is slow; the growing stage is a period of rapid growth; after growing stage, it enters the mature stage, in which the development is slow; finally reaches the limit and enters the decline stage. The fitting curve of the process is called the growth curve, and because of its S shape, it is called S-curve [13].

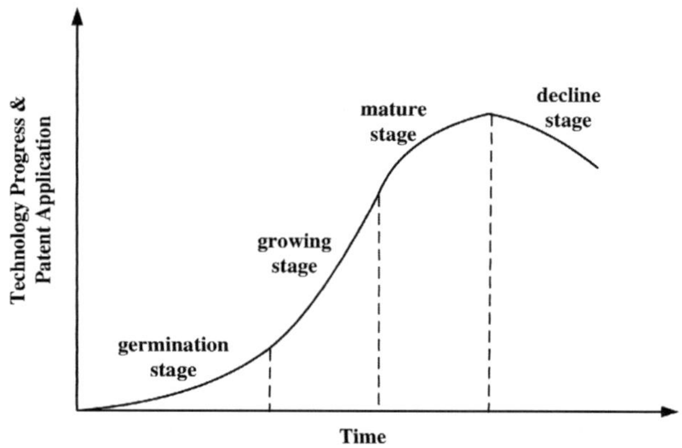

Figure 1. Technology Growth S-curve

The equation of the S curve is the Logistic model [14], as the Eq. (2) shows:

$$y = \frac{l}{1+\alpha e^{-\beta T}} . \qquad (2)$$

In the equation, y is the number of patent accumulation; α is the slope of the S curve, which is the growth rate of the S curve; β is the time point of the turning point (midpoint) in the growth curve; l is the saturation level of growth, that is, the saturation point (saturation); [l×10%, l×90%] is the time required for the growth and maturity.

The meaning of three parameters are as follows: (1)*saturation*: the maximum utility value generated by using a technique, that is, the highest value of the number of patent accumulation; (2)*growth time*: the time needed for producing the 10%~90% of the maximum utility value of a technology, i.e., the time needed for the period of growth and maturity; (3)*midpoint*: anti curve point of S-curve, that is, the 0 value point for two differential. These three parameters can be automatically calculated by the system. It is necessary to point out that the S curve model is a theoretical model of technology development, which does not take into account the influence of external factors that may bring changes to technological development. If there are some new emerging disruptive technologies or other changing factors, using S-curve to estimate the technology life cycle may cause some errors. In this paper, we only roughly estimate the technology life cycle, and the results also need to be corrected by the experts in technical field.

C. Data Source

In this study, the number of patent accumulation in the field of remote sensing around the world represents the development level of technology. The patents about remote sensing are retrieved by the patent retrieval tool—TI (Thomson innovation), which has the world's largest patent database, including patents from the United States, European countries, Japan, South Korea and so on, also containing the DOCdb (INPADOC) database and the Derwent World Patents Index (DWPI) database [15]. We use all the patents about remote sensing which were published before October 15, 2015 as the data source to research the technology development status of remote sensing industry.

III. TECHNOLOGY FORESIGHT OF REMOTE SENSING

Based on about 5027 patents related to remote sensing technology, we use the patent co-citation clustering method to cluster the patents, and get the current main technical directions of remote sensing. Then, we retrieve patents for the selected technical directions again, use the Logistic model to carry out the technology life cycle analysis and forecast the development trend of the remote sensing technology in the future.

A. Main Technical Directions of remote sensing

Get the first 30% of the highest cited patents in each year for co-citation clustering and visualization. Figure 2 is the patent co-citation clustering map. In this map, each cluster of nodes represents a patents group in which every patent is related to each other. It can represent a certain technical direction or a theme in the field. The number of nodes in a cluster represents the number of core patents contained in the technical direction. Also, it can represent people's attention to the technical direction in some way. Node's size represents patent's cited frequency; the greater the node is the higher the cited frequency is. Some different clusters may have similar topics, so we need to understand each cluster by manual analysis and summarize the main technical directions. Through the analysis of patents in the all clusters, we can draw the technical direction of each patents group (marked in the picture).

According to the patent co-citation clustering, in this paper 8 main technical directions in the remote sensing field from the perspective of patent application are summarized as follows: (1) "Fusion method of remote sensing image"; (2) "registration and correlation method of remote sensing

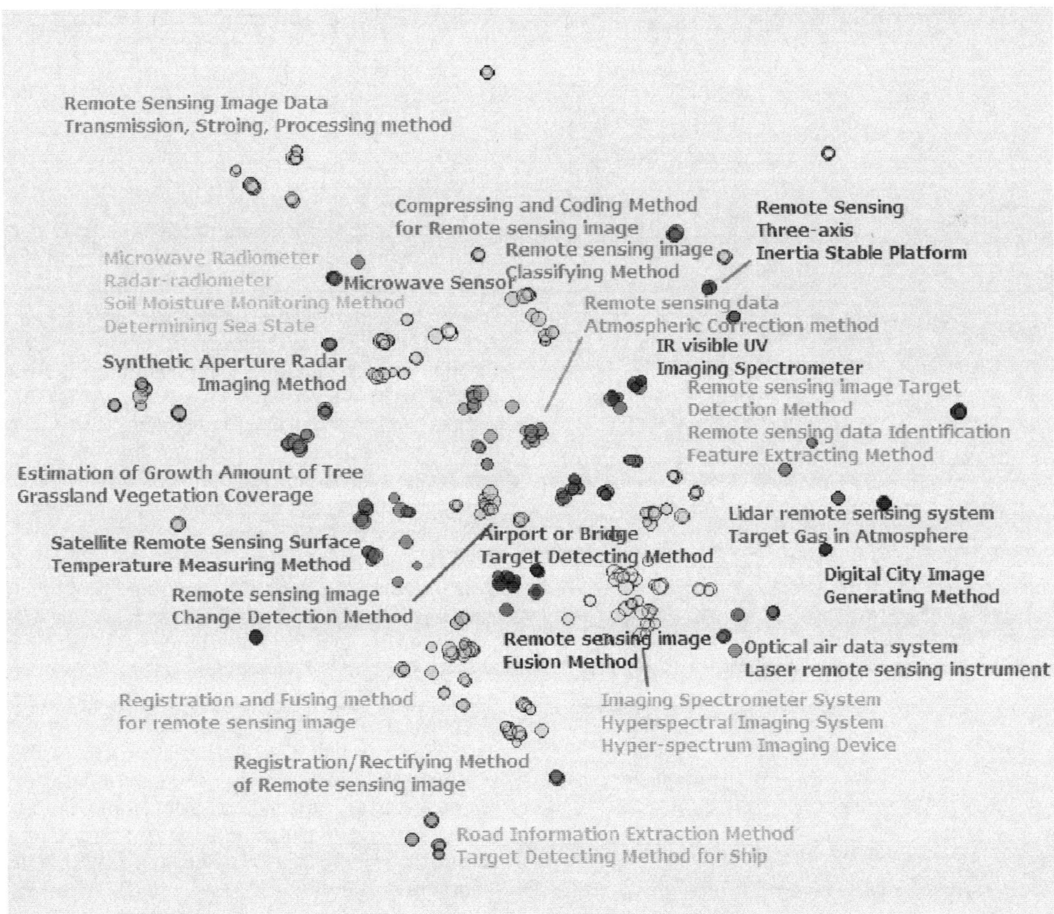

Figure 2. Patent Co-citation Clustering Map in the Field of Remote Sensing.

image"; (3) "object recognition and feature extraction method of remote sensing image"; (4) "changes detection method of remote sensing image"; (5) "remote sensing temperature measurement, inversion method"; (6) "imaging spectrometer & spectral imaging devices"; (7) "synthetic aperture radar/SAR"; (8) "Microwave remote sensor".

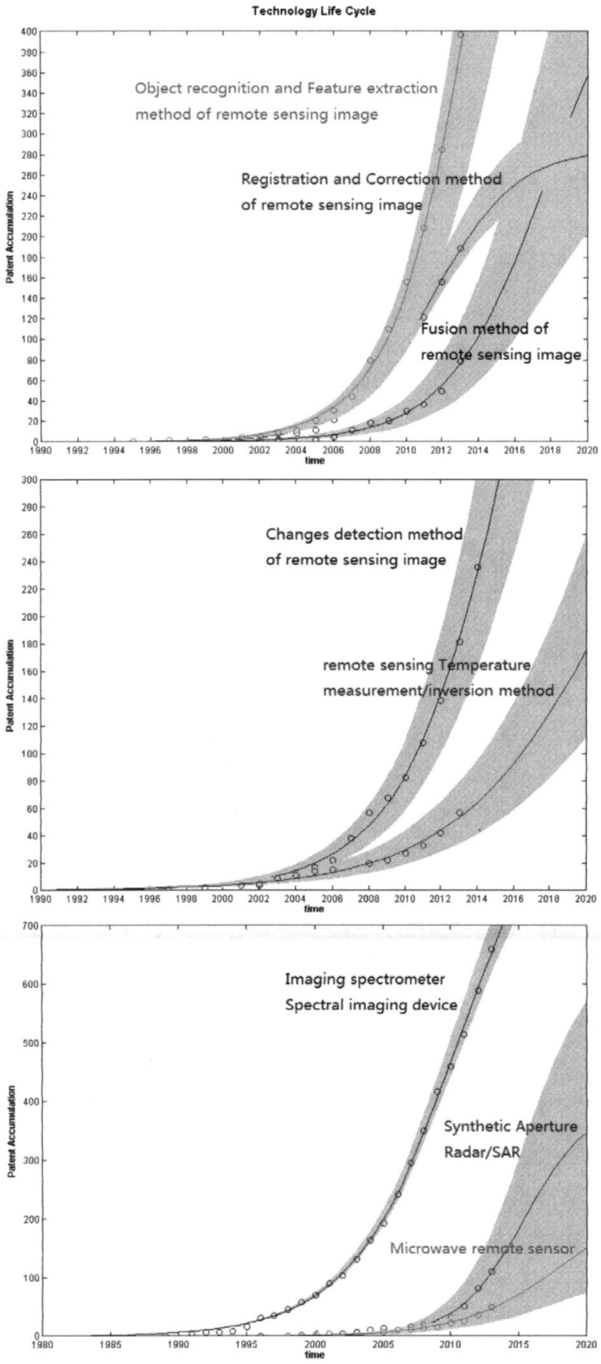

Figure 3. Logistic model of each technical direction.

B. *Results of Technical Life Cycle Analysis*

According to the Logistic model, we analyze the number of patent applications in the field of remote sensing. The growth curves of 8 technical directions are shown in Figure 3, which are fitted out by Loglet Lab2 [16]. The relevant parameters of Logistic Model are shown in Table I.

Taking "Fusion method of remote sensing image" as an example, the S curve and its implication are analyzed. From the beginning of 2003, there have been patents applications about remote sensing image fusion method. The system estimates that the growing stage needs 12 years, and the turning point will occur in 2018. Patent applications continued to grow until 2012, this period is the germination stage; then the technology goes into the growing stage until 2018, this period presents a trend of accelerated growth; from 2019 to 2025, patents about remote sensing image fusion show slow growth trend, but the total amount is still increasing, this period is mature stage; after this, patent growth will fall into recession, and the number of patents shows a decreasing trend.

TABLE I. PARAMETERS OF LOGISTIC MODEL

Code of Tech. Direction	Saturation	Midpoint	Growth Time
1	527.142	2017.933	12.135
2	285.587	2011.539	9.992
3	1388.207	2015.499	11.31
4	885.418	2017.381	14.346
5	541.418	2023.469	20.721
6	1036.318	2010.829	17.966
7	400.924	2015.443	10.743
8	248.668	2018.451	16.41

According to the method above, the S-curves of the 8 main technical directions are analyzed, and the distribution of their technical life cycle is obtained, as shown in Table Ⅱ. As can be seen in Table 1, from the perspective of patent, the 8 main technical directions in remote sensing have been through the germination stage. Among them, the technical directions in the growing stage are: (1) "Fusion method of remote sensing image"; (3) "object recognition and feature extraction method of remote sensing image"; (4) "changes detection method of remote sensing image"; (5) "remote sensing temperature measurement, inversion method"; (8) "Microwave remote sensor"; the technical directions in the mature stage are: (2) "registration and correlation method of remote sensing image"; (6) "imaging spectrometer & spectral imaging devices"; (7) "synthetic aperture radar/SAR".

It can be seen from the above data that remote sensing technologies have passed the stage of basic research, and most of the key technologies are in the stage of rapid growth. Technologies about "remote sensing imaging equipment" and "remote sensing image initial processing" are becoming mature. At present and in the near future, the key point of remote sensing technology development is the object-oriented, the demand-oriented, the high speed, efficient and automatic remote sensing image processing technology in later perid.

TABLE II. ESTIMATED TIME OF TECHNOLOGY LIFE CYCLE

Code of Tech. Direction	Germination stage	Growing stage	Mature stage	Decline stage
1	2003-2011	2012-2018	2019-2025	2026-
2	2001-2006	2007-2012	2013-2018	2019-
3	1995-2009	2010-2016	2017-2023	2023-
4	2002-2009	2010-2017	2018-2025	2026-
5	1997-2012	2013-2023	2024-2034	2035-
6	1989-2001	2002-2011	2012-2021	2022-
7	1996-2009	2010-2015	2016-2021	2022-
8	1998-2009	2010-2018	2019-2027	2028-

IV. CONCLUSION AND FUTURE WORK.

A. Conclusions

In this paper, we cluster more than 5000 patents related to remote sensing with the patent co-citation clustering method, and summary 8 main technical directions in this field as follows: (1) "Fusion method of remote sensing image"; (2) "registration and correlation method of remote sensing image"; (3) "object recognition and feature extraction method of remote sensing image"; (4) "changes detection method of remote sensing image"; (5) "remote sensing temperature measurement, inversion method"; (6) "imaging spectrometer & spectral imaging devices"; (7) "synthetic aperture radar/SAR"; (8) "Microwave remote sensor". Then, we retrieve patents for the selected technical directions again and use the Logistic model to carry out the technology life cycle analysis. Based on the analysis result, the distribution of their technical life cycle is obtained. It is cleared that 3 technical directions related to "remote sensing imaging equipment" and "remote sensing image initial processing" are becoming mature and other 5 directions related to “remote sensing image processing technology in later period” are in the stage of rapid growth.

With the results of technology life cycle analysis, we analyze the patents’ contents of each group deeply and make the following conclusions:

(1) Remote sensing technologies have passed the stage of basic research. Technologies related to "remote sensing imaging equipment" and "remote sensing image initial processing" are becoming mature. At present and in the near future, the key point of remote sensing technology development is the object-oriented, the demand-oriented, the high speed, efficient and automatic remote sensing image processing technology in later period.

(2) In early times, remote sensing technology was applied to the static object recognition, such as forest vegetation cover, coastline, airports, roads, bridges and so on. With the remote sensing technology being developed to “high temporal resolution”, “high spatial resolution”, and “wide scale”, the application of remote sensing is going towards disaster monitoring, sea state monitoring, ship target detecting, digital city, and so on.

(3) Patent applications related to remote sensing are in a rapid growth trend. The main technical directions of remote sensing are also in the growing stage, and nearly half of them are tending to be mature. Remote sensing patent applicants from the early military and scientific research institutions gradually extended to individuals and business organizations. The application range of remote sensing is from the early military, government to civilian, commercial. This shows that it is a good opportunity for the business development of remote sensing technology and the promotion of its industrialization. Remote sensing technology will have broad prospects for industrial development.

B. Future Works

(1) Extending data sources of technology foresight

In this paper, patent database is used as the data source of the technology foresight, which can include most of the research results from practical technical inventions around the world. However, there may be some time lags because it usually needs 2-3 years for a patent from the application to the general public. And if the patent search strategy is not complete, it will cause the research results to be not comprehensive. In addition to patents, there are also other kinds of technical information that are valuable and significant to the study on the future development trend of science and technology, such as literatures, business news, reports from the authoritative research institutions. In the future, we can make technology foresight using the combination of multi-source data, such as combining patents and scientific literature. Then we can use data mining to find the similarities and differences in the path of development from different perspectives, and search for the future potential technology opportunities.

(2) Combining the clustering analysis and text mining

This paper uses LinLog algorithm to realize the patent co-citation clustering analysis and visualization, but the analysis of clusters’ contents is hand finished, resulting in a larger workload. In the future, the text mining method can be introduced in the analysis of the clustering results, which can automatically show the technical direction of each cluster.

(3) Combining patent analysis and experts’ opinions

In most of the current technology foresight activities, patent analysis and experts’ opinions can not effectively combine. In the future works, we can carry out some expert investigations before the patent analysis, so that we are able to conduct a patent analysis or other quantitative analysis on issues that the experts are more concerned about. On the other hand, due to the development of science and technology involves many other issues, such as issues about economy and society, it is very complicated. The conclusions from patent analysis also need to be submitted to the experts for further analysis and study, in order to play the better role for technology foresight.

REFERENCES

[1] H. Z. Huang, "Application of Remote Sensing Technology in Agricultural Production in China", Scientific and Technical Information, vol. 24, 2010, pp46.

[2] G. F. Jing, "The Development of Remote Sensing Technology and the Analysis of the Industrialization", Geographic Information World, vol.3 (6), June 2007, pp.6-16.

[3] L. X. Zhao, "RFID Technology Foresight and Patent Strategy Research Based on Patent Analysis", Science and Technology Management, vol.33 (11), 2012, pp.24-30.

[4] H. G. Zhang, W. Y. Zhao, and R. H. Tan, "Product Technology Maturity Prediction Technique and Software Development Based on Patent Analysis,. China Mechanical Engineering, vol.17 (8) , 2006, pp. 823-827.

[5] T. B. Stuart and J. M. Polody, "Local search and the evolution of technological capabilities", Strategic Management Journal, vol.17, 1996, pp.21-28.

[6] A. D. Peng, "Research on Patent Classification Method and Related Problems Based on Co-citation", Information Science, vol.26 (11) , 2008, pp.1676-1684.

[7] Aljaber BS, Stokes N, Bailey J, Pei J. Document clustering of scientific texts using citation contexts. Information Retrieval, vol.13, 2010, pp.101-131.

[8] Xuezhao Wang , Yajuan Zhao, Rui Liu, Jing Zhang. "Knowledge-transfer analysis based on co-citation clustering", Scientometrics, vol. 97, 2013, pp.859-869.

[9] X. W. Wang, C. Liu, W. L Mao. "Technology Clustering Analysis Using Patent Co-citation Analysis: A Case Study of Apple Company", Science and Management, vol.5, 2014, pp.31-37.

[10] Andreas Noack, "Energy Models for Graph Clustering", Journal of Graph Algorithms and Applications, vol.11 (2), 2007, pp.453-480.

[11] J. Michael, McGuffin, "Simple Algorithms for Network Visualization: A Tutorial", TSINGHUA SCIENCE AND TECHNOLOGY, vol.17 (4), 2012, pp.383-398.

[12] D. B. Bradley, "Verhulst's Logistic Curve", Colledgr Mathematics Journal,vol.30(2) ,2000, pp.94-98.

[13] R. S. Campball, "Patent Trends as a Technological Forecasting Tool", World Patent Information, vol.3, 1983, pp.137-143.

[14] H. L. Yu, "To Predict the Development of Artificial Board Technology using TRIZ Theory S-curve Evolution Rule", Forestry Science and Technology, vol.7, 2009, pp.57-60.

[15] Thomson Innovation official website [EB/OL], [retrieved: 10,2015], http://www.thomsonscientific.com.cn/productsservices/thomsoninnovation/.

[16] Logistic Analysis: Loglet Lab 2 [EB/OL], [retrieved: 11,2015]. http://phe.rockefeller.edu/LogletLab/2.0/.

Introducing Mixed Tables

Lubomir Stanchev

Computer Science Department
California Polytechnic State University
San Luis Obispo, CA, USA
Email: lstanche@calpoly.edu

***Abstract*—Two approaches for extending relational database tables to allow storing uncertain and incomplete information have been proposed in the past. Grahne in 1984 introduced constraint tables that allow constraints to be attached to tuples and tables. Independently, Barbara et al. introduced in 1992 probabilistic tables that can contain random variables for some of the fields. In this paper, we combine the two approaches by introducing the concept of a *mixed table*: a table that allows storing both random variables and linear constraints on them.**

Keywords*–*c-tables; constraint databases; probabilistic databases; mixed tables.

I. Introduction

Most real-world information is incomplete or imprecise. For example, we may know that someone got good grades in algebra, but we may not know the precise grade. Similarly, we may know that a soldier is injured, but we may not know the extent of the injury. Or we may know that there is a 30% chance of rain tomorrow. Or maybe we know that there is a 90% probability that stock prices in the US will go down tomorrow if the Federal Reserve raises the key interest rate today. In this paper, we explore how such imprecise and probabilistic information can be represented in a tabular format without losing the richness of the data.

Many applications need access to incomplete information. For example, data mining algorithms can produce rules that have different levels of confidence. It is common for mobile sensors to produce conflicting information when operating in adverse weather conditions. Similarly, polling data is imprecise by nature. Storing such information in relational tables presents the advantage of allowing the use of exiting database technology, such as efficient querying, transaction control, logging and recovery, user authentication, and so on.

There is an obvious trade-off between the expressive power of the data representation and the complexity of query answering. For example, in the presence of Boolean constraints determining if a tuple belongs to every possible query result becomes as difficult as SAT [1], which is known to be NP-complete. Even in the absence of constraints, adding a random variable to every tuple that denotes the probability of the tuple existing (i.e., introducing *tuple-level uncertainty*) can make the problem of duplicate elimination over intermediate results #P-hard [2]. Fortunately, in most cases the high complexity is proportional only to the size of the incomplete information, which makes the algorithms practical when this size is limited. When this is not the case, Monte Carlo sampling algorithms that approximate the probability of a Boolean condition being true can be applied.

In this paper, we consider tables where random variables can occur for some of the fields. These are called probabilistic tables (or p-tables for short [3]). In addition, we allow constraints on these variables. Tables where constraints can be specified for some of the fields are called constraint tables (or c–tables for short [4]). We make the representation model even more expressive by considering bag semantics and allowing linear conditions over the random variables. This allows the tables to be closed under common relational algebra operations, such as projection, selection, join, duplicate elimination, and grouping and aggregation. We refer to such tables as *mixed tables* or *m-tables* for short. An example of an m-table is shown in Table I. The *global condition* field is part of every m-table. It specifies under what condition there will be tuples in the table. If the global condition is not satisfied, then the representation of the table will be empty. We assume that an empty condition is always true. A local condition is associated with each tuple. It specified the condition under which the tuple exists. In the example, either Bob or John goes to UCLA but not both of them because it is impossible that $x = 1$ and $x = 2$ at the same time. The variables y and x are random variable, where their distribution is shown in the lower part of Table I. For example, the random variable x shows that there is an equal probability that John or Bob studies in UCLA. Note that, as shown in Table I, every m-table can be represented using several relational tables (we will require that the random variables are initially independent and their distributions are discretized).

TABLE I. THE **Student** M-TABLE

name	*school*	*grade*	*local condition*
"John"	"UCLA"	y	$x = 1$
"Bob"	"UCLA"	"A"	$x = 2$

global condition:

value of y	*prob.*
"A"	0.6
"B"	0.3
"C"	0.1

value of x	*prob.*
1	0.5
2	0.5

In 1992, Rina Dechter wrote a survey paper on *constraint networks* [5] that shows how graph networks can be used to find the solution to a set of constraints. In 1985, Judea Pearl wrote a paper that introduces the concept of a *Bayesian network* for random variables [6]. The two concepts have been studies separately until Mateescu and Dechter introduced the concept of a *mixed network* [7]. This is a network that allows the specification of both constraints and dependencies between random variables. Here, we adopt the approach of the last paper and study how tables with linear constraints and random variables can be stored and queried. While c-tables with linear conditions [1] and p-tables [3] have been extensively studded, we are not aware of any research that combines the two concepts in the presence of linear conditions. The advantage of our approach is that most relational algebra operations are straightforward to perform and have good running times. One drawback of our approach is that some of the complexity is buried in the data representation.

In this paper, we define the precise semantics of an m-table as a set of relational tables. We then examine the problem of m-table simplification and deciding when two m-tables are equivalent, that is, when they represent the same set of tables. As part of this study, we show why it is impossible to create a canonical form for an m-table. We also define different relational algebra operations, such as projection, selection, inner join, union, monus, and duplicate elimination. For each operation, we present the formal semantics, show why this semantics is well justified, and show an algorithm for performing the operation. The basic idea is that performing a relational algebra operation on one or more m-tables should result in an m-table that represents the set of tables that we will get if we performed the relational algebra operation on the tables that are represented be the input m-tables. When this is the case, we will say that the relational algebra operation is *sound and complete*. In this paper, we closely follow the research that was presented in [8]. The novelty is that now we allow random variables to be part of a table. We also optimize some of the algorithms and elaborate on how the duplicate elimination operation can be performed.

In what follows, in Section II we present related research. Section III shows the formal semantics of m-tables and defines what does it mean for two m-tables to be equivalent. Section IV presents our algorithms for performing the different relational algebra operations on m-tables. Lastly, Section V summarizes the paper and highlights avenues for future studies.

II. Related Research

We start by presenting relevant research in the area of incomplete databases. It turns out that the problem of representing incomplete information is as old as the relational model itself [9], [10], [11], [12], [13]. Imielinski and Lipsi [14] were among the first to propose richer semantics for incomplete information. Before that, the only option was to put "null" when the value of a field of a tuple is unknown. Later, Libkin and Wong [15] extended the research to tuples with bag semantics. Grahne extensively studied the problem of representing incomplete information [4], while Reiter [16] and Yuan et al. [17] explored algorithms for querying tables with null values. Libkin [18] addressed the problem of querying incomplete databases, while Buneman et. all [19] showed how a table can represent one of several possibilities. The most expressive representation of incomplete information that we are aware of is [8]. It presents a system that supports bag semantics with grouping and aggregation.

We next turn our attention to papers on databases with statistical data. It turns out that probabilistic databases are also as old as the relational model [20], [21], [22], [23]. Barbara et al. [24] were the first to show how random variables can appear inside tables and how the different relational algebra operations can be performed on such tables. Ge at al. [25] show a general approach to storing and querying probabilistic objects that can contain any number of attributes, while Suciu et al. [2] show a comprehensive overview of the current state-of-the-art in probabilistic databases. In particular, Jampani et al. [26] show how to apply a Monte Carlo algorithm to approximate the distribution of the variables in the result of applying different relational operations, while other papers [27], [28], [29], [30], [31] show how these probabilities can be exactly computed. Note that, unlike most papers that use exclusively the tuple level uncertainty approach, we combine the tuple and attribute level uncertainty approaches. Although this approach increases the complexity of our data representation model, it allows for more compact representation of information. As a final remark, note that we allow linear constraints to be associated with tuples. This is a generalization of the approach of previous papers that allow lineage to be associated with each tuple [2].

III. Introducing M-tables

In this section, we present the syntax and semantics of a mixed table (a.k.a. m-table) and discuss the questions of m-table simplification, m-table equivalence, and the existence of a canonical form for m-tables.

Definition 3.1 (syntax of an m-table): An *m-table* contains three parts: a bag ot *m-tuples*, a single *global condition*, and the distribution of the random variables. An m-tuple t with attributes $\{A_i\}_{i=1}^{a}$ is a sequence of mappings from A_i to $D(A_i) \cup \mathbf{V}_i$ (called the *main part* and denoted as $main(t)$) plus a *local condition* (denoted as $lc(t)$), where i ranges from 1 to a. $D(A_i)$ is used to represent the domain of the attribute A_i, while $\mathbf{V}_i$ is a set of random variables over $D(A_i)$. We will allow local and global conditions over the system $\langle \mathbb{R}, \{>, =, +\}\rangle \cup \langle \mathbb{S}, \{=, \neq\}\rangle$, where $\mathbb{R}$ is the set of real numbers and $\mathbb{S}$ is the set of all strings. We will use $gc(T)$ to denote the global condition of the m-table T. Note that we require that the distribution of the random variables be discretized so that it can be stored in a tabular format.

We will follow the approach of Imielinski and Lipski [32] and define the *rep* function. It shows the set of relational tables that an m-table represents. The novelty is that we will also add a probability to each relational table that shows how likely it is that the particular table contains the correct data. We can think of each relational table as the interpretation of the m-table (or its random variables) under some possible world, where the sum of the probabilities over all possible worlds is equal to one. Note that, unlike [32], we adopt the closed world assumption. That is, we assume that tuples that are not part of a table do not belong to the table. We also apply bag semantics, that is, we allow duplicate tuples.

Definition 3.2 (semantics of an m-table): An m-table T represents the following set of relational tables and associated probabilities.

$$rep(T) = \{\langle v(T), p(v)\rangle : v \text{ is such that } p(v) > 0\} \quad (1)$$

The function v interprets the variables in T as constants in the corresponding domains. The expression $p(v)$ denote the probability that the mapping v occurs, where this probability can be computed from the probability distribution of the random variables. If the probability distribution of a random variable is missing, then we assume uniform distribution. We next define the function v for m-tuples.

$$v(t) = \begin{cases} v(main(t)) & \text{if } v(lc(t)) \wedge v(gc(T)) \\ \varnothing & \text{otherwise} \end{cases} \quad (2)$$

In the above formula, t is an m-tuple of the m-table T. The formula $v(main(t))$ means that we apply the interpretation v to all the variables in the main part of the m-tuple t. The function v is generalized to m-tables as follows, where $\{| \cdot |\}$ is used to denote a bag of elements.

$$v(T) = \{| \; v(t) : t \text{ is such that } t \in T \wedge v(t) \neq \varnothing \; |\} \quad (3)$$

The above definition differs from the definition in [8] because now a probability is associated with each of the relational tables that are represented by an m-table. While it is certainly possible to extend the definition and define ordering over m-tables, we leave this topic as an area for future research.

For completeness, we show the four possible representations of our example **Student** m-table in Table II. For example, there is a 15% probability that John is enrolled in UCLA and has a grade of "B" because there is a 50% probability that he is enrolled in UCLA and a 30% probability that his grade is a "B", where the two probabilities are independent.

TABLE II. THE RESULT OF APPLYING THE *rep* FUNCTION TO THE **Student** TABLE

name	*school*	*grade*	
"John"	"UCLA"	"A"	0.3⟩

name	*school*	*grade*	
"John"	"UCLA"	"B"	0.15 ⟩

name	*school*	*grade*	
"John"	"UCLA"	"C"	0.05 ⟩

name	*school*	*grade*	
"Bob"	"UCLA"	"A"	0.5 ⟩

Note that our definition of an m-table differs from a common approach in probabilistic databases where a probability of existence is assigned to each tuple (i.e., tuple level uncertainty [2]). However, we can compute the probability of existence of a tuple t by computing the value of $p(lc(t) \wedge gc(t))$. The function p computes the probability that is associated with a linear expression. The function can be computed using a mixed probability network, where Mateescu et al. propose both a precise algorithm and approximate Monte Carlo sampling algorithm for computing the probability [7]. We can apply this algorithm because the distribution of the random variables is discretized. The precise algorithm creates a graphical model where a node is created for every random variable and random variables that are correlated (i.e., are part of the same linear constraint) are connected with edges. It then examines how the distribution of one random variable affects the distribution of the connected in the graph random variables. The sampling algorithm approximates the probability of a linear condition being true by simply generating random interpretations according to the probability distribution of the random variables and calculating the percent of time that the linear condition is true. The Monte Carlo algorithm should be applied whenever it is unfeasible to apply the precise algorithm.

A. M-table Simplification and Equivalence

We start this subsection with an algorithm that simplifies a linear condition. The *simplify* algorithm is presented in Figure 1. It can be used to simplify the local conditions and global condition of an m-tuple. The algorithm converts the condition in disjunctive normal form and then normalizes each conjunction using the *normalize* algorithm from [33]. The algorithm has the property that it will convert each of the conjunctions into a canonical form. However, as we have shown in [1], a canonical form for a general linear constraint does not exist. Informally, the reason is that there are different ways to describe a linear point set as the union of polyhedras. The algorithm takes exponential time relative to the size of the condition, which is not necessarily a big concern because in practice most conditions are relatively small. Depending on the performance requirments, the algorithm can use the exact or approximate algorithm for calculating the p function.

Algorithm 1 *simplify*(θ)

```
if p(θ) = 0 then
    return false
end if
if p(θ) = 1 then
    return true
end if
θ_1 ∨ ... ∨ θ_n ← θ, where {θ_i}_{i=1}^n are conjunctions
for i ← 1 to n do
    θ_i ← normalize(θ_i)
end for
for i ← 1 to n do
    if θ_i ≡ true or p(θ_i) = 1 then
        return true
    end if
end for
θ ← false
for i ← 1 to n do
    if θ_i ≢ false and p(θ_i) > 0 then
        θ ← θ ∨ θ_i
    end if
end for
return θ
```

Figure 1. The algorithm for simplifying a linear condition.

Since a canonical form for m-tables does not exist, we can only simplify an m-table to make it more compact. The simplification algorithm is shown in Figure 2, where its main property is its correctness. That is, it does not change the set of relational tables that the input m-table represents.

The algorithm is identical to the algorithm from [1], where the only difference is that the *simplify* function considers the distribution of the random variables. The algorithm unifies tuples that are unifiable, which compacts the input m-table. Two m-tuples are unifiable when we know that exactly one of them can appear in any representation. For example, the two tuples in the example **Student** table are unifiable. Formal definition follows.

Definition 3.3 (m-tuple unification): The m-tuples t_1 and t_2 of the m-table T are unifiable exactly when the expression $lc(t_1) \wedge lc(t_2) \wedge gc(T)$ is not satisfiable.

The m-table simplification algorithm needs to consider all pairs of m-tuples and therefore will run in quadratic time relative to the size of the m-table. An example of applying the

Algorithm 2 *simplify*(T)

```
if simplify(gc(T)) ≡ false or p(gc(T)) = 0 then
    return empty table
end if
for all t ∈ T do
    if simplify(lc(t) ∧ gc(t)) ≡ false then
        remove t from T
    end if
end for
while ∃{t1, t2}, s.t. unifiable(t1, t2) do
    remove t1 and t2 from T
    crate a new m-tuple t
    X ← {x1, ... xn}, a set of new variables
    main(t) ← {x1, ..., xn}
    lc(t) ← (X = main(t1) ∧ lc(t1)) ∨ (X = main(t2) ∧ lc(t2))
    add t to T
end while
for all t ∈ T do
    lc(t) ← simplify(lc(t) ∧ gc(T))
    if lc(t) ≡ false then
        remove t from T
    else
        while main(t) contains a variable x and simplify(lc(t) ⇒ (x = c)) ≡ true do
            replace x with the constant c in main(t)
        end while
    end if
end for
gc(T) ← empty
return T
```

Figure 2. The algorithm for simplifying a mixed table.

simplify function to the **Student** table is shown in Table III. Note that the m-table can be further simplified by removing the random variable x and the conditions $x = 1$ and $x = 2$. However, this involves a more evolved linear expression simplification algorithm, such as the one presented in [8].

TABLE III. THE RESULT OF *simplify*(**Student**)

name	*school*	*grade*	*local condition*
n	"UCLA"	g	$(x = 1 \wedge n = \text{"John"} \wedge g = y) \vee$ $(x = 2 \wedge n = \text{"Bob"} \wedge g = \text{"A"})$

value of y	*prob.*
"A"	0.6
"B"	0.3
"C"	0.1

value of x	*prob.*
1	0.5
2	0.5

We will say that two m-tables are equivalent when they represent the same set of relational tables. A formal definition follows.

Definition 3.4 (m-table equivalence): Two m-tables T_1 and T_2 are equivalent when $rep(T_1) \equiv rep(T_2)$. We will write $T1 \simeq T_2$ to denote that two m-tables are equivalent.

The following theorem shows that the m-table simplification algorithm does not change the meaning of an m-table.

Theorem 3.1: For any m-table T, $T \simeq simplify(T)$.

Lastly, the following theorem shows a practical way to check for the equivalence of two m-tables.

Theorem 3.2: $T_1 \simeq T_2$ exactly when $simplify(T_1 - T_2) = \varnothing$ and $simplify(T_2 - T_1) = \varnothing$, where "$-$" is the monus relational algebra operation, which is defined in the next section.

IV. RELATIONAL ALGEBRA OPERATIONS

It is expected that the different relational algebra operations will have "nice" properties. In particular, we want the result of applying a relational algebra operation on one or more m-tables to be an m-table. We also expect the result of the operation to be consistent with the semantic of the input m-tables (see Definition 3.2). Precise definition of these properties follows. Note that we will say that the tables $\{T_i\}_{i=1}^n$ are *allowable* for the relational algebra operation q when $q(\{T_i\}_{i=1}^n)$ is well defined. For example, union is allowed only on tables that have identical attributes.

Definition 4.1 (closed RA operation): A relational algebra operation q with arity n is closed if an only if the result of applying q to any allowable m-tables $\{T_i\}_{i=1}^n$ is an m-table, that is, $q(T_1, \ldots, T_n)$ is always an m-table.

Definition 4.2 (sound RA operation): A relational algebra operation q is sound when it produces only correct answers. Formally, $rep(q(T_1, \ldots, T_n)) \subseteq q(rep(T_1, \ldots, T_n))$ for any allowable tables $\{T_i\}_{i=1}^n$.

Note that we will some times abuse notation and use $q(rep(T_1, \ldots, T_k))$ to define the result of applying the operation q to each table in the set $\{rep(T_i)\}_{i=1}^k$.

Definition 4.3 (complete RA operation): A relational algebra operation q is complete exactly when all correct answers appear in the result, that is $q(rep(T_1, \ldots, T_n)) \subseteq rep(q(T_1, \ldots, T_n))$ for any allowable m-tables $\{T_i\}_{i=1}^n$.

In order for a relational algebra to be *well defined*, it is required that all operations are closed, sound, and complete. We next define relational algebra over m-tables that is well defined, where the definition of completeness for the monus operation will have to be slightly adjusted.

A. Projection

In this subsection, we will define duplicate preserving projection, which we will denote as π^d. The more common duplicate eliminating projection can be achieved by applying the duplicate elimination operation to the result.

The algorithm is shown Figure 3, where the algorithm simply selects the desired fields. The following theorem is not hard to prove and it is based on a similar theorem in [1].

Theorem 4.1: The projection operation is well-defined and the result can be computed in time that is linear to the size of the input table.

Table IV shows the result of applying the duplicate preserving projection operation on the *name* and *school* fields of the example **Student** table. Note that the local condition field does not need to be included in the list of projected fields because it cannot be projected out.

Algorithm 3 Evaluating $\pi^d_{\mathbf{A}}(T)$

$S \leftarrow T$
for all $A \in attr(S)$ and $A \notin \mathbf{A}$ **do**
  if x is a random variable that appears only in A **then**
    remove the probability table for x
  end if
end for
for all $t \in S$ **do**
  remove attributes outside the set **A**
end for
return S

Figure 3. The algorithm for computing the projection over a mixed table.

TABLE IV. THE RESULT OF $\pi^d_{name,school}(\mathbf{Student})$

name	*school*	*local condition*
"John"	"UCLA"	$x = 1$
"Bob"	"UCLA"	$x = 2$

global condition:

value of x	*prob.*
1	0.5
2	0.5

B. Selection

Figure 4 shows how to apply the selection relational algebra operation to an m-table. It first replaces variables with constants where appropriate inside the main body of the table. It then adds the selection condition to all the local conditions. As a last step, the local conditions are simplified. Tuples that have a local condition that is false are removed. Similarly, tuples that have a local condition that is a tautology are left with empty local conditions. The following theorem is not hard to prove and it is based on a similar theorem in [1].

Theorem 4.2: The selection operation is well-defined and the result can be computed in time that is linear to the size of the input table plus the time to simplify the new local conditions.

Table V shows the result of applying $\sigma_{grade=\text{``A''}}(\mathbf{Student})$. The algorithm first substitutes the value for the attribute *grade* of the first tuple with "A" because we only keep tuples if the grade is "A". Then the selection condition is added to the local conditions. Note that the condition that is added to the second tuple is "A"="A", which is a tautology and is therefore removed by the *simplify* algorithm.

TABLE V. RESULT OF $\sigma_{grade=\text{``A''}}(\mathbf{Student})$

name	*school*	*grade*	*l. condition*
"John"	"UCLA"	"A"	$y =$ "A"$\wedge x = 1$
"Bob"	"UCLA"	"A"	$x = 2$

g.condition:

value of y	*prob.*
"A"	0.6
"B"	0.3
"C"	0.1

value of x	*prob.*
1	0.5
2	0.5

Algorithm 4 Evaluating $\sigma_\theta(T)$

$S \leftarrow T$
for all A_i such that θ has the form $(A_i = value \wedge \ldots)$ and $t.A_i = p$ **do**
  $t[A_i] \leftarrow$value
  if p does not appear anywhere else **then**
    remove the probability table for p
  end if
end for
for all $t \in S$ **do**
  $\psi(t) \leftarrow$ a substitution that substitutes every variable A_i with $t[A_i]$ (the value for the attribute A_i in t)
  $lc(t) \leftarrow simplify(lc(t) \wedge \theta_{\psi(t)})$
  if $lc(t) \equiv$ **true then**
    make local condition of t empty
  end if
  if $lc(t) \equiv$ **false then**
    remove t from S
  end if
end for
return S

Figure 4. The algorithm for computing selection over mixed table.

C. Natural Join

The algorithm for natural join is shown in Figure 5, where the algorithms for theta join and outer join are similar.

Algorithm 5 Evaluating $T_1(\mathbf{A}, \mathbf{B}) \bowtie T_2(\mathbf{B}, \mathbf{C})$

$T \leftarrow$ empty m-table with the attributes of $\mathbf{A} \cup \mathbf{B} \cup \mathbf{C}$
for all $t_1 \in T_1$ **do**
  for all $t_2 \in T_2$ **do**
    if $simplify(t_1[\mathbf{B}] = t_2[\mathbf{B}]) \not\equiv$ **false then**
      $t \leftarrow$ new tuple with attributes of T
      $main(t) \leftarrow \langle t_1, \pi^d_{\mathbf{C}}(t_2)\rangle$
      $lc(t) \leftarrow simplify(lc(t_1) \wedge lc(t_2) \wedge t_1[\mathbf{B}] = t_2[\mathbf{B}])$
      add t to T
    end if
  end for
end for
$gc(T) \leftarrow gc(T_1) \wedge gc(T_2)$
return T

Figure 5. The algorithm for natural join of mixed tables.

The above algorithm simply joins tuples from the two m-tables that are *joinable*. Two tuples are joinable when the local condition of the new tuple is satisfiable. When two tuples are joined, the new local condition is the conjunction of the join condition and the local conditions of the two tuples. As a final step, the global conditions of the two tables are merged using conjunction. The following theorem is not hard to prove and it is based on a similar theorem in [1].

Theorem 4.3: The natural join operation is well-defined and the result can be computed in time that is proportional to multiplying the sizes of the two tables times the time to perofrm the new linear condition simplification.

As is the case in relational databases, a join can be optimized using indexes. We leave the details as a topic for future research. Consider the **University** mixed table in Table VI. Table VII shows the result of the natural join of the **Student** and **University** tables. Note that the second tuple of the **University** table cannot join with any of the tuples in the **Student** table. Conversely, the first tuple of the **University** table joins with the two tuples in the **Student** table when z = "$UCLA$". In the tuple-level uncertainty model, one can compute that the *marginal probability* of the first tuple in the result (i.e., the probability of the tuple existing in a representation) is $0.5 * 0.6 = 0.3$. However, our model does not explicitly store the marginal probabilities of the resulting tuples.

TABLE VI. THE **University** M-TABLE

school	*local condition*
z	
Cal Poly	

global condition:

value of z	*prob.*
"UCLA"	0.6
"Univeristy of California Los Angeles"	0.4

TABLE VII. THE RESULT OF **Student** ⋈ **University**

name	*school*	*grade*	*local condition*
"John"	"UCLA"	y	$x = 1 \wedge z =$ "$UCLA$"
"Bob"	"UCLA"	"A"	$x = 2 \wedge z =$ "$UCLA$"

global condition:

value of y	*prob.*
"A"	0.6
"B"	0.3
"C"	0.1

value of x	*prob.*
1	0.5
2	0.5

value of z	*prob.*
"UCLA"	0.6
"Univeristy of California Los Angeles"	0.4

D. Union

Performing the duplicate preserving union of two m-tables is straightforward. Figure 6 shows the algorithm that simply merges the tuples of the two tables. The new global condition is the conjunction of the global conditions of the input tables.

Algorithm 6 Evaluating $T_1 \cup^d T_2$

$T \leftarrow$ empty m-table that has the attributes of T_1
for all $t_1 \in T_1$ **do**
  add t_1 to T
end for
for all $t_2 \in T_2$ **do**
  add t_2 to T
end for
$gc(T) \leftarrow gc(T_1) \wedge gc(T_2)$
return T

Figure 6. The algorithm for duplicate-preserving union of mixed tables.

The following theorem is not hard to prove and it is based on a similar theorem in [1]. Note that the m-table simplification algorithm can be applied to the resulting table in order to make it more compact, but this is not a requirement.

Theorem 4.4: The duplicate preserving union operation is well-defined and the result can be computed in time that is linear in the size of the input tables.

As an example, Table VIII shows the result of applying the duplicate preserving union on two copies of the *Student* table. The new table denotes that either we have two Bobs, or we have two Johns in UCLA, but not both.

TABLE VIII. THE RESULT OF **Student** $\cup^d$ **Student**

name	*school*	*grade*	*local condition*
"John"	"UCLA"	y	$x = 1$
"Bob"	"UCLA"	"A"	$x = 2$
"John"	"UCLA"	y	$x = 1$
"Bob"	"UCLA"	"A"	$x = 2$

global condition:

value of y	*prob.*
"A"	0.6
"B"	0.3
"C"	0.1

value of x	*prob.*
1	0.5
2	0.5

E. Monus

The duplicate-preserving monus operation is defined as follows $T_1 -^d T_2 = \{|t_{[k]} \mid t \in T_1 \wedge k = max(0, card(t, T_1) - card(t, T_2))|\}$. The *card* function returns the cardinality (a.k.a. number of appearances) of the tuple in the table, while $t_{[k]}$ denotes that the tuple t appears k times in the result. As expected, $t_{[0]}$ means that the tuple does not appear in the result.

We will define the algorithm that performs the monus operation using two two-dimensional arrays. Let $X[i, j]$ be the condition that must be true for the ith tuple in T_1 to delete the jth tuple in T_2. This condition is true under an interpretation that makes the main parts of the tuples the same and makes the local conditions of the two tuples and global conditions of the two tables true. Let $Y[i][j]$ be equal to 1 when the ith in T_1 is deleted by the jth tuple in T_2 and be equal to 0 otherwise. We will use Y to enforce the restriction that every tuple in T_2 can delete at most one tuple in T_1. Figure 7 shows the algorithm for performing the monus operation. The algorithm is an optimized version of the algorithm from [8]. Note that we do not specify the probability distributions of the two two-dimensional arrays of random variables and therefore uniform distribution is assumed.

The algorithm first removes tuples from T_2 that cannot delete tuples from T_1. It next copies tuples from T_1 that cannot be deleted by tuples from T_2 to the resulting set. As a final step, all the remaining tuples from T_1 are added to the result. For each of these tuples, a local condition is added that they will be part of the result only if they are not deleted by one of the tuples in T_2, where an interpretation of Y fixes which tuples in T_1 are deleted by which tuples in T_2.

The following theorem is not hard to prove and it is based on a similar theorem in [1].

Theorem 4.5: The monus operation is closed, sound, and it supports a version of completeness. Specifically, we need to modify the completeness condition as follows: $(Rep(T_1) - Rep(T_2)) \cup \{\varnothing\} \subseteq Rep(T_1 - T_2)$. The complexity of the operation is linear relative to the product of the sizes of the two tables plus the time to perform the new local condition simplification.

Algorithm 7 Evaluating $T_1 -^d T_2$

$V_1 \leftarrow T_1$
$V_2 \leftarrow T_2$
$R \leftarrow$ empty table that has the attributes of T_1
for all $t_1 \in V_1$ **do**
  if there is no tuple t_2 in V_2 such that $simplify(main(t_1) = main(t_2) \wedge lc(t_1) \wedge gc(t_1) \wedge lc(t_2) \wedge gc(t_2))$ **then**
    add t_1 to R
    remove t_1 from V_1
  end if
end for
for all $t_2 \in V_2$ **do**
  if there is no tuple t_1 in V_1 such that $simplify(main(t_1) = main(t_2) \wedge lc(t_1) \wedge gc(t_1) \wedge lc(t_2) \wedge gc(t_2))$ **then**
    remove t_2 from V_2
  end if
end for
$i \leftarrow 0$
for all $t_1 \in T_1$ **do**
  $j \leftarrow 0$
  for all $t_2 \in T_2$ **do**
    $X[i][j] \leftarrow simplify(main(t_1) = main(t_2) \wedge lc(t_1) \wedge gc(t_1) \wedge lc(t_2) \wedge gc(t_2))$
    $j \leftarrow j + 1$
  end for
  $i \leftarrow i + 1$
end for
$n \leftarrow$ number of tuples in V_1
$m \leftarrow$ number of tuples in V_2
$i \leftarrow 0$
for all $t \in V_1$ **do**
  $lc(t) \leftarrow lc(t) \wedge \neg(\bigvee_{j=1}^{m} (X[i,j] \wedge Y[i,j] = 1))$
  $i \leftarrow i + 1$
end for
$gc(R) \leftarrow \bigwedge_{j=1}^{m} (\bigvee_{i=1}^{n} (Y[1,j] = \ldots = Y[i-1,j] = Y[i+1,j] = \ldots = Y[n,j] = 0 \wedge Y[i,j] = 1))$
return $R \cup^d V_1$

Figure 7. The algorithm for subtracting mixed tables.

We had to modify the definition of completeness because we allow the empty set (a.k.a. $\varnothing$) to be a possible representation of an m-table. We believe that this is intrinsic problem associated with monus under the closed world assumption. Table IX shows the result of applying the monus operation on the m-tables *simplify*(**Student**) and **Student**. Applying the *simplify* algorithm to the new table will produce the empty set.

F. Duplicate Elimination

The duplicate elimination algorithm simply checks for pairs of m-tuples that have main parts that are unifiable and local conditions that are not excluding. The algorithm then adds the restriction to the output table that states that if the two tuples indeed have the same main part under some possible interpretation, then the local condition of only of the tuples can be satisfied. The formal definition of unifiable main parts is presented next.

TABLE IX. THE RESULT OF **Student** $-^d$ *simplify*(**Student**)

name	*school*	*grade*	*local condition*
"John"	"UCLA"	y	$x = 1 \wedge \neg($"John"$= n \wedge y = g \wedge ((x = 1 \wedge n =$ "John" $\wedge g = y) \vee (x = 2 \wedge n =$ "Bob" $\wedge g =$ "A"$)) \wedge Y[1,1] = 1)$
"Bob"	"UCLA"	"A"	$x = 2 \wedge \neg($"Bob"$= n \wedge g =$ "A"$\wedge ((x = 1 \wedge n =$ "John" $\wedge g = y) \vee (x = 2 \wedge n =$ "Bob" $\wedge g =$ "A"$)) \wedge Y[2,1] = 1)$

global condition: $(Y[1,1] = 1 \wedge Y[2,1] = 0) \vee (Y[1,1] = 0 \wedge Y[2,1] = 1)$

value of y	*prob.*
"A"	0.6
"B"	0.3
"C"	0.1

value of x	*prob.*
1	0.5
2	0.5

Definition 4.4 (unifiable main parts): Two tuples have main parts that are unifiable if these main parts can become equivalent under some possible interpretation. We will write *unifiable*$(main(t_1), main(t_2))$ when this is the case.

Details are shown in Figure 8, where we use δ to denote the duplicate elimination operation. The following theorem is not hard to prove.

Algorithm 8 Evaluating $\delta(T)$

$V \leftarrow T$
for all $t_1, t_2 \in V$ **do**
  if *unifiable*$(main(t_1), main(t_2))$ and $simplify(lc(t_1) \equiv (t_2)) \not\equiv$ **false then**
    introduce a new variable x
    $lc(t_1) \leftarrow lc(t_1) \wedge ((main(t_1) = main(t_2)) \Rightarrow (x = 1))$
    $lc(t_2) \leftarrow lc(t_2) \wedge ((main(t_1) = main(t_2)) \Rightarrow (x = 2))$
  end if
end for
for all new variable x **do**
  Add a table for the distribution of x. The possible values are 1 and 2 with probability 0.5 each.
end for
return V

Figure 8. The algorithm for duplicate elimination.

Theorem 4.6: The duplicate eliminating operation is closed, sound, and complete. The complexity of the operation is quadratic relative to the size of the table plus the time to execute the calls to the *simplify* function.

As an example, consider applying the duplicate eliminating operation on the table from Table VIII. The result is shown in Table X. We can apply the *simplify* function to the result to get back the **Student** table.

V. CONCLUSION AND FUTURE RESEARCH

We introduced the concept of a mixed table. This is a table that allows both random variables and linear constraints on them to be stored. To the best of our knowledge, we are the first paper to do so. We presented the semantics of a mixed table as

TABLE X. THE RESULT OF δ(**Student** $\cup^d$ **Student**)

name	*school*	*grade*	*local condition*
"John"	"UCLA"	y	$x = 1 \wedge z = 1$
"Bob"	"UCLA"	"A"	$x = 2 \wedge w = 1$
"John"	"UCLA"	y	$x = 1 \wedge z = 2$
"Bob"	"UCLA"	"A"	$x = 2 \wedge w = 2$

value of y	*prob.*
"A"	0.6
"B"	0.3
"C"	0.1

value of x	*prob.*
1	0.5
2	0.5

value of z	*prob.*
1	0.5
2	0.5

value of w	*prob.*
1	0.5
2	0.5

a set of relational tables, where a probability is associated with each representation. We extended the bag relational algebra from [8] to m-tables and showed that the new relational algebra is closed, sound, and complete. In summary, we believe that this paper can serve as a blueprint for a system for storing and querying m-tables.

As part of future research, we need to show how the different relational algebra operations can be performed efficiently. For example, indexes on the data can be used to execute the selection and join relational operations efficiently. We also need to follow the model from [8] and introduce algorithms for performing grouping and aggregation over m-tables.

REFERENCES

[1] L. Stanchev, "Bag Relational Algebra with Grouping and Aggregation over C-Tables with Linear Conditions," International Journal on Advances in Intelligent Systems, vol. 4, no. 3, 2010, pp. 258–272.

[2] D. Suciu, D. Olteanu, C. Re, and C. Koch, Probabilistic Databases. Morgan and Claypool Publishers, 2011.

[3] N. Dalvi, C. Re, and D. Sucu, "Probabilistic Databases: Diamonds in the Dirt," Communications of the ACM, vol. 52, no. 7, 2009, pp. 86–94.

[4] G. Grahne, The Problem of Incomplete Information in Relational Databases. Berlin: Springer-Verlag, 1991.

[5] R. Dechter, Constraint Networks. Encyclopedia of Artificial Intelligence, Second Edition, Wiley and Sons, 1992.

[6] J. Pearl, "Bayesian Networks: A Model of Self-Activated Memory for Evidential Reasoning," Seventh Annual Conference of the Cognitive Science Society, 1985, pp. 329–334.

[7] R. Mateescu and R. Dechter, "Mixed Deterministic and Probabilistic Networks," Annals of Mathematics and Artificial Intelligence, vol. 54, no. 1, 2008, pp. 3–51.

[8] L. Stanchev, "Querying Incomplete Information using Bag Relational Algebra," Proceedings of The Second International Conference on Information Process and Knowledge Management, 2010, pp. 110–119.

[9] J. Biskup, "A Formal Approach to null Values in Database Relations," Advances in Database Theory, 1981, pp. 299–341.

[10] E. Codd, "Understanding Relations (Installment 7)," Bulletin of ACM-SIGMOD, vol. 3, no. 4, 1975, pp. 23–28.

[11] ——, "Extending the Database Relational Model to Capture more Meaning," ACM Transactions on Database Systems, vol. 4, no. 4, 1979, pp. 397–434.

[12] J.Grant, "Null values in Relational Data Base," Information Processing Letters, vol. 6, no. 5, 1977, pp. 156–157.

[13] T. Imielinski and W. Lipski, "On Representing Incomplete Information in a Relational Data Base," Proceedings of the Seventh International Conference on Very Large Data Bases, 1981, pp. 388–397.

[14] ——, "Incomplete Information in Relational Algebra," Journal of Association of Computing, vol. 31, no. 4, 1984, pp. 761–791.

[15] L. Libkin and L. Wong, "Some Properties of Query Languages for Bags," Proceedings of Database Programming Languages, 1994, pp. 97–114.

[16] R. Reiter, "A Sound and Sometimes Complete Query Evaluation Algorithm for Relational Databases with Null Values," Journal of the ACM, vol. 33, no. 2, 1986, pp. 349–370.

[17] L. Yuan and D. Chiang, "A Sound and Complete Query Evaluation Algorithm for Relational Databases with Null Values," ACM Special Interest Group on Management of Data (SIGMOD), 1988, pp. 74–81.

[18] L. Libkin, "Query Languages Primitives for Programming with Incomplete Databases," Proceedings of the Fifth International Workshop on Database Programming Languages, 1995, pp. 1–13.

[19] P. Buneman, A. Jung, and A.Ohori, "Using Powerdomains to Generalize Relational Databases," Theoretical Computer Science, vol. 91, no. 1, 1991, pp. 23–55.

[20] E. Lefons, A. Silverstri, and F. Tangorra, "An Analytic Approach to Statistical Databases," International Conference on Very Large Data Bases, 1983, pp. 260–274.

[21] S. Ghosh, "Statistical Relational Tables for Statistical Database Management," IEEE Transactions on Software Engineering, vol. 12, no. 12, 1986, pp. 1106–1116.

[22] E. Gelenbe and G. Hebrail, "A Probability model of uncertainty in data bases," Second IEEE Conference on Data Engineering, 1986, pp. 328–333.

[23] R. Cavallo and M. Pittarelli, "The Theory of Probabilistic Databases," Proceedings of the Thirteen International Conference on Very Large Data Bases, 1987, pp. 71–81.

[24] D. Barbara, H. Garcia-Molina, and D. Porter, "The Management of Probabilistic Data," IEEE Transactions on Knowledge and Data Engineering, vol. 4, no. 5, 1992, pp. 487–502.

[25] T. Ge, A. Dekhtyar, and J. Gldsmith, "Uncertain Data: Representations, Query Processing, and Applications," in Advances in Probabilistic Databases. Springer-Verlag Berlin Heidelberg, 2013, pp. 67–108.

[26] R. Jampani, F. Xu, and M. Wu, "MCDB: A Monte Carlo Approach to Managing Uncertain Data," Proceeding of ACM Special Interest Group on Management of Data (SIGMOD), 2008, pp. 687–700.

[27] N. Fuhr and T. Rolleke, "A Probabilistic Relational Algebra for the Integration of Information Retrieval and Database Systems," ACM Transactions on Information Systems, vol. 15, no. 1, 1997, pp. 32–66.

[28] P. Agrawal, O. Benjelloun, A. D. Sarma, C. Hayworth, S. Nabar, T. Sugihara, and J. Widowm, "Trio: A System for Data, Uncertainty, and Lineage," Proceedings of Very Large Data Bases, 2006, pp. 1151–1154.

[29] N. N. Dalvi and D. Sucui, "Efficient Query Evaluation on Probabilistic Databases," Very Large Data Bases Journal, vol. 16, no. 4, 2007, pp. 523–544.

[30] P. Andritsos, A. Fuxman, and R. J. Miller, "Clean Answers over Dirty Databases: A Probabilistic Approach," Proceedings of the International Conference on Data Engineering, 2006, p. 30.

[31] L. Antova, C. Koch, and D. Olteanu, "MayBMS: Managing Incomplete information with Probabilistic World-set Decomposition," International Conference on Data Engineering, 2007, pp. 1479–1480.

[32] T. Imielinski and W. Lipski, "Incomplete Information in a Relational Data Base," Journal of ACM, vol. 31, no. 4, 1984, pp. 761–791.

[33] J. Lasssez and K. McAloon, "Applications of a Canonical Form of Generalized Linear Constraints," Journal of Symbolic Computations, vol. 13, 1992, pp. 1–24.

Knowledge Cluster Development through Connectivity: Examples from Southeast Asia

Hans-Dieter Evers
Center for Development Research (ZREF)
Rheinische Friedrich Wilhelms Universität Bonn, Germany
e-mail: hdevers@gmail.com

Thomas Menkhoff
Lee Kong Chian School of Business
Singapore Management University (SMU), Singapore
e-mail: thomasm@smu.edu.sg

Abstract— **Whereas since the 1990s national and regional planners saw the creation of knowledge clusters as a panacea for gaining a competitive advantage to propel a region or country into a higher stage of industrial development, recent research suggests that connectivity (e.g. through broadband penetration or joint research connections with collaborators elsewhere) is one of the enablers for socio-economic development. This paper will draw on the results of studies on knowledge clusters in Southeast Asian countries (Malaysia, Brunei, Singapore) as well as the relevant current literature to ask the question, whether knowledge clusters really contribute to regional development and if yes, under what circumstances. The paper will also draw on lessons learned from knowledge cluster initiatives in Organization for Economic Co-operation and Development (OECD) countries and highlight policy options to enhance connectivity in the context of knowledge cluster development.**

Keywords-knowledge clusters; connectivity; Southeast Asia.

I. INTRODUCTION

Not too long ago, Frances Anne Cairncross, a British economist, journalist, academic and a member of the Council of Economic Advisers for the Scottish Government, announced the "Death of Distance" [1]. She argued that the advances in telecommunications would effectively eliminate distance as a perceptible concept from our lives. This "death of distance," a determinant of the cost of communications, "will become the single most important economic force to reshape society over the next half century". Nothing could be further from the truth. Nobody will today negate the impact of the Internet and of broadband communications on society, culture and the economy, but space still matters. Industrial clusters, knowledge clusters and conceptions of space are still important factors, shaping economy and society. Why does distance still matter?

There are many answers to this intriguing question, but two stand out. The first has been propagated by Harvard Professor Michael Porter [38] [39] [40]. The competitive advantage of nations and regions depends on the formation of industrial clusters. "Clusters are geographic concentrations of interconnected companies, specialized suppliers and service providers, firms in related industries, and associated institutions (e.g. universities, standard agencies, and trade associations) in particular fields that compete but also cooperate. Such clusters are a striking feature of virtually every economy, especially those of more economically advanced areas" (Porter 2000:253). Not only that, the degree of clustering determines the competitiveness of a nation or region. Firms located in a cluster have an enhanced chance of profitability and are more competitive in contrast to firms located outside a cluster in splendid isolation. The main argument of earlier industrial location theory of Alfred Weber is resurrected, namely that transaction costs are lower in clusters than outside [49].

This mantra has been repeated over and over again by Porter and his followers and has led to massive research programmes figuring out the degree of clustering, the location of clusters and the best way to create and manage industrial clusters.

Meanwhile, a great number of studies have been conducted. According to the disciplinary home of the authors, there are coloured results. Geographers have emphasized location and proximity, sociologists emphasized social networks and knowledge sharing, and economists tend to look at economies of scale and transaction costs. At this stage it is extremely difficult to bring together the results of these studies and to draw final conclusions. It has, however, become clear that cluster formation and cluster competitiveness is a good deal more complex and complicated than advocates of Porterian cluster policies would have it. So far, it is not entirely clear whether clusters make firms more productive and thus more competitive, or more productive and competitive firms come together to form a cluster. This poses a dilemma for cluster policies or cluster governance. "Natural" clusters are possibly formed by highly competitive firms, but firms induced by government subsidies or active cluster management may not turn out to be more competitive at all despite being co-located in a cluster.

One finding of Porter type cluster analysis still holds, namely that despite increased broadband penetration and Internet connectivity clusters still emerge. The basic hypothesis that the higher the economic development of a country or region (in terms of the usual measurements), the higher the degree of industrial clustering appears to hold.

The big gap in our understanding of both the clustering process and the outcome of clustering still lies in a precise analysis of the inner workings of a cluster. In short, we need to know more about what makes a cluster tick, before a robust cluster policy can be designed. In Section II we highlight the importance of tacit knowledge in knowledge clusters, followed by what it takes in terms of knowledge management for clustering in close proximity to enable higher productivity (Section III+IV). Section V examines Singapore's maritime cluster and discusses the various ingredients for a cluster to become an innovation hub. In the conclusion, we make a case for the importance of governing connectivity as part of knowledge governance.

II. FROM INDUSTRIAL TO KNOWLEDGE CLUSTERS

Current cluster analysis is the foster child of industrial agglomeration theory, as developed by Alfred Weber a century ago [49] [50]. Taking the Ruhr District, the home of German heavy industries, as an example, he could show that the use of raw materials, like coal, water and iron ore, enticed basic industries and metal industries to crowd together to reduce transportation costs. Raw materials were heavier and therefore costlier to transport than finished products to customers. Markets and materials decide location of industries.

This "reduction of transaction cost" argument is still valid for manufacturing industries, but less so for the new and increasingly important raw material called "knowledge" [48]. Data, information and explicit knowledge can be transmitted through the Internet at low cost. Outsourcing data intensive work, like banking, bookkeeping, design and many other tasks has become frequent practice for both the manufacturing and service sectors. It is therefore surprising that in contradiction to the transaction cost argument, knowledge intensive industries still tend to cluster.

Knowledge clusters do not just consist of information and communications technology (ICT) or high-tech production units, but have to be combined with research institutes, R&D divisions of companies (incl. test-beds and labs), institutions of higher education and learning, like colleges and universities, and government support services.

With the rapid development of information and communication technology and the spread of fast Internet connection, knowledge is increasingly seen as the most important driver of development. While reaching the state of an industrial society is seen as the aim of many developing countries, the move towards a knowledge based economy and society has already engulfed the industrial world. The ICT based service sector is expanding and knowledge is regarded as a prime factor of production. Though production chains extend throughout the world, successful knowledge intensive industries are still found primarily in closely-knit knowledge clusters. The Silicon Valley, the Hyderabad ICT cluster or the biotech research cluster in Singapore are just a few of many examples of vibrant knowledge clusters. The cost for producing knowledge may be high, the cost of transferring data, information and knowledge is extremely low. If the venerable transaction cost argument does not hold, what then explains the emergence of knowledge clusters?

One argument refers to Nonaka's distinction between tacit and explicit knowledge [36]. Tacit knowledge is seen as the main ingredient of innovation in the fields of industrial production, marketing and organizational behaviour. While explicit knowledge can be easily transmitted, tacit knowledge or experience needs personal contacts to be disseminated [9] [19]. A concentration of experts and scientists leads to a "knowledge spill-over" between companies and in social networks and face-to-face contacts. This allows the transmission of valuable tacit knowledge, which is hard to pass on through the Internet. Even broadband enabled video conferencing is apparently not able to get tacit knowledge across and replace the stimulating excitement of personal encounters.

Porter and his followers, on the other hand, seem to be skeptical of this argument. Groupthink, for example, can discourage creativity and prevent the process of innovating [42]. Following Granovetter's distinction between strong and weak ties it could, indeed, be argued that weak social ties of pluralistic, open-ended networks are more likely to be innovative than tightly knit networks of like-minded persons [23]. In other words, clusters integrated by social networks are not necessarily more productive and innovative than clusters with broadband Internet communicating units. Empirical evidence is still scarce and a good deal more research will be necessary to draw robust conclusion.

Another still open issue is the scale and regional impact of clusters. As mentioned above, there appears to be a strong correlation between cluster formation and economic growth at the national level. The impact of cluster formation within regions or beyond is less well established.

III. K-CLUSTERS AS DRIVERS OF REGIONAL DEVELOPMENT

One important assumption of the European Cluster Initiative or the U.S. Cluster Mapping Project is that creating or supporting industrial clusters guarantees economic growth [13]. A study of the European Cluster Observatory concluded, "there is plenty of evidence to suggest that innovation and economic growth is heavily geographically concentrated" [47]. As summarized by Mitchell et al. as recently as 2014 "considerable evidence indicates that knowledge plays a key role in the performance and innovation of firms in clusters" (Mitchell et al. 2014:2198). This, they argue, is also true for small and medium-sized enterprises (SMEs), though they often lack the absorptive capacity to assimilate new knowledge, unless there are "knowledge brokers" using their social capital of contacts into their field of expertise (Mitchell et al. 2014:2204).

Another assumption is related to innovations as a driver of growth. Innovations are presumably more likely to occur in clusters rather than elsewhere. A survey of the European Commission (Europe INNOVA / PRO INNO Europe Paper N° 9, Commission Staff Working Document, p. 22) concluded, "cluster firms are more innovative than non-cluster firms. These innovative cluster companies are more than twice more likely to source out research to other firms, universities or public labs than were the average European innovative firms in 2004. This supports the view that clusters are encouraging knowledge sharing which may further stimulate innovation. Moreover, cluster firms patent and trademark their innovations more often than other innovative companies" (p. 22-23). The statistical evidence provided in these reports shows that most, if not all, clusters support innovations and regional economic growth [14].

Despite the robust statistical evidence, this assumption has recently come under attack. Clustering may even hinder innovations. As Maskell has pointed out [31], cognitive distance may be small in clusters, but when disparate knowledge is required, strong clustering may even prevent the exchange of necessary knowledge and therefor reduce innovative capacity (p. 924). When disparate knowledge is required, it will just not be available in a narrowly focused knowledge cluster because it might be blocked by a competing or differing school of thought.

In a review of the literature, Wolman and Hincapie draw attention to the fact that "all regions have clusters, but not all clusters produce high growth" [51]. The question is therefore: Why are some clusters and their companies and research institutions more innovative than others? What factors stimulate innovative behaviour and regional economic growth?

These questions have, despite Porterian rhetoric during the past 25 years [37-42], not yet be answered in full. The Porter doctrine can be summarized as follows:

- Cluster participation: (a) increasing the current productivity of constituent firms or industries, (b) increasing innovation and productivity growth, and (c) stimulating new business formation that supports innovation and expands the cluster [42]
- Clusters drive productivity and innovation. Firms that are located within a cluster can transact more efficiently, share technologies and knowledge more readily, operate more flexibly, start new businesses more easily, and perceive and implement innovations more rapidly [41]
- Clusters Drive Regional Performance: Job growth, higher wages, higher patenting rates; greater new business formation, growth and survival; resilience in downturns [37].

By repeating over and over again that clusters stimulate innovations and are a necessary precondition for growth, not all questions are automatically answered. Some doubt remains and many questions have been left open for further research. We will use examples from the existing extensive literature as well as from our own studies on the relatively under-researched areas of clusters in Southeast Asia and point into directions, in which answers may be found or where additional research will be necessary.

IV. Broadband and K-Clusters as Drivers of Regional Development

The existence of stable broadband connections is assumed by some authors to act as a driver for cluster formation. Fast Internet connections make video conferencing viable and an immediate exchange of data and information possible. Indeed it could be assumed that the extension of broadband connection makes firms less dependent on proximity externalities, i.e. on cluster formation. From a different perspective broadband connections could also be helpful in spreading the impact of cluster productivity to neighboring regions. The results of empirical studies are, however, not clear-cut. In a recent study, Mack concludes that "in some places, broadband appears to be an essential link that enables knowledge firms to strategically locate in lower cost counties and in close proximity to major knowledge centres. In other places, the availability of broadband Internet connections is unable to mitigate the negative externalities associated with locations in more remote areas of the country. From a policy perspective, this suggests that broadband should be viewed as a key component, but not the only component, of comprehensive local economic development plans" [30]. Her findings are depicted in a map, showing US counties with or without good broadband provision in relation to knowledge intensive industries.

A. Networks and Knowledge Hubs

As various surveys have shown, sharing and dissemination of knowledge within clusters is a major driver of innovations and growth [9] [19] [33] [45]. Several authors see this as a more or less automatic process. Knowledge workers and experts working in proximity in one location easily transmit knowledge, so the argument goes. There is a "knowledge spillover", leading almost automatically to higher productivity [1] [10]. Our studies in Indonesia [44] and Vietnam [6] show otherwise. Though automatic knowledge-spillover may happen, there are knowledge clusters with high kernel density, where knowledge sharing is low or totally absent. This is the case in Hoh Chi Minh City, which has a great number of research institutes and universities in close proximity, but hardly any knowledge exchange takes place [6] [16] [17].

This means that clustering in close proximity is not a sufficient precondition for higher productivity. Knowledge has to be managed, cooperation needs stimulation and appropriate institutions for knowledge sharing, on which productivity rests, have to be formed [9].

The Malaysian government has pursued an active cluster development agenda [20] by declaring several regions as "development corridors" [4] and creating a massive Multimedia Super Corridor next to the newly founded federal capital of Putrajaya [7] [25]. The two other successful knowledge driven industrial clusters are found in Penang and in Johore.

In our studies in Penang we found a high degree of clustering including ICT industry, universities and local and international research institutes and companies. Several companies had relocated to Penang from other countries, because of the availability of high-level manpower and access to services of support companies. Government agencies supported research projects and supported start-up companies [13] [15] [22] [26].

Another interesting case is Brunei Darussalam, a small resource rich country with practically no industrial base [2] [3] [18] [27]. We could identify only one dense knowledge cluster in the commercial district of the capital Bandar Seri Begawan, but the two major knowledge producing institutions University Brunei Darussalam, including several research institutes and the Institute Technology Brunei are actually located outside the major knowledge cluster [4]. Ongoing research by Purwaningrum (Institute of Asian Studies, UBD) shows that there is very little, if any, knowledge sharing between UBD, industry and government agencies. The so-called "triple helix" is not functioning and urgently needs to be managed.

V. Singapore's Maritime Cluster (SMC): Success through Connectivity and Collaborative Research & Development (R&D)

Quite a different story is the development of Singapore's maritime cluster enabled through decisive and visionary knowledge governance by institutions such as Singapore's Economic Development Board (EDB), the Maritime and Port Authority (MPA), Agency of Science, Technology and Research (A*Star) in collaboration with Jurong Town Corporation (JTC) as well as the Urban Redevelopment Authority (URA). JTC, for example, continues to offer future-oriented infrastructure solutions to its cluster customers in order to maintain and improve competitiveness. As far as the offshore sector is concerned, works are under way to increase Singapore's limited water land resource by building new wharves and jetty facilities.

A major corporate actor within the SMC is the Keppel group of companies [46], which employs over 30,000 employees in more than 30 countries (its workforce in Singapore comprises 1,500 people). Keppel Offshore & Marine's companies and yards are situated relatively close to each other within Singapore's SMC, which facilitates knowledge sharing, and creation, arguably key success factors in this business [5]. Incorporated in 2002, Keppel Offshore & Marine has over 300 years of combined experience from the three companies under its wings, namely Keppel Fels, Keppel Shipyard and Keppel Singmarine. With its key competency in the area of offshore engineering, Keppel FELS is the world's leader in offshore oil rig fabrication for international clients such as Petrobras in Brazil.

Keppel Offshore & Marine is well known for its innovative ultra deepwater solutions such as semisubmersibles, drilling tenders, or compact drill ships. Located in the tropics, it built icebreakers for customers in the West and fabricates ice-worthy jack-ups in collaboration with an international business partner. Its innovation capability in designing oil rigs is based on several specialized R&D departments such as the Deepwater Technology Group (DTG).

Keppel has forged R&D linkages with various stakeholders, which helps to create new knowledge and to innovate. Local collaboration partners include A*Star, Ngee Ann Polytechnic (NP), Nanyang Technological University (NTU) and National University of Singapore (NUS). The latter has established an offshore engineering program for young talent at the new Centre for Offshore Research & Engineering (CORE) in the Faculty of Engineering (NUS) together with the endowment of the Keppel Professorship in Ocean, Offshore and Marine Technology. An example of a joint Keppel-CORE project is: 'Improved Guidelines for the Prediction of Geotechnical Performance of Spudcan Foundations during Installation and Removal of Jack-up Units (InSafeJIP)'. To further enhance Singapore's leading role in the global market for oil and gas drilling units and offshore support vessels, Keppel collaborates with several international partners such as the Centre for Offshore Foundation Systems (COFS) at the University of Western Australia. Joint research areas include jack-up spudcan analysis, deep water anchoring systems and the application of geotechnical models in wind farm design.

A. Mapping the Density of the Increasingly Diverse SMC

According to industry observers, Singapore's status as a "dominant force in the offshore marine sector" in conjunction with related services does support the growth of the industry across the region (Indonesia, Malaysia, Philippines), "positioning it as a regional offshore marine hub for the Asia-Pacific" [24]. Like Dubai in the Middle East, Abuja in West Africa or Houston in the USA, Singapore is seen a "natural choice" for Asia driven in-part by a growing demand for oil and gas, the desire across Asia to be self-sufficient in oil and gas, offshore marine capabilities, business incentives and strong support for innovation and the development of R&D talent in key areas.

Over the past few years, Singapore's offshore marine cluster has expanded as evidenced by the emergence of several (complementary) sub-clusters such as oil companies, oilfield and seismic survey services, oil & gas equipment, shipyards and drilling contractors as well as oilfield chemicals. However, increasing diversity does not automatically imply new knowledge creation and collaborative innovation. One way of exploring the collaborative knowledge creation potential of such agglomerations and to delineate a knowledge cluster is to compile directories of firms (incl. research centres and institutions of higher learning). When combined with geospatial coordinates, this method helps to identify potential areas of agglomeration of knowledge transferring and producing organisations, which we define as knowledge clusters [21].

Our studies [33] show that there is a dense clustering of marine firms in the West of Singapore (Tuas) near the sea, which offers certain location advantages with potentially good linkage effects to other related industries in subclusters within the cluster. Proximity can have a positive effect on knowledge sharing which in turn can enhance new knowledge creation [9]. The density of Singapore's offshore marine cluster has been proactively shaped by various planning agencies such as URA, JTC and EDB who are doing their best in anticipating firms' long-term strategic business interests. Good knowledge governance and potential cluster synergies rest on strategic physical and economic planning approaches adopted by the respective planning agencies driven by Singapore's land scarcity.

The performance of a cluster depends on the extent of innovation related exchanges of knowledge, the quality of relationships to partners within and beyond the cluster as well as intra-organisational knowledge flows within cluster firms. Our findings suggest that firms located in the cluster comprising the central area / old harbour front might be a bit disadvantaged in the mid-term because they might lose their location advantages eventually in case the Tanjung Pagar port facilities will be moved closer to Tuas in the West to free up (valuable) land for expanding the business district further south [33].

B. From Cluster to 'Hub' Status

Increasing diversity does not automatically imply problem-free knowledge flows, new knowledge creation and collaborative innovation. For Singapore's offshore marine sector to become a powerful knowledge hotspot (hub) with regional and global significance, a sustainable local innovation system has to be nurtured characterised by high connectedness and high internal and external networking as well as knowledge creation and sharing capabilities. While empirical studies on the hub status of Singapore's offshore marine cluster are difficult to come by, there is some evidence that policy-makers continue to support and drive innovation in this sector. A key role is performed by the new Singapore Maritime Institute (SMI), a joint effort by MPA, the Agency for Science, Technology and Research (A*STAR) and the Economic Development Board (EDB) in partnership with local institutes of higher learning. SMI is developing strategies and programmes related to the academic, policy and R&D aspects of the maritime industry with an emphasis on shipping, port and maritime services, as well as offshore and marine engineering. It coordinates and aligns the strategic activities of the various maritime institutes at local institutes of higher learning and works to attract renowned academics and researchers to work in Singapore. It grooms local maritime talent and kickstarts more industry R&D projects. Collaborative R&D and capability development in key strategic areas such as subsea systems with local and international partners is seen as a viable strategy to achieve and retain Singapore's role as a global player in the offshore marine industry.

How is Singapore's quest to become a 'real' offshore technology hub progressing? Cluster theory argues that knowledge in form of innovations, patents and research papers as well as close cooperation between relevant knowledge institutions (both locally and internationally) are important to provide evidence for the knowledge hub function, including high knowledge productivity. We tried to shed light on the global standing of Singapore's offshore R&D as well as the external connections of Singapore-based researchers with the help of an output indicator of published journal articles. Only scientific research results in internationally recognized journals are counted. As a result not all projects of cooperation with local and international institutions are measured; only those documented in publications that are recognized, visible and accessible on the Web of Science. In the following, we shall present preliminary results of our analysis to better understand the global offshore R&D landscape.

Using the Web of Science and keywords such as offshore rigs, offshore engineering and dynamic positioning yielded 7,439 journal articles published between 2001-2011 spread over several categories such as Computer Science Information Systems, Electrical Engineering, Applied Mathematics, Automation Control Systems or Ocean Engineering. In terms of journal output, the top 5 countries appear to be the United States, the People's Republic of China, England, Germany and Japan. The top five research institutions are the Chinese Academy of Sciences, Russian Academy of Sciences, University California Berkeley, Indian Institute of Technology and the National University of Singapore (NUS).

In terms of external cooperative science connections (using an output indicator of joint journal articles to which Singapore researchers have contributed) between researchers from Singaporean institutions and elsewhere, India emerged on top of the list (4), followed by the People's Republic of China (2), Australia (2), Norway (2) and the United States (2). Important Singaporean educational institutions include the National University of Singapore (Faculty of Engineering, Department of Electrical & Computer Engineering; Centre for Offshore Research & Engineering; Department of Civil Engineering), Ngee Ann Polytechnic (Centre of Innovation - Marine & Offshore Technology) and corporate institutions such as Keppel Offshore & Marine and KeppelFELS.

A key capacity builder is the Centre for Offshore Research & Engineering (CORE) at the National University of Singapore (NUS) which has helped to enhance offshore geotechnical engineering according to observers. As in other clusters, building a full-time, world class academic group to work on offshore engineering, the transfer of knowledge from visiting experts to local talent and large-scale private sector engagement in terms of R&D funding are seen as important measures to further expand this field. While agencies continue to build up capacities in terms of offshore marine R&D, Keppel already has strong capabilities as indicated by the firm's reputation in the fabrication of jack-ups. Particular strengths with regard to knowledge-intensive technical ingredients/elements of offshore oil rig fabrication include Singapore's project management experience, the ability to deploy systems effectively, steel fabrication know how and availability of motivated manpower at competitive cost. Future (R&D) opportunities may include diversification into areas such as floating production systems and subsea production systems beyond the traditional focus on jack-ups, which bring in the revenues.

Our preliminary analysis suggests that Singapore is working hard towards becoming a global leader in offshore R&D. The ongoing investments into this sector and growing number of companies expanding their presence in the city-state such as Maersk Drilling are a result of turning visionary policy goals with regard to the country's enhanced (global) role in offshore marine R&D into reality. However, there are also challenges. As in other sectors, foreign scientists require certain incentives to set up shop in Singapore. While requirements for laboratory space and similar needs are relatively easy to fulfill in sectors such as biotechnology and life sciences, offshore marine scientists require special (at times huge) infrastructural facilities which in turn require space, sea water and land resources etc.

Furthermore one has to acknowledge the necessary organisational readiness in terms of being able to effectively absorb [11] [34] [52] new ideas generated within the organisation or 'externally' by cluster partners, for example through research & development, and to apply them in order to achieve innovation outputs. Key enablers to do so according to the two academics include exposure to relevant knowledge qua relentless networking, the presence of prior related knowledge so as to recognise the value of new knowledge and diversity of experience (the latter increases the scope for acknowledging external ideas and stimuli). Most if not all innovation frameworks propagated by innovation experts around the world have integrated research insights with regard to the power of absorptive capacity into their conceptual structure. Nevertheless, there are still many organisations 'out there' that remain weak or unsuccessful innovators, because they fail to absorb and make use of knowledge, learning opportunities and value networks.

If one translates the theory of absorptive capacity into practical recommendations for managers tasked to making innovation work, for example, qua innovative business models, the following recommendations emerge: Rethink the ways you deliver and capture value as well as how you deliver and monetize it! Leverage on your value networks and (re-)assess how you connect your organization with others (and their know how) to create more value! If innovation gaps are spotted, modify your value networks, e.g. by changing and innovating the supply chain as practiced by Samsung which developed a digital, more efficient operating model in order to better integrate its large and diverse number of logistic service providers (incl. carriers) globally or P&G famous for its continuous replenishment approach. Other 'older' supply chain innovations include the ocean shipping container (1956), the universal product code (1974), Toyota's integrated production system or FedEx' computerised tracking system developed from the mid-1980s onwards which provided near real-time information about package delivery.

VI. Conclusion: Knowledge Cluster Governance

We have looked critically at basic assumptions of the idea that cluster formation is a precondition for competitiveness, productivity, innovation and ultimately regional development. This position, promoted by Michael Porter, is summarized on the Website of the Harvard Business School as follows (as of November 2014): "Today's economic map of the world is characterized by "clusters." A cluster is a geographic concentration of related companies, organizations, and institutions in a particular field that can be present in a region, state, or nation. Clusters arise because they raise a company's productivity, which is influenced by local assets and the presence of like firms, institutions, and infrastructure that surround it". The basic assumption is that geographic concentration, e.g. clustering increases productivity, innovations and competitiveness. This assumption pervades the business literature. But is this assumption true? Yes and no. Clustering does, indeed, seem to have all these positive aspects, but the degree of clustering does not necessarily correlate with the degree of innovativeness or competitiveness. In other words, clustering is one, but not the only factor in translating clustering into regional economic development. One important aspect is "knowledge". Industrial clusters must contain knowledge clusters, but these knowledge clusters only function if they contain innovative, networked "knowledge hubs", i.e. if knowledge sharing takes place within a cluster and with other knowledge clusters elsewhere. For this to happen, connectivity in form of broadband connections, science cooperation, knowledge flows and so on as well as physical proximity via exchange of information in conducive 'places' such as coffee shops are some of the essential preconditions.

The availability of broadband connections has been identified as one important factor in turning cluster policies into a success [29] [30]. A recent macro study in the US evaluates the relationship between the spatial distribution of broadband providers and the presence of knowledge intensive firm clusters in US counties as "heterogeneous" and "localized": "From a policy perspective, this suggests that broadband should be viewed as a key component, but not the only component, of comprehensive local economic development plans" [29]. Broadband provision is the technological backbone of social networking and knowledge sharing. Proximity within clusters is still an important factor of productivity and regional development, if these conditions are fulfilled. Furthermore, one can not ignore the importance of absorptive capacity of both firms and individuals in recognizing the value of new information generated internally or sourced externally aimed at applying it effectively to value creation in business and society.

References

[1] L. Achtenhagen and R. Picard, "Challenges and success factors in media cluster development: a review of contemporary knowledge," Agglomeration, Clusters and Entrepreneurship: Studies in Regional Economic Development, pp. 221-251, 2014.

[2] M. N. I. Afzal and R. Lawrey, "KBE frameworks and their applicability to a resource-based country: The case of Brunei Darussalam," Asian Social Science, vol. 8(7), pp. 208-18, 2012a.

[3] —, "KBE frameworks and empirical investigation of KBE input-output indicators for ASEAN," International Journal of Economics and Finance, vol. 4(9), pp. 13-22, 2012b.

[4] S. Ariff Lim, H.-D. Evers, A. B. Ndah, and Farah Purwaningrum, “Governing Knowledge for Development: Knowledge Clusters in Brunei Darussalam and Malaysia." ZEF Working Paper Series 125, 2013.

[5] R. Boschma, “Role of proximity in interaction and performance: Conceptual and empirical challenges,” Regional Studies, vol. 39, pp. 41-45, 2005.

[6] T. Bauer, The Challenge of Knowledge Sharing – Practices of the Vietnamese Science Community in Ho Chi Minh City and the Mekong Delta, Berlin: LIT, 2011.

[7] T. Bunnell, Malaysia, Modernity, and the Multimedia Super Corridor: A Critical Geography of Intelligent Landscapes, London: RoutledgeCurzon, 2004.

[8] F. Cairncross, The Death of Distance, Cambridge,Mass.: Harvard Business School Press, 1997.

[9] Y. W. Chay, T. Menkhoff, B. Loh and H.-D. Evers, "What makes knowledge sharing in organizations tick?- An empirical study, " in Governing and Managing Knowledge in Asia, T. Menkhoff, H.-D. Evers and Y. W. Chay, Eds.. Singapore: World Scientific Publishing, pp. 301-326, 2010.

[10] Y. L. Chyi, Y. M. Lai and W. H. Liu, "Knowledge spillovers and firm performance in the high-technology industrial cluster," Research Policy, vol. 41(3), pp. 556-64, 2012.

[11] W. M. Cohen and D.A. Levinthal D. A., "Absorptive capacity: A new perspective on learning and innovation," Administrative Science Quarterly, vol. 35, pp. 128-152, 1990.

[12] A. B. Eisingerich, O. Falck and S. Heblich, “Firm innovativeness across cluster types,” Industry and Innovation, vol. 19(April), pp. 233-248, 2012.

[13] D. K. Eiteman, "Multinational firms and the development of Penang, Malaysia," The International Trade Journal, vol. 11(2), pp. 169-85, 1997.

[14] European Commission, Innovation Clusters in Europe: A statistical analysis and overview of current policy support. Brussels: European Commission, Enterprise and Industry Directorate-General, 2013.

[15] H.-D. Evers, "Penang as a knowledge hub," Penang Economic Monthly, vol. 6(11), pp. 36-38, 2011.

[16] H.-D. Evers and T. Bauer, "Emerging Epistemic Landscapes: Knowledge Clusters in Ho Chi Minh City and the Mekong Delta,” ZEF Working Paper Series 48, 2009.

[17] —, "Emerging epistemic landscapes: Knowledge clusters in Ho Chi Minh City and the Mekong Delta," in Beyond the Knowledge Trap: Developing Asia's Knowledge-Based Economies, T. Menkhoff, H.-D. Evers, Y. W. Chay, and E. F. Pang, New Jersey: World Scientific, 2011.

[18] H.-D. Evers, A. Banyouko and L. Yahya, "The Governance of Knowledge: Perspectives from Brunei Darussalam," Working Paper, Institute of Asian Studies, Universiti Brunei Darussalam, 2013.

[19] H.-D. Evers, S. Gerke and T. Menkhoff, Knowledge clusters and knowledge hubs: Designing epistemic landscapes for development," Journal of Knowledge Management, vol. 14(5), pp. 678 – 89, 2010.

[20] H.-D. Evers, R. Nordin Hans-Dieter and P. Nienkemper, "The Emergence of an Epistemic Landscape: Knowledge Cluster Formation in West-Malaysia," ZEF Working Paper Series 62., 2010.

[21] H.-D. Evers, P. Nienkemper and B. Schraven, “Measuring spatial density – Knowledge clusters in Malaysia”, in: Beyond the Knowledge Trap: Developing Asia's Knowledge-Based Economies, T. Menkhoff, H.-D. Evers, Y. W. Chay, and E. F. Pang, New Jersey: World Scientific, 2011.

[22] T. Menkhoff, H.-D. Evers, Y. W. Chay and E. F. Pang eds., “Beyond the Knowledge Trap: Developing Asia’s Knowledge-based Economies”, New Jersey: World Scientific Publishing, pp. 129-154. 2011

[23] S. Gerke and H.-D. Evers, "Looking East, Looking West: Penang as a Knowledge Hub," ZEF Working Paper Series No. 89, 2011.

[24] M. Granovetter, "The strength of weak ties," American Journal of Sociology, vol. 78, pp. 1360-80, 1973.

[25] C. Hayman, “Asia-Pac offshore marine potential – Singapore, with its commitments and leadership in sector, can help bring about collaborative development,” Business Times, February 17, 2012.

[26] T. Huff, "Malaysia's Multimedia Super Corridor and its first crisis of confidence," Asian Journal of Social Science, vol. 30(2), pp. 248-70, 2002.

[27] M. Kies and J. Revilla Diez," Regionale Innovationspotentiale in Südostasien - empirische Ergebnisse aus Singapur, Penang (Malaysia) und Bangkok (Thailand)," Geographica Helvetica vol. 59(1), pp. 7-19, 2004.

[28] R. Lawrey, "KBE frameworks and their applicability to a resource-based country: the case of Brunei Darussalam," Unpublished Ms., 2013.

[29] E. A. Mack, "Productivity and broadband the human factor," International Regional Science Review, vol. 36(3), pp. 392-423, 2013.

[30] —, "Broadband and knowledge intensive firm clusters: Essential link or auxiliary connection?" Papers in Regional Science, vol. 93(1), pp. 3-29, 2014.

[31] E. Mack and T. H. Grubesic, "Broadband provision and firm location in Ohio: An exploratory spatial analysis," Tijdschrift Voor Economische En Sociale Geografie, vol. 100(3), pp. 298–315, 2009.

[32] P. Maskell, "Towards a knowledge-based theory of the geographical cluster," Industrial and Corporate Change, vol. 10(4), pp. 921-20, 2013.

[33] T. Menkhoff, H.-D. Evers, Y. W. Chay and E. F. Pang (Eds.), Beyond the Knowledge Trap: Developing Asia's Knowledge-Based Economies. New Jersey, London, Singapore, Beijing: World Scientific, 2010.

[34] T. Menkhoff and H.-D. Evers, "Knowledge diffusion through good knowledge governance,” in Human Capital Formation and Economic Growth in Asia and the Pacific, edited by Wendy Dobson, London; New York: Routledge, Taylor and Francis Group, 2013.

[35] T. Menkhoff, "Using new external ideas to make innovation work," Business Times (August 15), 2014

[36] R. Mitchell, B. Boyle, J. Burgess, and K. McNeil, "“You can't make a good wine without a few beers”: Gatekeepers and knowledge flow in industrial districts," Journal of Business Research, vol. 67, pp. 2198-206, 2014.

[37] I. Nonaka, The Knowledge-Creating Company: How Japanese Companies Create the Dynamics of Innovation, New York: Oxford University Press, 1995.

[38] M. Porter, "Reshaping Regional Economic Development: Clusters and Regional Strategy (powerpoint presentation)," Harvard Business School: U.S. Cluster Mapping Launch Event, University of Minnesota, Minneapolis, MN, September 29th, 2014.

[39] M. Porter, "The economic performance of regions," Regional Studies, vol. 37, pp. 6-7, 2003.

[40] M. Porter, The Competitive Advantage of Nations, New York: The Free Press, 1990.

[41] —,"Clusters and the new economics of competition,” Harvard Business Review, vol. 76(6), pp. 77-90, 1998.

[42] —, "Clusters and Economic Policy: Aligning Public Policy with the New Economics of Competition," in ISC White Paper, November, Harvard Business School, 2007.

[43] —"Location, competition, and economic development: Local clusters in a Global Economy," Economic Development Quarterly, vol. 14(15), pp. 15-34, 2000

[44] R. C. Porter, The Economics of Water and Waste. A Case Study of Jakarta, Indonesia, Aldershot: Avebury Press, 1996.

[45] F. Purwaningrum, Knowledge Governance in an Industrial Cluster. The Collaboration between Academia-Industry-Government in Indonesia, Berlin and Zürich: LIT Verlag, 2014.

[46] F. Purwaningrum, H.-D. Evers and Yaniasih, "Knowledge Flow in the Academia- Industry Collaboration or Supply Chain Linkage? Case Study of the Automotive Industries in the Jababeka Cluster," Procedia - Social and Behavioral Sciences, vol. 52, pp. 62-71, 2012.

[47] M. Sabnani, More than Mettle by Keppel Offshore & Marine. Editions Didier Millet in association with Keppel Offshore & Marine Limited, 2007.

[48] Ö. Sölvell, C. Ketels and G. Lindqvist, The European Cluster Observatory: EU Cluster Mapping and Strengthening Clusters in Europe, Stockholm: Center for Strategy and Competitiveness, CSC, n.y..

[49] G. M. P. Swann, M. Prevezer and D. Stout (Eds.), The Dynamics of Industrial Clustering: International Comparisons in Computing and Biotechnology, Oxford: Oxford University Press, 1998.

[50] A. Weber, Reine Theorien des Standortes, Tübingen: Mohr Siebeck, 1990.

[51] —, Theory of the Location of Industries. Chicago: University ofn Chicago Press, 1981

[52] H. Wolma and D. Hincapie, "Clusters and Cluster-Based Development: A Literature Review and Policy Discussion," Working Paper, George Washington Institute of Public Policy, 2010.

[53] S. A. Zahra and G. George, "Absorptive capacity: A review, reconceptualization, and extension". Academy of Management Review, vol. 27(2), pp. 185-203, 2002.

Modeling the Interpretation of Sources of Norms

Tom M. van Engers
Leibniz Center for Law
University of Amsterdam
Amsterdam, The Netherlands
e-mail: vanengers@uva.nl

Robert van Doesburg
Immigration and Naturalisation Service
Rijswijk, The Netherlands
e-mail: r.v.doesburg@ind.minvenj.nl

***Abstract*—In this paper, the authors present their work on the development of a formal method for the interpretation of norms. This research is a continuation of the work reported in the eKNOW 2015 conference where we focused on a formal method to relate a set of norms described in natural language to the specification of a service based on these norms. In this paper, we focus on the modeling of the explicit interpretation of norms. These interpretation models are aimed to become components in our agent-role based simulations that allow to reason about the effect of norms in social reality. The method has been tested in a governmental organization for the specification of digital services. The method preserves the original concepts in sources of norms described in natural language, and delivers a translation of these norms to formal computational models. These models can be used to support institutional reasoning, i.e., reasoning about institutional facts and normative positions.**

Keywords-AI and Law; knowledge acquisition; knowledge representation; formal representation of norms; legal analysis; legal engineering; rule governance.

I. Introduction

Every organization's behavior is, in some way or the other, impacted by norms. These norms are either set by the organization's policies, by contractual agreements, or they are externally imposed. Governmental agencies that have responsibility for implementing law in various client-handling processes, have a particular interest in correct execution of norms.

Formalizing sources of norms, into formal computational models that can be used in information technology (IT), has been done in many different ways, and this has been object of study in the Jurix community and the Artificial Intelligence and Law (AI and Law) community. Both communities consist of experts from the field of Information Science and Law. For an overview of approaches, we refer to Bench Capon et al. [2].

While some of the approaches described by Bench Capon made it outside academia and resulted in practical applications, large-scale application within industries and government has not yet been accomplished due to various open issues. We will discuss some important issues, before we present our solution for some of these issues.

Marek Sergot was one of the first scholars that worked on legal knowledge based systems that were supposed to be closely aligned with sources of law [15][16]. He used the British Nationality Act as study case, a domain related to the field of Immigration Law, used in this paper.

Sergot used logic programs as his language for specifications. This language, based upon first order logic representation, can be used to express and reason with norms, but at the expense of sacrificing accuracy and reusability. This is a result of the task orientation of the method used.

Also, modal logics have been applied to the field of law. Next to their computational unattractiveness, thus far no one has been able to find the right translation of 'legal abilities'. Wierenga and Meijer [18] point at various approaches using some form of modal logic and give examples of problems that come with using modal logic for expressing norms.

A general problem for translating rules in logic is the disability to handle contrary positions and multiple contradictory interpretation models. Within the AI and Law community different conceptualizations have been developed, including formal models for argumentation and factor analysis of cases, also see [2].

With the approach presented in this paper, the authors aim to support large-scale applications in complex organizational contexts. Besides the problems addressed in literature, we also gathered requirements from our experience building large-scale applications of artificial intelligence (AI) in the legal domain for many years. The formal method for the interpretation of norms described in this paper, can be used to enable organizations to design IT-systems that support their business processes in a systemic way, and should allow for easy maintenance and easy implementation of changes. While developing our method, we have tested to what extent these requirements could be met, and we will report on our experiences in a future paper. Specifications of normative systems can also be used to control whether systems comply with norms or to support the internal and external communication on the interpretation of norms.

In this paper, we explain our method and its application in one concrete case: the application for a residence permit for international students in the Netherlands. Applying for and deciding on application is a process bounded by legal norms set by law. Though legal norms have some specific properties, the method presented in this paper holds for any organization applying norms.

Currently, many organizations recognize the huge economical potential that such a method could have. This most certainly holds for governmental institutions responsible for the execution of the law and applying legal norms to a massive number of cases. This allows us to cooperate with, and test our approach in many governmental agencies joined in the Manifesto Group, and in collaborative networks, such as the Blue Chamber [8] and the Netherlands Organisation for Scientific Research (NWO) [4].

Before going into the details of our approach, we will shortly sketch the general framework that has also been partly described in [6][7].

In section 2, a general framework of the work presented in this paper, is given. Section 3 contains an overview of the methods used. Section 4 contains an outline of a method for the interpretation of sources of norms, expressed in natural language. In section 5, a study case is presented, to illustrate the method for a formal interpretation of norms. In section 6, the results of the study case are presented. Section 7 contains a discussion on the results and an overview of future work.

II. The General Framework

In our approach, we separate three layers of reality that are interconnected (see figure 1). This model is an extended version of the three layers of reality model presented in [5]:

1. Sources of Norms
   This layer describes the components, structure and referential mechanisms that allow us to refer to the natural language sources describing the norms we want to 'translate' into formal computational models.
2. Institutional Reality
   This layer describes the interpretation of the sources of norms in the previous layer, using: states representing situations; legal positions; and acts regulated by norms. In this paper, we focus on this layer.
3. Social Reality
   The Social Reality layer describes agents, agent-roles, collaboration of agents, coordination, message passing, and other behavioral aspects of agents. This layer is used to describe and simulate behavior in societies regulated by norms. These norms can be used, e.g., to test (non-) compliance scenarios, and to predict effectiveness.

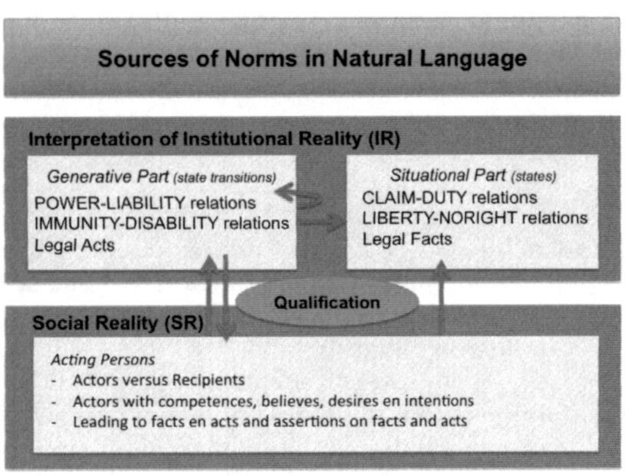

Figure 1. The Three Layers of Reality model.

In order to build a method for describing these three different layers, we have reconceptualized norms and normative systems, allowing us to model and analyze conflicting interpretations and to allow for simulating multiple interpretations in agent-role model based representations of social reality, see Sileno, Boer and Van Engers [17].

In the next section, we will briefly introduce the methods we use for modeling these three layers of reality.

III. Methods

A. Representing sources of law

The way we represent the normative sources is completely according to the state of the art standards (see CEN/Metalex [3]).

B. Fundamental legal concepts

The method for modeling the institutional content of normative sources is based upon the work of Wesley Newcomb Hohfeld, who introduced a set of fundamental legal conceptions in 1913, see Hohfeld and Cook [10]. Hohfeld's conceptualization of norms was meant to provide a solution for the ambiguity of the concepts 'right' and 'duty'. Hohfeld introduced a smallest set of legal conceptions to which, according to him, any and all 'legal quantities' could be reduced. But while Hohfeld was mainly aiming at understanding the positions between two adversarial parties in law cases, we aim to describe, analyze and understand (the consequences of) normative systems in general. This obviously includes individual cases consisting of two adversarial parties.

Hohfeld distinguished four, what he called Jural, or sometimes Legal, Relations: *Power-Liability* (1), *Immunity-Disability* (2), *Duty-Claimright* (3), *Liberty-Noright* (4). The term Jural Relation is probably chosen because Hohfeld, being a judge and professor in law, was mainly interested in applying his conceptual framework to cases of law in a judicial context. Other authors have chosen to either use the Legal or Jural Relations. Some have mixed these terms in their work, without giving an explanation for the difference between them, see for example [9]. For people in the field of law the terms *legal* and *jural* do have different meanings. We, however do not limit the application of our framework to either *legal* or *jural* norms. We address norms in general, including policies and social norms, therefore we use the term Normative Relations.

The Hohfeldian legal conceptions can only exist in pairs and describe relations between two people, each holding one of the rights in a pair. The *Power-Liability* and *Immunity-Disability* relations are generative: they can generate new Normative Relations. The *Duty-Claimright* and *Liberty-Noright* relations are situational: they can only be created and terminated by an act based on a generative Normative Relation.

C. Acts and facts

To be able to conceptualize normative systems in general, we express functional relations between complex objects (i.e., accessibility relations between possible worlds). To be able to do so we use acts and facts that are recognized by an institution: Institutional Acts and Institutional Facts. Institutional Acts play a pivotal role, as these acts connect the worlds in which certain Institutional Facts hold and certain Normative Relations exist. Generative Normative Relations (i.e., *Power-Liability* and *Disability-Immunity*) are expressed in a functional way, having a precondition, and a postcondition.

The formalization of norms stated in sources of norms, expressed in natural language, is being made explicit in an interpretation model derived from the original Hohfeldian framework. The resulting model contains the institutional interpretation of legal norms in a way that can be directly validated by legal experts (1), it can be used as a basis for a comprehensive representation of norms for clients of an institution (2), it is defeasible for clients and their legal representatives (3) and, it can be used to make a specification for IT services to support business processes (4). We have tested the applicability of this approach by modeling examples of various sources of law over the last couple of months and validated the results with experts.

D. Agent-base modeling

To model social reality, we have worked on different representation models enabling agent-role modeling and modeling social interaction between agents adapting such agent-roles. Also, various architectures and implementations of agent-role simulation environments have been tested, but as this is still quite preliminary work, in this paper, we will focus on the interpretation of norms from sources of norms, expressed in natural language and representing these in models of Institutional Reality.

IV. OUTLINE OF OUR METHOD TO MODEL A FORMAL INTERPRETATION OF SOURCES OF NORMS

Applying Hohfelds conceptualization for formalizing rules has been done before, e.g., by Allen and Saxon [1]. But rather than taking logic as formalization language like Allen and Saxon did, we have made a functional interpretation of the generative Normative Relations. The Institutional Reality model, describing an interpretation of the semantics of the content of the sources taken into scope, consists of two parts. First, the generative part describes the generative Normative Relations, i.e., *Power-Liability* and *Disability-Immunity* relations, as introduced by Hohfeld. Second, the situational part describes the Institutional Facts and situational Normative Relations, i.e., the *Duty-Claimright* and *Liberty-Noright* relations. The Generative Relations are conceptualized as functions with a precondition expressed in terms of Institutional Facts (iFACTs) and Situational Normative Relations, and a postcondition describing which iFACTs and/or Normative Relations are created or terminated. These Normative Relations can be either Situational or Generative Normative Relations. The function can only be executed if an Institutional Act (iACT) is recognized while the precondition is fulfilled.

As a result, we can build a graph of possible worlds, in which certain iFACTs and/or Normative positions hold, and in which every possible world has exits to other possible worlds that can be reached only by performing Institutional Acts while meeting the required precondition of that act. Institutional reasoning thus becomes a means-ends analysis problem that is commonly used in AI research since the early 1950s. Also, we can use graph analysis (topology) to inspect models of Institutional Reality, we can look for conflicts, missing iFACTs and so on. In this paper, we will focus on the creation of interpretation models, representing institutional reality. We will use a realistic example case from the domain of immigration as an illustration. The case addresses the issue of international students that apply for a study permit in the Netherlands. In the next section, we will explain the case and show interpretation models of the applicable legislation. The interpretation model shown, is actually used for realizing an eService at the Dutch Immigration and Naturalisation service (IND).

V. STUDY CASE

Students who do not have the Dutch Nationality and do not have the nationality of a EU Member state, have to apply for a residence permit to be able to study in the Netherlands. The application process for international students is one of the first services in a program that aims to digitalize all IND services. In an effort to support accountable services and agile implementation of policy changes, the IND is working on a formal method for the interpretation of norms. The analysis of the admission of, and the decisions on, applications for residence permits for international students, is one of the study cases used to develop a method for representing a formal interpretation of norms.

A. Applying for a residence permit in steps

In order to present our method for formalizing the interpretation of norms, the procedure for applying for a residence permit is described in steps. For every step, a short description of the legal context is given.

An international student that wants to come to the Netherlands has to apply for a residence permit. Applying for a residence permit, results in the creation of a liability for the IND to decide on the application. The liability to decide creates new duties for the IND:

1. When preparing a decision the administrative authority has the duty to acquire the necessary knowledge of relevant facts and of the interests to be weighed.
2. A decision must be based on sound reasoning.
3. A decision must be given within the time limit set by law.

Article 14, Alien Act (AA) gives Our Minister of Justice the power to grant, reject, or to disregard the application for granting a residence permit. Article 16, Alien Act explicitly states 11 grounds to reject an application. Article 4:5 of the General Administrative Law (GAL) gives the procedure of disregarding an application. Article 24, paragraph 2 the Alien Act gives Our Minister the power to disregard an application if no payment for the handling of the application has been made. Article 26 of the Alien Act gives Our Minister the duty only to grant a residence permit if the applicant fulfills all conditions. As a result the grounds for granting a residence permit can be derived from de absence of grounds to reject or disregard an application.

The relevant norms for the actions described above are described in natural language in sources of law. These sources do not have a functional structure and they include a lot of implicit references.

B. A formal analysis of norms

The formal analysis of norms requires the explicit description of an initial legal state. This state is the precondition that enables a legal act. Preconditions and legal acts are described in such a way that this act will always result in a one, and only one, postcondition. The postcondition can contain: the creation of new iFACT's and/or Normative Relations (1), and/or the termination of existing iFACT's and/or Normative Relations (2).

C. Examples of Normative Relations for deciding on applications for residence permits

The study case described above will now be presented in terms of our formal interpretation model. We present two representation formalisms, a vertical one and a graphical notation.

LEGAL SOURCE: Article 4:1 General Administrative Law
TEXT: "The application to issue a decision is submitted in writing to the administrative authority competent to decide on the application, unless otherwise provided by law."
NORMATIVE RELATION: NR.GAL.4:1
iACT: [to submit]
OBJECT: [the application to issue a decision]
POWER: [administrative authority]
LIABILITY: [applicant] (implicit)
PRECONDITION: (iFACT.GAL.4:1.written [the application to issue a decision is submitted in writing]) AND (iFACT.GAL.4:1.competent [the application is submitted to the administrative authority competent to decide on the application]) AND NOT (iFACT.GAL.4:1.provided [unless otherwise provided by law])
CREATING POSTCONDITION:
(iFACT.GAL.4:1.application [the application to issue a decision]) AND (NR.GAL.3:2 (DUTY: [the administrative authority] | CLAIMRIGHT: [the applicant]) [during the preparation of a decision the administrative authority acquires the necessary information concerning the relevant facts and the interests to be weighed]) AND (NR.GAL.3:46 (DUTY: [the administrative authority] | CLAIMRIGHT: [the applicant]) [a decision must be based on a valid motivation]) AND (NR.GAL.4:13.1.timelimit (DUTY: [the administrative authority] | CLAIMRIGHT: [the applicant]) [a decision must be given within the time limit set by law])

LEGAL SOURCE: Article 14, first paragraph, point a, Aliens Act
TEXT: "Our Minister is authorized to accept, to reject or to disregard the application for granting a temporary residence permit."

Notice that this sentence contains three acts. As a result the sentence describes three separate NORMATIVE RELATIONS to maintain a functional perspective: granting (1), rejecting (2) and disregarding (3).

1. NORMATIVE RELATION: NR.AA.14.1.a.grant
iACT: [to grant]
OBJECT: [the application for granting a temporary residence permit]
POWER: [Our Minister]
LIABILITY: [the alien]
PRECONDITION: (iFACT.AA.14.1.a.application [the application to grant a temporary residence permit]) AND (iFACT.AA.26.1.a [the alien has demonstrated that he fulfills all conditions for granting a residence permit])
CREATING POSTCONDITION:
(iFACT.AA.14.1.a.grant [the application to grant a temporary residence permit is disregarded])
TERMINATING POSTCONDITION:
(iFACT.AA.14.1.a.application [the application to grant a temporary residence permit])
2. NORMATIVE RELATION: NR.AA.14.1.a.reject
iACT: to reject
OBJECT: [the application for granting a temporary residence permit]
POWER: [Our Minister]
LIABILITY: [the alien]
PRECONDITION: (iFACT.AA.14.1.a.application [the application to grant a temporary residence permit]) AND (iFACT.GAL.3:46 [a valid motivation]) AND (iFACT.GAL.3:4.2 [the adverse consequences of a decision are not disproportionate to goals served by the decision for one or more parties involved])
CREATING POSTCONDITION:
(iFACT.AA.14.1.a.reject [the application to grant a temporary residence permit is rejected])
TERMINATING POSTCONDITION:
(iFACT.AA.14.1.a.application [the application to grant a temporary residence permit]) AND (NR.GAL.3:46 (DUTY: [the administrative authority] | CLAIMRIGHT: [the applicant]) [a decision must be based on a valid motivation])

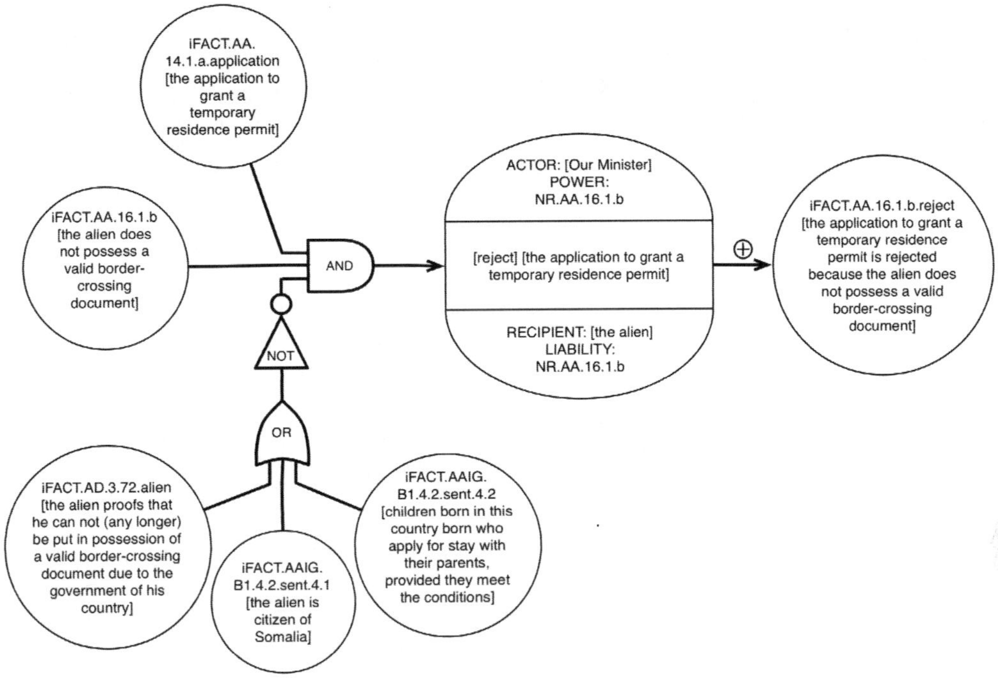

Figure 2. The graphical representation of the Normative Relation decribed in article 16, paragraph 1, point b of the Aliens Act.

3. NORMATIVE RELATION: NR.AA.14.1.a.disregard
iACT: [to disregard]
OBJECT: [the application for granting a temporary residence permit]
POWER: [Our Minister]
LIABILITY: [the alien]
PRECONDITION: (iFACT.AA.14.1.a.application [the application to grant a temporary residence permit]) AND (iFACT.AA.24.2.disregarding [if payment is not made, the application will be disregarded])
CREATING POSTCONDITION:
(iFACT.AA.14.1.a.disregarded [the application to grant a temporary residence permit is disregarded])
TERMINATING POSTCONDITION:
(iFACT.AA.14.1.a.application [the application to grant a temporary residence permit]) AND (NR.GAL.4:5 (POWER [to disregard] [application])

LEGAL SOURCE: Article 16, first paragraph, point b, Aliens Act
TEXT: "An application to grant a temporary residence permit as referred to in Article 14 may be rejected if:
b. the alien does not possess a valid border-crossing document."

NORMATIVE RELATION: NR.AA.16.1.b
iACT: to grant
OBJECT: [the application to grant a temporary residence permit]
POWER: [Our Minister]
LIABILITY: [the alien]
PRECONDITION: (iFACT.AA.14.1.a.application [the application to grant a temporary residence permit]) AND (iFACT.AA.16.1.b [the alien does not possess a valid border-crossing document]) AND NOT ((iFACT.AD.3.72.vreemdeling [the alien proofs that he can not (any longer) be put in possession of a valid border-crossing document due to the government of his country]) OR (iFACT.AAIG.B1.4.1.sent.4.1 [the alien is citizen of Somalia]) OR (iFACT.AAIG.B1.4.1.sent.4.2 [children born in this country born who apply for stay with their parents, provided they meet the conditions]))
CREATING POSTCONDITION:
(iFACT.AA.16.1.b.reject [the application to grant a temporary residence permit is rejected because the alien does not possess a valid border-crossing document])
Figure 2 gives the graphical representation of Normative Relation NR.AA.16.1.b.

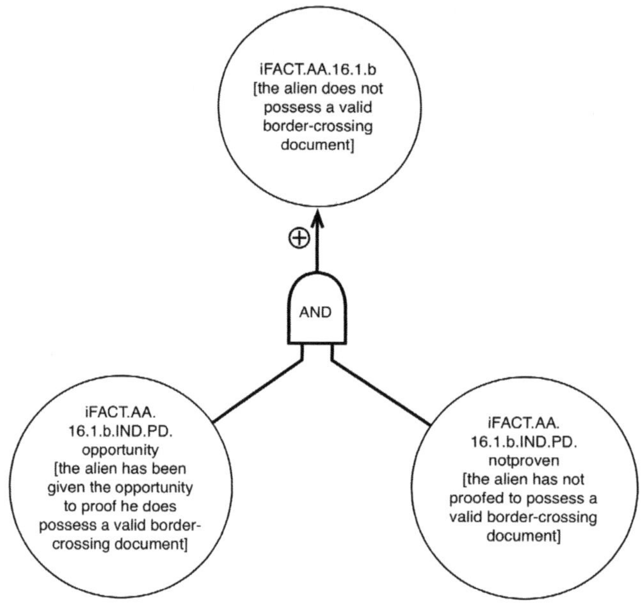

Figure 3. The graphical representation of de derivation of creation of iFACT.AA.16.1.b: 'the alien does not possess a valid border-crossing document.

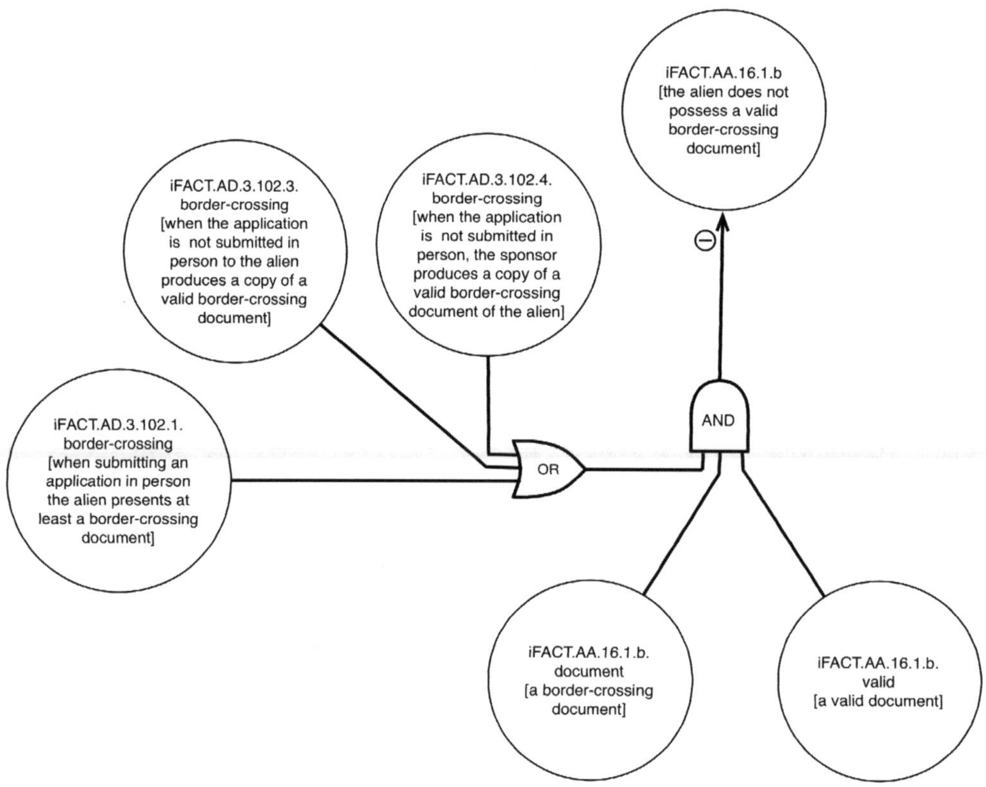

Figure 4. The grapical representation of the termination of iFACT.AA.16.1.b: 'the alien does not possess a valid border-crossing document.

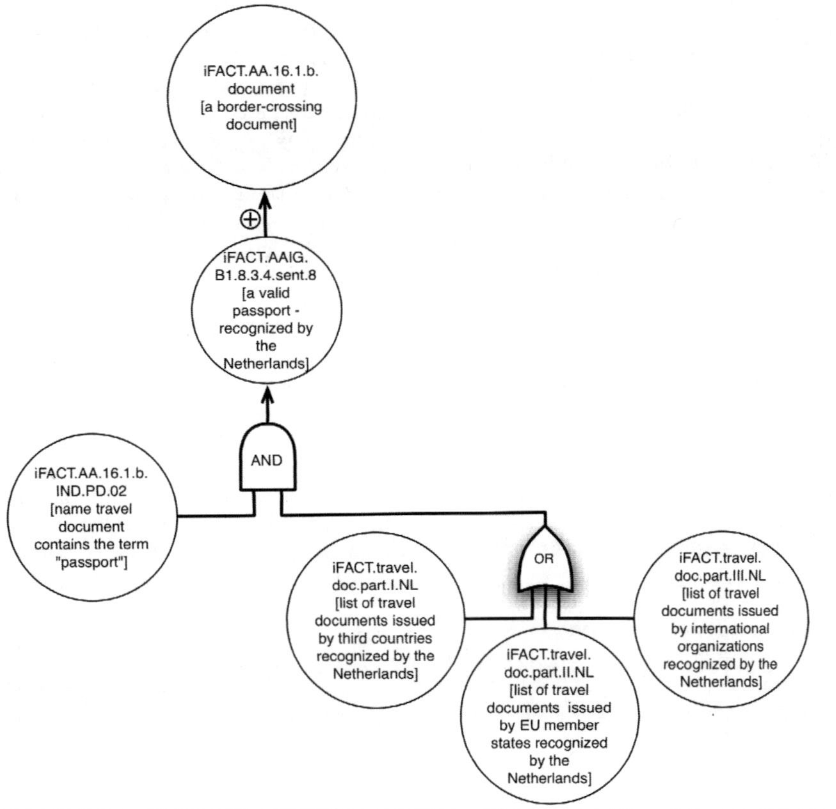

Figure 5. The grapical representation of the inconclusive policy descisions on traveldocuments that are not a 'passport'.

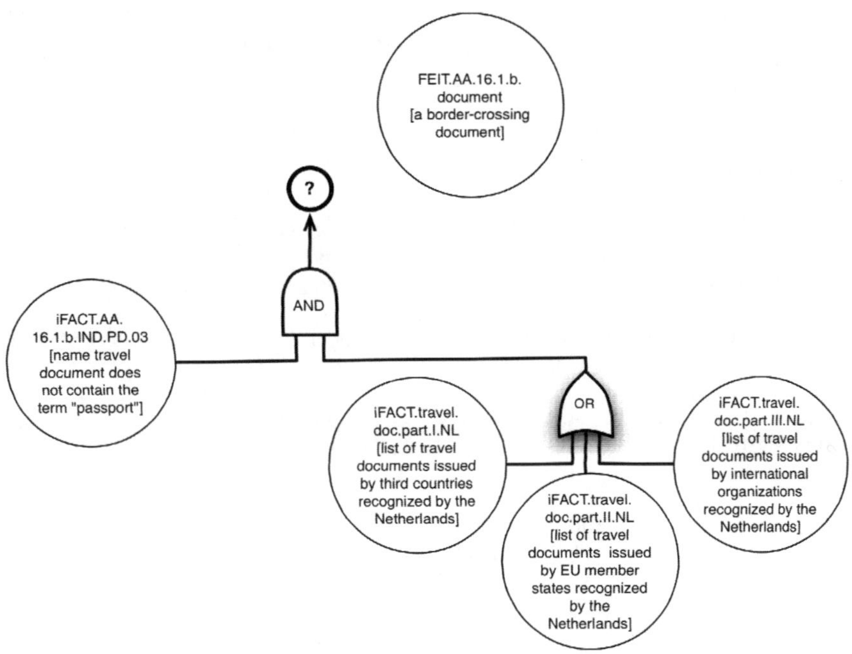

Figure 6. The grapical representation of the inconclusive policy descisions on traveldocuments that are not a 'passport'.

D. Establishing the existence or non-existence of iFACT's

The Normative Relations described above are practical because:

1. They can be traced back to specific words in legal sources.
2. They give an overview on the condition under which an iACT has a legal status and on exemptions.
3. The effect of the iACT is fully described, making it possible to formally describe the postcondition of the act.

However, the question what it takes for an iFACT to exist, or not, is still unclear. To answer this question a notation for deriving iFACTs, is developed. The derivation of iFACTs should be backed by legal sources or by policy statements. This can be illustrated by the derivation of the existence of iFACT.AA.16.1.b: [the alien does not possess a valid border-crossing document].

To be able to derive the existence or non-existence of iFACT.AA.16.1.b the following questions must be answered:

1. What is a border-crossing document?
2. What determines the validity of a border-crossing document?
3. How can an alien proof he possesses a border-crossing document?

Figure 3 shows the graphical representation of the derivation of the creation of the iFACT.AA.16.1.b. Figure 3 contains the concepts iFACT.16.1.b.IND.PD.opportunity and iFACT.16.1.b.IND.PD.notproven. These iFACTs represent policy decisions (PD) that do not yet exist, but are a formalization of the common knowledge procedure followed by IND employees to derive iFACT.AA.16.1.b [the alien does not possess a valid border-crossing document], The question whether iFACT.AA.16.1.b.IND.PD.opportunity and iFACT.AA.16.1.b.IND.PD.notproven should be formally established as IND implementation guidelines, is not yet answered.

Figure 4 shows the graphical representation of the derivation of the termination of iFACT.AA.16.1.b. It contains a breakdown of the sentence 'the alien does not possess a valid border-crossing document' into three parts: the document is 'a document belonging to the alien' (1), the document is 'a border-crossing document' (2) and the document is 'a valid document' (3).

Article 3.102 Aliens Decree (AD) gives three possibilities for the alien to proof he possesses a valid border-crossing document.

Figures 5 and 6 show the derivation of answer to the question what is 'a border-crossing document'. Figure 5 shows that any document that is a travel document recognized by the Netherlands, which contains the term 'passport' is considered to be a border-crossing document, based on Aliens Act Implementation Guidelines (AAIG) Volume B1, Chapter 8, paragraph 3.4, sentence 8. The list of travel documents recognized by the Netherlands can be found in three lists that are published under the authority of the European Commission. Figure 6 shows that the question whether a travel document that is recognized by the Netherlands and that does not contain the term 'passport' can not be answered based on sources of norms. Answering this question is, at present, left to the discretionary powers of IND officials.

Of all the aliens possessing a travel document and applying for a residence permit, more than 99% possesses a passport. In special situations, aliens possess a travel document that is not a passport – i.e., a refugee document or a seamen's book. To decide whether these travel documents are border-crossing documents, contextual information will be taken into account. For example: a seamen's book will probably not be accepted as a border-crossing document for an international student, because fulfilling the conditions for residing as an international student implies that the alien will leave the ship to study and doing so he will loose his valid seamen's book. The official will probably ask for a passport as proof for the possession of a valid border-crossing document. But this norm is not explicitly written down, probably because it concerns a situation that does not occur or is extremely rare.

VI. RESULTS

The method presented has been tested by analyzing regulations relevant for application of residence permits for foreign students and making decisions on these applications. The results are being used in the Digital Service Program of the IND that aims to have digitalized all IND services in 2017.

The analysis resulted in knowledge representations of legal knowledge that proofed to be comprehensible for multidisciplinary teams consisting of legal experts, policy advisors, administrators, knowledge workers and IT-experts (1), a list of anomalies in sources of law (2), specifications for executable knowledge models traceable to sources of law for inference engines (3), reusable components for specifications of related services (4).

A. Comprehensible representation of Normative Relations

Being able to validate the interpretation of norms with experts is an essential requirement of a formal method for the interpretation of norms in natural language. We have tested the comprehensiveness of the representations in sessions with legal domain experts and policy advisors. Legal experts and policy advisors considered the representation of norms in a functional perspective by determining a unique postcondition for an iACT, performed in an explicit precondition usefull. They understood the interpretation models without training and only needed some additional explanation. In some cases the models even caused changes in interpretations these experts acquired based on the sources of norms in natural language. Quantative information on the validation of models is not yet available. Also autonomous validation of legal experts without support, has not yet been tested. The first experiences suggest that autonomous validation is possible for legal experts that received some training using the method.

B. *Anomalies in sources of law*

Making an explicit interpretative model exposed anomalies in sources of law that, until now, remained undetected. The most important anomalies found are:

1. Mistakes in the registration of changes in sources of law. This results in faults in punctuation and in the adequate processing of changed references due to changes in sources of law. In article 16, paragraph 1, point e. we found a reference to the Infectious Diseases Act, that was replaced by the Public Health Act in 2008. The list of purposes of stay in article 3.4 Alien Decree (study is mentioned under point l.) refers to article 14, paragraph 2, Alien Act. Since a new paragraph 2 was introduced on June first 2013 the reference should have been changed to paragraph 3.
2. Incorrect interpretations due to multiple step implicit references. An example of this is the legal basis for accepting scholarships as independent means of support for students. The implementation guideline on which the power to recognize a scholarship as independent means of support refers to article 3.22 Alien Regulation that deals with sustainability. As a result there is no legal basis for accepting scholarships as means of support for students.

In current practice substantial investments in time and efforts are being made in order to detect and repair anomalies. Despite these efforts many anomalies remain undetected due to the lack of a proper method for interpreting sources of law, like the one presented in this paper.

These anomalies result in ambigious implicit interpretations, which may lead to incorrect judgments of cases. Incorrect judgements may lead to expensive lawsuits.

VII. Discussion and Conclusion

In [7], we described the scoping process that would enable us to efficiently work our way through the voluminous sources of norms. We discovered that the detailed modeling of the content of these sources helped us to discover 'lose ends', i.e., missing parts in these sources explaining essential things we needed to understand the meaning of the norms or the context in which those norms could/should be applied. Also, we discovered flaws in the referential structure of those sources.

The method presented in this paper, enabled us to make the interpretation of sources of norms, expressed in natural language, explicit. Domain experts, both legal experts and policy advisors, could not only work with those models, they were able to validate them and used them to start repairing the anomalies presented in Section 4 on the results of our analysis.

The method described in this paper, fits within a framework that also includes structuring sources of norms and modeling Social Reality. It is our aim to be able to understand how people understand norms, how we reason about them and how norms affect our society. The model of Institutional Reality is just a small step towards a better understanding of norms governed societies.

It is within our aims to set-up an ecological system where the agencies responsible for implementing regulations will make their models available to who ever wants to incorporate them in systems that are designed for other purposes. We have tested this with one of our master students, see [11], who has build a tax planning application for one of the big accountancy firms in the Netherlands, using an interpretation model that was made with help of the Dutch Tax Administration. This application, that was the result of a master thesis research project, of course was limited to a small piece of legislation, international Value Added Tax. But it showed that such an ecosystem is viable. To develop such an ecosystem is future work.

With this paper we hope to contribute to society, by allowing governmental agencies, non-governmental organizations and citizens to understand how norms are interpreted. This will also allow us to exchange ideas about solving conflicts in a civilized way, in case different opinions exist on the interpretation of sources of norms. Furthermore, it helps us to understand how one derives a different conclusion of the same set of facts, using a different interpretation model.

This brings us to the next topic, the role of the models of Social Reality that we develop using agent-role models. In most cases norms are created within a context where the people creating them have the power to enforce these norms, at least to a certain extend. It was outside the scope of this paper to discuss reward and punishments as instruments to promote certain behavior and discourage other. However if one creates norms, one would expect that these norms affect society in some way. In practical situations, e.g., in the field of law making, one would expect law-makers first to think well about the consequences of norms, before imposing them upon society. Nowadays, we have the computer power to actually simulate the effects of norms on society. The interpretation models of sources of norms described in this paper, play a pivotal role in creating the agent-role based simulations that we can develop to reason about the effects of norms in social reality.

The method presented in this paper, has been tested in a governmental organization for the specification of digital services. Also, we have applied it in other, smaller domains. Further application is planned, and we hope to learn from the experience with it. We have also planned to report on coder-independencies and natural language processing to support our method, similar to the work of De Maat [12][13][14], in the near future.

The method presented in this paper, preserves the original legal concepts described in natural language in sources of law, and delivers a formal translation of the norms contained in sources of law. This gives us a good basis for improving the agility of governmental agencies and others that use IT systems impacted by norms. At this stage we cannot give any numbers, but it would be interesting to measure the effect of using normative interpretation models for the explicit specification of actions by employees or requirements for IT-solutions in comparison to existing practices.

As for now, we have created a way to produce models that explicitly describe the interpretation of sources of norms, models that support institutional reasoning, i.e., reasoning about Institutional Facts and legal positions, and accounting for the reasoning.

In the future we will continue our work on completing our method. Constructing components that will allow us to simulate scenarios in social reality are amongst the new developments planned. We will also extend the domains in which we will test the usability of the current parts of our method. Foreseen extensions are in the field of tax administration, labor law (regulating flexible working hours in employment relations). Furthermore, we will work on the development of IT support for our method in co-operation with governmental organizations, businesses and the scientific community.

Our quest continues. In the spirit of Leibniz, who once dreamt of creating a calculus to solve disputes between people, we dream of offering the tools that help us to better understand the mechanisms of interpreting norms and settle disputes about them, thus keeping our society a civilized one.

ACKNOWLEDGMENT

The research reported upon in this paper, would not have been possible without the support of the Dutch Immigration and Naturalization Service.

REFERENCES

[1] L. E. Allen and C. S. Saxon, "Analysis of the logical structure of legal rules by a modernized and formalized version of Hohfeld fundamental legal conceptions", in A.A. Martino and F.S. Natali, editors, Automated Analysis of Legal Texts, pp. 385–450, 1986. Edited versions of selected papers from the Second International Conference on "Logic, Informatics, Law," Florence, Italy, September 1985.

[2] T. Bench-Capon et al., "A history of AI and Law in 50 papers: 25 years of the international conference on AI and Law", in Artificial Intelligence and Law Volume 20, Issue 3, pp. 215-319, 2012, doi: 10.1007/s10506-012-9131-x tt.

[3] CEN MetaLex. *Open XML Interchange Format for Legal and Legislative Resources*. [Online]. Available from: http://www.metalex.eu. 2016.04.02

[4] R. van Doesburg et al., Towards a Method for a Formal Analysis of Law, Study Case Report ICT with Industry workshop 2015, NWO 2016. [Online]. Available from: http://www.nwo.nl/over-nwo/organisatie/nwo-onderdelen/ew/bijeenkomsten/ict+with+industry+workshop/proceedings 2016.04.11

[5] T. M. van Engers, A. Boer, "Public Agility and Change in a Network Environment", in Judith Schossboeck, Noella Edelmann and Peter Parycek (Eds.,), JeDEM 3(1), pp. 99-117, 2011.

[6] T. M. van Engers and R. van Doesburg, "At your service, on the definition of services from sources of law", in Proceedings of the 15th International Conference on Artificial Intelligence and Law - ICAIL '15, pp. 221-225, 2015, doi:10.1145/2746090.2746115.

[7] T. M. van Engers and R. van Doesburg, "First steps towards a formal analysis of law", In Proceedings of eKNOW 2015, IARIA XPS Press, pp. 36-42, 2015.

[8] T. M. van Engers and S. Nijssen, "From legislation towards the provision of services", in Electronic Government and the Information Systems Perspective Lecture Notes in Computer Science, pp. 163-172, 2014, doi:10.1007/978-3-319-10178-1_13.

[9] L. Fiorito, "John R. Commons, Wesley N. Hohfeld, and the origins of transactional economics", in History of Political Economy, 42(2), pp. 267-295, 2010, doi:10.1215/00182702-2010-003.

[10] W. N. Hohfeld and W. W. Cook, Fundamental Legal Conceptions as Applied in Judicial Reasoning: And Other Legal Essays, New Haven, 1919 CT: Yale University Press.

[11] E. van Kampen, Introducing a Rule Based Approach for the Mapping and Determination of Legal Facts, Master Thesis, University of Amsterdam 2015.

[12] E. de Maat and R. Winkels, "Suggesting model fragments for sentences in Dutch laws", in Proceedings of Legal Ontologies and Artificial Intelligence Techniques, May 2010 pp. 19-28 [Online]. Available from: http://ssrn.com/abstract=2013146 [retrieved: 03, 2016].

[13] E. de Maat, Making Sense of Legal Texts, PhD-thesis, Sep. 2012, ISBN 978 90 5335.

[14] E. de Maat and T. M. van Engers. "Mission impossible?: Automated norm analysis of legal texts," in D. Bourcier, editor, Jurix 2003: The Sixteenth Annual Conference, Legal Knowledge and Information Systems, Amsterdam, IOS Press, pp. 143-144, Dec. 2003, ISBN: 978-1586033989.

[15] M. Sergot, F. Sadri, R. Kowalski, F. Kriwaczek, P. Hammond, and T. Cory, "The British Nationality Act as a Logic Program," in Communications of the ACM, Vol. 29, No. 5, pp. 370–386, May 1986, doi: 10.1145/5689.5920.

[16] M. Sergot, "Representing legislation as logic programs," Machine intelligence 11, J. E. Hayes, D. Michie, and J. Richards (Eds.), Oxford University Press, Inc., New York, NY, pp. 209-260, 1988, ISBN: 0-19-853718-2.

[17] G. Sileno, A. Boer, and T. M. van Engers, "Commitments, expectations, affordances and susceptibilities: Towards positional agent programming", PRIMA 2015: Principles and Practice of Multi-Agent Systems Lecture Notes in Computer Science, pp. 687-696, 2015, doi:10.1007/978-3-319-25524-8_52.

[18] R. J. Wieringa, and J.-J.Ch. Meyer, "Applications of Deontic Logic in Computer Science: A Concise Overview", in John-Jules Ch. Meyer and Roel J. Wieringa (Eds.), Deontic Logic in Computer Science: Normative System Specification. John Wiley & Sons, Chichester, UK, pp. 17-40, 1993, ISBN 9780471937432.

Recommendation Techniques on a Knowledge Graph for Email Remarketing

László Grad-Gyenge
Creo Group
Budapest, Hungary
laszlo.grad-gyenge@creo.hu

Peter Filzmoser
TU Vienna
Vienna, Austria
peter.filzmoser@tuwien.ac.at

Abstract—**The knowledge graph, which is an ontology based representation technique, is described to model the information necessary to conduct collaborative filtering, content-based filtering and knowledge based recommendation methods. Spreading activation and network science based recommendation methods are presented and evaluated. The evaluation measures are calculated on top list recommendations, where rating estimation is not necessary. In the experiment, click-through rates are measured and presented based on the email based remarketing activity of an electronic commerce system. Our primary result shows the improved recommendation quality of spreading activation based methods compared to the human expert.**

Keywords–knowledge graph; recommender system; spreading activation; network science; email remarketing

I. Introduction

The traditional classification of recommender systems [1] proposes three main categories as collaborative filtering, content-based filtering and knowledge based methods. By representing the information in an ontology specifically designed for the task, both the information necessary for collaborative, content-based and knowledge-base techniques can be represented in one knowledge base, as we introduce it, in the knowledge graph.

Graph based recommender systems are a promising alternative to representation learning and matrix factorization techniques. In our work, we propose an information representation technique, which is capable of representing heterogeneous information sources. Similar to ontologies, the knowledge graph is a heterogeneous, labelled, restricted multigraph. The novelty of our representation method is the ability to represent parallel edges between two nodes. By utilizing a multigraph, our primary intention is to be able to represent various interaction types between users and items in one data structure as opposed to existing knowledge representation techniques in this field. In our approach, we separate the representation of information from the calculation methods. We think that the elimination of these unnecessary interdependencies can lead to a clearer approach on the theoretical side.

In this paper, we compare our spreading activation based, personalized recommendations and the centrality measures of network science to the performance of the human expert. Our spreading activation based method defines an asymmetric proximity measure between a source node and other nodes in the network. As the method calculates the proximity of nodes, it is not a rating estimation based method (as collaborative filtering) and it is utilized to generate a list of recommendations. Network science based methods are applied in the cold start case, and recommend central items in the ontology.

Next to Web based advertisements, a well known medium of the remarketing era is the email. Sending offers to past or potential customers in newsletters is a common practice of the electronic commerce systems. The personalization of the list of the offered products has the potential to increase the performance of the newsletters. Also, the improvement of this remarketing activity leads to a higher customer engagement, hence it delivers a business value. On the other hand, as products valuable to the user are presented, the personalization of the newsletters leads to an increase in the service quality.

In our experiment, we evaluated recommender system based newsletters utilizing the information gathered on Booker [2], an electronic commerce system selling books. The newsletters are sent with the industrial grade email remarketing system, PartnerMail [3].

Related work is presented in Section II. Section III introduces the graph based knowledge base. Section IV describes the evaluated recommendation methods. A detailed description of the dataset can be found in Section V. The evaluation method is presented in Section VI. The results can be found in Section VII. Section VIII concludes the paper.

II. Related work

Graph based information representation is a known technique in this field. Cantador et al. [4] define a multi-layered graph approach and applies a clustering technique to derive recommendations. Kazienko et al. [5] work with a layered graph. In the field of recommender systems, graphs are typically involved to represent the social network. Guha et al. [6], Ziegler et al. [7], Massa et al. [8] and Jsang et al. [9] involve trust networks to enhance recommendation quality. Guy et al. [10], Konstas et al. [11] and He et al [12] calculate recommendations with the help of a social network.

Spreading activation is a known method in the field of recommender systems. Blanco-Fernandez et al. present a content based reasoning about the semantics of the user's preferences [13]. Their method is spreading activation based and the recommendations are calculated with the Hopfield Net algorithm. They emphasize that spreading activation can be helpful to avoid the overspecialisation. Hussein et al. introduce SPREADR, a spreading activation based technique to close the gap between context-awareness and self-adaptation [14]. Their method is also applied to adapt user interfaces [15]. Gao et al. define a prototype in their position paper incorporating user interests and domain knowledge in an ontology [16].

Codina et al. show a semantic recommender engine and also define a reasoning method to estimate user ratings on items to enhance the quality of rating estimations [17]. They define an item score as the weighted average of related concepts. An important aspect of their work is that they distinguish between explicit and implicit user feedback, which is also shown in Section V. Troussov et al. define a tag aware recommendation technique to investigate the decay and spreading parameters of spreading activation methods [18]. Alvarez et al. introduce ONTOSPREAD, a sophisticated, spreading activation technique in the scope of medical systems [19]. Jiang et al. present an ontology based user model and a spreading activation based recommendation technique [20].

III. Graph Based Representation

Cold start is a widely known, common problem of recommender systems. The most problematic situation of recommender systems is the lack of information, when there is no sufficient data available to deliver personalized recommendations for a newcoming user. To avoid this problem to the farthest possible extent, a general information representation method is used, which is capable of representing heterogeneous information. By representing heterogeneous information, the amount of information sources is increased. Following this strategy, our intention is to represent as much information as possible, in order not to constraint the recommendation methods in achieving high coverage.

The information is represented in a labelled, weighted, restricted multigraph, as $\mathcal{K}_u = (T_N, T_E, N, E_u, t_N)$ in the undirected case and $\mathcal{K}_d = (T_N, T_E, N, E_d, t_N)$ in the directed case. T_N is the set of node types, T_E is the set of edge types. N represents the set of nodes existing in the graph, $E_u \subseteq \{\{u, v, t\} | u \in N \wedge v \in N \wedge t \in T_E \wedge u \neq v\}$ represents the set of undirected edges between the nodes, $E_d \subseteq \{(u, v, t) | u \in N \wedge v \in N \wedge t \in T_E \wedge u \neq v\}$ represents the set of directed edges between the nodes. The function $t_N \subset N \times T_N$ assigns a node type to each node. At the moment, type assignments do not influence the final recommendation result and are introduced for completeness and further research.

IV. Recommendation Methods

In our experiment, we compare personalized and non-personalized recommendations. The personalized case is spreading activation based. In the non-personalized case, network science and human expert based recommendations are evaluated.

A. Spreading Activation

A spreading activation [21] based recommendation technique is used operating on $\mathcal{K}_u$ as introduced in Section III. Spreading activation is a well-known method in the field of semantic networks, neural networks and associative networks [22]. To recommend items with spreading activation, an iteration is started. In the first step the activation of the node representing the person to generate recommendations for is set to 1. This node is also called as source node. Then, in each iteration step all nodes distribute a part of their activation to the neighbouring nodes. The activation is divided equally along the receiving nodes. The parameter that determines the amount of activation distributed is called `spreading relax`. Before distribution, the activation is multiplied by the value of the parameter. A part of the activation is also kept at the node. The parameter that determines this amount is called `activation relax`. The iteration is conducted until the parameter `step limit` is reached.

After the iteration is finished, a relevance order is set up on the items. The relevance order is determined by the activation of the nodes after the last iteration step in the graph. Nodes of type `item` are selected and are sorted in descending order, by relevance. It means that nodes with higher activation value will be recommended with a higher priority.

B. Network Science

Network science [23] developed several centrality measures for nodes of networks. The aim of these measures is to express how central the position of a specific node is in a network by assigning numeric values to the nodes. Such measures are for example: degree centrality, closeness centrality, betweenness centrality and eigenvector centrality. Degree centrality counts the edges belonging to the node. Closeness centrality is the inverse of farness, which is the sum of the length of paths from the node to all other nodes. Betweenness centrality is the count of how many times a node lays on the shortest path between two nodes. Eigenvector centrality is proportional to the sum of the eigenvector centralities of its neighbours.

To calculate global recommendations, the above mentioned network science centrality measures are utilized on $\mathcal{K}_d$ and a relevance order is set up on the nodes of the network. The relevance order is prepared by sorting the nodes in descending by the specific centrality measure value.

C. Human Expert

In order to provide a baseline for our methods, human expert based newsletters are also involved in the experiment. The recommendations of the human expert are based on domain knowledge, experience on the market and publicly available top selling lists of competing on-line shops. For each campaign, the human expert provided a list of items to recommend. The list of items is treated as non-personalized recommendations; the same list of items is offered to all the users. Human expert based personalized recommendation is not feasible due to financial and capacity restrictions.

V. Dataset

In our experiment, the knowledge graph represents the information collected in the electronic commerce system. A representation method has been defined, which is capable to model all the available information present. Our software is integrated with the electronic commerce system, meaning that data is transferred to the knowledge base in real-time.

The knowledge graph contains persons, books, attributes, attribute categories and the relations between these entities. Each person and each book is represented with a node. Customer attributes are home town and birth year. These attributes are specified by the user and are not mandatory fields. Item attributes are author, publisher, year of publishing, number of pages and price. A book can have multiple authors. For each attribute value, a node is created and is bound with an edge to the appropriate node representing the person or item the specific attribute belongs to. In the case of number of pages

TABLE I. TYPES AND OCCURRENCES.

(a) Node types

Type	Count
Person	17 134
HomeTown	105
BirthYear	7
Item	117 367
Author	45 918
Publisher	6 351
YearOfPublishing	67
NumberOfPages	5
PriceCategory	5
ItemCategory	598

(b) Relation types

Type	Count
PersonBirthYear	8
PersonHomeTown	175
ItemAuthor	127 613
ItemCategory	30 800
ItemNumberOfPages	112 524
ItemPriceCategory	212 473
ItemPublisher	116 746
ItemYearOfPublishing	96 653
BoughtItem	22 064
OnWishList	2 972
ItemVisited	4 590
SubCategory	486

and price, value intervals are defined. In these cases, the nodes are created to represent the intervals instead of values.

In the electronic commerce system, the books are organized into categories. Such categories are for example "travel", "art" and "religion". A book can be assigned to multiple categories. The categories are organized into a hierarchical structure, meaning that most categories are subcategories of other categories. The category system and the book-category relations are also represented in the knowledge base.

In order to represent user interest in specific items, relations between persons and books are stored in the knowledge base. If a user visits the detailed information page of a book, a relation is inserted into the knowledge base to represent the implicit (not explicitly specified) interest of the user. If a user purchases an item (a more explicitly expressed interest), a relation is inserted into the knowledge base. In the electronic commerce system, users can put books on their wish-list to indicate that they are interested in buying the specific books later. Wish-lists are very useful information sources as they represent explicit interest expressed by the users. Wish-list relations are also stored in the knowledge base.

The information is represented in the knowledge base as defined in Section III. Table Ia presents the node types and occurrence counts in the knowledge base. Nodes of type `Person` represent people who are already users of the electronic commerce system and people who only signed up for the newsletter. Nodes of type `HomeTown` represent the home town of the users. Nodes of type `BirthYear` represent the birth year of the users, i.e. `1978`. Nodes of type `Item` represent the books available in the on-line shop, i.e. `Manga` and `Hieronymus Bosch`. Nodes of type `Author` represent the authors of the books, i.e. `Kurt Vonnegut` and `John Updike`. Nodes of type `Publisher` represent the publishers of the books, i.e. `Osiris Publishing` and `A & C Black`. Nodes of type `YearOfPublishing` represent the different years when books were published, i.e. `2007`. Nodes of type `NumberOfPages` represent number of pages intervals. The following intervals are defined `0-60`, `61-100`, `101-200`, `201-500` and `501-1000`. Nodes of type `PriceCategory` represent price intervals. The following intervals are defined by the expert of the electronic commerce system `0-1000`, `0-3000`, `1001-3000`, `3001-6000` and `6001-10000`. As the intervals are overlapping, a book can belong to multiple price categories. In this case multiple edge are created in the knowledge graph. Nodes of type `ItemCategory` represent item categories, i.e. `travel`, `art` and `religion`.

Table Ib presents relation types and occurrence counts in the knowledge base. Relations of type `PersonBirthYear` between nodes of type `Person` and nodes of type `PersonBirthYear` represent that the person was born in the specific year. Relations of type `PersonHomeTown` between nodes of type `Person` and nodes of type `HomeTown` represent that the person lives in the specific town. Relations of type `ItemAuthor` between nodes of type `Item` and nodes of type `Author` represent the author(s) of the specific book. Relations of type `ItemCategory` between nodes of type `Item` and nodes of type `ItemCategory` represent that the book belongs to the specific category. Relations of type `ItemNumberOfPages` between nodes of type `Item` and nodes of type `NumberOfPages` represent that the page count of the book falls in the specific page count interval. Relations of type `ItemPriceCategory` between nodes of type `Item` and nodes of type `PriceCategory` represent that the price of the book falls into the specified price category. Relations of type `ItemPublisher` between nodes of type `Item` and nodes of type `Publisher` represent that the book is published by the specific publisher. Relations of type `ItemYearOfPublishing` between nodes of type `Item` and nodes of type `YearOfPublishing` represent that the book has been published in the specific year. Relations of type `BoughtItem` between nodes of type `Person` and nodes of type `Item` represent that the person purchased the specific book. Relations of type `OnWishList` between nodes of type `Person` and nodes of type `Item` represent that the person put the specific book onto their wish-list. Relations of type `ItemVisited` between nodes of type `Person` and nodes of type `Item` represent that the person visited the Web page displaying details on the specific book. Relations of type `SubCategory` between nodes of type `ItemCategory` represent that the category is the sub-category of the specified one.

Table Ib shows that the knowledge base is sparse on person attributes but is rich on item attributes. The reason behind this is that while item attributes are available from the publishing companies, users do not take the time to specify their personal details. Unfortunately the wish-lists are also not densely populated. The knowledge base contains only a small amount of `ItemVisited` relations. The reason for this is that in order to maximize the book orders, the electronic commerce system does not make it mandatory to authenticate the users for purchasing or browsing. As the users are typically not authenticated, they cannot be identified and most of the `ItemVisited` relations are not recorded. Table Ib also shows that there are books with multiple authors in the database as the count of `ItemAuthor` relation is higher than the number of `Item` nodes. The count of `ItemNumberOfPages` and `ItemPublisher` is not the same. The reason for this is that the item attributes are not specified for each item. The relatively high number of `ItemPriceCategory` relations can be explained with the overlapping `PriceCategory` intervals.

The knowledge base is integrated with the electronic commerce system, meaning that changes made by the visitors in the database are immediately transmitted to the knowledge base of the recommender system. As the electronic commerce system is a system in production, it has several transactions per day. The node and relation counts per type indicated in Table Ia and Table Ib were recorded on 23 January, 2015.

VI. Evaluation

In our experiment, the methods described in Section IV are evaluated. As the recommender system software is integrated with the electronic commerce system, the information is transmitted to the knowledge base in real-time. The methods are evaluated with newsletters offering books to the users of the electronic commerce system. The books presented in each newsletter is selected by one of the methods. During the evaluation period, click-through events have been measured.

A. Newsletters Sent

To evaluate the recommendation techniques, 16 campaigns were conducted between 23 Jul, 2014 and 14 Jan, 2015. During the evaluation period 241 062 newsletters have been sent of which 35 229 newsletters have been opened.

TABLE II. Newsletter send dates.

Type	*Date sent*	*Type*	*Date sent*
Recommender System	2014-07-16	Human Expert	2014-09-22
Human Expert	2014-07-23	Recommender System	2014-09-26
Recommender System	2014-07-26	Human Expert	2014-10-02
Recommender System	2014-08-01	Human Expert	2014-10-09
Human Expert	2014-08-06	Recommender System	2014-10-15
Human Expert	2014-08-27	Human Expert	2014-10-22
Recommender System	2014-08-29	Recommender System	2014-10-31
Recommender System	2014-09-12	Recommender System	2014-12-14

Table II lists the newsletter campaigns. Column *type* contains the type of the campaign, column *Date sent* the date when the newsletters have been sent. The following campaign types are defined.

Recommender system based campaigns involve a personalized and a non-personalized recommendation method. The personalized method is utilized in the case, when there is enough information to offer a personalized list of books to the user. In this case, in our experiment, a spreading activation based technique as described in Section IV-A is evaluated. If there is not enough information to provide personalized recommendations, a non-personalized method is used as a fall-back solution. In this case, in our experiment one of the network science based methods as described in Section IV-B is evaluated.

Human expert based campaigns present the books selected by the human expert as described in Section IV-C to the users. In this case no fall-back solution is necessary as the human expert based method is a non-personalized method.

B. Evaluation Method

The behaviour of the users in the purchase process can be measured by several click-through events. In our experiment the click-through events are sequential. The steps of the process are the following: sending a newsletter, opening a newsletter, clicking on an item in a newsletter, ordering an item and paying for the item. During the evaluation period, the sales process is recorded and is measured. According to the mentioned steps, the following newsletter states are defined: `sent`, `opened`, `clicked`, `ordered` and `paid`.

In order to keep resource usage low, to conform industry standards and to be able to measure the click-through rate, the newsletters do not contain embedded images but image references. For security and privacy reasons, most of the state of the art email client software do not download remote images automatically. If the user is interested in more details of the message, the email client can be instructed to download and show the remote content in the message. As the image references point to our server, this user interaction will lead to a download event on the server side. This event can be monitored and the click-through event is recorded.

The next conversion, clicking on an book is an important step. By clicking on a book in a newsletter, the users click on a link. The links in a newsletter take the user first to our server. Each link in the newsletter contains a unique identifier. Based on this identifier our software records the click-through on the server and forwards the user to the detail page of the book in the electronic commerce system.

The detail page of the book also lets the user order the item, which event is forwarded to our software where the click-through event is recorded as the next conversion. If the user does not order the book in this work-flow event but visits the platform later and finalizes the order process, the order event will be forwarded to the evaluation software and the click-through event is to be recorded.

The electronic commerce system offers various payment methods like credit card, money transfer and cash. Cash based payments do not involve additional shipment cost, as in this case the user personally visits the store. Due to the lack of additional fees, in the economic environment the experiment is conducted in, cash based payment is the most frequently used method. The two consequences of cash based payment are the delay between the order and payment and the case of the unfinished purchase process. The first case is managed by our evaluation software. The latter case leads to a visible conversion rate between the order and payment steps.

C. Method Configurations

Human expert and network science based methods do not need configuration. Spreading activation requires three parameters as described in IV-A. Based on our past research results [24], `spreading relax`, `activation relax` is set to a constant value, 0.5. In the experiments various spreading activation configurations are defined as the value of the `step limit` parameter varies between 3 and 7. In a campaign only one method configuration is evaluated.

D. Recommendation List Filtering

In order to increase the recommendation quality, a post-processing is applied to the spreading activation and the network centrality measure based recommendation lists. The post-processing is specified by the human expert and is defined by the following rules

- a newsletter can contain at most 2 books from the same author,
- if a book is once presented in a newsletter, it won't be included into consecutive newsletters for two months,
- books already bought in the electronic commerce system are not inserted into the newsletter.

The above described rules can be understood as a filtering mechanism on the recommendation list. After the recommendation list is ordered by relevance, those n items are inserted into the newsletter, which items meet the described criteria, while keeping the relevance order.

VII. RESULTS

Table III summarizes the newsletters sent in the evaluation period. Each row represents the appropriate state of the newsletter according to the states described in Section VI-B. The columns define the type of the recommendation method as described in Section VI-A. The values present the number of newsletters. Due to space limitations, the summarized results are presented.

TABLE III. COUNT OF NEWSLETTERS PER STATE AND RECOMMENDATION METHOD TYPE

State	Spreading Activation	Network Science	Human Expert
Sent	66 148	72 884	102 030
Opened	11 700	9 206	14 323
Clicked	1 265	260	772
Ordered	24	0	17
Paid	17	0	6

The first row of the table shows an important property of the dataset, the high number of the cold start cases. In total, 66 148 personalized newsletters and 72 884 non-personalized newsletters were sent. It means that the proportion (52%) of the cold start case is relatively high, compared to, for example our experiments [24] on the MovieLens [25] dataset. The reason for the high proportion of cold start cases can be found in the high number of users signed up only to the newsletter as mentioned in Section V. As the nodes representing these users are not bound to the knowledge base by any edge, spreading activation based methods are not able to find a path between these nodes and the nodes representing books.

The most visible and important result of our experiment is visible in the last row of Table III representing newsletters resulting in a sale event. Spreading activation based newsletters lead to the highest number of purchase events, more than the human expert based newsletters. Unfortunately, network science based methods show a low performance, as network science based recommendations do not lead to a purchase event.

Table IV shows the click-through event rates between the different states of the evaluation process in each method type group presented in sub-tables. The rows represent the source state, the columns represent the destination state of the state transition. For example the value in the last column of the first row in Table IVa shows that 0.026% of all the sent, spreading activation based newsletters resulted in a purchase event.

The click-through rates presented in Table IV show that personalized newsletters clearly outperform the human expert, as 0.026% of all the sent personalized newsletters resulted in a purchase event, while this ratio is 0.006% for the human expert based method. The detailed click-through rates of personalized engines are higher than human expert based recommendations, except for one case, the `Clicked` to `Ordered` case. In this case, the click through rates are 1.897% compared to 2.202%. We would like to mention here that this state transition is being processed in the electronic commerce portal, which might influence the experiment.

TABLE IV. CONVERSION RATES OF METHOD TYPE GROUPS

(a) Spreading activation

	Opened	Clicked	Ordered	Paid
Sent	17.688%	1.912%	0.036%	0.026%
Opened		10.812%	0.205%	0.145%
Clicked			1.897%	1.344%
Ordered				70.833%

(b) Network Science

	Opened	Clicked	Ordered	Paid
Sent	12.631%	0.357%	0.000%	0.000%
Opened		2.824%	0.000%	0.000%
Clicked			0.000%	0.000%
Ordered				0.000%

(c) Human Expert

	Opened	Clicked	Ordered	Paid
Sent	14.038%	0.757%	0.017%	0.006%
Opened		5.390%	0.119%	0.042%
Clicked			2.202%	0.777%
Ordered				35.294%

Unfortunately, network science based methods show no activity after the `Clicked` state, as there is no click-through event from from the `Clicked` to the `Ordered` state for this method type. While the `Sent` to `Clicked` state transition rate of network science based methods (12.631%) is similar to the transition rate of other method groups (17.688% and 14.038%), the `Opened` to `Clicked` state transition rate (2.824%) is very low compared to other method types.

Comparing human expert based methods to spreading activation based engines, spreading activation shows a much higher conversion rate from the `Opened` to the `Clicked` state as 10.812% compared to 5.390% and from the `Ordered` to the `Paid` state as 70.833% compared to 35.294%. Referring to Section VI-B, the latter click-through rate involves additional resources from the users (picking up the books personally) and this difference shows a more stronger commitment of the users.

VIII. CONCLUSION AND FUTURE WORK

A graph based knowledge base containing heterogeneous information is defined. Three different groups of types of recommendation techniques are evaluated as spreading activation, network science and human expert. The methods are evaluated in an experiment with an electronic commerce system by sending personalized newsletters. During the experiment, click-through events are measured and presented in the paper. The results show that personalized newsletters outperform human experts and are also capable to increase business income.

Another important finding is that the application of network science measure methods does not lead to a purchase event. Jeong et al. [26] also conducted experiments in this field, and came to the conclusion that in order to increase the recommendation quality, network science measures should be combined with already existing methods. Our finding shows a similar result as the application of network science methods without combining with any additional information does not lead to high quality recommendations.

The most significant differences between the method types can be found at the state transition between the `Opened` to `Clicked` state and the `Ordered` to `Paid` state. In the case of network science methods we have information only in the case of `Clicked` to `Ordered` transition, as network science based methods do not even reach the `Ordered` state. The `Opened` to `Clicked` clicked transition rate shows somehow how relevant the recommended items are to the particular user, as this click-through event requires an explicit action from the user regarding to the item in interest. Network science based methods perform the worse at this state transition. Spreading activation based methods perform much better than human expert based methods indicating that spreading activation recommends more relevant items compared to the human expert.

As mentioned in Section VI, the last state transition involves additional resources from the user. In the economic environment the experiment is conducted in, the users are very cost sensitive, meaning that to eliminate shipping costs, instead of shipping, the personal pick-up is preferred. It means that the last transition step involves time and transportation costs from the users. The fact that spreading activation based methods outperform the human expert shows that the interpretation of the relevance of the recommended items draws additional factors of the evaluation method.

One of our next steps is to implement and evaluate collaborative filtering in the described evaluation environment. By its nature, the dataset contains no rating information, hence a binary variant of collaborative filtering should be implemented. Another interesting topic is the analysis of the impact of wishlists on the recommendation results.

A more technical problem is the user identification or authentication. We assume that by introducing a cookie or ETag based technique to identify returning users in the electronic commerce system, the number of edges of type `ItemVisited` can be significantly increased. Based on the additional information available, the recommendation method can be further investigated.

Utilizing neural networks and conditional random fields is also a possible direction of future research. By defining relations between nodes of the network on a more sophisticated level, the network can be able to more precisely adapt to the training data. Neural networks can be utilized with directed graphs.

REFERENCES

[1] D. Jannach, M. Zanker, A. Felfernig, and G. Friedrich, *Recommender Systems An Introduction*. Cambridge University Press, 2011.

[2] aLap. (2016, Apr.) Booker.hu Online Bookstore - Order a Book. [Online]. Available: http://www.booker.hu/

[3] CreoGroup. (2016, Apr.) PartnerMail. [Online]. Available: http://www.partnermail.eu/

[4] I. Cantador and P. Castells, "Multi-Layered Ontology-Based User Profiles and Semantic Social Networks for Recommender Systems," in *2nd Int. Workshop on Web Personalisation, Recommender Systems and Intelligent User Interfaces (WPRSIUI 2006) at the 4th Int. Conf. on Adaptive Hypermedia and Adaptive Web-Based Systems (AH 2006)*, Dublin, Ireland, June 2006.

[5] P. Kazienko, K. Musial, and T. Kajdanowicz, "Multidimensional Social Network in the Social Recommender System," *Trans. Sys. Man Cyber. Part A*, vol. 41, no. 4, pp. 746–759, Jul. 2011.

[6] R. Guha, R. Kumar, P. Raghavan, and A. Tomkins, "Propagation of trust and distrust," in *WWW '04: Proceedings of the 13th international conference on World Wide Web*. New York, NY, USA: ACM, 2004, pp. 403–412.

[7] C.-N. Ziegler and G. Lausen, "Propagation Models for Trust and Distrust in Social Networks," *Information Systems Frontiers*, vol. 7, no. 4-5, pp. 337–358, Dec. 2005.

[8] P. Massa and P. Avesani, "Trust-Aware Collaborative Filtering for Recommender Systems." in *CoopIS/DOA/ODBASE (1)*, ser. Lecture Notes in Computer Science, R. Meersman and Z. Tari, Eds., vol. 3290. Springer, 2004, pp. 492–508.

[9] A. Jøsang, S. Marsh, and S. Pope, "Exploring Different Types of Trust Propagation." in *iTrust*, ser. Lecture Notes in Computer Science, K. Stølen, W. H. Winsborough, F. Martinelli, and F. Massacci, Eds., vol. 3986. Springer, 2006, pp. 179–192.

[10] I. Guy, N. Zwerdling, D. Carmel, I. Ronen, E. Uziel, S. Yogev, and S. Ofek-Koifman, "Personalized recommendation of social software items based on social relations." in *RecSys*, L. D. Bergman, A. Tuzhilin, R. D. Burke, A. Felfernig, and L. Schmidt-Thieme, Eds. ACM, 2009, pp. 53–60.

[11] I. Konstas, V. Stathopoulos, and J. M. Jose, "On Social Networks and Collaborative Recommendation," in *Proceedings of the 32Nd International ACM SIGIR Conference on Research and Development in Information Retrieval*, ser. SIGIR '09. New York, NY, USA: ACM, 2009, pp. 195–202.

[12] J. He, "A Social Network-based Recommender System," Ph.D. dissertation, Los Angeles, CA, USA, 2010, aAI3437557.

[13] Y. Blanco-Fernández, M. L. Nores, A. Gil-Solla, M. R. Cabrer, and J. J. P. Arias, "Exploring synergies between content-based filtering and Spreading Activation techniques in knowledge-based recommender systems." *Inf. Sci.*, vol. 181, no. 21, pp. 4823–4846, 2011.

[14] T. Hussein, D. Westheide, and J. Ziegler, "Context-adaptation based on Ontologies and Spreading Activation," in *LWA 2007: Lernen - Wissen - Adaption, Halle, September 2007, Workshop Proceedings*, A. Hinneburg, Ed. Martin-Luther-University Halle-Wittenberg, 2007, pp. 361–366.

[15] T. Hussein and J. Ziegler, "Adapting web sites by spreading activation in ontologies," in *ReColl '08: Int. Workshop on Recommendation and Collaboration (in conjunction with IUI 2008)*, Gran Canaria, 2008.

[16] Q. Gao, J. Yan, and M. Liu, "A Semantic Approach to Recommendation System Based on User Ontology and Spreading Activation Model." in *NPC Workshops*, J. Cao, M. Li, C. Weng, Y. Xiang, X. Wang, H. Tang, F. Hong, H. Liu, and Y. Wang, Eds. IEEE Computer Society, 2008, pp. 488–492.

[17] V. Codina and L. Ceccaroni, "Taking Advantage of Semantics in Recommendation Systems." in *CCIA*, ser. Frontiers in Artificial Intelligence and Applications, R. Alquézar, A. Moreno, and J. Aguilar-Martin, Eds., vol. 210. IOS Press, 2010, pp. 163–172.

[18] A. Troussov, D. Parra, and P. Brusilovsky, "Spreading Activation Approach to Tag-aware Recommenders: Modeling Similarity on Multidimensional Networks," D. Jannach, W. Geyer, J. Freyne, S. S. Anand, C. Dugan, B. Mobasher, and A. Kobsa, Eds., 2009, pp. 57–62.

[19] J. M. Alvarez, L. Polo, P. Abella, W. Jimenez, and J. E. Labra, "Application of the Spreading Activation Technique for Recommending Concepts of well-known ontologies in Medical Systems," 2011.

[20] X. Jiang and A.-H. Tan, "Learning and inferencing in user ontology for personalized Semantic Web search." *Inf. Sci.*, vol. 179, no. 16, pp. 2794–2808, 2009.

[21] M. R. Quillian, "Semantic memory," in *Semantic Information Processing*, M. Minsky, Ed. Cambridge, MA: MIT Press, 1968, pp. 227–270.

[22] N. V. Findler, Ed., *Associative Networks: The Representation and Use of Knowledge of Computers*. Academic Pr, 1979.

[23] D. Easley and J. Kleinberg, *Networks, Crowds, and Markets: Reasoning About a Highly Connected World*. Cambridge University Press, 2010.

[24] L. Grad-Gyenge, P. Filzmoser, and H. Werthner, "Recommendations on a Knowledge Graph," in *MLRec 2015 : 1st International Workshop on Machine Learning Methods for Recommender Systems*, 2015, pp. 13–20.

[25] P. Resnick, N. Iacovou, M. Suchak, P. Bergstorm, and J. Riedl, "GroupLens: An Open Architecture for Collaborative Filtering of Netnews," in *Proc. of ACM 1994 Conference on Computer Supported Cooperative Work*. Chapel Hill, North Carolina: ACM, 1994, pp. 175–186.

[26] J. H. Jeong and J. W. Kim, "Personalized Recommendation Based on Collaborative Filtering with Social Network Analysis," in *International Conference on Information and Computer Applications*, ser. ICICA 2012, vol. 24. IACSIT Press, 2012, pp. 67–71.

Process Analysis and e-Business Adoption in Nigerian SBEs: A Report on Case Study Research

Olakunle Olayinka, Martin George Wynn, Kamal Bechkoum
School of Computing and Technology
University of Gloucestershire
Cheltenham, United Kingdom
e-mail: kunle@kunleolayinka.com, MWynn@glos.ac.uk, KBechkoum@glos.ac.uk

Abstract— **It is generally acknowledged that e-business technologies can provide internal value as well as opportunities to reach different local and international markets, for both large and small organisations. Although the use of web-based systems and technologies to improve business processes has increased steadily over the past decade, there remains a dearth of research in this field in developing countries such as Nigeria. This paper examines how e-business is being used in two Nigerian small businesses, using a process mapping technique, system profiling and two main models from the existing literature. The results indicate that these models provide a valid framework for the initial analysis of e-business in this environment, and that these companies are indeed benefitting from the deployment of e-business technologies, particularly in their customer facing processes and functions.**

Keywords- e-business; Nigeria; Small Business Enterprises; SBEs; process mapping; e-business models.

I. INTRODUCTION

The adoption of electronic business (e-business) technologies and processes has increased significantly in recent years [1][2]. In developed countries, research has shown that both large enterprises and small businesses have successfully adopted e-business technologies and processes to gain competitive advantage[3], transform business models [4], and improve relationships with customers and suppliers [5][6]. Various researchers have pointed out that the motivation for e-business adoption varies from organisation to organisation, though it often encompasses reducing transaction costs [7], improved access to global markets [8], or increasing bottom-line profit performance [9].

In developing countries such as Nigeria, there is a dearth of research on the adoption of e-business in Small Business Enterprises (SBEs). This research investigates e-business in Nigerian SBEs by using a process mapping approach to analyse the current situation in two SBEs. For the purposes of this research, SBEs are defined as enterprises which employ fewer than 50 persons, while Small to Medium Enterprises (SMEs) are defined as enterprises which employ fewer than 250 persons [10][11].

Following this brief introduction, Section II reviews relevant literature on e-business, e-business models, process mapping and the challenges faced by SBEs in Nigeria. Section III then describes the methodology employed in this study and Section IV presents and discusses some of the initial findings. Section V provides an initial analysis of these findings, and the final concluding section suggests how further research will adapt and improve existing models for application in the Nigerian business context.

II. LITERATURE REVIEW

The term e-business was used by IBM in 1997 to mean "the transformation of key business processes through the use of internet technologies" [12]. E-business can be viewed as the integration of web technologies with business processes and management practices to increase efficiency and lower costs [13][14]. Several recent studies have focused on the adoption of e-business technology and processes by SMEs in developed countries, including the UK [9][15], the USA [16], Australia [14] and in Canada [17]. However, there is still considerable debate in the existing literature on the value and productivity gain e-business has to offer to SBEs [9][18], who generally contribute significantly to a nation's economic growth by offering flexible employment opportunities [8], poverty alleviation [19], and enhance supply chain flexibility, and thereby support the country's overall GDP growth [20].

After rebasing its GDP in 2014, Nigeria became the largest economy in Africa, and the 26th largest economy in the world with a GDP of $509 billion [21][22], overtaking South Africa whose GDP at the time was $384.3 billion [20]. SMEs contributed about 46.5% to Nigeria's GDP with SBEs making up 99% of these SMEs in Nigeria. However, as an indication of the problems that need confronting in the uptake of e-business, it is worth noting that Nigerian businesses experience power outages about 5 to 10 times weekly, with each one lasting an average of one hour [23].

As a result of the increased use of the internet [24][25], and mobile networks penetration in Nigeria [26], current and potential customers of SBEs are not only equipped with desktop computers and laptops, but also with mobile devices such as iPads, Smart phones and tablets. The demand for e-business capabilities in Nigerian companies from customers is thus likely to increase, but very little research has explored the extent to which Nigerian SBEs are adopting e-business technologies and processes.

To date, most studies on e-business in Nigerian small businesses have focused primarily on e-commerce i.e., the buying and selling of good and services online, neglecting the potential of e-business in transforming business processes and core operations in the more traditional "bricks and mortar" companies [8][19]. In 2011, Olatokun and

Bankole [7] investigated the factors influencing e-business technology adoption by SMEs in Ibadan, a city in south western Nigeria. Data was collected by structured questionnaires administered to key personnel in 60 SMEs (30 adopters and 30 non adopters of e-business), and the results revealed that the age of SMEs was a significant influencing factor on whether e-business was used or not, while company size was of very little significance. It was the younger companies that constituted the majority of e-business users.

Process mapping has been applied as a tool to define and analyse processes in an organisation [27] and thereby to improve performance [28]. Researchers and systems analysts have applied this analytical tool in a number of different systems contexts. These range from the all-encompassing Enterprise Resource Planning (ERP) packages in large businesses [29][30] to e-business technology adoption in small businesses [9][31].

SMEs vary in structure, size and type of business, and the nature of e-business adoption will vary accordingly between businesses. The criteria and related models for assessing e-business need to accommodate these variations. For example, a small manufacturing company with one main customer is likely to focus more on internal efficiency gains, whilst an SBE with products with global potential is likely to focus more on online sales and marketing activities[32].

Various frameworks and models have been designed to both measure e-business adoption as well as aid e-business implementation. The DTI Adoption Ladder is one of the early e-business frameworks. It breaks down e-business adoption into 5 stages and suggests that organisations move through these stages in a sequential order [9][33]. Levy and Powell [34] proposed the "transporter model" as an alternative non-linear e-business adoption model for SMEs. This model suggests that different types of SMEs will view e-business adoption in different ways and identifies four dimensions of e-business deployment in an SME - brochureware, business opportunity, business network and business support.

In order to determine e-business adoption at individual process level – rather than at overall company level - the Connect, Publish, Interact, Transform (CPIT) model was developed by the UK Department of Trade and Industry [35]. This model offers a 2-dimensional matrix to evaluate the impact of e-business technologies across an organisation's main business processes. When compared with the Adoption Ladder, the CPIT model offers a more in-depth assessment of the impact of e-business on SME operations[9]. The Stages of Growth for e-business (SOG-e) model [36] is the combination of a six stage IT maturity model with a six stage Internet Commerce maturity model. However, somewhat akin to the CPIT model, the SOG-e model recognises that it is possible for an organisation to have different levels of e-business maturity in different areas of a business. A related model is that of Willcocks and Sauer [37] who identified 4 main stages through which organisations will pass as they develop and apply the skills needed for successful e-business deployment. The organization gains increased business value from e-business as it attains the new capabilities required to advance to the next stage.

While previous studies in developed countries have applied some of these methods and frameworks to evaluate e-business technology and process adoption in SMEs; to date, no study has applied similar methods in the analysis of e-business adoption in Nigerian SBEs. This research will attempt to apply some of these models to various Nigerian SBEs, using, as a starting point, a simple top level process mapping technique that has been applied in similar studies [9][31][38]. More specifically, it will address the following research questions (RQs):

RQ1. Can these mapping techniques and models of e-business adoption be usefully applied to SBEs in a developing world context?

RQ2. If so, what do they tell us about the use of e-business in these small businesses in Nigeria?

III. Research Methodology

Research projects usually adopt a particular philosophical stance based on a research paradigm, for example post-positivism, pragmatism, interpretivism or constructivism [39]. This philosophical stance has a major influence on the choice of research methods and approaches to be used in order to obtain relevant findings [40]. For the purposes of this research, an interpretivist paradigm is adopted, and the research approach is qualitative, using multiple case studies.

The case study method of research is well suited for observations where the researcher aims to probe deeply and analyse rigorously with a view to making generalisations about the wider population in which the unit being studied belongs [41][42]. Multiple case studies of Nigerian SBEs are investigated to assess and analyse e-business adoption in the country. The case studies were selected from a cross-section of SBE industry sectors in Lagos – Nigeria's most populous city and its economic capital. The use of multiple case studies adds greater weight to the research and makes research findings more convincing [43]. Qualitative data was gathered through questionnaires and semi-structured interviews with key personnel in the company case studies. The case studies were identified through the researcher's existing contacts with company owners and IT managers and all organisations selected for the study have already attempted to apply e-business within their organisations. This paper reports on the findings from just the first two case studies.

While this research is qualitative, exploratory and inductive in nature, some quantitative assessment of company turnover, number of staff and period of e-business usage was done. Necessary approval and consent from participatory organisations were sought and aliases have been used for company and individuals' names. Empirical evidence gathered from these organisations was developed and assessment made against selected models.

IV. Findings

ABC Laundries is a family business founded in 2010. It originated as a home based operation, but has now expanded to become a budget laundry and dry cleaning service for people living in Lagos. The company provides a wide range of laundry and dry cleaning services to people living in the Lagos Metropolis from its locations in Yaba and Surulere (urban areas within Lagos). With its main operations office in Surulere strategically located within the Lagos University Teaching Hospital, ABC Laundries is able to offer its laundry services to students and staff at the hospital, as well as pickup and delivery services to companies, corporate services, and guest houses across Lagos State. Currently, the company turns over circa 6 million Naira (£24,000) per annum, and employs 7 staff. (Staff wages are very low in comparison with developed world norms, averaging less than £1000 a year for these staff). The current business plan is to further increase revenue by expanding the company's customer base and increasing market share.

The management of ABC Laundries view e-business as a key enabler of corporate growth and, to this end, invested in a bespoke web-based system in 2013, to handle its key sales and marketing and financial management processes. Prior to this, most business processes were handled by a combination of paper based receipts, Excel spreadsheets and open source accounting tools. However, this became difficult to manage with the opening of a new branch in 2012, and this was the catalyst for investment in a new web portal. The key objectives of this investment were:

1. To provide a system where orders can be captured in real time at both locations.
2. To provide a mechanism to allow staff and customers to track the status of a laundry order from pickup to delivery.
3. To enable top-level financial reporting in real-time.
4. To maintain a database of customers and contact details.

The web portal was implemented in phases, adding new functionality as the old support systems were phased out. The key objectives have been met, with the addition of a few functionality enhancements. The web portal was built using PHP and the MYSQL database. Integration with email servers as well as SMS gateways has enabled emails and SMS notifications to be sent to customers.

GPY properties is a property development and marketing company founded in 2012. In the context of Nigeria's housing deficit and the acute absence of quality housing in the country, the company aims to help redress this imbalance through the provision of innovative, high quality and affordable homes.

The company originated as the property sales division of a larger consulting company called PYI Consulting Limited. However, as sales of developed properties increased, the owner decided to hive off the division into a separate corporate entity to focus on property development sales and marketing as its core business. In 2014, the company turned over about 20 million Naira (£80,000) and the forecast for 2015 is double this figure, due in part to the imminent completion a new state of the art private residential estate in Ogun State, Nigeria.

GPY Properties maintains a website mainly for marketing properties and showcasing its ongoing projects to customers and potential customers. The company also maintains a cloud based Customer Relationship Management (CRM) system for maintaining and analysing customer contact details.

From time to time, the company also advertises on Facebook and various other property aggregator websites. Invoice generation and other accounting activities are currently managed by Excel spreadsheets, but plans are in place to subscribe to a cloud based accounting solution; the Wave Accounting and Xero Accounting packages are possible solutions.

With three full time staff and twenty contract staff, the company has been able to automate most of its daily business activities concerning customer engagement, internal communication and product marketing.

V. Initial Analysis

Initial analysis of e-business deployment in the case study companies was undertaken through the combination of four models - process mapping, systems profiling, CPIT (a process based e-business model) and the Willcocks and Sauer e-business staged model. Previous research [8][34] indicates that the use of simple stage based models alone to determine the level of e-business use in an organisation is not sufficient, as different processes may be at different levels. However, even with models that examine technology deployment at process level, such as the CPIT model, there is still the need to adapt these to a small business environment, as the process definitions may not be appropriate to new SBEs [31]. This combination of pre-existing models, derived and adapted from previous research [9], is used as the conceptual framework for analysis of the case studies.

The web based system implemented at ABC Laundries now enables it to generate receipts and invoices at its sales desk on the fly, as well as manage the status of each laundry order throughout its lifecycle (i.e., from pickup/drop off to delivery/pickup). The company's business plan now entails the opening up of multiple locations across the State, and this will involve leveraging of further benefit from its web based system.

Using data from the questionnaire responses and semi structured interviews, seven core processes were identified in ABC Laundries (Fig. 1) - Laundry Operations, Financial Management, Sales & Marketing, Collection & Delivery Management, Stock & Procurement Management, Payroll & HR Management and Customer Services. At PGY properties, there were six core processes (Fig. 2) that the organisation performs – Financial Management, Constructor Liaison & Management, Customer Services, Property Sales and Marketing, Logistics & Procurement and Payroll & HR Management.

Systems profiling was applied to identify e-business systems currently in place in each process area. By employing a simple Red-Amber-Green assessment (Fig. 3 and Fig. 4), systems were assessed to indicate those in need of replacement, those that could possibly be retained and those that were deemed strategically and/or operationally sound. This procedure initiated the analysis of e-business systems at individual process level as well as indicating which processes are automated, semi-automated or non-automated.

Figure 1. Main business processes at ABC Laundries

A CPIT analysis of ABC Laundries (Fig. 5) then provided a more detailed view of the impact of e-business systems at process level. This revealed that e-business systems have made significant impact in the financial management and customer facing processes. Decision makers within the organisation are easily able to keep track of daily, weekly and monthly revenue from any of the two premises, or remotely, thus helping the organisation to plan effectively and take appropriate action when needed.

The sales and marketing process has also been made more efficient with the ability to automate and notify selected groups of customer via SMS or emails. There remain further benefits to be gained by automating the communication of marketing information to customers and by making relevant information available across processes. This may allow, for example, special offers to be made to customers in specific geographic locations, with high frequency of delivery, with a mind to keep delivery cost constant and increase orders to be delivered. This type of further development, which is akin to what, in a larger organization, would be termed Business Intelligence, would arguably move the company into the transformation stage on the CPIT model.

Figure 2. Main business processes at GPY properties

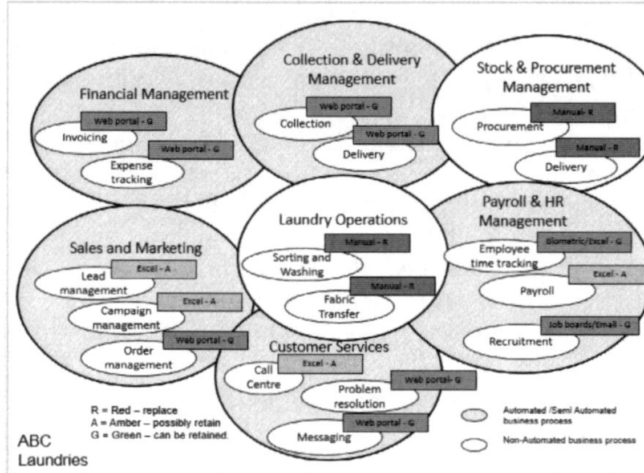

Figure 3. Main business processes, sub-processes and systems profiling at ABC Laundries

GPY Properties has been able to adopt e-business technologies without the need to use in-house IT staff, as it has been able to utilise a cloud based CRM tool. The CPIT Model for GPY Properties shows that its sales and marketing processes are well supported by e-business technology. According to the company's managing director, the strategy to advertise online has helped the company gather new leads - often people with very busy schedules, who would not normally have time to visit the company's office - as well as reach different geographical locations with its advertisements. This year, without doing any advert campaign specifically targeted at the northern part of Nigeria, the company has been able to make two property sales to individuals who live in this location, and a number of further sales are currently in the final stages of completion in this part of the country. One of the current subscribers to its flagship residential estate is a Nigerian who resides in Canada and who saw the advert on the company's Facebook page.

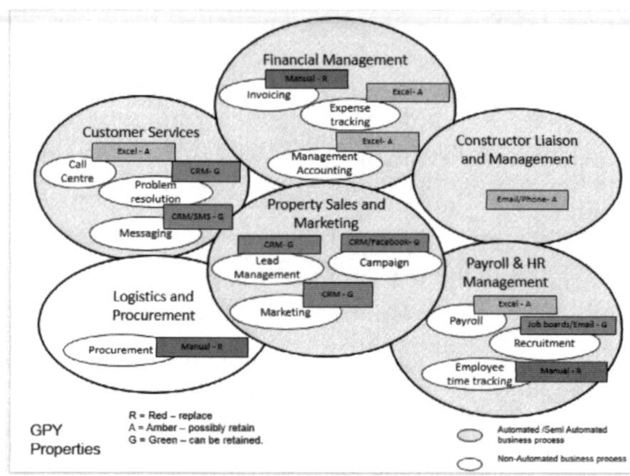

Figure 4. Main business processes and systems profiling at GPY Properties

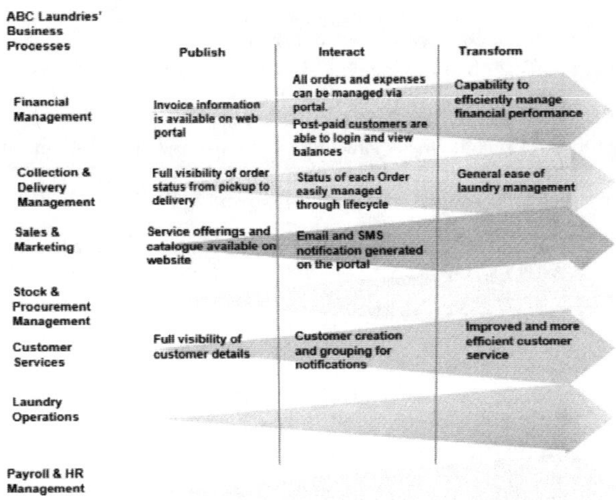

Figure 5. CPIT model applied to ABC Laundries

Nevertheless, Fig. 6 shows us that as of now, the deployment of e-business technologies at GPY Properties is restricted to the sales, marketing and customer service processes. The managing director has affirmed that the volume of data generated by the various departments in the other process areas does not justify further investment in e-business systems at present, although this may change as the organisation expands and takes up more construction projects.

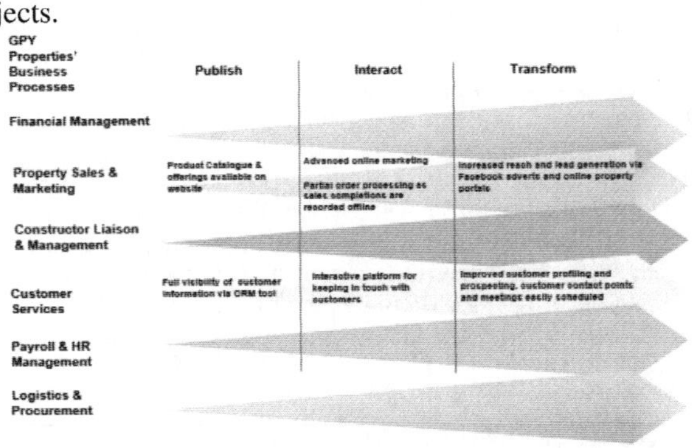

Figure 6. CPIT model applied to GPY Properties

Further, if we now look at these two companies against Willcocks and Sauer's model [37], the analysis suggests they are between stages 2 and 3 (Fig. 7), whereas other authors [44] have suggested that many small companies do not progress past stage 1 because they often do not see the benefit in investing in capital intensive e-business projects. This apparent contradiction is partly explained by the reduction in cost of e-business infrastructure in recent years, and, partly because of this, it has become a *de facto* norm to use e-business in the sales and marketing processes in many organisations, including SBEs. Moreover, in the two case study companies investigated here, the management sees e-business as a key enabler to growth. In ABC Laundries, in particular, their success with e-business to date can be attributed to the phased introduction of new e-business features which has helped the organisation derive value from relatively small scale, staged, expenditure. This has also allowed a phased upgrade in technology, accompanied by appropriate process improvement and staff training, before moving on to focus on another process. Similarly, at GPY Properties, the company has used cloud based systems that offer very low entry costs.

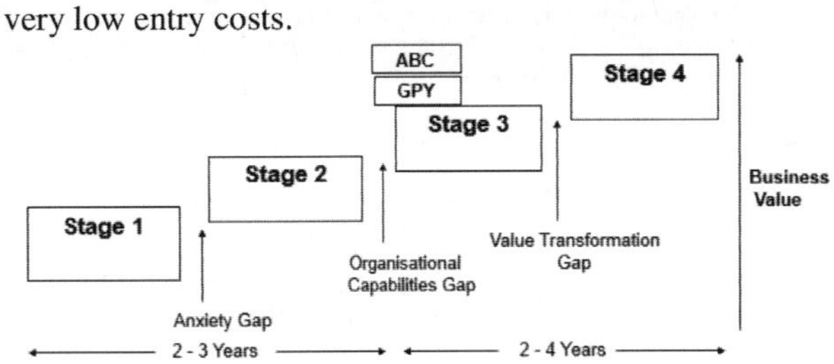

Figure 7. The Two Nigerian SBEs on the E-business Stage Model

Stage 1- Web Presence

- Develop presence
- Develop technology capability

Stage 2- Access Information and Transact Business

- Re-orientate business/technology thinking skills
- Build integrated approach with the web and business systems

Stage 3- Further Integration of Skills, Processes, Technologies

- Reorganise people/structures
- Reengineer processes
- Remodel technology infrastructure

Stage 4- Capability, Leveraging, Experience and Know-How to Maximise Value

- Customer-focused organisation

VI. CONCLUSION

The analysis of the two case studies indicates that e-business technologies and processes are being adopted by Nigerian SBEs, and that existing e-business models can be usefully applied to assess e-business operations in these companies. So, in answer to the RQs noted earlier in this paper, this research suggests that the e-business adoption models, developed to gauge the impact of e-business in the developed world over a decade ago, are of value today in a developing world context. Although the definition of e-business has evolved, the process mapping technique and the application of models like CPIT can give a clear framework and point of departure for the assessment of e-business in countries like Nigeria; and they clearly show that e-business technologies are bringing value to the studied SBEs, particularly in the customer facing processes, which mirrors the early deployment of e-business in the developed world.

Future research will now focus on how these models can be advanced and refined to provide an enhanced analytical framework for understanding and progressing e-business deployment in Nigeria. In particular, the three dimensions of change discussed above in relation to ABC Laundries – technology deployment, process improvement, and people skills enhancement – will be incorporated into a new combined model of e-business implementation. These dimensions of change have been identified by other authors [45] [46] with regard to information systems projects in developing world contexts, and this provides a theoretical platform for further investigation of these concepts in current and future case studies of e-business in Nigerian SBEs.

REFERENCES

[1] E. M. Agwu, "An investigative analysis of factors influencing E-business adoption and maintenance of commercial websites in Nigeria," Basic Res. J. Bus. Manag. Accounts ISSN 2315-6899 Vol. 3, 2014, pp. 5–16.

[2] A. Yee-Loong Chong, K.-B. Ooi, H. Bao, and B. Lin, "Can e-business adoption be influenced by knowledge management? An empirical analysis of Malaysian SMEs," J. Knowl. Manag., vol. 18, no. 1, 2014, pp. 121–136.

[3] B. A. Wagner, I. Fillis, and U. Johansson, "E-business and e-supply strategy in small and medium sized businesses (SMEs)," Supply Chain Manag. An Int. J., vol. 8, no. 4, 2003, pp. 343–354.

[4] T. Oliveira and M. F. Martins, "Understanding e-business adoption across industries in European countries," Ind. Manag. Data Syst., vol. 110, no. 9, 2010, pp. 1337–1354.

[5] T. Oliveira and M. F. Martins, "Firms Patterns of e-Business Adoption: Evidence for the European Union-27," Electron. J. Inf. Syst., vol. 13, no. 1, 2010, pp. 47–56.

[6] D. Sharma and M. Ranga, "Mobile customer relationship management-A competitive tool," Excel Int. J. Multidiscip. Manag. Stud., vol. 4, no. 7, 2014, pp. 37–42.

[7] W. Olatokun and B. Bankole, "Factors Influencing Electronic Business Technologies Adoption and Use by Small and Medium Scale Enterprises (SMES) in a Nigerian Municipality," J. Internet Bank. Commer., vol. 16, no. 3, 2011, pp. 1–26.

[8] M. Taylor and A. Murphy, "SMEs and e-business," J. small Bus. Enterp. Dev., vol. 11, no. 3, 2004, pp. 280–289.

[9] M. G. Wynn, P. Turner, and E. Lau, "E-business and process change: two case studies (towards an assessment framework)," J. Small Bus. Enterp. Dev., vol. 20, no. 4, 2013, pp. 913–933.

[10] European Commission, The new SME definition: user guide and model declaration. Office for Official Publications of the European Communities, 2005.

[11] Small and Medium Enterprises Development Agency of Nigeria, "National Policy on Micro, Small and Medium Enterprises," 2014.

[12] D. Chaffey, E-business and E-commerce Management: Strategy, Implementation and Practice. Financial Times Prentice Hall, 2007.

[13] V. Bordonaba-Juste, L. Lucia-Palacios, and Y. Polo-Redondo, "Antecedents and consequences of e-business adoption for European retailers," Internet Res., vol. 22, no. 5, 2012, pp. 532–550.

[14] A. Prananto, J. McKay, and P. Marshall, "Lessons learned from analysing e-business progression using a stage model in Australian Small Medium Enterprises (SMEs)," ACIS 2004 Proc. , 2004, p. 75.

[15] C. Parker and T. Castleman, "New directions for research on SME-eBusiness: insights from an analysis of journal articles from 2003-2006," J. Inf. Syst. Small Bus., vol. 1, no. 1, 2007, pp. 21–40.

[16] H. D. Kim, I. Lee, and C. K. Lee, "Building Web 2.0 enterprises: A study of small and medium enterprises in the United States," Int. Small Bus. J., vol. 31, no. 2, 2013, pp. 156–174.

[17] P. Ifinedo, "Internet/e-business technologies acceptance in Canada's SMEs: an exploratory investigation," Internet Res., vol. 21, no. 3, 2011, pp. 255–281.

[18] A. Basu and S. Muylle, "Assessing and enhancing e-business processes," Electron. Commer. Res. Appl., vol. 10, no. 4, 2011, pp. 437–499.

[19] D. O. Faloye, "The adoption of e-commerce in small businesses: an empirical evidence from retail sector in Nigeria.," J. Bus. Retail Manag. Res., vol. 8, no. 2, 2014, pp. 54–64.

[20] Bloomberg Business, "Nigerian Economy Overtakes South Africa's on Rebased GDP," Bloomberg Business, 2014. [Online]. Available: http://www.bloomberg.com/news/articles/2014-04-06/nigerian-economy-overtakes-south-africa-s-on-rebased-gdp. [Accessed: 18-March-2016].

[21] The Economist, "Nigeria: Africa's new Number One | The Economist," 2014.

[22] World Bank, "Nigeria Economic Report: Improved Economic Outlook in 2014, and Prospects for Continued Growth Look Good," 2014. [Online]. Available: https://www.worldbank.org/en/country/nigeria/publication/nigeria-economic-report-improved-economic-outlook-in-2014-and-prospects-for-continued-growth-look-good. [Accessed: 18-March-2016].

[23] E. I. Ohimain, "Can Nigeria Generate 30% of her Electricity from Coal by 2015," Int. J. Energy Power Eng., vol. 3, no. 1, 2014, p. 28.

[24] Internet Live Stats, "Internet Users by Country," 2014. [Online]. Available: http://www.internetlivestats.com/internet-users-by-country/. [Accessed: 18-March-2016].

[25] Vanguard Nigeria, "Nigeria has 48m active internet users – NITDA," 2014. [Online]. Available: http://www.vanguardngr.com/2014/10/nigeria-48m-active-internet-users-nitda/. [Accessed: 18-March-2016].

[26] Paul Budde Communication Pty Ltd, "Nigeria - Mobile Market - Insights, Statistics and Forecasts," Paul Budde Commun. Pty Ltd, 2015.

[27] J. M. Jacka and P. J. Keller, Business Process Mapping: Improving Customer Satisfaction. Wiley, 2009.

[28] S. Biazzo, "Process mapping techniques and organisational analysis: Lessons from sociotechnical system theory," Bus. Process Manag. J., vol. 8, no. 1, 2002, pp. 42–52.

[29] H. Akeel and M. G. Wynn, "ERP Implementation in a Developing World Context: a Case Study of the Waha Oil Company, Libya," in eKnow 2015 7th International Conference on Information, Process and Knowledge Management, 2015, no. A, pp. 126–131.

[30] M. G. Wynn and M. Rezaeian, "ERP implementation in manufacturing SMEs: Lessons from the Knowledge Transfer Partnership scheme," InImpact J. Innov. Impact, vol. 8, no. 1, 2015, pp. 75–92.

[31] M. Wynn and E. Tipton, "The Deployment of Service Management Systems in SMEs--Three Case Studies," in SERVICE COMPUTATION 2011 : The Third International Conferences on Advanced Service Computing, 2011, pp. 149-156.

[32] P. Taylor, "The Importance of Information and Communication Technologies (ICTs): An Integration of the Extant Literature on ICT Adoption in Small and Medium Enterprises," Int. J. Econ. Commer. Manag., vol. 3, no. 5, 2015, pp. 274-295.

[33] A. Gunasekaran, Modelling and Analysis of Enterprise Information Systems. IGI Pub., 2007.

[34] M. Levy and P. Powell, “Exploring SME internet adoption: towards a contingent model,” Electron. Mark., vol. 13, no. 2, 2003, pp. 173–181.

[35] Department of Trade and Industry, Business in the Information Age: International Benchmarking Study 2003. Booz Allen Hamilton, London, 2003.

[36] J. McKay, A. Prananto, and P. Marshall, “E-business maturity: The SOG-e model,” in Proceedings of the 11th Australasian Conference on Information Systems (ACIS), 2000, pp. 6–8.

[37] L. P. Willcocks and C. Sauer, Moving to e-business. Random House Business Books, 2000.

[38] M. Wynn and O. Olubanjo, “Demand-supply chain management: systems implications in an SME packaging business in the UK,” Int. J. Manuf. Res., vol. 7, no. 2, 2012, pp. 198–212.

[39] J. W. Creswell, Research Design: Qualitative, Quantitative, and Mixed Methods Approaches, Fourth edi. SAGE Publications, 2013.

[40] M. B. Davies, Doing a Successful Research Project: Using Qualitative or Quantitative Methods. Palgrave Macmillan, 2007.

[41] R. B. Burns, Introduction to Research Methods. SAGE Publications, 2000.

[42] D. Silverman, Interpreting Qualitative Data. SAGE Publications, 2015.

[43] R. K. Yin, Case Study Research: Design and Methods. SAGE Publications, 2003.

[44] M. Levy, P. Powell, and P. Yetton, “SMEs: aligning IS and the strategic context,” J. Inf. Technol., vol. 16, no. 3, 2001, pp. 133–144.

[45] R. Heeks, "Information Systems and Developing Countries: Failure, Success, and Local Improvisations", Journal of Information Society, Vol.18 (2), 2002, pp. 101-112.

[46] A. Bakeer and M. Wynn, “E-Business In The University Sector: A Case Study From Libya”, The Marketing Review, Vol 15, No 4, 2015, pp. 465-481.

The Strategic Value of Interorganization Information Systems: A Resource Dependency Perspective

Philippe Marchildon and Pierre Hadaya
Department of Management and Technology
ESG-UQAM
Montréal, Canada
e-mail: marchildon.philippe@courrier.uqam.ca
hadaya.pierre@uqam.ca

***Abstract*—Over the past three decades, numerous studies have shown that the adoption of interorganizational systems (IOS) has enabled organizations to obtain a competitive advantage. Yet, recent information systems (IS) resource-centered studies now question the strategic value of IOS, arguing that they have become easily imitable necessities. However, these studies are mainly efficiency oriented and do not assess the effectiveness impacts of IOS. Hence, the objective of this paper is to bring clarity on the strategic value of IOS by demonstrating that IOS can indeed be used to achieve organizational effectiveness. To do so, we anchor our work on the resource dependency theory (RDT), which explicitly posits effectiveness as the main driver of organizational performance. Accordingly, the literatures on business relationships, organizational performance, RDT and IOS are examined to propose a research model, its related hypotheses, and methodological aspects regarding its empirical validation. Finally, the proposed model's anticipated contributions are discussed.**

Keywords-dyadic business relationship; dependence; effectiveness; resource dependency theory; interorganizational information systems.

I. INTRODUCTION

To stay competitive in today's uncertain dynamic environment, organizations are increasingly relying on their partners to accomplish complex tasks that are impossible to achieve independently [1][2]. This new dynamic, where organizations are outsourcing their activities in which they are less competent [3], is modifying the links bounding a firm to its business counterparts [4] and creating a state of greater interdependence between social actors present in the environment [5]. This new dynamic is also translating in the emergence of new interorganizational forms such as virtual enterprises and integrated supply chains [6][7], to harness benefits from closer and stronger partnerships [8], which, in turn, have put to the forefront the use of interorganizational information systems (IOS). IOS are computer networks that support information exchange across organizational boundaries [9]. They have been extensively adopted and relied upon by organizations to obtain a competitive advantage over their competitors. Abnormal rents derived from such systems are assumed to stem from their ability to allow information to flow quickly and transparently across multiple interorganizational boundaries making it visible to all supply chain partners and in turn improving the performance of business relationships [10]. Despite these stated benefits, recent findings from information systems (IS) resource-centered studies now question the strategic value of IOS, arguing that they have become easily imitable necessities [11][12][13][14].

The proliferation of new interorganizational forms has also changed organizational practices in regards to performance assessment by shifting the locus of organizational performance from efficiency to effectiveness considerations. Indeed, organizations forced to transact with one another to complete their activities are no longer the sole master of their destiny and are thus subject to external influence and demands when making strategic decisions. Effectiveness, defined as the organization ability to satisfy the demands of those in its environment from whom it requires support for its continued existence [5], is thus becoming a critical measure of organizational performance. Furthermore, the shift from efficiency to effectiveness considerations has exacerbated the recent questioning of IOS strategic value. Indeed, findings from IS studies suggest that incentive to adopt an IOS are only efficiency bounded (i.e., reduction of transaction cost, increase productivity) [15][16]. Thereby, using such resources would be of little value in an effectiveness prized context and further validates the recent questioning of their strategic value.

Despite these criticisms on the strategic value of IOS, we must emphasize that resource-centered studies in the IS field are for the most part efficiency oriented and do not assess the effectiveness impacts of IOS [17]. Such a state suggests that much is still to learn in this area and that discarding the strategic value of IOS based on an half complete picture would be mistaken. The present paper is in line with this consideration and aims to bring clarity on the strategic value of IOS by demonstrating that IOS can be used to achieve organizational effectiveness. To do so, we anchor our work on the resource dependency theory (RDT), which is the only resource-based theory (e.g., resource based view theory, relational view theory, knowledge based view theory) that explicitly takes into consideration the interdependencies between social actors and posits effectiveness as the main driver of organizational performance and competitive advantage. More precisely, the underlying premise of this paper is that an organization may shift the nature (i.e., structure) of its business relationship with a trading partner from an arm's length to an integrated stance [18][19][20][21] by using an IOS, which in turn will enable the organization to be effective (i.e., to satisfy the demands of its partner from whom it requires support for its continued existence).

The rest of the paper is organized as follows. First, in Section 2, we illustrate the key differences between efficiency and effectiveness measures of operational performance. Then, in Section 3, we rely on the tenets of RDT to identify how an organization may change the nature of its business relationship with a partner from an arm's length to integrated stance to achieve organizational effectiveness. Next, based on these theoretical underpinnings we present our research model and its related hypothesis in Section 4. This is followed, in Section 5, by a discussion of the research methodology that will be used to validate our research model. Lastly, Section 6 concludes the paper by presenting the anticipated theoretical and practical contributions of the study as well as its limits and future research avenues.

II. LITTERATURE REVIEW

A. *Organizational Performance: Efficiency vs. Effectiveness*

Efficiency and effectiveness are clear distinguishable domains of organizational performance [22]. Efficiency is an internal standard of organizational performance [5] that refers to an input-output ratio or comparison [22]. In turn, effectiveness is externally oriented [5] and refers to an absolute level of either input acquisition or outcome attainment [22]. Effectiveness measures of performance imply a valued evaluation, usually based on how well the organization is meeting the needs or satisfying the criteria of evaluators [5]. As such, in a context like today's competitive environment, where interdependencies between social actors play a critical role, effectiveness measures are more suitable to assess organizational performance than efficiency measures due to their external focus. In the particular case of this study, evaluators consist of the external partners upon which an organization depends.

B. *Resource Dependency Theory*

Resource dependency theory posits that organizations are defined at the activity level, making activities under the control of an organization its core and purpose [5]. To complete their activities, organizations are assumed to rely on resources present in their environment. Resources can include anything perceived as valuable by an organization; from materials to access to markets [23]. The reliance on these resources poses the problem of their procurement, which is exacerbated by the fact that no organization is believed to be self-contained or to have the total control over it's required operational components or resources [5]. Therefore, differences in firm resource endowments exist and persist over time and define the structure of an organization's environment. In turn, environmental characteristics or patterns of resource endowments create interdependencies between organizations for resource procurement and forces them to transact with one another [23].

Exchanges between partners caused by the environmental structure are not all balanced. In fact, in dyadic settings, asymmetry due to the unequal importance of the exchange for each organization may be present [23]. Asymmetry in a relationship is determined by the respective dependence level of each party upon the other [24]. According to [5], three factors must be weighted to assess an organization's level of dependence towards another. First, the importance of the resource exchanged for the organization (i.e., the extent to which the organization requires the resource for continued operations and survival). Second, the extent to which the organization from which the resource will be acquired has discretion over the resource allocation and usage. Third, the extent to which there are few alternatives or other organizations from which the resource can be obtained. Hence, an organization for which the resource exchanged is highly important, and that has limited discretion over the resource and few alternatives from which it can obtain the resource is considered to be dependent upon its exchange partner.

In turn, asymmetry or different levels of dependence in an exchange will confer to the less needy partner a certain power over its more dependent counterpart exposing the later to the influence and the demands of the former [24]. Hence, an organization's level of dependence upon a partner measures the potency of its partner. In other words, it measures how much the dependent organization must take into account its partner's demands, and also how likely the dependent organization will consider its partner's demands in its decision making process [5].

To deal with a partner's demands and ensure its survival (i.e., to be effective), an organization can take three types of actions [5]. As noted by [25, p. 88], "The first alternative is to comply with such influence. The second response is to evade these demands. The last alternative is to alter external demands by modifying its relationships with external actors". RDT focuses mainly on this last alternative. More precisely, RDT posits that an organization will aim to shift the nature (i.e., structure) of its relationship with a significant partner from an arm's length to an integrated stance. In doing so, an organization will increase its external partner's stakes in the relationship, which in turn will alleviate power asymmetries and secure access to critical resources. Two types of strategies can be used to achieve this aim [25]: (1) ownership alteration strategies such as vertical integration, horizontal integration and diversification that involve the acquisition of the needed external resource and, thus, eliminate interdependencies [5]; and (2) quasi-hierarchical strategies that do not involve a change in ownership, but rather the creation of quasi hierarchical relations (e.g., joint ventures, interlocking boards of directors, associations, cartels and the formation of social norms) to more formally govern interfirm relationships [23].

III. Conceptual Framework

Based on the theoretical background presented above, the premise of this paper is that IOS usage may be used by an organization to implement a quasi-hierarchical strategy in its attempt to increase its partner's stake in the relationship, alleviate power asymmetries and secure access to the critical resources it requires for its continued existence. This Section exposes the three hypotheses tied to our research model shown in Figure 1.

A. Hypothesis #1

According to the tenets of RDT, to be effective, a dependent organization should develop a close interorganizational relationship – a particular type of quasi-hierarchical strategy – with its business counterpart in order to balance the asymmetrically dependent relationship and make it more symmetrical and interdependent [5]. Finding stemming from the field of marketing, which has a well established tradition of examining organizational dependence in business relationships, support this assertion. Indeed, several authors have demonstrated that the dependence of one party upon another entices the former to integrate its activities with the later [26][27][28]. For example, to ensure that it continues to have access to the resources provided by its less needy partner, a dependent organization is more likely to have a long-term orientation and significantly invest in its relationship with its partner [26][27][29]. Such investments often take the form of bounding behaviours, which include adding value to goods exchanged and developing specialized procedures in ordering, shipping and servicing [30]. Conceptually one can think of such investments involving people, products and procedures as creating exit barriers in the business relationship [27], which would create switching costs for the less needy organization if it decided to change trading partner.

These bounding behaviors also include relationship-specific IOS usage. For example, a dependent supplier may use an IOS to facilitate timely and accurate information sharing, which should add value to the exchange relationship by reducing redundant workload for their customer [31]. It is important to note that these offsetting investments in dyadic relationships are themselves transaction-specific assets since their value would be greatly diminished if one of the partners was to switch and decide to exchange with a source different than the original partner. Thus, IOS usage may be seen as a particular type of quasi-hierarchical strategy that balances asymmetrically dependent relationship. Based on the arguments mentioned above the following hypothesis is formulated:

Hypothesis #1: The greater the organization's level of dependence upon the trading partner, the greater its level of IOS usage with that trading partner.

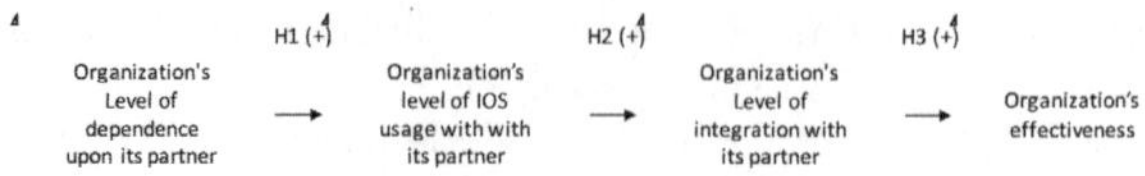

Figure 1. Research Model.

B. Hypothesis #2

Various mechanisms facilitating the integration between trading partners have been identified in the organization theory literature [32]. As noted by [33, p. 171), these mechanisms include "standardizing work (i.e., common and clearly specified procedures and tasks), standardizing output (i.e., clearly specified results or output of work), standardizing skills and knowledge (i.e., standardized training and expertise), standardizing norms (i.e., establishment of common values, beliefs, and expectations), direct supervision (i.e., someone not directly doing the work, but being responsible for coordinating the activities), planning (i.e., establishment of schedules governing activities of different units), and mutual adjustment (i.e., people or units adapting to each other during their work processes)". In turn, numerous studies in the IS field have demonstrated that IOS usage allow for the implementation and/or optimization of these mechanism facilitating integration between partners [34]. Indeed, IOS are recognized to enhance the formalization, the content and the amount of information exchanged between business partners [21]. More precisely, by requiring standard protocols for data communication, IOS usage introduces the need for the establishment of a formal agreement between the trading partners, which in turn fosters the standardization of work and certain outputs. Furthermore, by formalizing communication processes and procedures as well as by providing a superior capacity for data transmission, IOS usage also enhances the speed, the accuracy and completeness of interorganizational communication [35], which in turn optimizes several other mechanisms facilitating partner's integration. For example, by allowing the information to flow effectively across organizational boundaries [36][37], IOS usage enables a manufacturer to promptly react to unexpected events caused by their suppliers/customers as well as to advise them of changes in planning, which fosters rapid mutual adjustment between partners [38][39][40]. Improvements in interorganizational communication derived from IOS usage also increase speed of feedback and error correction between supply chain partners [40] thereby facilitating the supervision of activities across organizational boundaries. In addition, sharing information through IOS gives integrated partner's accurate and precise information on future material requirements [39], and thus improves their planning and scheduling [41][42]. Based on these previous arguments, the following hypothesis is formulated:

Hypothesis #2: The greater the organization's level of IOS usage with the trading partner, the greater its level of integration with that partner.

C. Hypothesis #3

The positive relationship between an organization's pursuit of a quasi-hierarchical strategy and its effectiveness has been demonstrated in several studies. For example, [43] demonstrated that, by integrating its activities with those of its trading partner, an organization can be more innovative and be more prone to develop new business opportunities. In addition, [44] also revealed that, by integrating its activities with those of its trading partner, an organization can be more effective. Based on these previous arguments, the following hypothesis is formulated:

Hypothesis #3: The greater the organization's level of integration with the trading partner, the greater its effectiveness.

IV. METHODOLOGY

As our research is still in progress, this Section explains the methodological framework we have devised, but not yet used, to test our research model. More precisely, we present our intended research setting, data collection procedures, survey instrument and data analyses procedures.

A. Research Settting

An important part of the research design was to identify an industry where: (1) new interorganizational forms established to harness the benefits of closer and stronger partnerships exist, (2) effectiveness is a valued measure of organizational performance, and (3) the level of IOS adoption is high. One example of such industry came to our attention: the aerospace industry. Indeed, recent studies have shown that organizations from this industry are increasingly developing integrated supply chains and strong business partnerships to fulfill market demands [45]. As such, effectiveness is highly valued in this industry [45]. Lastly, recent studies have also shown that the adoption level of IOS by firms in this industry is amongst the highest [46]. Accordingly, the unit of analysis of this study is the business relationship between a manufacturer pertaining to the aerospace industry and one of its customers.

B. Data Collection

Data will be collected by means of a field survey. Conceptually, a researcher can decide to study a business relationship through the perspective of the supplier, the customer or both parties [47]. In the present research, the perspective of the manufacturer (i.e., the supplier) will be adopted. We will follow the key informant approach and collect data from one sales professional at each supplier because specialists in this boundary role are most likely to be knowledgeable about study constructs [48]. These sales professional will be identified from a Canadian governmental database, which lists all the manufacturers pertaining to the Canadian aerospace industry. They will be asked to focus on a specific customer relationship for the sale of a specific component/resource when answering the survey. Lastly, to ensure the anonymity of our respondents all collected data will be anonymized.

C. Survey Instrument

The survey instrument will include measures specifically developed for the purpose of this study as well as measures drawn and/or adapted from the literature. Existing scales for the manufacturer's level of dependence upon its customer were deemed inappropriate as they do not account for the three dimensions identified by [5]. Also, measures of organizational effectiveness are non existent. Thus, we will develop appropriate scales for each of these constructs by following the three-stage approach proposed by [49].

Scales for the remaining constructs (those related to the manufacturer's level of IOS usage with its customer, and the manufacturer's level of integration with its customer) will adapted from the literature. More precisely, the manufacturer's level of IOS usage with its customer will comprise three dimensions, namely volume, diversity and depth and will be measured with scales adapted from [50]. The manufacturer's level of integration with its customer will include four dimensions, namely joint actions, assistances, monitoring and information exchange [51] and will be measured using scales adapted from [52] (joint actions), [53] (assistance), [54] (monitoring), and [55] (information exchange).

D. Data Analyses

Structural equation modeling (SEM) will be used to analyze this study's data. One important particularity of this approach is that it allows for the simultaneous evaluation of both the quality of the measurement and the construct interrelationships [34]. In addition, the use of SEM will allow us to test both the direct and indirect effects of dependent constructs on organizational effectiveness as well as to assess if the process of IT value creation is sequential as implied by our model.

A two-phase analytical procedure will be employed. In the first phase, a confirmatory factor model (i.e., the measurement model) will be used to measure the fit between the theorized model and observed variables, whereas in the second phase, results of the measurement model will be used to create a path-analytic model to investigate the relationships hypothesized in this study [56].

V. CONCLUSION

The objective of this project is to bring clarity on the strategic value of IOS by demonstrating that IOS can be used to achieve organizational effectiveness. To do so, a research model anchored on RDT is proposed. Results tied to the empirical testing of this model should prompt important theoretical and practical contributions as well as future research avenues despite certain limits.

A. Theoretical Contribution

First, by measuring organizational effectiveness rather than organizational efficiency, the present study will broaden our understanding IOS impacts and consequently our understanding of their strategic value. Second, this study will complement previous IS resource-centered research by providing insights on how to use a particular IS strategic resources, namely IOS. Traditionally, IS resource-centered research have been concerned with identifying strategic resources rather than explaining how they should be used. Such predisposition and lack of guidelines to turn valuable IS resources into competitive advantages may lie on the extensive reliance on the resource-based-view perspective, which doesn't cover this critical aspect. As such, the present study, anchored on RDT, significantly departs from previous research endeavors by being one of the few to both identify and define how a particular IS strategic resource, the IOS, can be used to alleviate dependence asymmetries in business relationships.

B. Practical Contributions

From a practical stance, anticipated findings should help organizations to better manage their portfolio of interorganizational relationships by identifying: (1) key organizational partners, (2) how to alleviate the influence of these partners through interorganizational integration and (3) the critical role of IOS in this integrating process. As such, managers will be able to effectively cope with partner demands, and hence ensure the survival of their organization.

C. Limits and Future Research Avenues

The theoretical and methodological contents presented above suggest a few limits and related future research avenues. First, our study sample is specific to manufacturers involved in a customer relationship for the sale of an important component/resource. To address this limit, future research should be undertaken in order to replicate our research efforts in different settings with different types of resources. For example, it could be interesting to replicate our research efforts within the context of manufacturer-supplier relationships where the manufacturer aims to acquire an IT resource in exchange of a monetary compensation. Second, the present study does not take into consideration the different types of IOS used to support the manufacture-customer relationship (e.g., dyadic, multilateral). Future research initiatives could thus be undertaken to extend the present work by investigating whether or not the use of different types of IOS may lead to different findings. For example, it would be interesting to see if the dependence between two business partners can influence the choice of a particular type of IOS. Third, our research considers only the perspective of the manufacturer. To address this limit, we recommend that future research on dyadic relationships should investigate the viewpoint of both partners in the business relationship. Such an endeavor would generate more accurate findings by, amongst other things, assessing interdependence between the partners, which better reflects the reality of business relationships than only capturing the level of dependence of a single partner towards the other.

REFERENCES

[1] J. H. Dyer and H. Singh, "The Relational View: Cooperative Strategy and Sources of Interorganizational Competitive Advantage," Academy of Management Review, vol. 23, no. 4, 1994, pp. 660-679.

[2] W. W. Powell, "Neither Market nor Hierarchy: Network form of Organization," Research in Organization Behavior, vol. 12, 1990, pp. 295-336.

[3] M. Sobrero and E. B. Roberts, "Strategic Management of Supplier-Manufacturers Relations in New Product Development," Research Policy, vol. 31, 2002, pp. 159-182.

[4] M. Bensaou, "Interorganizational Cooperation: The role of Information Technology an Empirical Comparison of U.S. and Japanese Supplier Relations," Information Systems Research, vol. 8, no. 2, 1997, pp. 107-124.

[5] J. Pfeffer and G. R. Salancik, The External Control of Organizations: A Resource Dependence Perspective, New York, NY: Harper & Row, 1978.

[6] L. A. Lefebvre and É. Lefebvre, "E-commerce and Virtual Enterprises: Issues and Challenges for Transition Economies," Technovation, vol. 22, no. 5, 2002, pp. 313-323.

[7] P.-M. Léger, L. Cassivi, P. Hadaya, and O. Caya, "Safeguarding Mechanisms in a Supply Chain Network," Industrial Management and Data Systems, vol. 106, no. 6, 2006, pp. 759-777.

[8] B. A. Weitz and S. D. Jap, "Relationship Marketing and Distribution Channels," Journal of Academy of Marketing Science, vol. 23, no. 4, 1995, pp. 305-320.

[9] V. Choudhury, "Strategic Choices in the Development of Interorganizational Information Systems," Information Systems Research, vol. 8, no. 1, 1997, pp. 1-24.

[10] P. Hadaya and L. Cassivi, "The Role of Joint Collaboration Planning Actions in a Demand-Driven Supply-Chain," Industrial Management & Data Systems, vol. 107, no. 7, 2007, pp. 954-978.

[11] N. G. Carr, "IT doesn't matter," Harvard Business Review, vol. 81, no. 5, 2003, pp. 41–49.

[12] E. K. Clemons and M. C. Row, "Sustaining IT Advantage: The Role of Structural Differences," MIS Quarterly, vol. 15, no. 3, 1991, pp. 275-292.

[13] F. J. Mata, W. L. Fuerst, and J. B. Barney, "Information Technology and Sustained Competitive Advantage: A Resource-Based Analysis," MIS Quarterly, vol. 19, no. 4, 1995, pp. 487–505.

[14] A. Paulraj, A. A. Lado, and I. J. Chen, "Inter-Organizational Communication as a Relational Competency: Antecedents and Performance Outcomes in Collaborative Buyer–Supplier Relationships," Journal of Operation Management, vol. 26, no. 1, 2008, pp. 45-64.

[15] S. Barrett and B. Konsynski, "Inter-Organization Information Sharing Systems," MIS Quarterly, vol. 6, 1982, pp. 93-105.

[16] T. W. Malone, J. Yates, and R. I Benjamin, "Electronic Markets and Electronic Hierarchies," Communications of the ACM, vol. 30, no. 6, 1987, pp. 484-497.

[17] W. Oh and A. Pinsonneault, "On the Assessment of the Strategic Value of Information Technologies: Conceptual and Analytical Approaches," MIS Quarterly, vol. 31, no. 2, 2007, pp 239–265.

[18] J. Y. Bakos and E. Brynjyoolfsson, E. "From Vendors to Partners: Information Technology and Incomplete Contracts in Buyer-Supplier Relationships," Journal of Organizational Computing, vol. 3, no. 3, 1993, pp. 301-329.

[19] V. Grover, J. Teng, and K. Fiedler, "Investigating the Role of Information Technology in Building Buyer-Supplier Relationships," Journal of the Association for Information Systems, vol. 3, no. 1, 2002, pp. 217–245.

[20] R. L. Stump and V. Sriram, "Employing Information Technology in Purchasing: Buyer-Supplier Relationships and

Size of the Supplier Base," Industrial Marketing Management, vol. 26, no. 2, 1997, pp. 127–136.

[21] L. R. Vijayasarathy and D. Robey, "The Effect of EDI on Market Channel Relationship in Retailing," Information & Management, vol. 33,no. 2, 1997, pp. 73-86.

[22] C. Ostroff and N. Schmitt, "Configurations of Organizational Effectiveness and Efficiency Source," Academy of Management Journal, vol. 36, no. 6, 1993, pp. 1345-1361.

[23] J. Tillquist, J. L. King, and C. Woo, "A Representational Scheme for Analyzing Information Technology and Organizational Dependency," MIS Quarterly, vol. 26, no. 2, 2002, pp. 91-118.

[24] T. Casciaro and M. J. Piskorski, "Power Imbalance, Mutual Dependence, and Constraint Absorption: A Closer Look at Resource Dependence Theory," Administrative Science Quarterly, vol. 50, no. 2, 2005, pp. 167-199.

[25] C. L. Iacovou, "Interorganizational Systems as an Uncertainty Reduction Strategy: A Resource Dependence Perspective," The fifteen conferecne of the Administrative Science Association of Canada (ASAC), 1994, pp. 45-51.

[26] R. F. Lusch and S. W. Brown,"Interdependency, Contracting, and Relational Behavior in Marketing Channel," Journal of Marketing, vol. 69, no. 4, 1996, pp. 19-38.

[27] S. Ganesan, "Determinants of Long-Term Orientation in Buyer-Seller Relationships," Journal of Marketing, vol. 58, no. 2, 1994, pp. 1-19.

[28] J. B. Heide and G. John, "The Role of Dependence Balancing in Safeguarding Transaction-Specific Assets in Conventional Channels," Journal of Marketing, vol. 52, no. 1, 1988, pp. 20-35.

[29] L. Buchanan, "Vertical Trade Relationship: The Role of Dependence and Symmetry in Ataining Organizational Goals," Journal of Marketing Research, vol. 29, no. 1, 1992, pp. 65-75.

[30] R. M. Emerson, "Power-Dependence Relations," American Sociological Review, vol. 27, no. 1, 1962, pp. 31-41.

[31] C. C. Hsu, V. R. Kannan, K. C. Tan, and G. K. Leong, "Information Sharing, Buyer-Supplier Relationships, and Firm Performance," International Journal of Physical Distribution & Logistics Management, vol. 38, no. 4, 2008, pp. 296–310.

[32] S. Glouberman and H. Mintzberg, "Managing the Care of Health and the Cure of disease—Part II: Integration," Health Care Management Review, vol. 26, no. 1, 2001, pp. 70–84.

[33] H. Barki and A. Pinsonneault, "Toward a Construct of Organizational Integration," Organization Science, vol. 16, no. 2, 2005, pp. 165-179.

[34] M. Subramani, "How Do Supplier Benefit From Information Technology Use in Supply Chain Relationships?," MIS Quarterly, vol. 28, no. 1, 2004, pp. 45-73.

[35] L. W. Stern and P. J. Kaufmann, "Electronic Data Interchange in Selected Consumer Goods Industries: An Inter-Organizational Perspective," In R.D. Buzzel (Ed.), Marketing in an Electronic Age, Boston, MA: Harvard Business School Press, 1985.

[36] J. I. Cash and B. R. Konsynski, "IS Redraws Competitive Boundaries," Harvard Business Review, vol. 63, no. 2, 1985, pp. 134-142.

[37] S. Kekre and T. Mukhopadhyay, "Impacts of Electronic Data Interchange on Quality Improvement and Inventory Reduction Programs: A Field Study," International Journal of Production Economics, vol. 28, no. 3, 1992, pp. 265–282.

[38] R. O'Callaghan, R. Kaufmann, P. J. Konsynski, and R. Benn, "Adoption Correlates and Share Effects of Electronic Data Interchange Systems," Journal of Marketing, vol. 56, no. 2, 1992, pp. 45-55.

[39] K. Srinivasan, S. Kekre and, T. Mukhopadhyay, "Impact of Electronic Data Interchange Technology on JIT Shipments," Management Science, vol. 40, no. 10, 1994, pp. 1291–1304.

[40] E. T. G. Wang, J. C. F. Tai, and H. L. Wei, "A Virtual Integration Theory of Improved Supply-Chain Performance," Journal of Management Information Systems, vol. 23, no. 2, 2006, pp. 41-64.

[41] C. A. Hill, C. P. Zhang, and G. D. Scudder, "An Empirical Investigation of EDI Usage and Performance Improvement in Food Supply Chains," IEEE Transactions on Engineering Management, vol. 56, no. 1, 2009, pp. 1-15.

[42] Z. Shi, "Exploring the Roles of Transaction Costs Reduction and Explicit Coordination in Mediating the Impacts of IOS Use on Buyer Benefits," Journal of Information Technology Management, vol. 18, no. 2, 2007, pp. 1-17.

[43] N. R. Sanders, "IT Alignment in Supply Chain Relationships: A Study of Supplier Benefits," Journal of Supply Chain Management, vol. 41, no. 2, 2005, pp. 4-13.

[44] A. Gunasekaran, C. Patel, and E. Tirtiroglu, "Performance Measures and Metrics in a Supply Chain Environment," International Journal of Operations & Production Management, vol. 21, no. 1, 2001, pp. 71-87.

[45] R. R. Bales, R. S. Maul, and Z. Radnor, "The Development of Supply Chain Management within the Aerospace Manufacturing Sector", Supply Chain Management: An International Journal, vol. 9, no. 3, 2004, pp. 250-255.

[46] Forrester Research, "Canadian Online B2B Trade Poised to Reach C$272 Billion in 2005", Press releases, 2001.

[47] J. C. Anderson and J. A. Narus, "A Model of Distributor Firm and Manufacturer Firm Working Partnerships," Journal of Marketing, vol. 54, no. 1, 1990, pp. 42-58.

[48] L. W. Phillips and R. P. Bagozzi, "On Measuring the Organizational Properties of Distribution Channels: Methodological Issues in the Use of Key Informants," Research in Marketing, vol. 8, 1986, pp. 313–369.

[49] G. C. Moore and I. Benbasat, "Development of an Instrument to Measure the Perception of Adopting an Information Technology Innovation," Information Systems Research, vol. 2, no. 3, 1991, pp. 192-222.

[50] B. Massetti and W. R. Zmud, "Measuring the Extent of EDI Usage in Complex Organizations: Strategies and Illustrative Examples," MIS Quarterly, vol. 30, no. 3, 1996, pp. 331-345.

[51] R. A. Robicheaux and J. E. Coleman, "The Structure of Marketing Channel Relationships," Journal of the Academy of Marketing Science, vol. 22, no. 1, 1994, pp. 38-51.

[52] R. Gulati and M. Stych, "Dependence Asymmetry and Joint Dependence in Interorganizational Relationships: Effects of Embeddedness on a Manufacturer's Performance in Procurement Relationships," Administrative Science Quarterly, vol. 52, no. 1, 2007, pp. 32-69.

[53] T. G. Noordewier, G. John, and J. R. Nevin, "Performance Outcomes of Purchasing Arrangements in Industrial Buyer-Vendor Relationships," Journal of Marketing, vol. 54, no. 4, 1990, pp. 80-93.

[54] R. L. Stump and J. B. Heide, "Controlling Supplier Opportunism in Industrial Relationships," Journal of Marketing Research, vol. 33, no. 4, 1996, pp. 431-441.

[55] J. B. Heide and A. S. Miner, "The Shadow of the Future: Effects of Anticipated Interaction and Frequency of Contact on Buyer-Seller Cooperation," Academy of Management Journal, vol. 35, no. 2, 1992, pp. 265-291.

[56] G. S. Kearns and A. L. Lederer, "A Resource-Based View of Strategic IT Alignment: How Knowledge Sharing Creates Competitive Advantage," Decision Sciences, vol. 34, no. 1 , 2003, 2003, pp. 1-29.

Creating a Minimal Information Vocabulary for a Reproducible Method Description A Case in Column Chromatography

Dena Tahvildari
Computer Science Department
VU Amsterdam
The Netherlands
Email: d.tahvildari@vu.nl

Anne Vissers
Laboratory of Food Chemistry
Wageningen University
The Netherlands
Email: anne.vissers@wur.nl

Guus Schreiber
Computer Science Department
VU Amsterdam
The Netherlands
Email : guus.schreiber@vu.nl

Jan Top
Food & Biobased Research
Wageningen UR
and VU Amsterdam
The Netherlands
Email : jan.top@wur.nl

***Abstract*—Descriptions of experimental methods in scientific publications are often incomplete or inadequate. In these cases, the experimental work cannot be reproduced or verified due to lack of information. To facilitate the documentation of lab methods, in some domains minimum information guidelines have been developed. If implemented, these guidelines ensure that the information about the method can be easily verified, analysed and clearly interpreted by a wider scientific community. However, there is an evident lack of automated documentation tools to create and edit laboratory reports that follow these guidelines and at the same time do not impose a too rigid framework on the scientist. This paper describes the very first step towards the development of semantically rich but free-text editor for creating descriptions of experimental methods. We created and evaluated the vocabulary for reporting a column chromatography experiment, which is developed using the MIAPE guidelines. Our goal is to check if we can use the MIAPE guidelines in the food chemistry domain.The ultimate use of the vocabulary is in semantically enriched editorial software. An editor should give knowledge-based guidance to the author and semi-automatically add meta-data. The first step in designing such editor is to construct supporting vocabularies and evaluate their use in the domain of interest. Our initial application domain is laboratory of food chemistry.**

Keywords–MIAPE; vocabulary; material and method sections; HPLC; reproducibility; laboratory experiments.

I. Introduction and Objective

Transparency and reproducibility are recognized as essential features of science [1][2]. The quality of methodology descriptions are important factors for transparency and reproducibility. Therefore, providing adequate research documentation is an important task of a scientist.

In this paper, we discuss the very first step towards creating a semantic support for writing a reproducible method description, which intends to allow researchers to perform this task effectively and efficiently. The notion of research reproducibility has different interpretations, varying between different research fields. Research reproducibility commonly implies that, as an ultimate product of scientific investigation, research papers must be accompanied by a detailed description of the computational or experimental environment that are used to produce the result. According to Clarebout's principle [3] "An article [...] in a as a means for scholarly communication is not the scholarship itself; it is merely advertising of the scholarship. The actual scholarship is the complete software development environment and the complete set of instructions that generates the results". This idea promotes that research data, algorithms, codes and protocols are not simply ancillary information, but first class scholarly products as important as the paper itself. We define the term reproducibility as "the ability to investigate a phenomenon using the similar conditions as in the original experiment". We emphasize that the conditions do not need to be identical, but only similar, since slight variations are essential for scientific understanding of a phenomenon.

We focus on reproducibility in the context of laboratory research. There can be two reasons for an experiment not to reproduce the same phenomenon:

1) the hypothesized mechanism does not manifest itself, even having all conditions right (falsification)
2) the conditions under which the hypothesized effect can manifest itself have not been adequately fulfilled

The second condition can result from a poor description of the experimental conditions. This is why the scientific method requires explicit records of "all" experimental conditions. Having a report of the precise experimental process, and data is necessary to explain why some result has been found, why results could be different or be same as the results found in a different condition. For repeating a mechanism, it is important to know which assumptions and conditions must hold for the mechanism to manifest itself. In addition to serving scientific integrity, another reason for having details of an experiment is to make the transition to applications. For example, a Standard Operating Procedure (SOP), is intended as a step-by-step instruction to achieve a predictable, standardized, desired result, often within the context of a longer overall process.

Although a full account of the experimental conditions would be ideal, this cannot be achieved in practice. It is not possible to describe literally all details that possibly might be of influence; what's worse, scientists are usually not inclined to allocate time and effort to the "administrative" task of creating extensive documentation. Transparency in documentation is costly for scientists – in terms of time and effort. Taking into account that only the "essential" conditions need to be registered, the question is how researchers can be supported to realize which are these essential conditions that are sufficient to perform a "similar" experiment. When asked for, most scientists embrace transparency and reproducibility as disciplinary norms and values of science [4]. Therefore, one might expect that providing full documentation of methods and data is routine in daily practice. Yet, a growing body of evidence suggests that this is not the case [5][6]. It is becoming increasingly clear that the current publication model falls short in promoting transparency and reproducibility. A recent Nature report from researchers at the Amgen corporation showed that only 11% of the academic research in the literature are reproducible. Individual motivation and personal efficiency gain are other variables in promoting reproducibility and transparency of scientific methods [7][8].

In the present publication model, the conditions under which an experiment is performed are described in the "material and method" section of a scientific article. This section should provide information about the materials, procedures and critical steps that are used in the course of an experiment, such that the procedure can potentially be reproduced as faithfully as possible [9].

Minimum information guidelines (MIAPE) have been developed in various research domains to facilitate documentation [10]. Although they provide valuable guidance for reporting the necessary information about the method, they are rather high level, and do not give the detailed and context-specific support that is needed at the time of writing a method description. We think that a semi-automated use of minimum information guidelines in editorial applications could improve the quality of laboratory reports and method sections of publications, while limiting the time and effort needed to produce these.

Our approach to solve the quality problem of laboratory method reports and (potentially) lab protocols – in terms of transparency and reproducibility – relies on the use of the Semantic Web technologies and formal methods. We believe that in order to provide support for scientific authors, the first step would be to create a formal model of the underlying domain knowledge. A structured vocabulary or ontology can help to provide context-dependent suggestions to authors. We emphasize that we do not address the quality of the argumentation followed, nor the soundness of the research method.

In this study, we start off by exploring the minimum information guidelines for reporting a column chromatography technique in the food chemistry domain. Our hypothesis is that terms occurring in the guidelines should be present in the method sections of published papers. In the second section of this paper, we present relevant literature regarding the problem, and current approaches. In the third section of the paper, we briefly familiarise our readers with high performance liquid chromatography techniques as the first case study. Our approach to create the first draft of the vocabulary is presented in section 4. Section 5 is dedicated to results of the term frequency measurements. Finally, we discuss the results and provide some hypotheses for further testing in section 6.

II. Related work

Several initiatives have identified the problem of inadequate reporting and have proposed solutions. The National Centre for the Replacement, Refinement and Reduction of Animals in Research (NC3R) assessed methodological reports in the literature for in-vivo research. They evaluated 271 publications and showed that only 60% of the articles included information about the number and characteristics of the animals (strain, sex, age, weight) and approximately 30% of the articles lacked detailed descriptions of the statistical analyses used. Built upon this study, the ARRIVE [11] [12] guidelines were developed for reporting in-vivo experiments, pertaining to animal research.

To promote scientific reproducibility, the FORCE11 community has published a set of recommendations for minimal data standards for biomedical research and published a manifesto to improve research communication. The BioSharing initiative contains a large registry of community standards for structuring and curating data sets. It has made significant strides towards the standardization of data via its multiple partnerships with journals and other organizations [13].

The most relevant work to our research is an initiative in the Proteomic community. The problem of accurate methodological reporting is addressed by developing the minimum information documentation guidelines (MIAPE guidelines) as a standard, along with the development of MIAPE-supported software tools. For example, the ProteRed MIAPE Web toolkit was developed to fulfill the lack of bio-informatics tools to create and edit standard file formats and reports. It allows these to be embedded in proteomics research work flows. This system is able to verify if the report fulfills the minimum information requirements of the corresponding MIAPE modules while highlighting missing information and inconsistencies in a report. In other words, this system works as a MIAPE compliance checker and has been designed to support the validation of experimental meta-data [14].

Our approach is similar to the ProteRed compliance checker in terms of using semantics. However, we intend to develop MIAPE-CC vocabularies and use it in editorial applications that are frequently used by scientists, such as Microsoft Word. We believe that in order to enable researchers to provide a reproducible method description with low cost, we need to develop a knowledge base of reporting requirements and apply them in the most frequently used scholarly communication tools [15].

III. Case description

This section describes high-performance liquid chromatography (HPLC). We have selected this technique as a use case to build a vocabulary and select reference articles. HPLC is a chromatographic method that is used to separate a mixture of compounds in analytical chemistry and biochemistry so as to identify, quantify or purify the individual components of the mixture. HPLC can be used in the following applications, on small scale (analytical) and large scale (preparative):

1) Mixture characterization (analytical)
2) Water purification (preparative)
3) Pre-concentration of trace components (preparative)

Examples of HPLC chromatography types are:

1) Ion-exchange chromatography of proteins
2) Ligand-exchange chromatography
3) Reversed phase chromatography
4) Size exclusion chromatography

The sample mixture to be separated and tested is sent into a stream in the mobile phase percolating through the column. There are different types of columns available with sorbents of varying particle sizes and materials. For most types of chromatography, the mixture has interaction with the sorbent, also known as the stationary phase. The separation depends on the balance between compound affinities for the sorbent (As) and for the mobile phase (Amp). To separate compounds, a constant flow of mobile phase over the column is applied, which changes in composition gradually. When "As" is less than "Amp", the compound detaches from the sorbent and travels in the mobile phase stream towards the detector. The time that the compound needs to emerge at the detector is referred to as the retention time. For each component in the mixture, this depends on its chemical nature, the characteristics of the column and the composition of the mobile phase. Changes in these conditions yield different retention times. The retention time is measured under specific conditions and together with data from specific detectors used, is considered as the identifying characteristic of a given analyte.

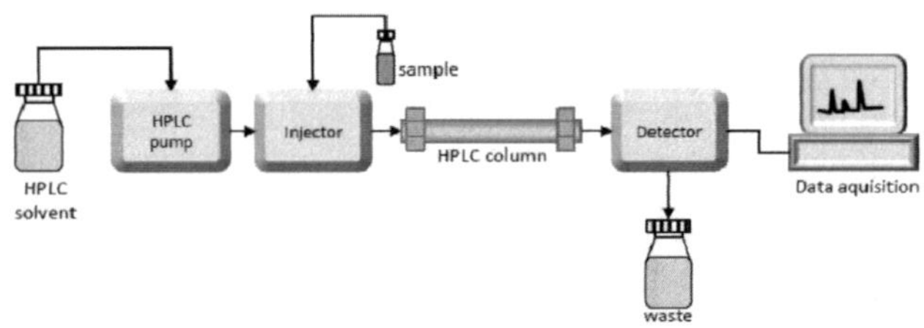

Figure 1. Components of a chromatographic process

The preparation of the mobile phase affects the quality of separation. The mobile phase might contain acids like formic, phosphoric or trifluoroacetic acid or salts to force components into their non-charged states and increase column retention. A pump is used to generate a specified flow of the mobile phase. Although manual injection of samples is still possible, most HPLC systems are now fully automated and controlled by computer software (e.g., XCalibur). The injector, or auto sampler, introduces the solvent into a phase stream that carries the sample into the column, which is under high pressure and contains specific packing material needed to affect separation. The packing material is referred to as the stationary phase because it is held in place by the column hardware. A detector is used in these experiments to see the separated compound bands width as they elute from the column. The information is sent from the detector to a computer software which generates the chromatogram. The mobile phase exits the detector and is either discarded as waste in analytical chromatography, or collected in case of preparative chromatography. Figure 1 schematically presents a the fundamental components of a chromatographic process.

In an HPLC experiment, data about cleaning the column, system calibration, retention time, sample components, and graphs that are generated by the HPLC system and the detector are analysed and documented in XCalibur. This software enables scientists to gather, analyse, visualize the information about the chromatogram. Although XCalibur has features for creating metadata about the experiment, we have observed that it's added value for documenting the experiments, has not been fully realized by the scientists. The reason is not known to us; however, we are interested to understand the functionality and usability of this software for the future use.

IV. METHOD

This section describes how we extracted terms from the guidelines and how the resulting vocabulary was evaluated in the food chemistry domain. We should indicate that the "quality" of the vocabulary is determined by the degree to which it assists scientists in the considered domain to create reproducible method descriptions in an efficient manner. However, the first measure for the quality is the extent to which the terms contained in the vocabulary occur and convey the intended meaning in published method descriptions. We explicitly do not use the "method sections" as sources for the creation of vocabulary, but only for the evaluation of our vocabulary in the domain of Food Chemistry. This is to guarantee the independence of our method from the specific set of method sections we selected. The MIAPE-CC is our starting point for creating a vocabulary in the considered domain [16]. Table I presents the seven categories, each representing an essential part of an experimental setup. It covers a column chromatography experiment from the selection and configuration of a column, through the selection of a suitable mobile phase and verification of the relevant performance characteristics, to the collection of fractions and associated detector readings. We manually extracted the main concepts from the guideline. In total, 83 terms were extracted. Table II provides an example of the main categories and the associated terms. In the next step we measured the occurrence of the extracted terms in the material and method sections. The library of Wageningen University (The Netherlands) kindly provided us a list of articles from laboratory of food chemistry that cover five predefined criteria.

TABLE I. The MIAPE-CC CLASSIFICATION

MIAPE-CC CLASSIFICATION	
Class	Description
global descriptors	All the general information about the experiment, such as the date on which the work described was initiated and etc
sample	Description of the source, such as means of collection, volume, concentration or previous step of processing.
equipment	Description about the type of column and the chromatography system that are being used.
mobile phase	The mobile phase is the phase that moves in a definite direction. It may be a liquid, or a gas (GC), or a super critical fluid.
column run process	The total time of the column run with appropriate units.
pre and post run process	a description of the purpose of the process, such as equilibration, calibration or washing (this may be part of the column run, as one step or as preconditioning of the column prior to use).
column output	a description about the output that is selected for detection and/or fraction.

TABLE II. EXAMPLE TERMS EXTRACTED FROM MIAPE-CC

general description	equipment	sample	mobile phase
date stamp	column	name	name
responsible person	type	volume	constituent
contact	manufacturer	concentration	concentration
affiliation	dimension	molecular mass	pH

- the journal that cover topics related to food chemistry,

- the journal that do not have MIAPE-CC module as reporting guidelines requirement,
- articles submitted by researchers from Wageningen University,
- articles that are published in the time range from 2000 to 2014,
- articles that use column chromatography as a purification technique.

We deliberately excluded journals that explicitly require the compliance to the MIAPE-CC, since they might give a too positive impression of the use of terms from the guideline. We selected authors from Wageningen University as participants of the test group in our study. From 28 journals in total, specialized in food chemistry, 62 articles were retrieved. From these articles, we extracted the "Material and Method" sections – sometimes entitled "Experimental Method". Since the articles were retrieved in PDF format, we used Apache PDFBox [17] to parse and extract the method segments and stored them in plain text format. We created a CSV file including the title and the articles' DOIs. The collected method descriptions were marked as relevant by an expert from food chemistry domain. This set of method sections forms our corpus to evaluate the use of MIAPE-CC vocabulary. By counting how frequent each term occurs in the corpus, we can see how well the terminology required by MIAPE-CC is used by scientists. We used two packages from the RStudio toolbox for this experiment. The "tm" package was used to create the corpus and to pre-process the textual corpus. To have a more accurate mapping we transformed all tokens to the lower case. To prevent getting wrong mappings to commonly used words, we removed all stop words from our corpus [18]. The "qdap" package designed for quantitative discourse analysis was used to create a function – "termco" – to conduct the string mapping from our terms to the tokens [19]. The data and code are accessible through the Github (https://github.com/denatahvildari/MIAPE.git). The folder contains files related to the MIAPE-CC guideline, the developed vocabulary, the selected publications, and the R code used for the term occurrence experiment.

V. Result

The word occurrence measurement showed that from 83 terms in the vocabulary, 40 terms never occurred in any of the method description sections (48%). The 43 remaining terms occurred at least in one method section (51%). Table III provides the detailed results of the term occurrence experiment. The concept equipment contains 24 terms and it represents information about the product details for column, physical characteristics of column, and the chromatography system used for separation. From this class, 91% of the terms are not identifiable. Another interesting result is related to the concept 'column output'. Outputs of a run process are 'fraction' and 'detection'. Consider 'fraction' as an example. Descriptions about the start time and end time of fractionating process, and the size of fraction are essential information in this category. We observed that 55% of terms representing this concepts are not detected by our method. In the next section we discuss our observations and possible explanations for this result.

TABLE III. TERM OCCURRENCE PER CATEGORY

Class	Never occurred terms	Occurred terms
General descriptor	4	1
Sample	9	8
Equipment	22	2
Mobile Phase	0	2
Column Run	0	5
Pre and Post Run processes	2	6
Column output	13	9

VI. Discussion

To gain some insight about this result, we consulted a domain expert and qualitatively analysed the data by inspecting the selected method sections. Our goal was not to find additional terms, but to identify generic patterns that explain the above results. We provide some explanations for these results. Only one term related to the MIAPE-CC category "general descriptors" occurred. The reason is that information about the name, contact, the date that the experiment was conducted, and the institutional role of the experimenter are not usually included in the "material and method" sections of publications. Information about the date is mostly documented in the scientists' laboratory notebooks. In the present model for publishing an article, this information can be found in the header along with the title of the paper. Authors do not see the necessity to report it in the method sections. This is common practice. The present underlying assumption is that this type of information is not assumed to be part of the experimental conditions needed for reproducibility.

General information about samples and equipment such as name, manufacturer, model, and type is not detected by our method. The reason is that authors do not use the top level class terminology such as "manufacturer" to report the provenance of their experimental materials or equipment. They simply mention the name of the manufacturer. For example, consider the following sentence:

"Branched sugar arabinon was obtained from British Sugar – Mcleary."

With our method, we searched for the term "manufacturer" and did not notice the fact that the British Sugar is an instance of the class 'manufacturer'.

Information about the mobile and stationary phases is crucial for describing a column chromatography experiment. However, the occurrence of these terms was not frequent in the selected 62 publications. As it is observed, the authors use synonyms when referring to the mobile phase, such as "solution", "eluent" and "solvent". For the same reason as described in the second observation, authors only mention the name of the mobile phase; for example, "solution (A): Water and solution (B): (ACN) Acetonitrile, Methyl cyanide". The term stationary phase was not frequently used. The stationary phase is the substance fixed in place for the chromatography procedure. In HPLC chromatography, the stationary phase is the same as the column and packing materials.

Terms representing the physical characteristics of the column were mentioned using abbreviations. For example, the inner diameter of the column is presented as "ID".

Information about the run processes are mostly mentioned along with information related to the column. In the MIAPE-CC model these concepts are categorised in separated classes.

The MIAPE-CC model indicates that for describing the column output, authors should mention the description about the detector that is used and how the fractionating procedure was done, if the experiment has gone through iterations. We could identify the detection equipment and some of the related terms such as the "wavelength". However, the term "trace" never occurred. The reason is that a 'trace' is being used for a specific type of a detector which is called "PDA". In our selected publications this type of detector was never used.

VII. Conclusion and Future Work

In this paper, we argue that the reproducibility of an experimental method description is indebted to the existence of minimum information about that experiment. The minimum information guidelines specify all the details of an experiment such as materials, instruments, units of measure, characteristics of the column run processes and the possible deviations from the protocol. However, they are not highly adopted by researchers. This is partly because of the natural language nature of these guidelines, which does not allow for any computational support. This means that for reporting an HPLC experiment, a researcher still needs to follow extensive instructions and check too many lines to know which information is essential for describing a column run process. We believe that the existence of formal representations of these guidelines could improve their usage. We envision that if the vocabulary is applied in a software tool that scientists use on a daily basis, the transparency of the laboratory reports and consequently the reproducibility of the method can improve.

We investigated the MIAPE-CC guideline for reporting a column chromatography experiment and identified the main concepts and the associated terms. We evaluated its use in our domain of interest, which is food chemistry. Through an experiment we measured the occurrence of 83 terms from 7 categories in 62 method sections of published papers. The results indicate that half of the terms occurred at least in one of the descriptions. We mention that these results are not self-descriptive – meaning that the occurrence of terms does not guarantee the correct use of them, and also the absence of terms does not necessarily manifest the quality of the report. We realized this through a qualitative analysis and by consulting the domain experts. We learned that the our present method does not recognize the synonyms, abbreviations, instances and the existing relations. This is caused by the limitations in the model. Our analysis give a clear indication how to extend the vocabulary. With respect to its ultimate use, the present vocabulary is also limited in the sense that it does not present any semantic relations. These relations are needed when providing suggestions on missing information to authors when creating method sections or laboratory reports. We conclude that MIAPE is a good starting point for creating the required vocabulary, but it needs to be further elaborated. We should also mention that the sample size of the method description sections seems small (N=62), as some of the reviewers kindly pointed out, therefore results might not be conclusive. We take this remark into consideration for the next measurements. Nevertheless we see that even this small sample provided useful insight. The next step is to extend the vocabulary. For this, we use the Rapid Ontology Creation (ROC+) method. This tool is designed to be used by the domain experts, who do not have expertise in knowledge engineering. The method consists of two sessions, in which domain experts come together and jointly discuss, document and agree upon relevant terms and relations in their domain [20]. Moreover, we are looking into additional statistical methods to evaluate the mapping between the vocabulary and the method sections.

Acknowledgment

The authors would like to acknowledge the help of Prof. dr. Harry Gruppen and his team at Wageningen University.

References

[1] M. McNutt, "Reproducibility," Science, vol. 343, no. 6168, 2014, pp. 229–229.

[2] E. Miguel, C. Camerer, K. Casey, J. Cohen, K. M. Esterling, A. Gerber et al., "Promoting transparency in social science research," Science (New York, NY), vol. 343, no. 6166, 2014, p. 30.

[3] J. B. Buckheit and D. L. Donoho, Wavelab and reproducible research. Springer, 1995.

[4] M. S. Anderson, B. C. Martinson, and R. De Vries, "Normative dissonance in science: Results from a national survey of us scientists," Journal of Empirical Research on Human Research Ethics, vol. 2, no. 4, 2007, pp. 3–14.

[5] J. P. Ioannidis, M. R. Munafo, P. Fusar-Poli, B. A. Nosek, and S. P. David, "Publication and other reporting biases in cognitive sciences: detection, prevalence, and prevention," Trends in cognitive sciences, vol. 18, no. 5, 2014, pp. 235–241.

[6] L. K. John, G. Loewenstein, and D. Prelec, "Measuring the prevalence of questionable research practices with incentives for truth telling," Psychological science, 2012, p. 0956797611430953.

[7] A. Cabrera, W. C. Collins, and J. F. Salgado, "Determinants of individual engagement in knowledge sharing," The International Journal of Human Resource Management, vol. 17, no. 2, 2006, pp. 245–264.

[8] C. Drummond, "Replicability is not reproducibility: nor is it good science," 2009.

[9] A. De Waard, "The future of the journal? integrating research data with scientific discourse," 2010.

[10] "The Minimum Information About a Proteomics Experiment (MIAPE)," 2010, URL: http://www.psidev.info/node/91 [accessed: 2016-04-13].

[11] "ARRIVE guidelines," 2010, URL: https://www.nc3rs.org.uk/arrive-guidelines [accessed: 2016-04-13].

[12] C. Kilkenny, W. J. Browne, I. C. Cuthill, M. Emerson, and D. G. Altman, "Improving bioscience research reporting: the arrive guidelines for reporting animal research," Animals, vol. 4, no. 1, 2014, pp. 35–44.

[13] N. A. Vasilevsky, M. H. Brush, H. Paddock, L. Ponting, S. J. Tripathy, G. M. LaRocca et al., "On the reproducibility of science: unique identification of research resources in the biomedical literature," PeerJ, vol. 1, 2013, p. e148.

[14] J. A. Medina-Aunon, S. Martínez-Bartolomé, M. A. López-García, E. Salazar, R. Navajas, A. R. Jones et al., "The proteored miape web toolkit: a user-friendly framework to connect and share proteomics standards," Molecular & Cellular Proteomics, vol. 10, no. 10, 2011, pp. M111–008 334.

[15] P. E. Bourne, T. W. Clark, R. Dale, A. de Waard, I. Herman, E. H. Hovy, and D. Shotton, "Improving The Future of Research Communications and e-Scholarship (Dagstuhl Perspectives Workshop 11331)," Dagstuhl Manifestos, vol. 1, no. 1, 2012, pp. 41–60. [Online]. Available: http://drops.dagstuhl.de/opus/volltexte/2012/3445 - Retrieved on 16.03.2016

[16] C. F. Taylor, N. W. Paton, K. S. Lilley, P.-A. Binz, R. K. Julian, A. R. Jones, W. Zhu, R. Apweiler, R. Aebersold, E. W. Deutsch et al., "The minimum information about a proteomics experiment (miape)," Nature biotechnology, vol. 25, no. 8, 2007, pp. 887–893.

[17] "Apache PDF Box," 2010, URL: https://pdfbox.apache.org/ [accessed: 2016-04-13].

[18] I. Feinerer, "Introduction to the tm package text mining in r," 2015.

[19] "Search For and Count Terms," 2010, URL: http://finzi.psych.upenn.edu/library/qdap/html/termco.html [accessed: 2016-04-13].

[20] D. J. Willems, N. J. Koenderink, and J. L. Top, "From science to practice: Bringing innovations to agronomy and forestry," Journal of Agricultural Informatics, vol. 6, no. 4, 2015, pp. 85–95.

Implementing Integrated Software Solutions in Iranian SMEs

Maryam Rezaeian and Martin Wynn
School of Computing and Technology
University of Gloucestershire
Cheltenham, UK
Email: MaryamRezaeian@connect.glos.ac.uk
Email: MWynn@glos.ac.uk

Abstract – **There has been little research on information systems in Iranian companies, and this paper helps to address this by examining the implementation and functioning of integrated software solutions in two small to medium sized enterprises in Iran. This is of particular interest now that the sanctions on trade with Iran have been removed, which will inevitably lead to increased sales opportunities for western technology companies in the country. This study uses a process mapping and systems profiling approach to establish the current status of software implementation in these manufacturing companies. It investigates the underlying information systems strategy and examines how this has been implemented in the core process areas of these companies. The outcome of these major systems projects is assessed, and comparisons are drawn between these Iranian based "Total Systems" software products and similar products more widely available in the developed world.**

Keywords – Enterprise Resource Planning; Total Systems; Iranian SMEs; information systems; ERP; process change; IS strategy.

I. Introduction

The first Enterprise Resource Planning (ERP) software packages came to the market in the 1980s, and have been widely implemented in the developed world, particularly by large corporations. Since the turn of the century, there has been an increase in the use of these integrated software systems by small to medium sized enterprises (SMEs) in the developed world [1]. This has been paralleled – part cause, part effect – by an increase in the number of ERP vendors specifically geared to the requirements and budgets of SMEs. In the developing world, the uptake of these new systems has been slower, for a number of reasons, including the lack of the human and financial resources needed for such projects, and the non-availability of sales and support offices for many of the main ERP vendors in developing world countries. Nevertheless, the use of ERP packages in developing world countries has accelerated in recent years, but the current literature suggests that there have been both significant failures [2] as well as successes [3].

One interesting development in Iran has been the emergence of integrated software solutions developed in the country, by and large for the home business market (Table 1). These are sometimes called "Total Systems," being produced and sold by Iranian software companies. The term "ERP" is also used, but these products are usually more customizable than western based ERP products to specific user requirements, and are also available in both the Parsi language, as well as English. The sanctions on trade with the West have further encouraged Iranian companies to look inside their country for integrated software solutions. This article examines the implementation of two such packages in Iranian SMEs and discusses the underlying information systems (IS) strategy.

TABLE I. HOME GROWN TOTAL SYSTEMS PACKAGES IN IRAN (INDICATING VENDOR WEB ADDRESSES)

BEHKO	http://www.behko.com/?page_id=96
GREEN/ GALAX	http://www.greendataware.com/about/history/
PARS ROYAL	http://parsroyal.net/products
MEDAR GOSTARESH	http://www.itorbit.net/
HAMKARAN SYSTEM	http://www.systemgroup.net/products/%D8%B1%D8%A7%D9%87%DA%A9%D8%A7%D8%B1-%D8%AF%D9%88%D9%84%D8%AA
RAYDANA SYSTEM	http://www.danabarcode.com/
EADEGOSTAR	http://ideagostarco.net/Page/About
EADEPARDAZAN	http://www.eadepardazan.com/pages/ltr/LTRDefault.aspx?pid=2&lang=2
RAYVARZ	https://rayvarz.com/about-us
FARAGOSTAR	http://www.faragostar.net/automation/
PARNIAN PARDAZESH PARS	http://www.parnianportal.com/OA/Pages/Home.aspx
BARID SAMANEYE NOVIN	http://www.baridsoft.ir/products/integrated-approach/office-automation

This introductory section is followed in Section II by a discussion of the background to this paper. In Section III, a brief description of the case study methodology used in this research is given. The final two sections – Sections IV and V - focus on the case study findings and analysis.

II. BACKGROUND

ERP is a modular but integrated software system which automates business processes, shares common data, and produces and accesses information in a real time environment [4]. ERP software can be implemented in stages, module by module, and therefore be used to integrate previously isolated IT systems and functional departments within a company. ERP is also viewed by some researchers [5] [6] as a fundamental method for achieving best practice within business operations – the implementation of an ERP package requiring the application of certain disciplines within main business processes. As Koch has noted, "ERP attempts to integrate all departments and functions across a company on to a single computer system that can serve all those departments' particular needs" [4]. According to Turban *et al.* [7], ERP not only provides business discipline, it also allows the alignment of IT deployment with overall business strategy and business goals. Implementing ERP thus may also require change in core processes, often termed business process reengineering or "BPR" [8].

There remain divergences of opinion regarding the suitability of systems developed in the Western world in a developing world context. When discussing IS in the developing world, Gomez and Pather [9] observe that there is a lack of literature and evaluation studies, and the World Bank view that "analysts and decision makers are still struggling to make sense of the mixed experience of information technologies in developing countries" is highlighted by other authors [10]. In spite of uncertainty and failure in the adoption of information systems (IS), the overall deployment of ERP and IS in general is increasing in the developing world.

Increasing professional skills and training is viewed as a key element for successful IS project delivery by Noudoosbeni et al. [11], who argue that lack of planning and management as well as inadequate training led to IS project failure in Malaysian companies. Research of companies in Iran [12] [13] [14] highlight a range of issues that have hampered IS deployment in general in the country - lack of managerial skills, low IT maturity, poor training, poor internet access, governmental policies, and poor business planning; but there is very little literature on the more specific issues faced by SMEs attempting to implement ERP software. Other researchers [15] [16] suggest that the lack of human capability and economic conditions in developing countries lead to IS failure and prevent overall economic growth. There nevertheless appears to be a significant market for ERP software in SMEs in the developing world. The studies of Dezar and Ainin [17] and Arabi et al. [18] indicate that 90% of businesses in developing countries are SMEs; but adoption of ERP systems by SMEs in developing countries is a new activity, in part due to the high expense and technical complexity of such systems.

Iran is an interesting example of the potential of ERP systems in a developing world country. Talebi [19] reports that the great majority of businesses in Iran are micro, small and medium-sized enterprises. According to Molanezhad [20], the majority of SMEs in Iran are in the manufacturing sector. He also suggests that due to the location of Iran in the Middle East, its access to Russia, Europe and Asia, and its considerable market size, ERP systems have significant potential in supporting Iranian SMEs grow their business and increase their employment. This potential has been reinforced by the recent international agreement on nuclear development in Iran, and the subsequent opening up of trading with the West. Hakim and Hakim [21] assert that "IT, as a new industry in Iran, has not found its rightful place within organizations, as the managers are still adamant and adhere to the traditional management systems, and show resistance to the required organizational and infrastructural changes".

Research by Heeks [22] suggests there are several main elements of change that are important in implementing new IS in developing world environments. He identified people, process, structure and technology as key dimensions of what he termed the "design-actuality gap". Heeks' model can be used in various business change contexts, and in this paper it is used to support the analysis of the implementation of the integrated software systems in the two case study companies. Other authors [23] have adopted a similar approach in looking at structures that are embedded in both packages and organisations in trying to assess the reasons for misalignments between IS strategy and the overarching business strategy of the organisation.

The process mapping technique can help the researcher assess systems deployment at process level. It generates a sequence of maps that are used in identifying the information systems that are used in defined business areas. While process mapping is used as a framework to identify the business processes and sub-processes, it can also be used as a point of reference for assessing the functionality of the information systems themselves. This "systems profiling" encompasses a review and assessment of functionality, reporting capabilities, user interface and soundness of the underlying technology [24].

Within this context, and in accordance with the research aims and objectives given above, this research addresses the following questions:

1. What is the nature of the Iranian Total Systems products and do they parallel the modular structure typical of their western ERP counterparts?
2. How successful has the implementation of these products been in supporting the growth of selected case study companies?

III. RESEARCH METHOD

The case study is a widely used research method within business research. Bryman and Bell [25] argue that the case study is particularly appropriate to be used in combination with a qualitative research method, allowing detailed and intensive research activity, usually in combination with an inductive approach as regards the relationship between theory and research. The case study is also appropriate for a combination of qualitative methods, which is of particular relevance to this study of information systems in two SMEs, where mapping and profiling techniques are combined with questionnaire and interview material. Saunders, Lewis and Thornhill [26] argue that case studies are of particular value for explanatory or exploratory investigation, such as that pursued in this research.

The case studies under investigation are manufacturing SMEs in Iran. This paper reports on the initial findings from two case studies, but additional cases are currently being researched, which will allow stronger conclusions to be drawn in due course. Aliases are used because of confidentiality issues. The first case study is the Isfahan Bus Company, which was founded in 1985 as a family business in Najafabad in Isfahan province. The company designs, manufactures and sells a range of buses, vans and spare parts and currently employs 350 staff. The second case study is Electronic Transmission Systems, a company employing 160 staff which was founded in 1978, and is another family business in the Isfahan province. The company designs, manufactures and distributes electronic vehicles, E-bikes, differential transmission systems (for Pride, Nissan Jounior and Tiba engines), and pinion and gear differential systems and parts.

Data collection to date has been achieved through questionnaires, interviews, and documentary evidence. Yin [27] suggests that the utilisation of multiple sources of evidence is one way of increasing the construct validity of case studies. A detailed structured questionnaire was filled in by two respondents in one case study and three in the second company and follow-up interviews have been conducted with the questionnaire respondents. The job roles of these respondents were:

Isfahan Bus Company

Head of IT: he was heavily involved in supporting main departments in specifying their requirements and in package selection. In implementation phase, he had regular meetings with department heads to progress check and make sure they understood the implementation process.

Head of quality control and engineering: he was on the steering group that was responsible for selecting and implementing the Total Systems solution. As main user and responsible for overall project quality, he represented individual departmental needs, and met with the head of IT regularly.

Head of commercial department: he worked closely with the head of IT in the selection and implementation processes, identifying and planning training for most of the staff.

Electronic Transmission Systems

Head of IT: he was involved in selecting the Total Systems package, but all main decisions were made by the company director

Head of human resources: he was not involved in the software selection process but has played an important role in post implementation in reviewing and proposing training needs for new systems users.

The questionnaire responses and follow-up interviews have clarified the processes and sub-processes that are central to the companies' business operations, and allowed a mapping of current technology deployment in each process area. More specifically, the topics included in the questionnaire can be categorised as follows:

a) Company information: basic company data, company profile, size, operations and other general information.
b) Company processes: the company's main business processes and also the secondary processes (sub-processes within each main process area).
c) Information systems: the deployment of information systems and the underpinning technical architecture.
d) Current systems status: the functionality of the main information systems and general satisfaction levels in different departments that use them.
e) Problems and challenges: key problems or issues, both from a technical perspective and from the point of view of the end user; integration and interfacing of systems, report quality, systems performance.

Questionnaires and interviews were conducted in Parsi and have been translated into English.

IV. Case Study Findings

This section will apply process mapping and systems profiling to the two manufacturing SMEs in Iran.

Case Study 1: The Isfahan Bus Company (IBC)

IBC has six major top level business processes and a number of sub-processes. These are briefly outlined below, along with the information systems which currently support them (Figure 1).

The *manufacturing process* comprises three sub-processes: production planning and production, quality control, and engineering. Production planning is automated via the materials requirements planning (MRP) module of the BEHKO system. This systems module assesses the requirements for production against current company stock and suggests replenishment works orders for the appropriate dates and quantities to meet production requirements. The system takes account of current stock levels, outstanding orders, and minimum purchase order quantities. It will suggest a schedule of what should be made and when, what should be purchased and when, and current and future loading of production lines, by resource by week. This sub-process includes the bill of materials (BOM) function. When the MRP module receives an order, it will also create a list of required components to make that order. The MRP module also has additional forward planning functionality. It has the capability to plan requirements for meeting new orders and rescheduling existing orders.

In contrast, the quality control and engineering sub-processes are only partly automated. These sub-processes are supported by Microsoft Excel and Access to monitor, store and report upon key events and stock transactions. These include inspection and testing records, and inventory transactions for engineering parts.

The *sales and marketing process* is also supported by the BEHKO system. There are two sub-processes – sales management and marketing management, supported, respectively, by the BEHKO sales management module (that encompasses customer records, sales orders, price lists and quotation functions) and the BEHKO customer relationship management (CRM) module.

A customer record includes customer details, customer status, and customer discounts, and is linked to the sales ledger which shows outstanding invoices and displays these along with other real time data from BEHKO so that sales and purchasing staff have a total up-to-date view of pertinent financial data for each customer. The sales order function allows the entry and editing of sales order information and the generation of sales reports. The quotation function allows the processing of requested quotes for business and the generation of quotation reports to send to customers. The BEHKO CRM module provides the systems functionality to manage and report upon sales contacts, prospects, existing customers and suppliers, in support of improved customer service and better information availability across the internal customer facing processes.

The purchasing and procurement process centres on purchasing management and related operations. Purchasing management is supported by the BEHKO purchasing module, which provides a full range of purchasing functions. After the MRP module calculates requirements to fulfill a works order, a purchase requisition is generated electronically to be accessed by the purchasing department

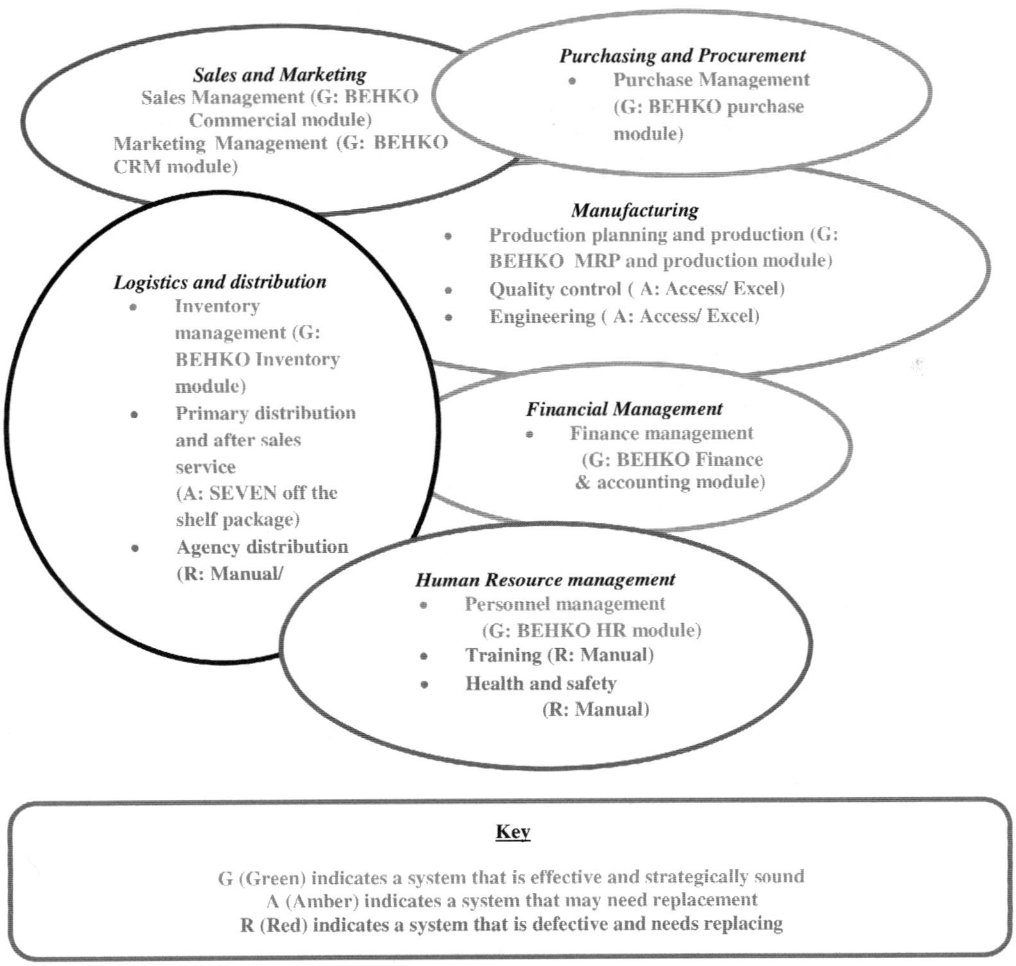

Figure 1. Main Business Processes and IS profiling at IBC

and processed as a purchase order on the system; copies are also made available electronically to the finance department. The BEHKO purchasing module generates unique supplier reference codes and provides purchase reports for each supplier. It also has the capability to assess suppliers' credit worthiness and overall supply performance, and also attach picture, voice or any other document to supplier files.

The *financial management* process is again supported by a BEHKO systems module – the finance and accounting module. This system reports the current sales order book (accounts receivable), purchase order book, outstanding purchase invoices and staff payments (accounts payable), alongside the company general ledger and cash management transactions. This system assesses current outstanding sales orders to raise sales invoice to customers, and matches goods received notes against purchase orders and purchase invoices. The module defines the financial period start and end dates and can accommodate a variety of foreign currencies and exchange rates.

The *logistics and distribution* process has three sub-processes - inventory management, primary distribution and aftersales services, and agency distribution. Inventory management is automated via the BEHKO stock control system. The primary distribution and aftersales services sub-process manages customers' orders to ensure customer delivery and post sales service. It is supported by an off the shelf after sales information systems package called SEVEN. The agency distribution sub-process involves the sale of spare parts for buses and other vehicles via company agencies located in different cities in Iran. This process is partly manual and partly automated by use of spreadsheets.

The *human resource (HR) management* process can be subdivided into three main sub-processes: personnel management handles employee records (including payment, staff absence and leave, and timesheet recording) and this is centrally managed and automated using the BEHKO HR systems module. There are also the staff training and health and safety sub- processes, which are mainly manual.

The information system strategy adopted at IBC has been to implement modules of the BEHKO total system in the core process areas of the business, some of which have been customized to meet the specific requirements of the company. BEHKO is an Iranian software company, and its selection was based on functionality, language – it uses both Parsi and English – and easy access for systems support and

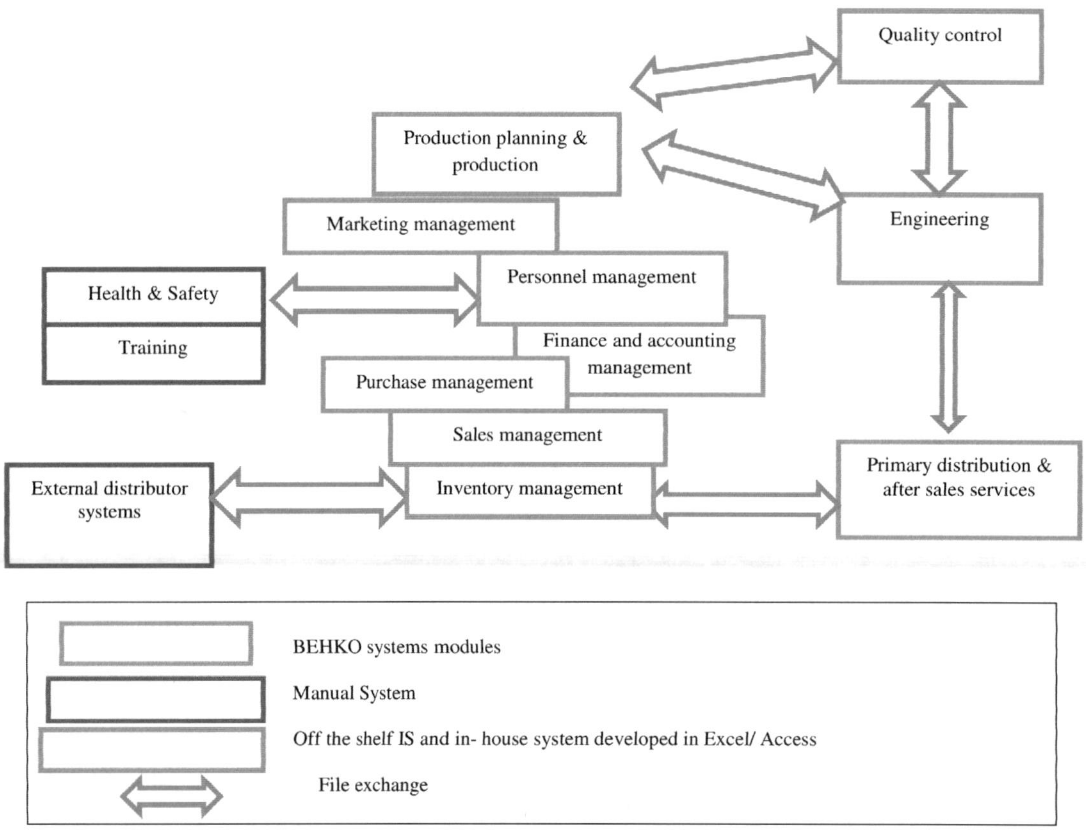

Figure 2. Systems Interfaces at IBC

upgrade. IBC pursued a phased implementation to enable a careful phasing out of previous systems and a managed exchange of data between old and new systems. In addition, it allowed staff to adapt to the changes in systems and procedures in an orderly and controlled manner. Many modules were customised based on requested requirements specified by senior management in each process area. In all, it took three years to implement the system, but even now some sub-processes are still manual or are supported by using spreadsheets and semi-automated file exchanges (Figure 2).

Although the BEHKO system modules are well integrated, there is no effective integration with the stand alone SEVEN system, or with the MS Excel and MS Access applications. The BEHKO system is developed in C++ and uses the SQL database and is administered by senior managers who have access to all system generated reports and invoices. These reports include key business performance information, providing an overview of all sales, purchases, stock levels, financial data and staff reports.

The current IS strategy at IBC was adopted in 2008 in support of the company's business strategy to expand production and drive up bottom-line company profit. The strategy was a formal decision made by a committee comprising selected managers from across all departments - commercial, finance, production, engineering, quality control, and the IT manager. Previous systems were a mix of off the shelf packages and end-user applications. The initial focus was to be on the in the logistics and distribution process area, to establish consistent inventory product codes and simplify and standardise product information for both internal processes and also for customer facing sales and marketing departments. After a successful six month parallel run of old and new systems in this area in 2008, the BEHKO systems modules were introduced in stages, completing in 2012. The software vendor continues to provide support and upgrades, IBC is now planning a major upgrade to the BEHKO ERP product in 2017. This package includes improved functionality which should allow the replacement of the SEVEN package and other standalone applications.

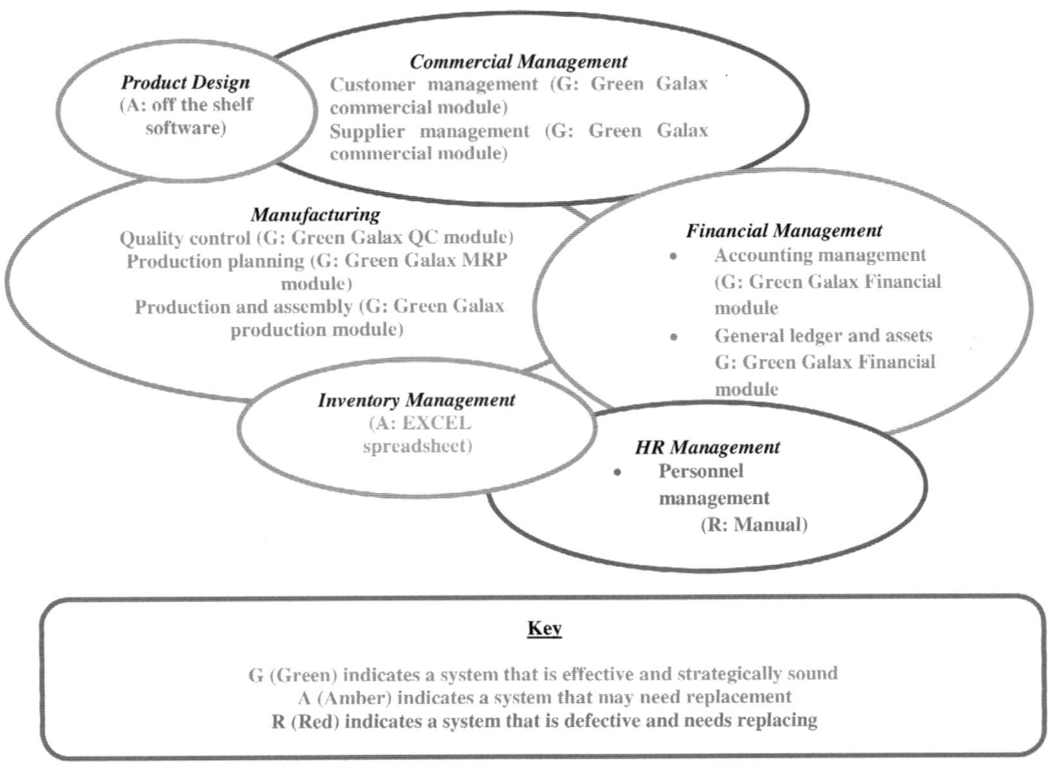

Figure 3. Main Business Processes and IS profiling at ETS

Case Study 2: Electronic Transmission Systems (ETS)

Initial process mapping suggests there are six top level business processes, and each process has several sub-processes. The processes are depicted in Figure 3, along with the information systems which currently support these business processes.

The *manufacturing process* comprises three sub-processes: quality control, production planning, and production and assembly. The quality control sub-process encompasses the inspection of both purchased and manufactured parts and products, and the recording and monitoring of test results. The GREEN/GALAX quality control module records and manages all data associated with product sampling, testing and results recording and reporting. Security aspects are supported by systems controls on access, allowing only staff with the required skills and competence levels to undertake inspection testing.

The production planning sub-process is automated with the GREEN/GALAX materials requirements planning (MRP) module, which determines the quantity and timing of component purchases. MRP stores the bills of materials and explodes these into requirements, based on received orders, and will then compare the demands to available company stock to generate necessary procurement requirements. The production and assembly sub-process encompasses production control and final inspection operations. The GREEN/GALAX production module also provides time estimates for parts delivery at production line and for final inspection of finished products. The production team can attach drawings of product designs and technical specifications to job sheet records.

The *inventory management* process covers stock control and is partly automated with MS Excel spreadsheets monitoring manufactured and component products in and out of the stockrooms. The *product design* process is automated with a range of off the shelf design and planning software packages, including Catia V5R18, MSC Super Forge, Master CAM 9.0, Autodesk Mechanical desktop 2007, Power Mill 6.0, Primavera Project planner, MS project 2007, and Minitab 13.0. This process encompasses the design and drawing of company products based on received orders and customer specifications.

The *commercial management* process has two sub-processes - customer management and supplier management – and both are supported by the GREEN/GALAX commercial management module. This module supports the categorization and management of both customers and suppliers, and recording of relevant details. The *financial management* process is similarly supported by a GREEN/ GALAX module. There are two sub-processes: accounts management, and general ledger and asset management. The system manages financial activities, financial figures and reports and invoices; it contains the ledgers for sales and purchase transactions, and records company assets, liabilities, owners' equity, revenue, and expenses.

The *human resource management* process covers personnel management, including employee records, staff absence and leave, and timesheets. The process is mainly manual. Employees have their own identity and attendance card, which are checked and monitored by security guards at

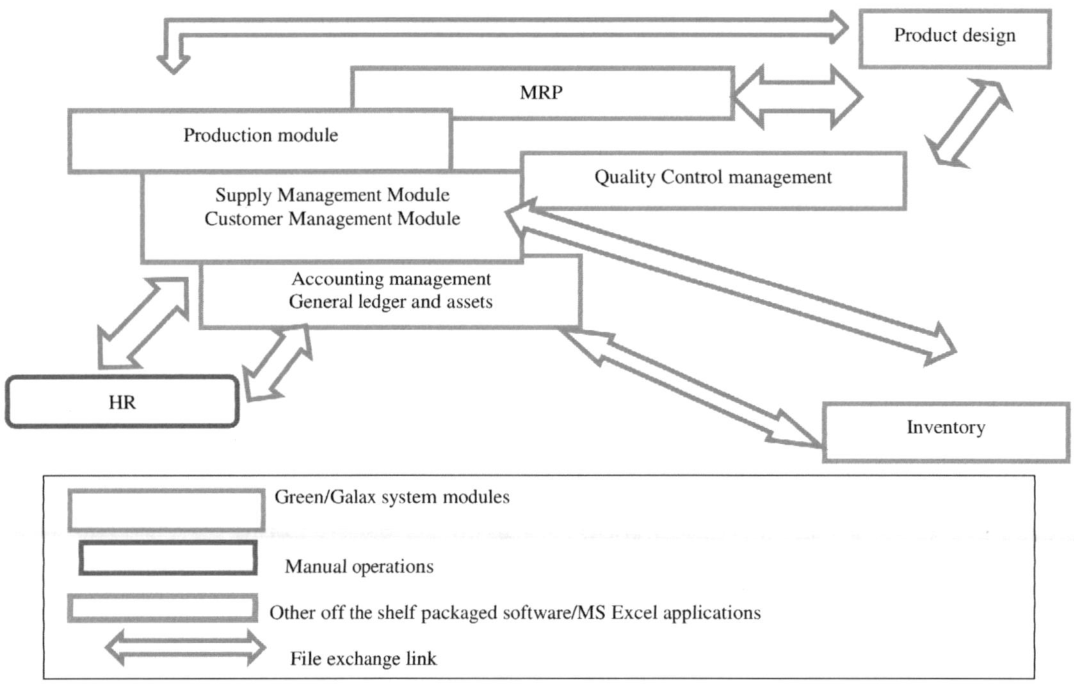

Figure 4. Systems Interfaces at ETS

the company entrance. Annual leave is also authorised and recorded by a manual, paper-based system.

The information system strategy adopted at ETS is based on the GREEN/GALAX Total Systems package, combined with point solutions developed in MS Excel. The choice of the main software system again was influenced by the fact that it was available in the Parsi language and there was easy access to software support and technical advisors.

The current IS strategy was adopted in 2014 and was a formal decision made by the IT manager in conjunction with the company director. Modules of the GREEN/GALAX were implemented simultaneously in core business functions. Unfortunately, training was poor and insufficient and there have been significant user issues with some departments reverting to previous semi-manual processes. There also remain a number of file exchange operations whereby data is extracted from the GREEN/GALAX system and input into standalone applications for inventory management and product design (see Figure 4). In 2015, external consultants were engaged to review the status of the ERP project and specifically to provide training and user support. Despite this initiative, there remain significant issues to address. The implementation of new modules has not been adequately coordinated with changes in people capability. The HR system needs to be automated and integrated with finance and the accounting department to prevent duplication and data inconsistencies in payroll. Similarly, the inventory management module of the GREEN/GALAX system needs to be ushered in to provide consistent product codes and enhance the capability and functionality of company business activities. The company needs to address the training issue to encourage and support staff in using all of the available functions in the new system.

V. CONCLUDING REMARKS

The current information system strategies at both IBC and ETS have some similarities. Both companies elected to adopt a Total Systems package, from Iranian based software suppliers, to provide the benefits of integrated systems and consistent management information to support company growth aspirations. In both companies, however, some of the old legacy systems remain in some core process areas, and these should be replaced in the near future with appropriate Total Systems modules.

There were significant differences between the two companies' strategy implementation approaches. At IBC, the strategy development and its implementation was agreed to, and guided by, a cross-departmental steering group that carefully managed a staged implementation, providing the necessary training and support for end-users. At ETS, the package selection process was more the result of discussions between the IT manager and the company director, and lacked cross-company involvement and support. Implementation was simultaneous in most process areas, increasing the risk of systems problems and data issues. This was compounded by the absence of adequate training and support for end-users, which left the project in a parlous state. Only recently has the engagement of third party support helped to provide much needed training and bed in the new systems modules.

This initial analysis reinforces the findings of Heeks [22] and other recent studies [28][29] that suggest large scale technology implementation, even in SMEs, must be accompanied by appropriate process improvement and an upgrade in people skills to accommodate the new ways of working that are often introduced with new systems modules. At IBC, where a cross-departmental steering group guided and controlled the project, this was largely achieved; but at ETS, the lack of a similar project management capability constituted a major risk to successful project outcomes, which is only now being adequately addressed.

The research outcomes also provide some interesting insights into the ERP market in Iran, where, with international sanctions now lifted, the opportunities for western based ERP vendors are likely to be enhanced. However, the home-grown Total Systems packages, which exhibit a similar modular structure to the ERP packages used in the West, have an established user base which is likely to grow, in the short-term at least, given the benefits of customisation and bi-lingual operation that most of these packages offer. Nevertheless, the research to date is just a "snapshot" of the current situation and recent history in two small manufacturing SMEs and it is unwise to make broader generalisations from just these two cases. To address this limitation, other company case studies are now being undertaken, and it is expected that this will allow the development of an implementation model for ERP products in the specific environment of Iranian manufacturing SMEs, that will be useable in future systems projects in the country.

REFERENCES

[1] M. Wynn, "Information systems strategy development and implementation in SMEs", Management Research News, Vol. 32 (1), pp. 78 – 90, 2009.

[2] A. Hawari and R. Heeks, "Explaining ERP failure in a developing country: a Jordanian case study", Journal of Enterprise Information Management, Vol. 23 (2), pp. 135-160, 2010.

[3] M. Moohebat, M. Jazi, and A. Aseni, "Evaluation of ERP implementation at the Esfahan Steele Company", International Journal of Business and Management, Vol. 6 (5), pp. 236-250, 2011.

[4] C. Koch, "The ABCs of ERP", CIO Magazine, Dec 1999.

[5] C. Soh and S. Sia, "An institutional perspective on sources of ERP package organization misalignments", Journal of Strategic Information Systems, Vol.13 (4), pp. 375-397, 2004.

[6] K. Boersma and S. Kingma, "Developing a cultural perspective on ERP", Journal of Process Management, Vol. 11 (2), pp. 123- 136, 2005.

[7] E. Turban, E. McLean, J. Wetherbe, N. Bolloju, and R. Davison, Information Technology for Management – Transforming Business in the Digital Economy, 3rd ed., John Wiley & Sons, New York, 2002.

[8] M. Hammer and J. Champny, Re-engineering the Corporation: A Manifesto for Business Revolution, Harper Business, New York, 1993.

[9] R. Gomez and S. Pather, "ICT evaluation: are we asking the right questions?", Electronic Journal of Information

Systems in Developing Countries (EJISDC), Vol. 50 (5), pp. 1-14, 2012.

[10] S. Batchelor, S. Evangelista, S. Hearn, M. Pierce, S. Sugden, and M. Webb, ICT for Development: Contributing to the Millenium Development Goals – Lessons Learnt from Seventeen infoDev projects, Wasington DC: World Bank, 2003.

[11] A. Noudoosbeni, N. Ismail, and H. Jenatabadi, "An effective end-user knowledge concern training method in enterprise resource planning (ERP) based on critical factors (CFS) in Malaysian SMEs," International Journal of Production Economics, Vol. 115 (2), pp. 72-85, 2010.

[12] A. Shahin, S. Sadri, and R. Gazor, "Evaluating the Application of Learning Requirements Planning Model in the ERP project of Esfahan Steel Company", International Journal of Business Management, Vol. 5 (2), pp. 33-43, 2010.

[13] P. Hanifzade and M. Nikabadi, "Framework for Selection of an Appropriate e- Business Model in Managerial Holding Companies: case study: Iran Khodro", Journal of Enterprise Information Management, Vol. 24 (3), pp. 237-267, 2010.

[14] A. Amid, M. Moalagh, and A. Ravasan, "Identification and classification of ERP critical factors in Iranian industries," Journal of Information Systems, Vol. 37, pp. 227-237, 2011.

[15] M. Warschauer, "Dissecting the Digital Devide: A case study in Egypt", The Information Society, Vol.19 (4), pp. 7-24, 2003.

[16] R. Wade, "Bridging the Digital Divide: New Route to Development or New Form of Dependency?", Journal of Global Governance, Vol. 8 (4), pp. 443- 466, 2002.

[17] S. Dezar and S. Ainin, "ERP implementation success in Iran: examining the role of systems environment factors", World Academy of Science, Engineering and Technology, Vol. 42, pp. 449-455, 2010.

[18] M. Arabi, M. Zameri, K. Wong, H. Beheshti, and N. Zakuan, "Critical Success Factors of Enterprise Resource Planning Implementation in Small and Medium Enterprises in Developing Countries: A Review and Research Direction", Proceedings of Industrial Engineering and Service Science, 2011, http://www.academia.edu/1083186/Critical_Success_Factors_of_Enterprise_Resource_Planning_Implementation_in_Smalland_Medium_Enterprises_in_Developing_Countries:_a_Review_and_Research_Direction/ [Retrieved: March, 2016]

[19] K. Talebi, "How should the entrepreneurs of SMEs in Iran change their style in a business life cycle?", Iranian Journal of Management Studies (IJMS), Vol. 1 (1), pp. 10-17, 2007.

[20] M. Molanezhad, "A Brief Review of Science and Technology and SMEs Development in Iran", The inter-sessional panel of the United Nations commission on science and technology for development, 2010.

[21] A. Hakim and H. Hakim, "A practical model on controlling ERP implementation risks", Journal of Information Systems, Vol. 35, pp. 204-214, 2012.

[22] R. Heeks, "Information Systems and Developing Countries: Failure, Success, and Local Improvisations", Journal of Information Society, Vol.18 (2), pp. 101-112, 2002.

[23] C. Soh and S Kien Sia, "An institutional perspective on sources of ERP package-otrganisation misalignments", Journal of Strategic Information Systems, Vol.13, pp. 375-397, 2004.

[24] M. Wynn and O. Olubanjo, "Demand-supply chain management: systems implications in an SME packaging business in the UK", International Journal of Manufacturing Research, Vol 7 (2), pp. 198-212, 2012.

[25] A. Bryman and E. Bell, Business Research Methods, 3rd edition, Oxford: Oxford University Press, 2011.

[26] M. Saunders, P. Lewis and A. Thornhill, Research methods for business students, 5th ed., 2009, England: Pearson Education Limited.

[27] R. K. Yin, Applications of Case Study Research. 3rd ed., 2012, London: SAGE Publications, Inc

[28] H. Akeel and M. Wynn, "ERP Implementation in a Developing World Context: a Case Study of the Waha Oil Company, Libya", The Seventh International Conference on Information, Process and Knowledge Management, Lisbon, eKnow, Feb 2015. ThinkMind, ISBN: 978-1-61208-386-5; ISSN: 2308-4375.

[29] M. Wynn, P. Turner, A. Banik, and A. G. Duckworth, "The impact of customer relationship management systems in small businesses", Strategic Change, Vol. 25, 2016 (forthcoming).

A Semantic Layer for Urban Resilience Content Management

Ilkka Niskanen, Mervi Murtonen
Technical Research Centre of Finland
Oulu/Tampere, Finland
Ilkka.Niskanen@vtt.fi,
Mervi.Murtonen@vtt.fi

Fiona Browne, Peadar Davis
School of Computing and Mathematics
Ulster University
Jordanstown, Northern Ireland, UK
f.browne@ulster.ac.uk
pt.davis@ulster.ac.uk

Francesco Pantisano
Smart System Infrastructures
Finmeccanica Company
Genova, Italy
francesco.pantisano@finmeccanica.co

Abstract— **Content Management refers to the process of gaining control over the creation and distribution of information and functionality. Although there are several content management systems available they often fail in addressing the context specific needs of end-users. To enable more task specific and personalized support we present a semantic content management solution developed for the domain of urban resilience. The introduced semantic layer is built on top of an existing content management system and by utilizing domain specific annotation and categorization it facilitates the management of heterogeneous and large content repository. In addition, the enhanced semantic intelligence allows better understanding of content items, linkages between unstructured information and tools, and provides more sophisticated answers to users' various needs.**

Keywords- content management; semantic technologies; heterogeneous data repository

I. INTRODUCTION

The field of Content Management (CM) refers to the process of gaining control over the creation and distribution of information and functionality. Concisely, an effective Content Management System (CMS) aims at getting the right information to the right people in the right way. Usually CM is divided into three main phases namely collecting, managing, and publishing of content. The collection phase encompasses the creating or acquiring information from an existing source. This is then aggregated into a CMS by editing it, segmenting it into components, and adding appropriate metadata. The managing phase includes creating a repository that consists of database containing content components and administrative data (data on the system's users, for example). Finally, in the publishing stage the content is made available for the target audience by extracting components out of the repository and releasing the content for use in the most appropriate way. [1]

Currently, there are several commercial and open-source technologies available that are applied to address different content management needs across various industries including healthcare [12], and education [15], for example. However, the standard versions of the existing solutions are not always capable of supporting end-users in their specified context to reach their particular goals in an effective, efficient and satisfactory way [2]. For instance, the included content retrieval mechanisms are often implemented using traditional keyword based search engines that are not adapted to serve any task specific needs [3][4][5].

One of the main issues to be resolved is how to convert existing and new content that can be understood by humans into semantically-enriched content that can be understood by machines [6]. The human-readable and unstructured content is usually difficult to automatically process, relate and categorize, which hinders the ability to extract value from it [7]. Additionally, it results in the restriction of development of more intelligent search mechanisms [6]. To address some of the above described deficiencies, semantic technologies are being increasingly used in CM. In particular, the utilization of domain specific vocabularies and taxonomies in content analysis enables accurate extraction of meaningful information, and supports task-specific browsing and retrieval requirements compared to traditional approaches [6]. Furthermore, semantic technologies facilitate creating machine-readable content metadata descriptions, which allows, for example, software agents to automatically accomplish complex tasks using that data. Moreover, semantically enhanced metadata helps search engines to better understand what they are indexing and providing more accurate results to the users [9].

The HARMONISE platform, developed in the FP7 EU HARMONISE [17] project is a domain specific CMS that provides information and tools for security-driven urban resilience in large-scale infrastructure offering a holistic view to urban resilience. A database contained by the system manages an extensive set of heterogeneous material that comes in different forms including tools, design guidance and specifications. The platform aims at serving as a 'one-stop-shop' for resilience information and guidance and it contains a wealth of information and tools specifically designed to aid built environment professionals. While the platform and the hosted toolkit are aimed to be used by a variety of potential end-users from planners and urban designers to construction teams, building security personnel and service managers, the specialized problem domain and heterogeneous content repository poses significant challenges for users to effectively retrieve information to accomplish their tasks and goals.

In this paper the Semantic Layer for the HARMONISE (SLH) approach is introduced. The SLH is a semantic content management solution developed to address many of the above discussed challenges related to domain specific content management. It is implemented on top of the HARMONISE platform and it aims at offering more task specific and personalized content management support for end-users. Additionally, by utilizing domain specific annotation and categorization of content the SLH facilitates the management of heterogeneous and large content repository hosted by the HARMONISE platform.

The semantic information modelling allows better understanding of platform content, linkages between unstructured information and tools, and more sophisticated answers to users' various needs. Moreover, the semantic knowledge representations created by the layer help end-users to combine different data fragments and produce new implicit knowledge from existing data sets. Finally, by utilizing Linked Data [18] technologies the SLH fosters interoperability and improves shared understanding of key information elements. The utilization of interconnected and multidisciplinary knowledge bases of the Linked Data cloud also enables applying the solution in other problem areas such as health care or education.

The rest of paper is organized as follows. Section II provides a through description of the HARMONISE platform and its application area. In Section III the architecture and different components of the SLH are described. Section IV provides a Use Case example demonstrating the functionality of the SLH. Finally, Section V concludes the paper.

II. THE HARMONISE CONTENT MANAGEMENT PLATFORM

At present there exist a number of content management systems that enable publishing, managing and organizing electronic documents. For example, Drupal [19] and WordPress [20] are well-known, general-purpose CM solutions providing such basic CM features such as user profile management, database administration, metadata management, and content search and navigation functionalities [2]. These tools provide functionality to create and edit a website's content often with easy-to-use templates for digital media content publishing.

As stated above, the HARMONISE platform is a CMS specifically tailored for the domain of urban resilience. The system provides information and tools for security-driven urban resilience in large-scale infrastructure and contains a variety of interactive elements allowing users to both import and export data to and from the platform and personalize the platform to their own needs. The core functionalities of the HARMONISE platform are implemented using ASP.NET web application framework and it utilizes Microsoft SQL 2012 database to store content items.

An important part of the HARMONISE content management platform is the Thematic Framework [10] that was created to structure information within the platform and to guide end-users through an innovative step-by-step search process. The Thematic Framework is set out in Fig. 1 below.

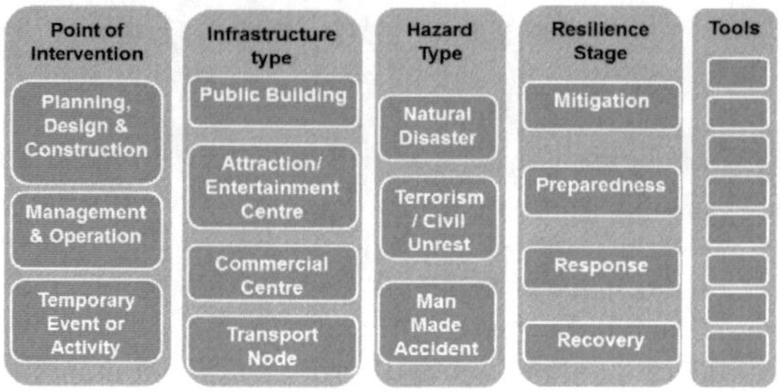

Figure 1. The Thematic Framework (adopted from [10])

By unpacking resilience into a number of key layers the Thematic Framework provides the necessary taxonomy needed for realizing effective domain-specific content annotation and categorizing functionalities, as later discussed. The objective of the domain-specific annotation is to allow users to easily identify and access information and tools within the platform, and to search the platform according to their unique needs or interests.

III. THE SEMANTIC LAYER

As earlier described, the HARMONISE content management platform hosts a large portfolio of urban resilience related content. However, finding relevant information and tools from such a knowledge base with conventional information retrieval methods is usually both tedious and time consuming, and tends to become a challenge as the amount of content increases [6]. Often users have difficulties in grouping together related material or finding the content that best serve their information needs, especially when content is stored in multiple formats [11].

In general, the existing CMSs usually lack consistent and scalable content annotation mechanisms that allow them to deal with the highly heterogeneous domains that information architectures for the modern knowledge society demand [8]. The semantic layer described in this study aims at addressing the above mentioned challenges by integrating semantic data modelling and processing mechanisms to the core HARMONISE platform functionalities. For example, the application of semantic mark-up based tagging of web content enables expressively describing entities found in the content, and relations between them [6]. Moreover, by utilizing the Linked Data Cloud links can be set between different and heterogeneous content elements and therefore connect these elements into a single global data space, which further facilitates interoperability and machine-readable understanding of content [13].

The main features of the SLH are divided to four parts. First, the metadata enrichment part produces information-rich metadata descriptions of the content by enhancing content with relevant semantic metadata. Second, the semantic metadata repository implements the necessary means for storing and accessing the created metadata. The third component of the SLH realizes a semantic search feature. In more detail the search service aims at returning more meaningful search results to the user by utilizing both keyword-based semantic search and "Search by theme" filtering algorithm that restricts the searchable space by enabling users to select certain categories from the Thematic Framework. The final part, content recommendation, combines information about users' preferences and profile to find a target user neighborhood, and proactively recommends new urban resilience tools/resources that might be of potential interest to him/her. In Fig. 2 the logical architecture of the SLH is represented.

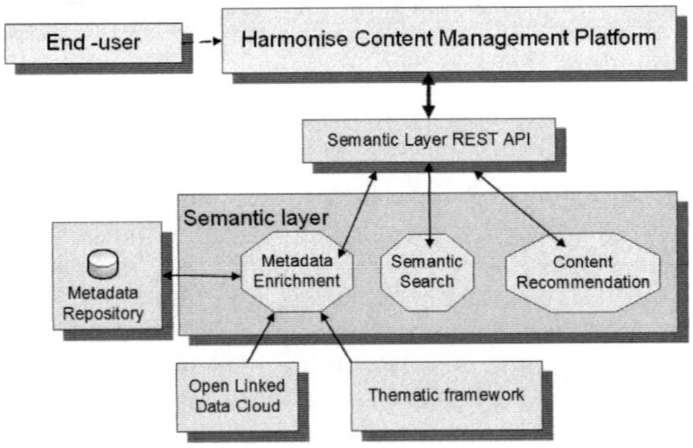

Figure 2. The logical architecture of the SLH

The following sections describe the logical architecture in more detail.

A. Semantic Layer REST API

The Semantic Layer REST API provides the necessary interface for the HARMONISE Platform to interact with the SLH. It enables, for example, to transmit query requests from the platform to the SLH or retrieve content recommendations personalized for a particular user.

B. Metadata Enrichment

The purpose of the Metadata Enrichment service is to produce information-rich metadata descriptions of the content that is uploaded to the HARMONISE platform. Enhancing content with relevant semantic metadata can be very useful for handling large content databases [1]. A key issue in this context is improving the "findability" of content elements (e.g. documents, tools).

The enrichment process is based on tagging. A tag associates semantics to a content item, usually helping the user searching or browsing through content. These tags can be used in order to identify the most important topics, entities, events and other information relevant to that content item. The tagging data is created by analyzing the uploaded content and the metadata manually entered by the user. This information consist e.g. title, keywords, Thematic Framework categories, topics, content types and phrases of natural language text.

In the metadata analysis the following three technologies that provide tagging services are utilized: ONKI [21], DBPedia [22] and OpenCalais [23]. The ONKI and DBPedia knowledge bases provide enrichment of the human defined keywords by utilizing Linked Data reference vocabularies and datasets. The Metadata Enrichment service utilizes the APIs of the above mentioned technologies to search terms that are somehow associated to the entities defined by a user.

The extracted terms fall into three categories: similar, broader and narrower. The similar terms are synonyms to the original entities whereas broader terms can be considered as more general concepts. The narrower terms represent examples of more specific concepts compared to the original entity. Each of the acquired terms contains a Linked Data URI that can be accessed to get more extensive description of that term. By enriching the human defined keywords with additional concepts and Linked Data URIs more comprehensive and machine-readable information about uploaded content items can be generated.

The uploaded content items are also examined using the OpenCalais text analyzer tool. Using such mechanisms as natural language processing and machine learning the tool allows analyzing different text fragments contained by the uploaded content item. As a result, OpenCalais discovers entities (Company, Person etc.), events or facts that are related to the uploaded content element.

In the final part of the metadata enrichment process the metadata elements created by different tools are merged as a single RDF (Resource Description Framework) metadata description and stored to the metadata database.

C. Semantic Metadata Repository

The database technology used for storing the semantic metadata of content is OpenLink Virtuoso [26]. Virtuoso is a relational database solution that is optimized to store RDF data. It provides good performance and extensive query interfaces [16] and was thus selected as the metadata storage to be used in the SLH.

D. Semantic Search

The Semantic Search service aims at producing relevant search results for the user by effectively utilizing the machine-readable RDF metadata descriptions created by the Metadata Enrichment service. Unlike traditional search engines that return a large set of results that may or may not be relevant to the context of the search, the Semantic Search analyses the results and orders them based on their relevancy. Thus, users are emancipated from performing the time-consuming work of browsing through the retrieved results in order to find the content they are looking for.

The Semantic Search service is implemented as a Java web application composed of three main components (see Fig. 3):

- RESTful Web Service: based on Apache CXF framework, it represents the semantic search service front-end. It receives the search queries from the HARMONISE platform and returns the list of search results provided by the underlying components;
- Semantic Search Service Core (SSS Core): component based on Java/Maven project, customized to manage all the core processes (data indexing, content search, content retrieving, results formatting);
- Semantic Search Engine: component based on Apache Solr [24] enterprise search platform, in charge of the indexing and the search processes. When a new content

is uploaded to the HARMONISE platform it reads from the Virtuoso database the data produced by the semantic content enrichment service in order to create the index to query on. When a user submits a query the semantic search engine queries the index in order to find the documents that best match the user request parameters.

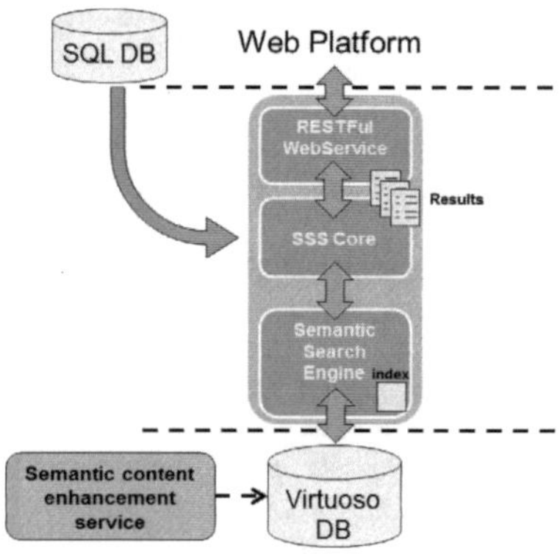

Figure 3. Logical architecture of the semantic search service

The Semantic Search service relies on the Solr search engine [25] in order to search across large amount of content metadata and pull back the most relevant results in the fastest way. Solr is a document storage and retrieval engine, which uses Lucene's inverted index to implement its fast searching capabilities. Unlike a traditional database representation where multiple documents would contain a document ID mapped to some content fields containing all of the words in that document, an inverted index inverts this model and maps each word to all of the documents in which it appears. Solr stores information in its inverted index and queries that index to find matching documents.

In the Semantic Search service, the Solr index is constructed according to the Metadata Repository data structure. In more detail, a sample of the following data fields are encompassed in the index: Id (document identifier on Virtuoso DB); Upload date (date when the document has been uploaded); Topics (list of topics from the Thematic Framework); Permissions (list of user groups allowed to view the document), Description (description of the document) and Tags (list of tags added by the metadata enhancement service).

The search results provided by the Semantic Search service are ranked according to the relevancy scores that measure the similarity between the user query and all of the documents in the index. The results with highest relevancy scores appear first in the search results list.

The scoring model is composed by the following scoring factors:

- Term Frequency: is a measure of how often a particular term appears in a matching document. Given a search query, the greater the term frequency value, the higher the document score.
- Inverse Document Frequency: is a measure of how "rare" a search term is. The rarer a term is across all documents in the index, the higher its contribution to the score.
- Coordination Factor: It is the frequency of the occurrence of query terms that match a document; the greater the occurrence, the higher is the score.
- Field length: the shorter the matching field, the greater the document score. This factor penalizes documents with longer field values.
- Boosting: is the mechanism that allows to assign different weights to those fields that are considered more (or less) important than others.

E. Content Recommendation

Similar to the Semantic Search, the Content Recommendation Service (CRS) is based on semantic modelling of content resources. The aim of the content recommendation service is to improve user experience in terms of the search functionality and the filtering of relevant information through the utilization of collaborative filtering.

The CRS utilizes user profiles which are created and maintained by the HARMONISE platform. The CRS combines information about users' preferences and profile to find a target user neighborhood, and recommend new urban resilience tools/resources that might be of potential interest to him/her. Ordered weighted average and uniform aggregation operators are applied to fuse user information and obtain global degrees of similarity between them. The user profiles contain information about user's preferences and favorite content, for example. It also includes the content item IDs that have been already recommended for that particular user. This information is then utilized when content recommendations are created for different users. An overview of the CRS algorithm is provided in Fig. 4. Fig 4 illustrates how user preference and user profile similarity are fused together along with a weighted sum to provide a ranked list of recommendation tailored to the user.

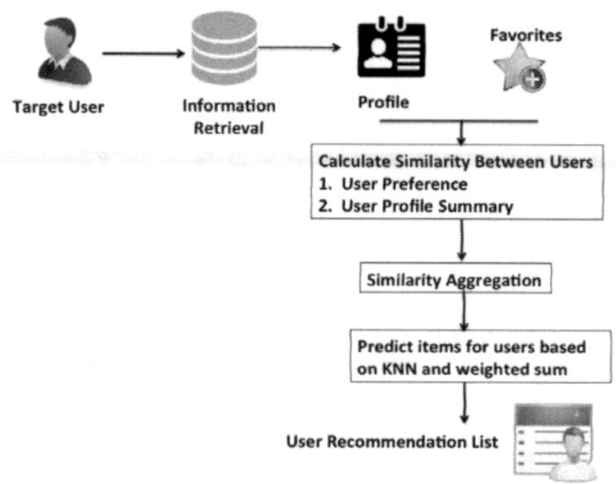

Figure 4. Overview of the CRS Algorithm

The CRS is triggered by the HARMONISE platform through the 'get recommendation' method provided by the Semantic Layer REST API. The ID of the user is transmitted as a method parameter. Once the recommendation service receives the ID, it retrieves the user profile of the user from the database and analyses the information it contains. It extracts, for example, the topics and research areas the user is interested in. Additionally, the profession, areas of expertise and relevant user groups are retrieved from the user profile. The algorithm then identifies similar users based upon the user profile using the Jaccard [14] index. Similarity between users is also measured by taking into consideration their profile similarity using the ordered weighted sum. Both these measures are fused using a similarity aggregation approach.

The actual recommendation generation process is carried out by comparing the user profile data with the semantic content metadata descriptions. Similarly as in the search algorithm described in the previous section, the content items whose metadata is associated with e.g. terms, topics or research areas as contained by the user profile are included to the initial recommendation results. Of course, the content items that have already been recommended for the user are excluded from the results list. Subsequently, the recommendation results are analyzed using the ranking model introduced by the Semantic Search. Using K-nearest neighbors, the content items that gets the highest score is returned to the platform as the most highly recommended content item.

IV. USE CASE EXAMPLE

The functionality of the SLH is demonstrated with a Use Case example in which a user uploads a document into the HARMONISE content management platform and tries to retrieve it with the search functionality. Additionally, the recommendation service is verified by creating a user profile that is interested in topics relevant to the uploaded content. The content item used in the Use Case example is an electronic manual that presents tools to help assess the performance of buildings and infrastructure against terrorist threats and to rank recommended protective measures. This kind of guidance document is a typical representative of a content item managed by the HARMONISE platform.

Once the user has provided necessary input in the upload form the content description is transmitted to the Metadata Enrichment component that processes the collected data and forms an RDF metadata description of the content. It was noted that the returned semantic content metadata contained five keywords that are enriched with 81 broader or narrower and 26 similar terms. Moreover, the content is annotated with several categories defined by the Thematic Framework.

Once the enriched metadata is stored to the Semantic Metadata Repository, and indexed by the Semantic Search service, it can be tried to be retrieved with the search functionality. The content retrieval is tested with the 'Resilience Search Wizard' feature provided by the SLH. The wizard allows to define keywords and to select those categories from the Thematic Framework that are considered as relevant to the uploaded content. The utilized search parameters are shown in the search wizard screenshot illustrated in Fig. 5.

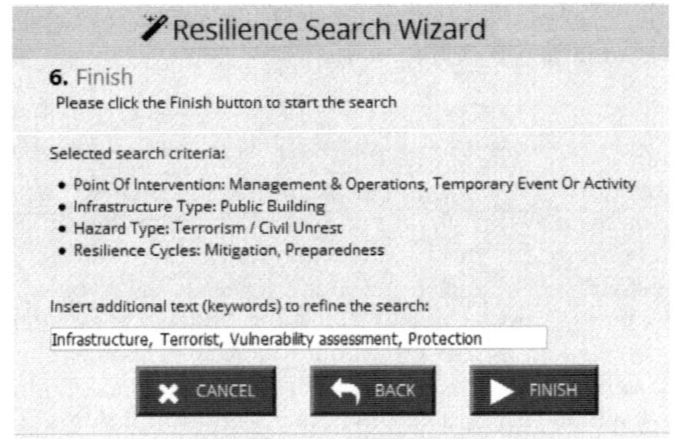

Figure 5. Search parameter definition

As earlier explained, the search functionality is able to sort the results based on their relevancy. Fig. 6 represents the most highly ranked search results returned by the search service. As can be seen, the applied ranking algorithm identified the uploaded electronic manual document as the second relevant search result for the given search query. In total, the search functionality found 24 results with the defined search parameters.

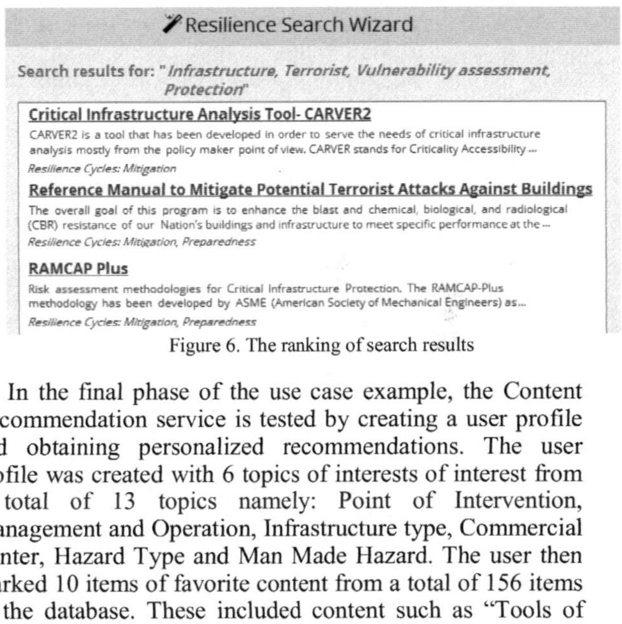

Figure 6. The ranking of search results

In the final phase of the use case example, the Content Recommendation service is tested by creating a user profile and obtaining personalized recommendations. The user profile was created with 6 topics of interests of interest from a total of 13 topics namely: Point of Intervention, Management and Operation, Infrastructure type, Commercial Center, Hazard Type and Man Made Hazard. The user then marked 10 items of favorite content from a total of 156 items in the database. These included content such as "Tools of Regional Governance" and "Flood management in Linares Town". For the first step in the recommendation algorithm, Jaccard index is utilized to compute the degree of similarity between the favourite content and profile information of the user entered and all the users of the HARMONISE system. In the second step, a KNN algorithm is applied to identify the 5 most similar neighbors. Based on neighbor users, we compute for each item not marked as a favorite by the user, a predicted rating. This is used to construct an ordered recommendation list to the target user, which in this case study was a list of 5 recommendations including documents based on "Key issues of Urban Resilience", "Building urban resilience Details" and "Resilience: how to build resilience in your people and your organization".

V. CONCLUSION

In this work, we introduce a developed semantic content management system for the domain of urban resilience. This system utilizes semantic technologies to manage an extensive set of heterogeneous material that comes in different forms including tools, design guidance documentation and specifications. Moreover, the developed approach enables the creation of machine-understandable and machine-processable descriptions of content items. This has resulted in an improved shared understanding of information elements and interoperability.

The described approach was implemented on top of an existing content management system. With the effective utilization of Linked Data based analysis tools and domain specific content annotation mechanisms it offers task specific and personalized content management support for end-users. The enhanced intelligence has provided better understanding of urban resilience content, linkages between unstructured information and tools, and more sophisticated answers to users' various needs.

With minimal adjustments the introduced semantic layer could be utilized also in other problem domains. For a new CMS to integrate with the semantic layer requires only creating a well described domain specific taxonomy and implementing the technical means for communicating with the provided REST API.

Up to this point, the HARMONISE platform and the SLH have been tested by HARMONISE project partners and other invited domain specialists who have evaluated the system in terms of usability, perceived usefulness and the relevancy of received search and recommendation results. Next, the evaluation process will encompass final tests where the approach will be used in problem area specific case studies with various end user groups.

The future work also includes further refining the HARMONISE platform and the SLH on the basis of the feedback received from the case studies. Additionally, the graphical appearance of the platform's user interface as well as the usability of individual components will be improved.

REFERENCES

[1] B. Boiko, Content management bible, John Wiley & Sons, 2005.

[2] N. Mehta, Choosing an Open Source CMS: Beginner's Guide. Packt Publishing Ltd, 2009.

[3] D. Dicheva and D. Christo, "Leveraging Domain Specificity to Improve Findability in OER Repositories." Research and Advanced Technology for Digital Libraries. Springer Berlin Heidelberg, pp. 466-469, 2013.

[4] S. K. Patel, V. R. Rathod, and S. Parikh, "Joomla, Drupal and WordPress-a statistical comparison of open source CMS." Trendz in Information Sciences and Computing (TISC), 3rd International Conference on. IEEE, 2011.

[5] C. Dorai and S. Venkatesh, "Bridging the semantic gap in content management systems." Media Computing. Springer US, pp. 1-9, 2002.

[6] J. L. Navarro-Galindo and J. Samos, "The FLERSA tool: adding semantics to a web content management system." International Journal of Web Information Systems 8.1: pp. 73-126, 2012.

[7] A. Kohn, F. Bry, and A. Manta, "Semantic search on unstructured data: explicit knowledge through data recycling." Semantic-Enabled Advancements on the Web: Applications Across Industries: Applications Across Industries, 194, 2012.

[8] R. García, J. M. Gimeno, F. Perdrix, R. Gil, and M. Oliva, "The rhizomer semantic content management system", In Emerging Technologies and Information Systems for the Knowledge Society pp. 385-394, Springer Berlin Heidelberg, 2008.

[9] D. R. Karger and D. Quan, "What would it mean to blog on the semantic web?" The Semantic Web–ISWC 2004. Springer Berlin Heidelberg, pp. 214-228, 2004.

[10] S. Purcell, W. Hynes, J. Coaffee, M. Murtonen, D. Davis, and F. Fiedrich, "The drive for holistic urban resilience" 9th Future Security, Security Research Conference, Berlin Sep. 16- 18, 2014.

[11] A Vailaya, M. A. Figueiredo, A. K. Jain, and H. J. Zhang, "Image classification for content-based indexing". Image Processing, IEEE Transactions on, 10(1), pp. 117-130, 2001.

[12] S. Das, L. Girard, T. Green, L. Weitzman, A. Lewis-Bowen, and T. Clark, "Building biomedical web communities using a semantically aware content management system". Briefings in bioinformatics, 10(2), pp. 129-138, 2009.

[13] M. Hausenblas, "Exploiting linked data to build web applications." IEEE Internet Computing 4, pp. 68-73, 2009.

[14] R. Real and J. M. Vargas, "The probabilistic basis of Jaccard's index of similarity." Systematic biology, pp. 380-385, 1996.

[15] N. W. Y Shao, S. J. H Yang, and A. Sue, "A content management system for adaptive learning environment." Multimedia Software Engineering, Proceedings. Fifth International Symposium on, IEEE, 2003.

[16] O. Erling and I. Mikhailov. "RDF Support in the Virtuoso DBMS", Networked Knowledge-Networked Media. Springer Berlin Heidelberg, pp. 7-24, 2009.

[17] The HARMONISE project (Available online at: http://harmonise.eu/) [accessed: 13.4.2016]

[18] Linked Data (Available online at: http://linkeddata.org/) [accessed: 13.4.2016]

[19] Drupal (Available online at: https://www.drupal.org/) [accessed: 13.4.2016]

[20] WordPress (Available online at: https://wordpress.org/) [accessed: 13.4.2016]

[21] ONKI - Finnish Ontology Library Service (Available online at: http://onki.fi/) [accessed: 13.4.2016]

[22] DBpedia (Available online at: http://dbpedia.org/) [accessed: 13.4.2016]

[23] OpenCalais (Available online at: http://www.opencalais.com/) [accessed: 13.4.2016]

[24] Solr (Available online at: http://lucene.apache.org/solr/) [accessed: 13.4.2016]

[25] Apache Lucene Core (Available online at: https://lucene.apache.org/core/) [accessed: 13.4.2016]

[26] Virtuoso Universal Server (Available online at: http://semanticweb.org/wiki/Virtuoso) [accessed: 13.4.2016]

TripleSent: a Triple Store of Events Associated with their Prototypical Sentiment

Veronique Hoste[1], Els Lefever[1], Stephan van der Waart van Gulik[2] and Bart Desmet[1]

[1]LT3 Language and Translation Technology Team
[2]Centre for Logic and Philosophy of Science
Ghent University, Belgium
email: firstname.lastname@ugent.be

***Abstract*—The current generation of sentiment analysis systems is limited in their real-world applicability because they cannot detect utterances that implicitly carry positive or negative sentiment. We present early stage research ideas to address this inability with the development of a dynamic triple store of events associated with their prototypical sentiment.**

Keywords—sentiment detection; triple store; implicit sentiment; natural language processing.

I. INTRODUCTION

In the last decades, state-of-the-art research in natural language processing (NLP) has made a shift from rule-based to statistical corpus-based approaches, which require high-quality electronic text corpora. Supervised and unsupervised statistical approaches to structure and interpret patterns in text and speech have been successfully developed on such corpora. Examples include part-of-speech taggers, parsers, named entity recognition, machine translation, speech recognition, text classification and summarization, sentiment analysis, etc. Some of these tasks can be performed with near-human accuracy (e.g., part-of-speech tagging), whereas for more complex tasks, such as sentiment analysis, performance is limited by the amount of available knowledge.

In sentiment analysis, the objective is to automatically determine the sentiment (positive, neutral or negative) expressed in an utterance, e.g., (a) *"I love to go shopping"*, (b) *"Coke tastes great"*, (c) *"I bought the mattress a week ago, and a valley has formed"*. Most state-of-the-art sentiment analysis systems combine a statistical approach with lists of subjective words (*"love"*, *"great"*), such as the MPQA (Multi-Perspective Question Answering) [1] lexicon. As a result, they are capable of detecting expressions of sentiment only if they can learn them from annotated corpora or sentiment lexicons. While current sentiment analyzers can deal with expressions that address sentiments explicitly, as in examples (a) and (b), they **struggle with sentiments that are only implicitly present in so-called polar facts**, as is the case in example (c) [2]. Current systems fail to detect polar facts, which implicitly carry positive or negative sentiment. This is problematic, because implicit sentiment has been shown to account for more than half of the sentiment in certain domains (e.g., product reviews, *"Web surfing drains the battery"*, or financial reporting, *"Fed lowers interest rates"*) [3]. Progress in the automatic detection of ironic utterances such as *"Going to the dentist tomorrow yippee"*, in which the expressed sentiment is not to be understood in its literal sense, also suffers from the lack of common sense knowledge [4][5].

As this severely limits the real-world applicability of the current generation of sentiment analyzers, we aim to investigate the feasibility of developing a dynamic triple store of events associated with their prototypical sentiment. Such common-sense knowledge could then complement other knowledge sources (e.g., sentiment lexicons) and other types of features derived from training data in a classification-based approach to sentiment analysis or irony detection.

Knowledge bases, such as WordNet, DBPedia, Freebase, OpenCyc, SUMO and Open Mind Common Sense, which store and structure lexical and factual knowledge in machine-readable formats, have been instrumental for the success of complex language understanding applications, such as the IBM Watson question answering system [6]. They are an essential resource for tasks that involve factual analysis, such as summarization, wikification, question answering and textual entailment. For sentiment analysis, however, there is an additional need for knowledge about the prototypical sentiments people hold towards entities and events. As "prototypical" sentiment, we consider sentiments that are commonly associated with a certain event, an event being the combination of a verb and a direct, indirect or prepositional object. Certain events may entail multiple prototypical sentiments, depending on perspective. As an example, the sentence *"Fed lowers interest rates"* will be considered prototypically positive for people who want to take out a loan, but it can also be considered negative in that it may cause inflation.

The remainder of this ideas paper is organized as follows. In Section 2, we propose the methodology we intend to use to build a knowledge base of events and their prototypical sentiment. In the last section, we present some prospects for future work beyond the construction of the knowledge base.

II. RESEARCH OBJECTIVES

We conceive TripleSent as consisting of two interacting layers: a **knowledge base** and a **reasoner**. The knowledge base contains events for which the prototypical sentiment is known with a high certainty. This information is stored in the form of sentiment triples. For example, the negative sentiment commonly associated with *"going to the dentist"* can be formally captured by the sentiment triple <visit-dentist, has-sentiment, negative> (note that there is some notational abuse here to facilitate the reader). The reasoner, on the other hand, is capable of inferring sentiment for events that are not stored in the database. When a user asks for the prototypical sentiment for "visit the oncologist", the reasoner combines information from factual knowledge bases like WordNet [7] (which knows that oncologists, like dentists, are a kind of doctor) with the sentiment information from the triple store, to (conditionally) infer the expected sentiment triple <visit-oncologist, has-sentiment, negative>. Some of the inferences can be truly 'conditional' because whenever new, more reliable information contradicting the inferred triple is added or generated, the reasoner will need to revoke the inference (and all other inferences that rely on it). Like human reasoning, this requires a non-monotonic logic approach (see Objective 2).

Objective 1: Event extraction and enrichment

To kick-start the knowledge base, events will be collected for which the sentiment is known. These events will be obtained by extracting patterns for highly explicit sentiment expressions (e.g., *"I hate"* or *"I love"*) or from large web data crawls (e.g., commoncrawl.org), which will subsequently be syntactically and semantically parsed to extract events and sentiment triples. In the same vein, we will investigate leveraging existing large parsed datasets to extract high-confidence sentiment triples with minimal human intervention, using pattern-based and supervised sentiment analysis techniques [8]. Events for which both polarities are found frequently in the data will initially not be considered for further processing and will be investigated in more detail to understand the nature of this ambiguity. Given the linguistic diversity with which events can be expressed, the usefulness of the resulting triple store will also heavily depend on the ability to automatically handle orthographic variation (as for example in *"pediatrician"*, *"paediatrician"* or *"pediatrist"*), and syntactic and semantic synonymous structures (e.g., *"visit"*, *"going to"*, *"seeing"*, etc. *"a pediatrician"*).

In order to allow for the creation of new sentiment triples, explicit sentiment triples present in the knowledge base will be linked to ontological information provided by lexical resources and factual knowledge bases such as WordNet and DBPedia, respectively.

Objective 2: Opinion inferencing

The reasoner can infer all kinds of new sentiment triples from already known triples using (decidable) fragments of first-order predicate logic. However, in order to enable TripleSent to also deal with the expected sentiment for events that are not yet stored in the database, the reasoner should allow dynamic, conditional inferences of unseen triples. For example, starting from the explicit sentiment triple <visit-oncologist, has-sentiment, negative>, the reasoner relies on WordNet information like <oncologist, is-a, medical specialist> to (provisionally) derive <visit-medical-specialist, has-sentiment, negative>, and, again by relying on WordNet information, to (provisionally) derive <visit-dentist, has-sentiment, negative> and <visit-podologist, has-sentiment, negative>. Note that the last sentiment attribution is debatable, and can be revoked in the (future) presence of other, more reliable triples (stating explicitly, for example, that prototypical visits to podologists are not negative). For the implementation of this type of reasoning, we will evaluate different non-monotonic logic approaches, such as default logic [9], adaptive logics [10] or answer set programming [11].

In order to evaluate the event extraction, event enrichment and opinion inferencing, we will manually annotate test corpora by relying both on expert annotators and crowdsourcing. For the evaluation of the event extraction, we will assess precision both for the event extraction and the sentiment attached to these events. In order to also enable the measuring of recall, we will furthermore rely on an existing corpus for irony detection annotated with event-sentiment annotations [12]. As in previous annotation efforts, it was shown that crowdsourcing is a reliable and very cost-effective means of collecting human knowledge, we will also investigate the use of a **crowdsourcing methodology to validate and enrich the output of the platform**. Inferred sentiment triples will be presented to a crowd of human annotators who indicate what they consider to be the prototypical sentiment for the given event. This could provide additional high-confidence triples to be stored, contradicting evidence to inform non-monotonic decisions (e.g., exceptions such as <visit-podologist, has-sentiment, neutral>), and grounding that can be used in a feedback loop to improve the inference engine.

III. CONCLUSION AND FUTURE WORK

To date, there is a complete lack of reusable and dynamically growing knowledge bases linking events to implicit sentiment, which can be used for research and development in opinion inferencing. The TripleSent platform including the knowledge base and the automatic reasoner will open new perspectives in NLP research and can push the state-of-the-art in semantic text processing and inferencing, and more specifically in NLP applications such as sentiment analysis and irony detection.

REFERENCES

[1] J. Wiebe, T. Wilson, and C. Cardie, "Annotating expressions of opinions and emotions in language", Language Resources and Evaluation, vol. 39, issue 2-3, 2005, pp. 165-210.

[2] B. Liu, "Sentiment Analysis and Opinion Mining", Morgan & Claypool Publishers, May 2012.

[3] M. Van de Kauter, B. Desmet, and V. Hoste, "The good, the bad and the implicit: a comprehensive approach to annotating explicit and implicit sentiment", Language Resources and Evaluation, Springer Netherlands, vol. 49, 2015, pp. 685-720.

[4] E. Riloff, et al., "Sarcasm as Contrast between a Positive Sentiment and Negative Situation", Proceedings of the 2013 Conference on Empirical Methods in Natural Language Processing (EMNLP 2013), 2013, pp. 704-714.

[5] C. Van Hee, E. Lefever, and V. Hoste, "LT3: Sentiment Analysis of Figurative Tweets: piece of cake #NotReally", Proceedings of the 9th International Workshop on Semantic Evaluation (SemEval 2015), 2015, pp. 684-688.

[6] D. Ferrucci, et al., "Building Watson: An overview of the DeepQA project", AI Magazine, vol. 31, no. 3, 2010, pp. 59-79.

[7] C. Fellbaum, "WordNet: An Electronic Lexical Database", Cambridge, MA: MIT Press, 1998.

[8] C. Van Hee, M. Van de Kauter, O. De Clercq, E. Lefever and V. Hoste, "LT3: Sentiment Classification in User-Generated Content Using a Rich Feature Set", Proceedings of the 8th International Workshop on Semantic Evaluation (SemEval 2014), 2014, pp. 406-410.

[9] R. Reiter, "A logic for default reasoning", Artificial Intelligence, vol. 13, no. 1, 1980, pp. 81-132.

[10] D. Batens, "A General Characterization of Adaptive Logics", Logique et Analyse, vol. 44, no. 173-175, 2003, pp. 45-68.

[11] M. Blondeel, S. Schockaert, D. Vermeir, and M. De Cock, "Fuzzy Answer Set Programming: An Introduction", Soft Computing: State of the Art Theory, vol. 291, 2013, pp. 209-222.

[12] C. Van Hee, E. Lefever, and V. Hoste, "Exploring the Realization of Irony in Twitter Data", Proceedings of the Tenth International Conference on Language Resources and Evaluation (LREC'16). European Language Resources Association (ELRA), accepted for publication.

[13] O. De Clercq, et al., "Using the Crowd for Readability Prediction". Natural Language Engineering, vol. 20, no. 3, 2014, pp. 293-235.

WordNet Exploration and Visualization in Neo4J - A Tag Cloud Based Approach

Enrico Giacinto Caldarola*†, Antonio Picariello*, Antonio M. Rinaldi*‡
*Department of Electrical Engineering and Information Technologies
University of Naples Federico II, Napoli, Italy
†Institute of Industrial Technologies and Automation
National Research Council, Bari, Italy
‡IKNOS-LAB Intelligent and Knowledge Systems
University of Naples Federico II, LUPT
Email: enricogiacinto.caldarola@unina.it, antonio.picariello@unina.it, antoniomaria.rinaldi@unina.it

***Abstract*—In the Big Data era, the visualization of large data sets is becoming an increasingly relevant task due to the great impact that data have from a human perspective. Since visualization is the closer phase to the users within the data life cycles phases, there is no doubt that an effective, efficient and impressive representation of the analyzed data may result as important as the analytic process itself. Starting from previous experiences in importing, querying and visualizing WordNet database within Neo4J and Cytoscape, this work aims at improving the WordNet Graph visualization by exploiting the features and concepts behind tag clouds. The objective of this study is twofold: first, we argue that the proposed visualization style is able to put order in the messy and dense structure of nodes and edges of WordNet, showing as much as possible information from the lexical database and in a clearer way; secondly, we think that the tag cloud approach applied to the synonyms rings reinforces the human cognition in recognizing the different usages of words in a language like English. The ultimate goal of this work is, on the one hand, to facilitate the comprehension of WordNet itself and, on the other hand, to investigate techniques and approaches to get more insights from the visual representation and analytics of large graph databases.**

***Keywords*–WordNet; Big Data; Data and Information Visualization; Neo4J; Graph Database; NoSQL.**

I. Introduction

A subtle difference exists between *data* and *information*. The first is raw, it simply exists and has no significance beyond its existence (in and of itself) [1]. Data are just numbers, bits of information, which '*...have no way of speaking for themselves. We speak for them. We imbue them with meaning.*' [2]. On the contrary, information is data that has been given meaning by way of relational connection, by providing context for them. Even more subtle is the distinction between *Data Visualization* and *Information Visualization*. If the main goal of the first one is to communicate information clearly and efficiently to users, involving the creation and study of the visual representation of data – i.e., "information that has been abstracted in some schematic form, including attributes or variables for the units of information" [3] – the main task of the second one is the study of (interactive) visual representations of abstract data to reinforce human cognition. The abstract data may include both numerical and non-numerical data, such as text and geographic information. Beyond Information Visualization, an other outgrowth field is *Visual Analytics* that can be defined as 'the science of analytical reasoning facilitated by interactive visual interfaces.' [4]. Today, in many spheres of human activity, massive sets of data are collected and stored. As the volumes of data available to various stakeholders such as business people or scientists increase, their effective use becomes more challenging. Keeping up to date with the flood of data, using standard tools for data management and analysis, is fraught with difficulty. The field of visual analytics seeks to provide people with better and more effective ways to understand and analyse these large datasets, while also enabling them to act upon their findings immediately, in real-time [5]. Thus, the challenges that the Big Data imperative [6][7] imposes to data management severely impact on data visualization. The "bigness" of large data sets and their complexity in term of heterogeneity contribute to complicate the representation of data, making the drawing algorithms quite complex. Just to make an example, let us consider the popular social network Facebook, in which the nodes represent people and the links represent interpersonal connections; we note that nodes may be accompanied by information such as age, gender, and identity, and links may also have different types, such as colleague relationships, classmate relationships, and family relationships. The effective representation of all the information at the same time is really challenging. The most common solution is to use visual cues, such as color, shape, or transparency to encode different attributes. In this regard, tag clouds are a popular method for representing variables of interest (such as popularity, frequency of occurrence of a term, and so on) in the visual appearance of the keywords themselves using text properties such as font size, weight, or color [8]. Since the study conducted in this paper consists in the visual representation of WordNet as a large graph in Neo4j [9] and Cytoscape [10], a particular attention is paid to *Graph Visualization*, referring to other well-known works in the literature for a complete review of the techniques and theories in Information Visualization [11][12].

Graphs are traditional and powerful tools for visually representing sets of data and the relations among them by drawing a dot or circle for every vertex, and an arc between two vertices if they are connected by an edge. If the graph is directed, the direction is indicated by drawing an arrow. The pioneering work of W. T. Tutte [13] was very influential in the subject of graph drawing, in particular he introduced the use of linear algebraic methods to obtain graph drawings. Basically, there are generally accepted aesthetic rules to draw a graph [14], which include: distribute nodes and edges evenly, avoid edge crossing, display isomorphic substructures in the same manner, minimize the bends along the edges. However, since it is quite impossible to meet all rules at the same time, some of them conflict with each other or they are very computationally expensive, practical graphical layouts are usually the results of compromise among the aesthetics. There exists different graph visualization layouts in literature, such as: the Tree Layout, the Space Division Layout, the Matrix Layout and the Spring Layout[15], to mention a few. The latter will be used in this work and it is worth to spending few words on it. Spring layout, also known as *Force-Directed* layout, is a popular strategy for general graph visualization. The strategy consists in modeling the graph as physical systems of rings or springs. The attractive idea about spring layout is that the physical analogy can be very naturally extended to include additional aesthetic information by adjusting the forces between nodes. As one of the first few practical algorithms for drawing general graphs, spring layout is proposed by Eades in 1984 [16]. Since then, his method is revisited and improved in different ways [17]. Mathematically, Spring layout is based on a cost (energy) function, which maps different layouts of the same graph to different non-negative numbers. Through approaching the minimum energy, the layout results reaches better and better aesthetically pleasing results. The main differences between different spring approaches are in the choice of energy functions and the methods for their minimization. Specifically concerning the visualization of WordNet, there are not many works in the literature. In [18], the authors make an attempt to visualize the WordNet structure from the vantage point of a particular word in the database, this in order to overcome the down-side of the large coverage of WordNet, i.e., the difficulty to get a good overview of particular parts of the lexical database. An attempt to apply design paradigms to generate visualizations which maximize the usability and utility of WordNet is made in [19], whereas, in [20] a radial, space-filling layout of hyponymy (IS-A relation) is presented with interactive techniques of zoom, filter, and details-on-demand for the task of document visualization, exploiting the WordNet lexical database. The visualization approach used in this work uses the Spring layout to draw the graph-based representation of WordNet in Cytoscape and a tag cloud-based strategy to represent the synonim rings from WordNet. Moreover, as a general rule the principled representation methodology we agree on is the *Visual Information Seeking Mantra* presented by Scheiderman in [21]. It can be summarized as follows: "overview first, zoom and filter, then details-on-demand".

The reminder of the paper is organized as follows. Section II describes the WordNet meta-model, while Section III, after a clarification of ground concepts related to WordNet landscape, describes how WordNet has been imported in Neo4J and its visualization in Cytoscape. Section IV goes to the hearth of this work *rationale* by illustrating the way a tags cloud approach is used to effectively draw the graph of WordNet synonyms rings in Cytoscape. Finally, Section V draws the conclusion summarizing the major findings and outlining future investigations.

II. WordNet Case Study

The case study presented in this paper consists in the *reification* of the WordNet database inside the Neo4J GraphDB. WordNet [22][23] is a large lexical database of English. Nouns, verbs, adjectives and adverbs are grouped into sets of cognitive synonyms (synsets), each expressing a distinct concept. Synsets are interlinked by means of conceptual-semantic and lexical relations. In this context, we have defined and implemented a meta-model for the WordNet reification using a conceptualization as much as possible close to the way in which the concepts are organized and expressed in human language [24]. We consider concepts and words as nodes in Neo4J, whereas semantic, linguistic and semantic-linguistic relations become Noeo4J links between nodes. For example, the hyponymy property can relate two concept nodes (nouns to nouns or verbs to verbs); on the other hand a semantic property links concept nodes to concepts and a syntactic one relates word nodes to word nodes. Concept and word nodes are considered with *DatatypeProperties*, which relate individuals with a predefined data type. Each word is related to the represented concept by the ObjectProperty *hasConcept* while a concept is related to words that represent it using the ObjectProperty *hasWord*. These are the only properties able to relate words with concepts and vice versa; all the other properties relate words to words and concepts to concepts. Concepts, words and properties are arranged in a class hierarchy, resulting from the syntactic category for concepts and words and from the semantic or lexical type for the properties. The subclasses have been derived from the related categories. There are some union classes useful to define properties domain and codomain. We define some attributes for Concept and Word respectively: Concept *hasName* that represents the concept name; *Description* that gives a short description of concept. On the other hand Word has Name as attribute that is the word name. All elements have an ID within the WordNet offset number or a user defined ID. The semantic and lexical properties are arranged in a hierarchy. in Table I some of the considered properties and their domain and range of definition are shown.

TABLE I. PROPERTIES

Property	Domain	Range
hasWord	Concept	Word
hasConcept	Word	Concept
hypernym	NounsAnd VerbsConcept	NounsAnd VerbsConcept
holonym	NounConcept	NounConcept
entailment	VerbWord	VerbWord
similar	AdjectiveConcept	AdjectiveConcept

The use of domain and codomain reduces the property range application. For example, the hyponymy property is defined on the sets of nouns and verbs; if it is applied on the set of nouns, it has the set of nouns as range, otherwise, if it is applied to the set of verbs, it has the set of verbs as range. in Table II there are some of defined constraints and we specify on which classes they have been applied w.r.t. the considered properties; the table shows the matching range too.

Sometimes the existence of a property between two or more individuals entails the existence of other properties. For example, being the concept dog a hyponym of animal, we can assert that animal is a hypernymy of dog. We represent this characteristics in OWL, by means of property features shown in Table III.

TABLE II. MODEL CONSTRAINTS

Costraint	Class	Property	Constraint range
AllValuesFrom	NounConcept	hyponym	NounConcept
AllValuesFrom	AdjectiveConcept	attribute	NounConcept
AllValuesFrom	NounWord	synonym	NounWord
AllValuesFrom	AdverbWord	synonym	AdverbWord
AllValuesFrom	VerbWord	also_see	VerbWord

TABLE III. PROPERTY FEATURES

Property	Features
hasWord	*inverse* of hasConcept
hasConcept	*inverse* of hasWord
hyponym	*inverse* of hypernym; *transitivity*
hypernym	*inverse* of hyponym; *transitivity*
cause	*transitivity*
verbGroup	*symmetry* and *transitivity*

III. Importing WordNet in Neo4J and Visualizing It in Cytoscape

The WordNet lexical database has been imported in Neo4J [25] and afterward visualized in Cytoscape according to a procedure similar to that described in a previous work by the authors [26]. In a nutshell, the procedure consists in accessing the WordNet files through the JWI (Java Wordnet Interface) APIs [27][28], collecting all the information about *synsets*, *words* and *word senses* in four different csv files, and finally, loading all the csv lines in Neo4J through the Neo4J *LOAD CSV* macro. Compared to the previous one, this work focuses on the visualization of WordNet and the most expensive part of the work has consisted in defining a Cytoscape custom style to represent the *synonyms rings* as tag clouds in an effective and clear way. This surely represents the novelty of this approach. We preferred to load WordNet objects from JWI APIs and serialize them in custom csv files, which were then imported throughout Cypher macros, instead of using already existing WordNet RDF serialization [29], because, this way, we could add some useful information in the csv lines like the *word frequency*, the *polysemy*, and so forth, for the sake of the successive representation in Cytoscape. And that is also why we prefer to create a custom tool to import the WordNet database in Neo4J instead of using already existing tools. Before diving into the procedure details, it is worth to clarify the distinction and provide some useful definitions coming from JWI APIS about *synsets*, *synsets (or synonyms) rings*, *index words* and *word senses*. Figure 1 try to put light on this. As discussed in the previous section, a synset is a concept, i.e., an entity of the real world (both physical or abstract) meaning something whose meaning can be argued by reading the *gloss* definition provided by WordNet. Its meaning can be also understood by analysing the semantic relations linking it to other synsets or by the synset (or synonyms) ring. This one is a set of words (hereafter mentioned as index words) generally used in a specific language (such as English) to refer to that concept. The term synset itself is used to refer to set of synonyms meaning a specific concept. On the contrary, an index word is just a term, i.e., a *sign* without meaning; so that, only when we link it to a specific concept we obtain a word sense, i.e., a word provided with a meaning. An index word has got different meanings according to the context in which it is used and because of a general characteristic of languages: the *polysemy*. For example, the term *home* has nine different meanings if it is used as noun, and so, it belongs to nine different synsets. In fact, the WordNet answer when we search for *home* is the following:

1. (430) home, place — (where you live at a particular time; "deliver the package to my home"; "he doesn't have a home to go to"; "your place or mine?")
2. (350) dwelling, home, domicile, abode, habitation, dwelling house — (housing that someone is living in; "he built a modest dwelling near the pond"; "they raise money to provide homes for the homeless")
3. (116) home — (the country or state or city where you live; "Canadian tariffs enabled United States lumber companies to raise prices at home"; "his home is New Jersey")
4. (43) home — (an environment offering affection and security; "home is where the heart is"; "he grew up in a good Christian home"; "there's no place like home")
5. (38) home, nursing home, rest home — (an institution where people are cared for; "a home for the elderly")
6. (36) base, home — (the place where you are stationed and from which missions start and end)
7. (7) family, household, house, home, menage — (a social unit living together; "he moved his family to Virginia"; "It was a good Christian household"; "I waited until the whole house was asleep"; "the teacher asked how many people made up his home")
8. (7) home plate, home base, home, plate — ((baseball) base consisting of a rubber slab where the batter stands; it must be touched by a base runner in order to score; "he ruled that the runner failed to touch home")
9. (3) home — (place where something began and flourished; "the United States is the home of basketball")

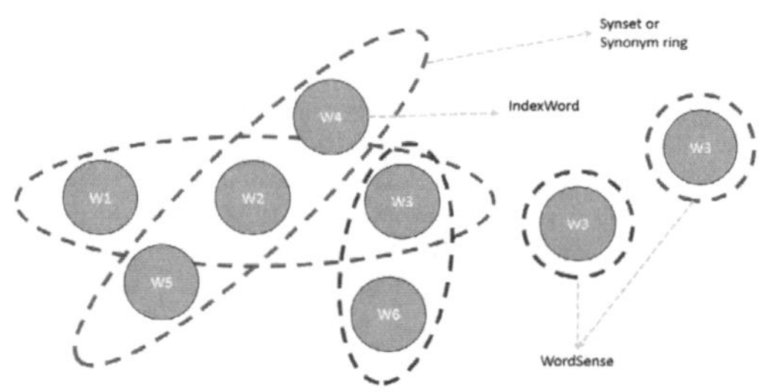

Figure 1. WordNet synsets, index words and word senses.

In addition to synsets glosses, WordNet gives us some useful statistic information about the usage of the term *home* in each synset. The position of the term in each synonyms ring tell us how usual is the use of the term to signify that concept. The position of the term in each synset is a measure of the usage frequency of the term for each concept: higher the position, higher the frequency. Moreover, by counting the number of synsets which a term belongs to, it is possible to obtain its polysemy (e.g., the number of possible meanings of *home*). JWI is able to tell us all this information about synset and word senses. In particular, for each synset we have collected the following fields in the csv files:

1) *Id*: the univoque indentifier for the synset;
2) *SID*: the Synset ID as reported in the WordNet database;
3) *POS*: the synset's part of speech (POS);
4) *Gloss*: the synset's gloss which express its meaning;
5) *Level*: the hieararchical level of synset in the whole WordNet hierarchy.

For word senses we have collected the following fields:

1) *Id*: the univoque indentifier for the word sense;
2) *POS*: the word's part of speech (POS);
3) *polysemy*: the word polysemy;
4) *frequency*: the word frequency of the word sense as previously explicated.

A third csv file stores the semantic links existing between synset by reporting the IDs of the source and target synset and the type of semantic link existing between them, such as hypernym, hyponym, meronym, etc.

In addition to the previous files, a final file lists the links between each word sense and each synset. This file is very simple, it just contains a line for each pair (Word Sense, Synset) in WordNet. Other minor and not significant fields have been added for the sake of the visualization in Cytoscape, such as *label* (a human readable label for the nodes) and *dimension* (used to suggest a plausible diameter for the Synset node representation according to its depth in the WordNet hierarchy). The code to convert WordNet synsets into csv tables is available at https://github.com/eureko/WordNetToCSVFiles/.

In order to import all the information contained in the csv files and translate them into a graph data structure inside Neo4J [9], the meta-model described in Section II has been used. Each synset and word sense have been converted into a node of the graph with label respectively: *Synset* and *WordSense*. Each semantic relation has become an edge between two synset nodes with the *type* property expressing the specific semantic relation holding between the concepts. Finally, the word sense nodes have been connected to their related concepts nodes through a specific relation. This allows to effectively represent synonyms ring through the Neo4J web visualizer. For example, Figure 2 shows the results of the following Cypher query:

```
match (a: WordSense {POS: 'NOUN'})-[r]->(c: Synset)
        where (c)<-[]-(: WordSense {label: 'home'})
                return a,r,c
```

The figure reports nine synset rings for the term *home*. The filled circles represents the synset and contain the synset gloss definition, while the white circles around contain the word terms used to signify such synset.

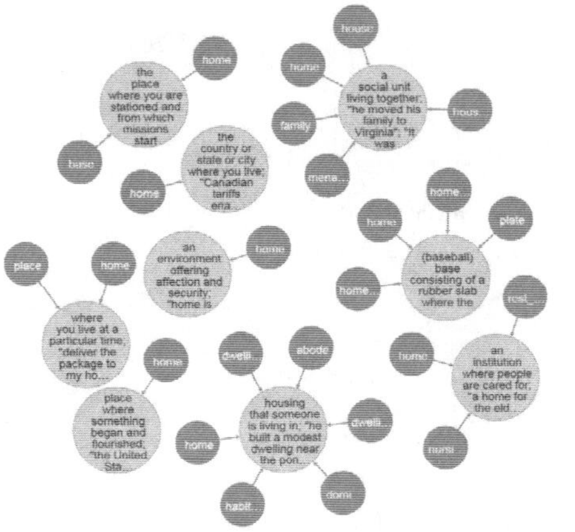

Figure 2. WordNet synset rings containing the 'home' word

IV. THE TAG CLOUD-BASED REPRESENTATION OF WORNET SYNONYMS RINGS

The work described in this paper has encountered challenges that are quite close to the typical Big Data scenario. In fact, this version of WordNet graph (v. 2.1) includes 117597 synsets rings containing 207106 word senses conveyed by 155327 index words, 283837 semantic relations (cfr., Section II) linking synsets each other and 207016 semantic-lexical links between index words and synsets. With these big numbers,

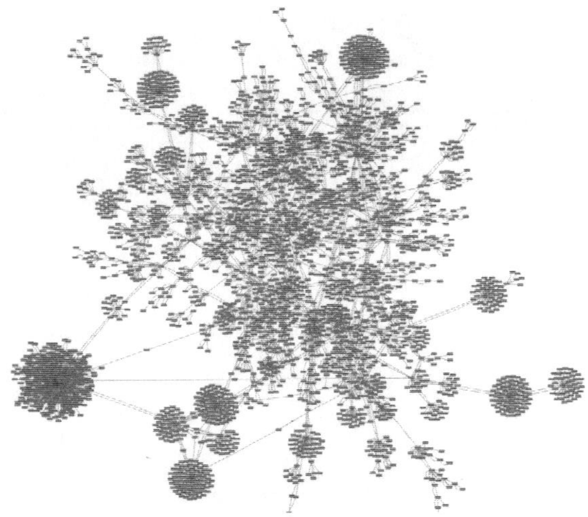

Figure 3. Large scale representation of 5000 relations and 3404 synsets in WordNet

the manipulation, the querying and the visualization of the graph become quite challenging. The visualization of the entire structure of WordNet in terms of all synsets, words, semantic and lexical relations in a way that is elegant and intelligible at the same time, is a *chimera*, due to the performance issues of the visualization tools, in particular when sophisticated drawing algorithms are used, and to the strongly connected nature of information to be represented, which often results in a messy and dense structure of nodes and edges. Just to have an idea, Figure 3 shows a representation of an excerpt of WordNet (5000 semantic relations over 3404 synsets) obtained from *Cytoscape* v.3 graph visualization tool. The Neo4j running instance has been accessed via a specific plug-in, namely cyNeo4j, that converts the query results into Cytoscape table format and then create a view according to a custom style and a selected layout like the *Force-directed graph drawing algorithm* before mentioned. The resulting figure is more considerable for global analysis, or for its look and feel, than for actual information that you can retrieve from it. Nevertheless, thanks to the force-directed algorithm, it is possible to observe agglomerates of nodes and edges which correspond to specific semantic categories and can help users in zooming the desired semantic area.

Thus, it is necessary to simplify the representation of the network by following some functional and esthetic criteria. In this regard, we have selected some simple representation criteria, listed as follows:

1) the efficiency of the visualization, i.e., avoid the information redundancy and the proliferation of useless signs and graphics as much as possible;
2) the effectiveness of the visualization, i.e., grant that the graphical representation of the network covers the whole informative content of the WordNet graph-based implementation;
3) the clearness of visualization, i.e., use light colors, such as gray, light blue, dark green, etc. with a proper level of brightness and with an appreciable contrast.

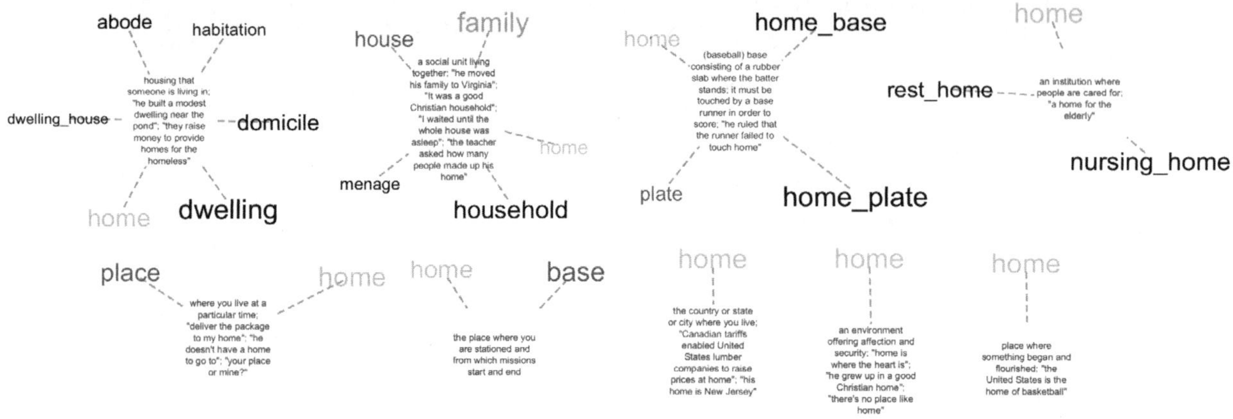

Figure 4. WordNet synset rings containing the 'home' word with the customized style in Cytoscape

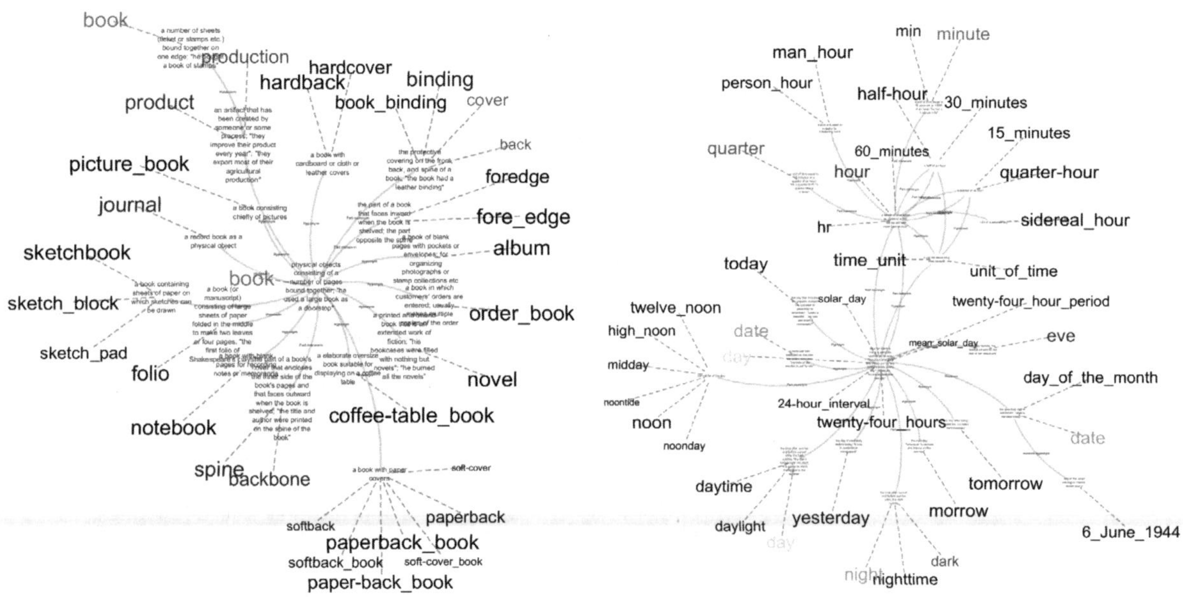

(a) Something about *book*.

(b) Something about *time*.

Figure 5. WordNet excerpts in Cytoscape with custom style.

Furthermore, the adoption of tag cloud based representation for the synonyms rings brought us to use the statistical linguistics measures of *polisemy* and *frequency* of a term as visual cues in drawing the word signs attached to a certain synset. Technically, higher the frequency of the word sense, larger is the font used to represent such word in the corresponding synonym ring, as well as, higher is the polysemy of a word in the whole WordNet, lighter is the shade of gray used to tag such word. All the word senses are connected to the corresponding synset through a blank gray line and each synset is represented through a short text containing its gloss. Semantic relations between synsets are represented through a transparent green arc showing a label that report the type of the semantic link (e.g., hypernym, hyponim, meronym, etc.). Figure 4 shows the application of the style rules described above to the same cypher query from *home* mentioned in the previous section. For each sense of the term *home*, the figure shows the tag cloud based representation. Some considerations arise from the figure above. The lighter gray used for the term 'home' is due to its high polysemy (9). This color is intentionally weak to demonstrate how vague is the term alone without a context making it meaningful. Things get worse, for example, with terms like *head* or *line* with a polysemy equal to 33 and 29 respectively. On the contrary, the term *home_plate* is large in size and as a strong gray shade because of its low polysemy (1) and high frequency when used in the context of baseball.

Figures 5(a) and 5(b) show more representations of WordNet excerpts to fully demonstrating the customized style resulting from this work. The figure are obtained through the following Cypher query where 'keyword' is substituted with *book* and *time*:

```
MATCH (a: WordSense {label: '<keyword>'})-[r]->
        (b: Synset)-[t: semantic_property]->
                (f: Synset)<-[s]-(c: WordSense)
        return a,r,b,t,f,s,c
```

The figures above also highlights the semantic relations existing between synsets showing a more complete representation of WordNet with the new visualization style described in this work.

V. Conclusion and Future Work

Starting from previous experiences in importing, querying and visualizing WordNet in Neo4J and Cytoscape, a tag cloud based approach has been proposed in this paper as a new solution to make more effective and intelligible the representation of the WordNet graph. The results shown in this work are twofold: first, the new visualization style is able to put order in the messy and dense structure of nodes and edges of WordNet, showing as much as possible information from the lexical database and in a clearer way; secondly, the tag cloud approach is able to reinforce the human cognition in recognizing the different usages of words in English, w.r.t. the concepts they are related to. In fact, the proposed solution not only shows the synsets and the semantic relations holding between them, but also gives clues about the frequency of use of the synonyms for each synset. Future investigation may surely go in the direction of improving the criteria to simplify the WordNet representation with an evaluation for the visualization methods also validated by usability tests in which the user can express a consensus whether the representation is friendly or not, and the information inside WordNet is easily accessible or not. Finally, according to other studies, which aim at improving the tag cloud with semantics [30] and adding multimedia information to the knowledge representation model [31], we will investigate on the use of semantic properties and more efficient metrics to measure the relatedness among WordNet terms, also applying other visual features to combine these information and improve the quality of WordNet visualization.

References

[1] G. Bellinger, D. Castro, and A. Mills, "Data, information, knowledge, and wisdom," 2004.

[2] N. Silver, The signal and the noise: Why so many predictions fail-but some don't. Penguin, 2012.

[3] M. Friendly, "Milestones in the history of data visualization: A case study in statistical historiography," in Classificationthe Ubiquitous Challenge. Springer, 2005, pp. 34–52.

[4] J. J. Thomas and K. A. Cook, Illuminating the Path: The R&D Agenda for Visual Analytics National Visualization and Analytics Center. National Visualization and Analytics Center - U.S. Department of Homeland Security, 2005.

[5] D. A. Keim, J. Kohlhammer, G. Ellis, and F. Mansmann, Mastering the information age-solving problems with visual analytics. Florian Mansmann, 2010.

[6] E. G. Caldarola, A. Picariello, and D. Castelluccia, "Modern enterprises in the bubble: Why big data matters," ACM SIGSOFT Software Engineering Notes, vol. 40, no. 1, 2015, pp. 1–4.

[7] E. G. Caldarola, M. Sacco, and W. Terkaj, "Big data: The current wave front of the tsunami," ACS Applied Computer Science, vol. 10, no. 4, 2014, pp. 7–18.

[8] S. Bateman, C. Gutwin, and M. Nacenta, "Seeing things in the clouds: the effect of visual features on tag cloud selections," in Proceedings of the nineteenth ACM conference on Hypertext and hypermedia. ACM, 2008, pp. 193–202.

[9] Neo Technology Inc. Neo4j: The world's leading graph database. [Online]. Available: http://neo4j.com (2016)

[10] M. E. Smoot, K. Ono, J. Ruscheinski, P.-L. Wang, and T. Ideker, "Cytoscape 2.8: new features for data integration and network visualization," Bioinformatics, vol. 27, no. 3, 2011, pp. 431–432.

[11] R. Spence, Information visualization. Springer, 2001, vol. 1.

[12] R. Mazza, Introduction to information visualization. Springer Science & Business Media, 2009.

[13] W. T. Tutte, "How to draw a graph," Proc. London Math. Soc, vol. 13, no. 3, 1963, pp. 743–768.

[14] H. Purchase, "Which aesthetic has the greatest effect on human understanding?" in Graph Drawing. Springer, 1997, pp. 248–261.

[15] T. M. Fruchterman and E. M. Reingold, "Graph drawing by force-directed placement," Softw., Pract. Exper., vol. 21, no. 11, 1991, pp. 1129–1164.

[16] P. Eades, "A heuristics for graph drawing," Congressus numerantium, vol. 42, 1984, pp. 146–160.

[17] E. R. Gansner and S. C. North, "Improved force-directed layouts," in Graph Drawing. Springer, 1998, pp. 364–373.

[18] J. Kamps and M. Marx, "Visualizing wordnet structure," Proc. of the 1st International Conference on Global WordNet, 2002, pp. 182–186.

[19] C. Collins, "Wordnet explorer: applying visualization principles to lexical semantics," Computational Linguistics Group, Department of Computer Science, University of Toronto, Toronto, Ontario, Canada, 2006.

[20] ——, "Docuburst: Radial space-filling visualization of document content," Knowledge Media Design Institute, University of Toronto, Technical Report KMDI-TR-2007-1, 2007.

[21] B. B. Bederson and B. Shneiderman, The craft of information visualization: readings and reflections. Morgan Kaufmann, 2003.

[22] C. Fellbaum, "Wordnet," The Encyclopedia of Applied Linguistics, 1998.

[23] G. A. Miller, "Wordnet: a lexical database for english," Communications of the ACM, vol. 38, no. 11, 1995, pp. 39–41.

[24] A. M. Rinaldi, "A content-based approach for document representation and retrieval," in Proceedings of the eighth ACM symposium on Document engineering. ACM, 2008, pp. 106–109.

[25] J. Webber, "A programmatic introduction to neo4j," in Proceedings of the 3rd annual conference on Systems, Programming, and Applications: Software for Humanity. ACM, 2012, pp. 217–218.

[26] E. Caldarola, A. Picariello, and A. M. Rinaldi, "Big graph-based data visualization experiences - the wordnet case study," in Proceedings of the 7th International Joint Conference on Knowledge Discovery, Knowledge Engineering and Knowledge Management, 2015, pp. 104–115.

[27] M. A. Finlayson, MIT Java Wordnet Interface (JWI) User's Guide, Version 2.2.x, 2013.

[28] ——, "Java libraries for accessing the princeton wordnet: Comparison and evaluation," in Proceedings of the 7th Global Wordnet Conference, Tartu, Estonia, 2014.

[29] Wordnet RDF. [Online]. Available: http://wordnet-rdf.princeton.edu/ (2016)

[30] A. M. Rinaldi, "Improving tag clouds with ontologies and semantics," in IEEE International Workshop on Text-Based Information Retrieval (TIR'12) in conjunction with DEXA12. IEEE, 2012.

[31] ——, "A multimedia ontology model based on linguistic properties and audio-visual features," Information Sciences, vol. 277, 2014, pp. 234–246.

Evolutionary Social Knowledge Graphs for Individual and Organizational Learning

Christoph Greven, Hendrik Thüs, Mohamed Amine Chatti, Ulrik Schroeder
Learning Technologies Research Group
RWTH Aachen University
Aachen, Germany
email: {greven, thues, chatti, schroeder}@cs.rwth-aachen.de

Abstract—**Knowledge has been identified as one of the most important resources that grants organizations certain competitive advantages. Hence, while dealing with problems like the demographic change, organizations are trying to preserve the knowledge of their members. Its informal and network character, as well as its little half-life demand high standards to record, store and maintain the knowledge which needs to be consider for the development of an appropriate knowledge tool. This paper presents a novel knowledge management system which addresses the scattered, distributed, flexible and interrelated nature of knowledge. It therefore brings different important aspects together and utilizes the personal knowledge management of individuals in working processes together with social collaboration methods for a global organizational learning process. The three reflection layers promote a continuous feedback loop resulting in high quality knowledge maturing. The paper mainly concentrates on the essential underlying architecture and knowledge structure that only makes the learning process possible.**

Keywords-Knowledge Management System; Informal Knowledge; Network Knowledge; Knowledge Graph; Knowledge Evolution; Organizational Learning; Reflection.

I. INTRODUCTION

Since time immemorial, society tries to impart new knowledge to their posterity and therefore finds appropriate ways to capture it. As, over time, the kind and form of knowledge changed, the methods and techniques to store it changed accordingly. Knowledge itself is a controversial topic and scientists have many different ideas and views on it. But when it comes to a concrete software tool to deal with it, knowledge needs to be stored somehow. That is where traditional knowledge management systems fail because they are not able to map the complex characteristics that knowledge nowadays has. They are not considering the multimodality, flexibility, interrelation, and short life. As a consequence, a lot of potential remains unused or even gets lost.

The lost capacities are also sensed by the economy. While resource management in general has always been an important issue for the efficiency, companies start to realize that, beside traditional sources like money or workforce, expertise or knowledge is a new resource and good that drastically impacts their competitiveness. Having employees with a lot of expertise means an enormous advantage on the market. Hence, it is not astonishing that companies start to manage their knowledge like all other resources to keep, maintain, and expand their knowledge.

There is a common consensus on the significance of knowledge for economic success. However, its extraction and collection is not as easy. Organizations as well as society have to face different recent problems: the running demographic change, an enormous information overflow, overspecialization in special fields instead of heaving general problem-solving competency, the high percentage of tacit knowledge which is not tangible from outside, little exchange of experience which is often related to missing communication possibilities, a lack of knowledge application after trainings or workshops, no feedback for the authors from the real practitioners, little reusability of knowledge due to the rigid old structures, very slow publication procedures of new knowledge, for example owed to only annually meeting committees, or very specialized and often mobile workplaces that require considerably different demands.

Regarding the learning or knowledge management process, there are different challenging phases. First, the knowledge is in the employees' minds. The largest share is not factual but tacit knowledge. Thus, it is difficult to make this knowledge explicit and verbalize or formalize it. Second, employees that have certain competency do not communicate and share it. The most valuable knowledge is useless if anyone can access it. Last, the knowledge needs to be kept up to date and be adapted regarding the latest changes. A quality assurance of the individual knowledge is mandatory to eliminate errors and misconceptions.

All the present problems can be addressed by aspects of knowledge management systems. Therefore, this paper presents a novel learning management system that owns the potential to help out of misery. Thereby it presents the overall process of knowledge management but clearly focusses on the underlying unique architecture and structure which makes this kind of interactions possible.

The remainder of this paper is structured as follows: Section 2 gives a brief overview about recent knowledge management approaches. Section 3 introduces and explains the knowledge management process and hence the individual as well as organizational learning. The concrete underlying structure which defines how knowledge is finally represented and treated is depicted in Section 4. As this is the major part of this paper, different aspects like knowledge entities, relational behavior, versioning or access management are described in more detail. Section 5 gives some information regarding evaluation efforts. Finally, Section 6 concludes the approach so far and gives an outlook of future procedures and possible extensions.

II. Knowledge and Learning

Organizations had high hopes in knowledge management when it came up in the 90s. The topic knowledge management has been discussed a lot in literature and there are various different opinions on it. Earlier discussions are about whether to understand knowledge as a thing [1][2][3] that can be stored like in simple information management. Others see it as a standardized process that learners always pass through but which is not really flexible. One example is the well-known SECI model [4] which seems to be flexible at a first glance but which is not indeed. More recent approaches are concentrating on the knowledge worker himself and realize knowledge as well as learning as highly personal. Personal knowledge management puts the learner and his tacit, implicit knowledge in focus [5][6][7]. In contrast to earlier understanding of knowledge management, this is steered by the user and hence following a bottom-up instead of a traditional top-down approach. Still, the nature of today's knowledge cannot be mapped.

Today, organizational structures like companies invest enormous amounts of money in education and training. Still, those efforts cannot prevent regular incidents with e.g. breakdowns appearing in the public media every now and then. Many of those effects are owed to omissions of knowledge management and a corresponding quality assurance. Especially traditional organizations are only slowly adapting their management strategies and often count on outdated approaches such as simple learning content or asset management systems. Although, such systems got more interactive with the new possibilities of the Web 2.0 focusing on the worker a lot more, platforms like wikis are still struggling in the professional working environments. They cause additional expenses and the active involvement of people is hard. Personal learning environments try to address the individuality of the learners and their tacit knowledge, but in most cases they are only a set of enforced tools that do not fit in naturally. Further aspects like workplace mobility make knowledge management even more difficult while the new powerful mobile devices offer a lot of still unused potential. Systems for mobile distribution of digital documents [8] or question and answering systems [9] show that companies are trying to find a way out, but that the overall transfer and integration of new approaches is rather slow. And nevertheless, not all current problems like the short half-life, dispersion and fragmentation or interrelation of knowledge are addressed.

The approach presented in this paper is based on the Learning as a Network theory [10] which unites the concepts of network learning, complexity theory, and double loop learning. It regards learning and working as one thing and addresses the challenges described.

III. Evolutionary Knowledge Progession

The idea behind the whole concept is a 3-layered knowledge reflection process which promotes personal learning, naturally leading to organization learning as well. As depicted in Figure 1, the process concentrates on the single knowledge worker and his knowledge. As a certain knowledge maturity or quality has been reached in one phase, it can be raised to the next level. At the same time, experiences on higher levels always reproduce a knowledge flow backwards.

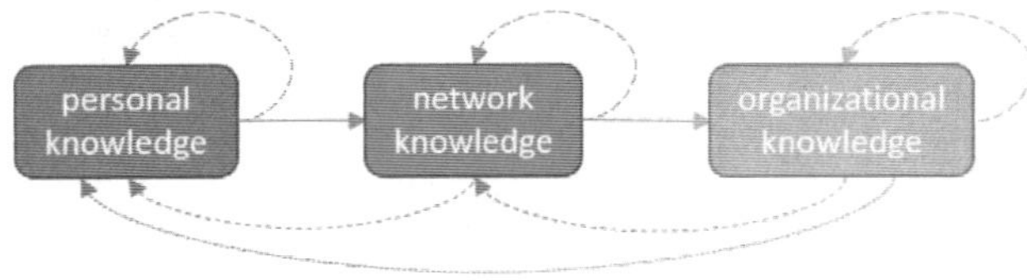

Figure 1. Three-layered knowledge reflection loop.

The first phase starts with the personal knowledge management and learning process of each individual. The individual refers to official material like instruction rules, documentations, guidelines, or trainings in his everyday working process. While using it in his every day work, he gains experience and has the possibility to create his very own multimedia notes and aids. With the help of his newly gained knowledge, he can solve similar problem situations in future. By and by, he changes, enhances and corrects his thoughts in this feedback loop which results in high quality working aids. At any time, the individual can decide to exchange his knowledge with a selected group of peers allowing them to participate in his experience.

In the second phase, knowledge is communicated amongst the personal knowledge networks of the individuals. Discussions come about and argue on certain approaches, understanding or best practices that have been experienced by the individuals. Besides the open dialog, users also have the possibility to rate all kinds of material available, from official guidelines to answers to comments. The new insights gained from the discourse influence the knowledge in the network as well as the personal opinions so that parts are revised resulting in a higher quality.

In the third and last phase, the created knowledge should flow back to the original authors so that it can be didactically reworked and integrated in the official organizational knowledge. As new versions, it can be published for all the workforce again where it represents the basis for future working processes. The overall continuous feedback loop starts again. Intelligent methods help editors to find and discover problem areas or highly valuable knowledge in the system.

In principle, the presented process is generic and can be applied in various kinds of scenarios. The related project – Professional Reflective Mobile Personal Learning Environments (PRiME) – in which this model has been developed, concentrates on mobile field services that profit the most [11]. An according architecture of mainly mobile clients of visualizers and manipulators communicate with a central knowledge repository through service interfaces. The mobile application ecology thereby supports the personalization of each individual and can be flexibly adapted to the current needs of the worker [12][13]. The presented process appears to be unspectacular, but to really establish such a continuous feedback loop, many different aspects need to be considered. The next section explains the underlying complex knowledge structure step by step, for without no system would have been possible.

IV. REALIZATION

This section gives more details on the concrete realization and implementation which is the foundation for the before mentioned knowledge process. Therefore, the different knowledge entities are explained, relationships are introduced, the versioning is described, annotations and ratings are pointed out, and finally the authorization system is explained. The paper does not restrict to a fixed technological implementation as a selection of such heavily depends on the application scenario and environment.

A. *Entities*

In whichever way knowledge is generated or understood, when it comes to a concrete implementation it has to be stored in a data base somehow. The system supports the separation of concerns and concentrates on the content and its structure and not on its visual representation. The own knowledge structure is format-less and does not contain general style information. Figure 2 shows a very simplified class diagram of the elements and relations that are introduced in the following sections. There are two major entities which represent different aspects of the knowledge.

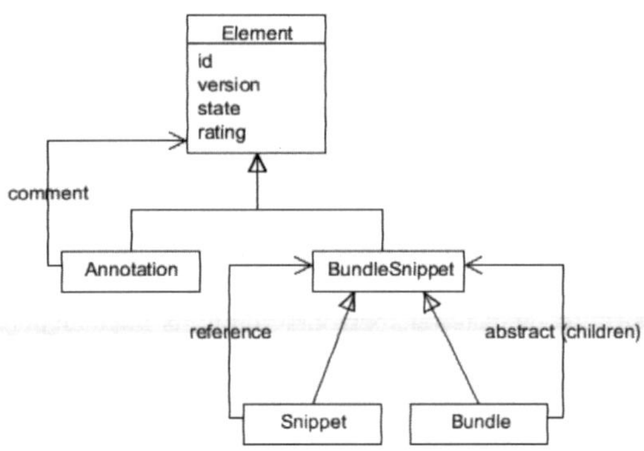

Figure 2. Simplified CD of knowledge structure.

1) Snippets

Snippets are multimedia-based atomic units of knowledge. A single snippet might cover a paragraph, an image, a short video, an engineering detail drawing, a 3D-model, and so forth. It is self-contained and from a semantic point of view it would not make sense to split it up any further. Snippets are reduced to content and do not address possible visual presentation. Hence, they abdicate the most formatting and style information and are restricted to those that contribute to the actual content. That are, e.g., structural information like listings or tables or style information like bold or underline. Beside the content, snippets hold further meta information like an abstracting title, information about the author, etc. Summarizing, they represent a smallest semantic unit of concrete, directly applicable content.

2) Bundles

Bundles are logical, semantic units that are thought to group an order of knowledge entities such as snippets, or bundles themselves. That means it is a recursive data structure which allows to set up several layers of bundles and snippets. It can be understood as a tree where the inner nodes are bundles and the leaves are snippets whereas leaves are allowed on every level. Bundles do not contain content themselves but such as snippets they hold some additional meta information, e.g., a title. They can be compared to chapters or sections in a book, where text (snippets) may be placed on each level as, e.g., an introduction of the section, or inside a section. Bundles are logical groupings of content and form an enclosed object themselves regardless of the surrounding content and where they are to be found. Summarizing one could say that bundles mainly realize a named list of references to sub-elements.

B. *Relations*

The previous sections introduced snippets as content holders and bundles as semantic structures. Without any relational associations they were lose, incoherent pieces without any use. And as already mentioned, the most important aspect of today's knowledge is still missing: interrelations. That is why the system offers different kinds of relationships between elements that all have a special semantic. Simplified, one can first think of bidirectional associations (see next section for more details). The first and most important relation has been implied before already. It is the parent-child relation of bundles (parent) and bundles or snippets (children). The recursive component allows a hierarchical representation of knowledge in a tree-like structure. Through the relation, bundles are able to somehow abstract and aggregate their subtree and make it usable as a whole. Official documents or training exercises are arranged the same way: there is a general topic which is split up in subtopics, and so forth. Although traditional documents have a tree structure (also see Section 4.H), once they are in the system they (or parts of them) can be reused in different contexts. That means they can be embedded via the parent-child relation in other bundles resulting in potentially more than one parent for each bundle and hence many simultaneous interwoven trees.

Oftentimes, knowledge refers to some other knowledge. As an example, specifications often contain phrases like "see chapter x" or "as in figure y". There is a corresponding relation – namely references – which allows snippets to cross-ling additional elements which do not even need to be in the same tree. As a result, the trees-structure becomes a real graph. Additionally, there are further relations which are of minor importance. For example, there is a "based on" association telling that this element or its version is based on content in some other snippet, bundle or comment (see Section 4.B for more details). In particular, this can be used to "thank" a user for his contribution.

C. *Versioning and States*

For a knowledge management system that also offers official material like documentations, instruction rules, guidelines, etc. it is important to keep track of the changes that have been done in the system. That is, e.g., related to the responsibility of the authors. Hence, a complex versioning system has been created which covers the system's entities and their relations.

Elements, i.e., bundles and snippets, are uniquely defined by their id and their version number. Newly created elements get a novel id and start with version 0. As soon as new versions are created, new physical elements are injected, having the same id but an increased version number. This way, the history of one single element can be traced by showing all elements with the same id and all the different versions. Essentially, a new snippet version means a changed content (or meta information like its title). It is to be created when the knowledge atom needs to be updated, changed or enhanced. In contrast, a new bundle version means a changed structure (or its meta information). As a bundle only defines its children and hence the subtree in the hierarchy, adapting it means adding, ordering, or even removing a child element.

The whole knowledge structure is based on the directive that the newest version of an element is understood to always be the best version of it. At least in relation to the current state of knowledge in the system. That has big implications on the whole process and structure. As stated before, knowledge is not represented redundantly. There are no copies of elements but multiple usage of an element is realized by multiple relations to one single element. Considering the "the newer the better" rule it would be comfortable if relations always addressed the newest versions of elements as all previous versions are thought to describe the same issue but in a less optimal way. That is how the system has been implemented. This implies, that as soon as an element is changed into a new version, all other elements which have relations to the changed element are now directly referring to the new version. As an example, one can think of an exploded view of a machinery which is used in a book's chapter and in a workshop presentation. In case the image needs to be corrected, the new version is immediately included in the book and presentation as well. The versioning together with the referencing keeps the knowledge structure very flexible and adaptable.

The authoring process of creating new versions commonly includes a phase, where elements are under construction but not yet finished to be accessible for everyone. That is not covert in the system so far. To satisfy this requirement, elements are extended via states. The idea behind states is to describe in which maturity phase an element is. When a new version is created due to changes of the current element, the version number is incremented. Furthermore, the element is *working* state then. All temporal independent changes of the element are directly applied and do not result into a new version until the author has finished his work. And yet it is no different if changes are done within a minute or over several weeks. The working state also has some other influences. For example, working versions of elements cannot be found by someone who does not own authoring rights. The element remains in working state until it is actively published by an author. That means the version number stays the same while the state is changed to *published*. At this point of time, the element reached an official character of quality and is accessible for the target group. From then on it is not possible to adapt the element, and changes result in new working versions with incremented version numbers respectively. Besides the *working* and *published*, there are other states, for example *initial* for automatically imported elements with additional restrictions. Figure 3 shows the different versions/states of an element and the possible transitions.

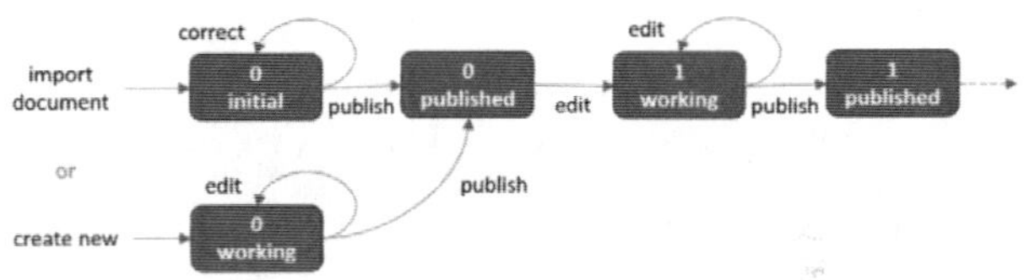

Figure 3. Knowledge versioning process.

The versioning of the bidirectional relations and the different states do not mesh with each other very well. The structure of elements and relations is thought to have one best element for each knowledge issue. The concept of non-published new versions leads to a violation as there is a coexistence of two elements describing the same things at a time. Of course, it would not make sense to show both of them in the tree or link the new version already as it has not been finalized yet. To address this challenge, it has been decided to slit the bidirectional relations up into two unidirectional relations, which are not synchronized at the same time but with a delay of the different state transitions.

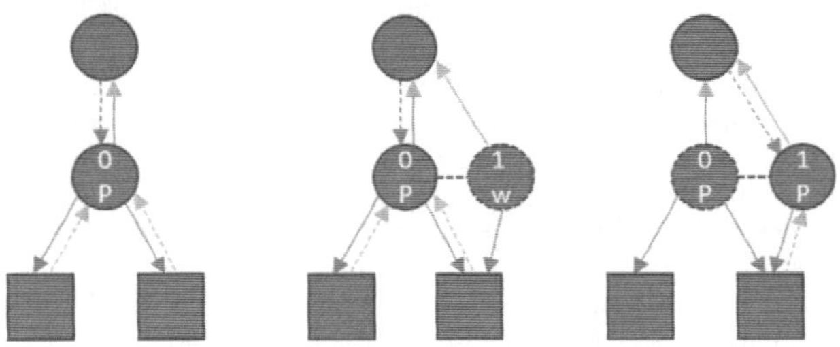

Figure 4. Evolving Knowledge Graph.
Left: published bundle (version 0) with two children and one parent bundle.
Middle: one snippet is deleted in working version 1 of bundle.
Right: updated bundle (version 1) is published.

Figure 4 shows an example of one root bundle, containing one other bundle, containing two snippets itself. One can see that the return paths of the middle bundle's relations (dashed) are only set the moment the element is published. When being in working state, it only adapts or rather creates the relation parts of which it is the owner (solid). The figure also shows how the child relation (green) of the top bundle is altered on publish. Splitting up the bidirectional relations added some complexity as there two independent structures by the going and returning part of the relations. But since the modification process of the relations follows strict rules, it is a good tradeoff.

D. *Annotation System*

At the beginning of this section, the two main entities snippets and bundles have been introduced. Actually, there is one more element which has a deep impact on the utilization of the whole system. In contrast to snippets and bundles, which represent something official or thought trough in the system, annotations are personal notes of individual users. Just like snippets, they are multimedia objects. The creation of annotations via certain tools is very easy so that users can ad-hoc record audio, take a photo, create a video, list some issues, create a sketch, etc. Thus, it is easy to grab non-formal situational knowledge. Furthermore, a short description can be added explaining the note in some detail. The real profit is earned when annotations are stuck at any other knowledge element in the system. I.e., with the help of annotations the user is able to create his own working aids and extend the global knowledge with his own experience. For the moment, his annotations are private and can be seen by himself only. Nevertheless, it seems as if they are part of the available knowledge graph. Whenever the user works with the available material, from now on he directly receives his embedded annotations as additional help. As soon as the aids are believed to be valuable enough, the user has the possibility to share them with a self-determined group of other users (see sections 4.F and 4.G). Annotations can even be used to comment on already available annotations of other users encouraging discourses and allowing the author of the knowledge element to receive useful feedback and insights. That means the system avails communication and exchange of knowledge where it was not possible before, e.g., due to a job profile like field services. On the one hand, helpful contributions can be used to improve the knowledge in future versions. On the other hand, the author realizes misconceptions he would not have known otherwise and has the chance to respond to them. From an architectural point of view, the annotation structure is infinitive, but due to usability the level of annotations is limited to 2 levels via the program logic. That way, answers to annotations on elements are still possible but discourses do not get too complex and unclear. As already mentioned, annotations are similar to snippets although they serve a different purpose. The likeness can be used in such a way that an element's author can use annotations as templates for new elements or improved versions. That way he can easily embed, e.g., a photography of a mechanic taken of a machine. The mechanic himself gets involved in the process and can identify with the new material due to his input.

E. *Rating System*

Besides annotations, knowledge workers have another possibility to interact with the available knowledge. An extra rating system has been integrated into the structure which allows users to rate all kinds of elements, i.e., snippets, bundles and annotations. While ratings on annotations and snippets refer to the content or the remark, a rating of a bundle expresses the quality of the compilation. For example, that includes which subsections a chapter has, how subsections are ordered, whether the collection of elements is semantically complete, etc. Due to the rating system, it is very easy for users to communicate their thoughts without too much effort. Still, the input can be used to advice high quality knowledge and identify problem areas to contribute to an overall quality assurance. As users do not vote too much and if they do they do not tend to down-vote, the graphical user interface needs to assure a quick access of a simple rating mechanism like, e.g., positive stars. This is also very important for the authors and all users in the system. The awareness of activities in the system has a motivating effect on its participants and their willingness to contribute.

F. *Diverse Group System*

Annotations and other elements can be share with selected peers. To achieve this and to simplify the communication and distribution of material, a diverse group system has been created. Groups are collections of peers in the system and designed in a rather generic way. Via different characteristics, such as visibility or admission procedures, it is possible to easily create various different kinds of groups. It is feasible to have personal unidirectional friend lists which are only visible for the user himself, circles like in google+, groups which are used for commonalities such as working locations or occupational profiles, more formal groups that may represent a successfully passed training, groups that reproduce department structures, and so forth. Table 1 shows some possible types of groups regarding some of their features. They are used for communication purposes as well as access management of knowledge elements in the system as described next.

TABLE I. GROUPS AND THEIR FEATURES

Feature \ Group	Personal Friends List	Group of Colleagues	Official Department	Working Location
Open	No	No	No	Yes
Visible for all	No	No	Yes	Yes
Applicable	No	Yes	No	No
Invitable	No	Yes	No	Yes

G. *Access Rights Management*

Not only from an organizational point of view it makes sense to restrict the users' access to selected content. This is reasonable if there is, e.g., security-related material for which's use the worker is not educated. The presented group system is an optimal basis for the needed rights management. In the knowledge system, the creator is in full control of his knowledge and has the power to grand additional rights. As there is no one system-wide privileged author, it depends on the element and the current situation whether some user owns this authoring role or not. Access rights are related to single elements and hence for every snippet or bundle – at least in principle – it could be different. Of course, the user interfaces simplify the process such that authors can adapt the access for a whole (tree) structure at once. Besides the special *creator* role which allows to retain full power over a created element, there are several other roles. There is a right to *read* and show elements, and a right to *write* and change an element. Access rights cannot only be assigned to a single user but also to groups. That way it is very easy to allow a certain group of people to use some material, e.g., the handouts of a workshop. As soon as more people pass the corresponding training, they only need to be invited to the group which is already authorized. Another *manage* right allows users to allocate rights to other users and pass the power. For example, his makes sense if there is committee that is responsible for some knowledge. One last special right is called *REFERER*. The owner of this right is able to only add read access to others. That becomes important if authors want to include elements of other authors into their bundles. Commonly, they would not have power about the rights allocation of the included elements. To still be able to offer reading rights to their audience, they can get the REFERER right which enables them to add readers to foreign material. Table 2 summarizes all different rights again.

TABLE II. ACCESS RIGHTS

Access Right	Declaration
CREATOR	Implies all the access rights and cannot be revoked
READ	Find and read-out element
WRITE	Change element
MANAGE	Grant and revoke other rights
REFERER	grant READ rights

H. Linkage of Traditional File Formats

The cold-start problem is a negative effect which many new software systems suffer from. That occurs, when there is too little data in the system to really use it effectively. However, employees need their material and cannot trust in a system that only covers some aspects. The risk of falling back into old habits and not accepting the system as a whole is too high. Also, organizations already have an enormous mass of material in digital file formats of traditional tools like MS Word, MS PowerPoint, and others. Hence, it would be a tremendous help to transfer those into the new system structure.

Different importers have been created that take, e.g., a MS Word's docx file and convert it into the system's internal structure of snippets, bundles, etc. The modules analyze the original document and utilize different kinds of information to build up the hierarchy. For example, the different levels of headlines can be used to recognize the different bundle levels, or paragraphs can be used to determine text units for snippets. This automation disburdens the human authors a lot. As it is not possible to create an automatism for all theoretically possible inputs, the modules only generate suggestions which are stored via a special initial state. Authors then have the chance to correct the material in regard to inaccurately detected elements. That means combining snippets that should have been recognized as one, splitting up material in further units, and so forth. After publishing the new structures, they are ready to be used like structures that have been created from scratch in the system. Elements in the system are neither restricted to their former visualization nor to their previous format.

Summarizing, the presented knowledge structure represents a network of knowledge elements (snippets, bundles, annotations) and their interrelations. Version control realizes a constant graph evolution and still allows to reproduce the history of knowledge. Social aspects like annotations and rating together with the group system are the basis for lively exchange of knowledge between peers. Via the rights and roles management, it is very easy to grant access to different users. To overcome the start-up problems, import modules are able to automatically transform traditional documents into the new knowledge structure.

V. EVALUATION

The presented approach has been developed in connection with a project named Professional Reflective Mobile Personal Learning Environments (PRiME). It is a joint research project of the Learning Technologies Research Group from RWTH Aachen University and DB Training, Learning & Consulting from Deutsche Bahn AG. It is sponsored by the Federal Ministry of Education and Research via the German Aerospace Center. Although the system developed in PRiME is designed in a generic way to fit many different scenarios, the most benefitting job profiles are mobile field services. As proof of concept, we address a first group of mobile mechanics from the car inspection service of the long-distance passenger transport DB Fernverkehr AG, as well as related trainers, training developers and specialist author. The mostly qualitative evaluations in form of interviews and work tasks show broad acknowledgement and positive feedback from all involved roles. It also emerged, that in principal the current traditional processes are similar to the proposed ones but so far very uncomfortable and slow in comparison to the new possibilities in the PRiME system. Current employees make their own way to cope with the addressed problems and look for workarounds or their very own tricks anyway. Thus, the need for an organization-wide uniform solution is clearly there.

Further quantitative evaluations with, e.g., questionnaires in combination with some broader field studies are running at the moment. First figures adumbrate that the implemented system and its underlying model can really embed in the everyday work life and naturally support the workers in their working process. The results will be published accordingly.

VI. CONCLUSION AND FUTURE WORK

Knowledge has been identified as a very important resource that greatly impacts the competitiveness. Hence, there are endeavors to improve the collection, distribution and the enhancement of knowledge and manage it like any other good.

In this paper, we introduced a promising approach that unites different – so far independent – aspects like complexity, network character, social aspects, and quality assurance together into one process and model to naturally fit in and characterize the real knowledge process. The underlying structure has been explained in more detail and allows the distribution of official knowledge, the record of tacit knowledge, sharing it with peers, and improving it due to an annotation and rating system. The whole system results in a three-layered learning process starting with the personal individual, over his social network to the whole organization. This continuous process of knowledge evolution and maturation has some additional benefits:

- Knowledge does not leave the organization with its members and hence does not need to be reproduced again and again.
- The concept promotes a mentality to work together and benefit from one another instead of destructive competition.
- By their contribution, knowledge workers feel involved and can identify easily with the organization.
- The organization's focus is more on its employees and their abilities.
- Due to their participations, users enjoy respect and appreciation.
- Users have the chance to communicate and experience social aspects that have not been possible before.
- Very high reusability of knowledge by virtue of the atomic elements and their linkage.
- Faster publication procedures of official knowledge as authorities can concentrate on point by point enhancements.
- Authors get to know about misconceptions and can reveal them.
- Authors can fall back on an enormous collective know-how and quality assurance a lot faster due to the high involvement.

The presented knowledge system is already able to map the whole knowledge process from individual to organizational learning. Nevertheless, there are many aspects that can and should be enhanced. The introduced structure can cope with the spread and cross-linked character of the knowledge. Still, one idea is to add more semantic meaning to elements by, e.g., introducing categories or types of knowledge units to improve its discovery and offer it more selective. It has to be further researched if it is possible to deduce concepts or taxa from the structural content in different areas of application. Once formalized, ontologies can then abet improvements in, e.g., identifying situationally important knowledge.

Content can be created from scratch or traditional file formats can be imported by specific modules, as described before. Even if the whole management and usage process is represented in the system, there are still situations where other formats outside of PRiME are needed. That could be a PowerPoint presentation in a workshop or a Word document for external companies that do not have access to the system. Analog to the import modules, export modules will be able to generate traditional documents back from the special systems own structure.

The current employees are used to their present toolset which is in most companies the Microsoft Office Suite. Instead of forcing them to use yet another system, there are approaches to develop assistance systems that integrate PRiME into their common working environment. As an example, plugins for their text editors can help to stick with some guidelines to gain the maximum profit and less rework from the import modules.

Learning Analytics is a powerful tool that allows better learning data analyses. On the one hand, it can improve the automated feedback for authors so that they see points of failure or misconceptions at a glance. On the other hand, it can optimize the user's handling of material in his working process. Further collection of context data [14] like time, location, situation, etc. can help to offer the right knowledge which is required for the individual in his current unique situation. Ideally, it could dispense with former traditional searching.

Aside the mentioned aspects, there are many more possible extensions or improvements which could also cover topics like assessment. It remains to be seen how the system will be accepted in long-term studies and if there are other aspects of higher priority such as the improvement of user motivation.

REFERENCES

[1] P. Hildreth and C. Kimble, "The duality of knowledge," Information Research, Vol. 8 No. 1. 2002.

[2] C. Kimble, Paul Hildreth and Peter Wright, "Communities of practice: going virtual," in Y. Malhotra (Ed.), Knowledge Management and Business Model Innovation, Idea Group Publishing, Hershey (USA)/London (UK), pp. 220–234. 2001.

[3] Y. Malhotra, "Integrating knowledge management technologies in organizational business processes: Getting real time enterprises to deliver real business performance," in Journal of Knowledge Management, Vol. 9 No. 1, 2005, pp. 7–28.

[4] I. Nonaka and H. Takeuchi, "The Knowledge-Creating Company: How Japanese Companies Create the Dynamics of Innovation," Oxford University, New York. 1995.

[5] G. E. Gorman and D. J. Pauleen, "The Nature and Value of Personal Knowledge Management," in D. J. Pauleen and G. E. Gorman (Eds.), Personal Knowledge Management: Individual, Organizational and Social Perspectives. Gower Publishing Limited, Farnham Surrey, England, pp. 1-16. 2011.

[6] L. Prusak and J. Cranefield, "Managing your own Knowledge: A Personal Perspective", in D. J. Pauleen and G. E. Gorman (Eds.), Personal Knowledge Management: Individual, Organizational and Social Perspectives. Gower Publishing Limited, Farnham Surrey, England, pp. 99-114. 2011.

[7] D. Snowden and D. J. Pauleen, "Knowledge Management and the Individual: It's Nothing Personal", in D. J. Pauleen and G. E. Gorman (Eds.), Personal Knowledge Management: Individual, Organizational and Social Perspectives. Gower Publishing Limited, Farnham Surrey, England, pp. 115-128. 2011.

[8] "DB Regio und DB Training gewinnen Deutschen Bildungspreis 2013", https://www.db-training.de/dbtraining-

de/start/news1/6012202/bildungspreis2013.html. reviewed: March, 2016.

[9] J. Finken, D. Krannich, and B. Tannert, “Kodin-Kfz - A Collaborative Diagnosis Network,” in Proceedings of ICL 15th International Conference on Interactive Collaborative Learning. Sept. 2012, Villach, Austria. IEEE Conference Publications. 2012, pp. 1–3.

[10] M. A. Chatti, U. Schroeder, and M. Jarke, “LaaN: Convergence of Knowledge Management and Technology-Enhanced Learning,” in Learning Technologies, Vol.5 No.2. 2012, pp.177-189.

[11] C. Greven, M. A. Chatti, H. Thüs, and U. Schroeder, “Context-Aware Mobile Professional Learning in PRiME,” in “Mobile as Mainstream - Towards Future Challenges in Mobile Learning : 13th World Conference on Mobile and Contextual Learning”. Springer. 2014, pp. 287-299.

[12] C. Greven and U. Schroeder, “²SIMPLE: Symbiotic Interrelated Seamless Integrated Mobile Personalizable Learning Environments,” in Proceedings of DeLFI Workshops 2015. 2015, pp 232-243

[13] C. Greven et al., “Seamless Application Ecologies as Mobile Personal Learning Environments,” in “DeLFI 2015 – Die 13. E-Learning Fachtagung Informatik der Gesellschaft für Informatik e.V”. 2015, pp. 57-69.

[14] Thüs et al., “Mobile learning in context,” in Int. J. Technology Enhanced Learning, Vol. 4, Nos. 5/6, 2012, pp. 332-344.

Recommendation-Based Decision Support for Hazard Analysis and Risk Assessment

Kerstin Hartig and Thomas Karbe

Institute for Software Engineering - TU Berlin
10587 Berlin, Germany
Email: {kerstin.hartig, thomas.karbe}@tu-berlin.de

Abstract—**Since 2011, automotive companies have to adhere to the functional safety standard ISO 26262. One important safety activity described in the standard is the hazard analysis and risk assessment, which is strongly expert-driven, and therefore expensive, time consuming, and dependent from the individual expert's opinion. In this paper, we present a decision support system for hazard analyses in order to increase their consistency and efficiency. The system automatically combines results from finished analyses and supporting information in a knowledge base and searches it for useful recommendations during a new hazard analysis and risk assessment.**

***Keywords*–Decision Support; Advisory System; Recommendation System; Spreading Activation; Hazard Analysis.**

I. INTRODUCTION

In 2011, the automotive functional safety standard ISO 26262 "Road Vehicles - Functional Safety" [1] was published. Since then, the individual safety processes of automotive companies were adapted and now each new system for a car is developed according to the ISO 26262. The *hazard analysis and risk assessment* (HARA) is one of the first activities of the safety lifecycle. In this analysis, experts examine the systems with respect to its functions, possible malfunctions, and the consequences of those malfunctions in different situations. For many systems in the automotive domain nearly identical systems exist for other series vehicles. However, a simple copy-paste approach is not feasible. Even small changes in a system could lead to completely different analysis results.

Since the ISO 26262 is still a very young standard, there are not many tools to support it appropriately. According to [2], the experience of experts is still the main means to conduct a proper HARA. In order to reduce the workload of the domain experts and to increase the consistency of HARA projects for similar systems, we propose a recommendation system that bases its recommendations on already completed analyses, and that therefore makes optimal use of the reuse potential. The system automatically creates a knowledge base that combines information from other HARA projects with complementary information, e.g., synonym dictionaries. When an expert is working on a new HARA, the system proposes knowledge artefacts that could be useful for the actual or next analysis step, together with an explanation. Relevance in the knowledge base is determined by a mechanism called *spreading activation* that leverages the relationships between concepts in a semantic network. In Section II of this paper, we cover the basics and the related work for the topics HARA, spreading activation, and semantic web technologies. In Section III, we discuss the two phases of our proposed recommendation system. Finally, in Section IV, we summarize our results and present multiple possibilities to continue research in this area.

II. BASICS AND RELATED WORK

In this section, we shortly introduce the main concepts and tasks for conducting a HARA. Furthermore, we describe spreading activation and its application as semantic search technique. In a third part, we present selected applications of semantic web technologies that have been applied in non-web environments and are related to our approach.

A. Hazard Analysis and Risk Assessment (HARA)

According to ISO 26262, HARA is a method for identifying and assessing hazards and specifying safety goals in order to reduce risks down to an acceptable level [1]. The HARA workflow consists of several steps, which can be tailored individually.

The initial input is a collection of documents related to an item of interest, e.g., description, interfaces, architecture. In subsequent steps, the item functions to be examined are defined, their potential malfunctions are identified, relevant driving situations are assigned, and hazardous situations are derived. The impact and consequences of each hazardous situation are determined and their risk is classified by the specific parameters. Their evaluation leads to the assignment of an Automotive Safety Integrity Level (ASIL) and results in appropriate safety goals. Higher ASILs usually require higher efforts in providing functional safety. HARA strongly relies on expert knowledge, usually involving several experts from different departments and is usually a very complex and time-consuming analysis.

B. Spreading Activation

Spreading activation has its origin in the fields of psychology and psycholinguistics. It was used as a theoretical model to explain semantic memory search and semantic preparation or priming [3]–[5]. A semantic network was defined as an explanatory model of human knowledge representation. In such a network, concepts are represented by nodes and the associations between concepts as links [4]. Over the years, spreading activation evolved into a highly configurable semantic search algorithm and found its application in different fields [6]. Spreading Activation is capable of both identifying and ranking the relevant environment in a semantic network.

The processing of spreading activation is usually defined as a sequence of one or more iterations, so-called pulses. Each node in a network has an activation value that describes its current relevance in the search. In each pulse, activated nodes spread their activation over the network towards associated concepts, and thus mark semantically related nodes [6]. If a termination condition is met, the algorithm will stop. Each pulse consists of different phases in which the activation values are computed by individually configured activation functions.

Additional constraints control the activation process. Fan-out constraints limit the spreading of highly connected nodes because a broad semantic meaning may weaken the results. Distance constraints reduce activation of distant nodes, because distant nodes are considered to be less associated to each other. There are many other configuration details such as decays, thresholds, and spreading directions. In the survey, Crestani argues that spreading activation is capable of providing good results, but the effectiveness highly depends on the availability of a representative network as well as techniques for automated network building [6]. Therefore, the approach presented in this paper aims at both the automated creation and the semantic enrichment of the network.

C. *Applications of Semantic Web Technologies*

In 2001, Tim Berners Lee coined the term *Semantic Web* [7], which envisions extensive sharing and reuse of semantically enriched data over the web. To support this vision, organizations and initiatives such as the W3C elaborate on development and standardization of knowledge and semantic technologies, including RDF and OWL. While those technologies are created with the web in mind, they are useful in other domains as well.

One area of application is the *semantic desktop*, which aims at transferring semantic web technologies to the user's desktop [8]. Schumacher et al. even apply spreading activation in semantic desktop information retrieval [9]. Semantic desktop technologies primarily focus on interconnecting different desktop applications for personal or group information management, e.g., implemented in the NEPOMUK Project [10]. Similarly, we want to combine semantic web technologies and spreading activation, but focus on providing recommendations for safety analyses such as HARA. Álvarez et al. examined spreading activation techniques for information retrieval in RDF graphs and ontologies [11]. They introduced the OntoSpread Framework to support configuration and execution of the algorithms and applied it in a medical recommendation system [12]. However, they utilized existing ontolgies whereas our approach includes the overall process of creating and searching semantic networks in order to provide step-by-step guidance through the analysis process by problem-specific recommendations.

III. APPROACH FOR A RECOMMENDATION SYSTEM FOR DECISION SUPPORT

A. *Approach*

We propose an approach to enhance a HARA tool with semantic technologies in order to provide the user with recommendations. One such analysis tool is medini analyze [13], in which the HARA projects used in this paper were conducted. However, our approach is independent from a concrete tool and applicable to any tool with a known structure, e.g., meta model, class diagram. The approach consists of two phases: the building phase and the search phase, each of which comprises three steps (see Figure 1). The building phase includes building the knowledge base on model and instance level and a post-processing step for semantic enrichment. The search phase includes the identification and evaluation of relevance, generation of recommendations and providing explanations.

Throughout the remainder of this paper, we will make use of the following concrete scenario when explaining each step.

Example: A safety engineer adds a new function, namely "operate directional indicator", during a HARA. The engineer queries the system for functions in order to see, which related functions have been used in earlier HARA projects. Next to finished HARA projects, the system contains knowledge about synonyms. One entry in this synonym collection is, that "directional indicator" and "turn signal" have the same meaning. Therefore, one of the provided recommendations should be the function "activate turn signal right", which has been used in a finished HARA project.

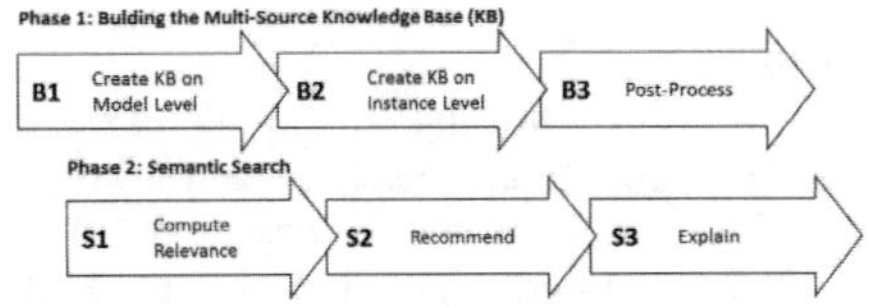

Figure 1. Phases and Steps of the Approach.

B. *Building Phase: Multi-Source Knowledge Base*

Optimally, recommendation detection should be conducted on a knowledge base containing extensive expert's knowledge. This knowledge originates from different sources, most importantly from already completed analyses. Additional information, such as glossaries, synonyms, feature models, or other domain-specific background knowledge can help to find potentially useful semantic relationships between different artefacts. Therefore, our proposed knowledge base has an extensible modular structure, consisting of multiple so-called *knowledge blocks*. Creating this knowledge base automatically bypasses the main obstacles for successful application of spreading activation, i.e., dependance on the representativeness of networks and automated network building [6].

Each block consists of both the model representation of the knowledge and their instances. Therefore, we require both the XML schema definition and the data provided in XML as input. A block contains relations between concepts within the block, as well as relations to other blocks, stitching multiple blocks to one piece. These so-called cross-block relations are identified and set whenever a new block is included.

1) Automatic Generation of the OWL Model (B1): The main knowledge block for a tool-based recommendation system is given by the data structure of the tool itself, usually available through meta models or class diagrams. In this paper, the target language for the semantic representation is Web Ontology Language (OWL), a W3C standardized description language with formal semantics for representing and computing knowledge. However, the approach is applicable to any other target structure based on RDF Graph. In OWL, we can describe information as classes, properties, instances, and data values [14]. Given XML schema definitions of a meta model and other information sources, we can apply mapping techniques to create an OWL model. In [15], Bohring and Sauer propose an XSD to OWL mapping to capture the XML schema semantics while translating the schema constructs to OWL. Similar transformation approaches are described in several other publications, e.g., [16][17]. We slightly adapt the existing mappings for our specific transformation.

Example: In our example, we provide, additionally to the tool meta model, a collection of synonyms as second knowledge block. Synonyms are easy enough to explain in the example, but carry semantic meaning, and therefore have a visible impact. Synonyms are represented by a class with a name attribute and a reflexive *synonym* association. In the same beforementioned fashion, we apply our transformation. This results in an *owl:class Synonym* and a symmetric object property *hasSynonym* as well as a datatype property for the synonym name (see upper right side of Figure 2).

2) Automatic Import of OWL Instances (B2): Now, we want to fill the created OWL model with instance data. The import can be technically implemented using an XML to OWL transformation [15].

Example: For the scenario, we import the instances "turn signal" and "directional indicator" of type *Synonym* and connect them by a *hasSynonym* link. Furthermore, we include the instance "activate turn signal right" of type *Function*, among others (see Figure 2).

3) Stitching Multi-Source Knowledge Blocks (B3): Knowledge blocks need to be interconnected in order to capture known semantics. Proper stitching is essential, since it represents the actual semantic enhancement of the knowledge base. Usually, stitching knowledge blocks requires domain knowledge to decide which concrete concepts need to be connected. However, once this decision is made, the linking process can be automated via stitching rules. The resulting OWL representation including the model and instance level consists of an underlying RDF graph which is composed of a set of RDF triples [18]. Each triple consists of a subject, a predicate, and an object which read as a statement, e.g., "Function *hasMalFunction* Malfunction". The OWL to RDF graph mapping is standardized by the W3C [19].

Example: We stitch the HARA block and the synonym block by introducing a new relation *hasSynonymConnection*. This relation links all instance nodes that contain a synonym instance name with that synonym instance (see Figure 2).

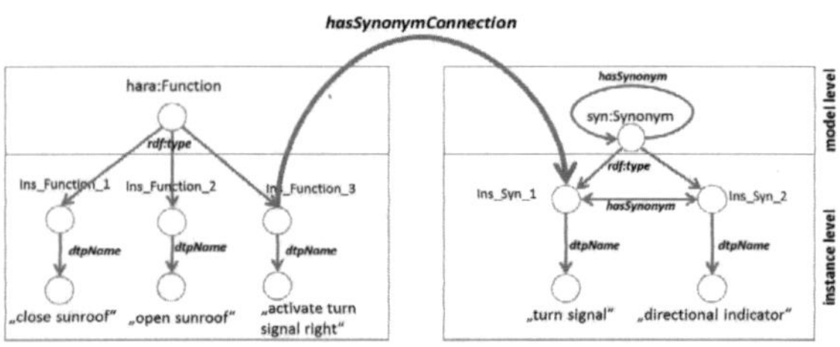

Figure 2. Knowledge Base with Knowledge Blocks for HARA and Synonyms.

C. Search Phase: Semantic Search Concept

Searching the knowledge base is conducted in three steps (see Figure 1). Firstly, we apply a spreading activation algorithm to identify the context of our specific search, i.e., the relevant subnetwork. This step reduces the search space and ranks the visited nodes by their relevance. Secondly, we filter the most relevant nodes in the resulting subnetwork by the sought-after type. As a result, we generate recommendations for the user in order to support their decisions. In a third step, we provide explanations for the recommendations.

1) Spreading Activation (S1): Since spreading activation algorithms are highly configurable and profit from domain- and problem-specific configurations, we apply the following configuration settings: The termination criteria are a specified amount of pulses, the full activation of the graph, as well as a threshold for the total activation value transmission of a pulse. In case of convergence the spreading will stop. We additionally apply fan-out and local distance constraints to limit the activation broadcast of highly connected nodes and decrease the activation depending on the path distance. We apply a pulse constraint to reduce the spreadable activation values over the time in order to achieve convergence with increasing pulse count. Most importantly, we apply path constraints utilizing the semantic relevance of properties.

Example: In our scenario, we privilege the synonym knowledge block because the knowledge of two words meaning the same thing can boost the search. In order to emphasize their importance, we attach higher weights to the associated properties *hasSynonymConnection* and *hasSynonym*. Figure 3 depicts our search scenario. The engineer added the function

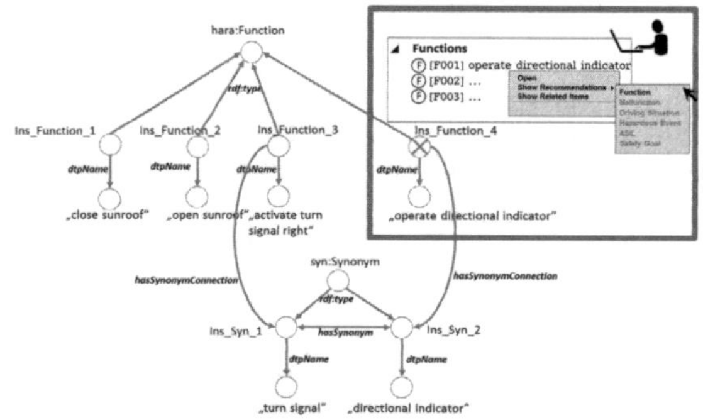

Figure 3. Recommendation Query.

"operate directional indicator" and now searches for associated functions.

Figure 4 depicts the semantic network before (a) and during five pulses (b-f) of the spreading in our network. Starting point

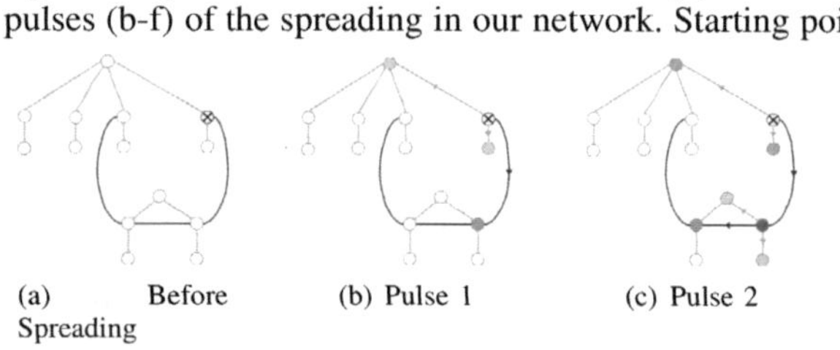

(a) Before Spreading (b) Pulse 1 (c) Pulse 2

(d) Pulse 3 (e) Pulse 4 (f) Pulse 5

Figure 4. Semantic Network before and during spreading activation pulses.

is the crossed node, which stands for the newly added function. Since synonym property edges receive higher weights, they are represented by darker color. Activation spreads in pulses over the network whereas higher activation of nodes is represented by darker color. Over the pulses, the faster activation over priorized edges and limitations by fan-out constraints at nodes with lots of branches can be observed. The result is a semantic network with nodes ranked by relevance.

2) Recommendations through Type-Specific Filtering (S2): Recommendation requests are specific to a concrete artefact type. Therefore, we filter the relevant subnetwork resulting from the spreading step by the sought-after type sorted by their assigned activation value representing their relevance regarding the specific query.

Example: The filtered subnetwork, depicted in Figure 5, only contains instances of the artefact type *Function*. The node that represents the function "activate turn signal right" has the highest relevance, and therefore is the first recommendation generated for our scenario.

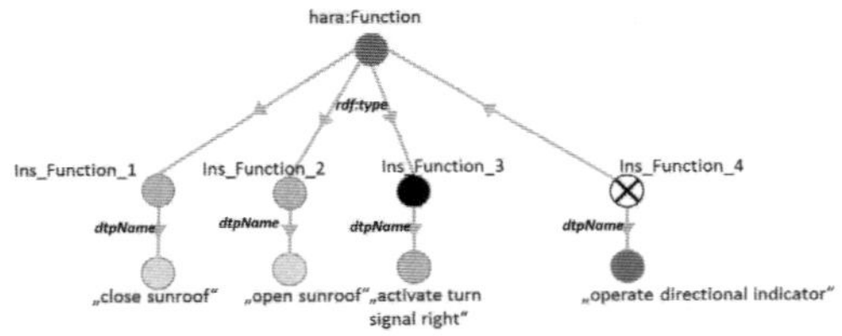

Figure 5. Filtering by Types for Identification of Recommendation.

3) Explanations (S3): For user acceptance, the origins of the resulting recommendations must be transparent. Thus, decision support for HARA can profit from appropriate explanations. Explanation can be derived by evaluating the activation history and find the path sequence that contributed most to the activation of a specific node. Optimizing the explanation given for each recommendation is work in progress and will be examined in our future research work.

Example: In the presented example, the explanation is obvious: The function "activate turn signal" is the highest ranked recommendation, because "turn signal" and "directional indicator" are synonyms, and therefore have the same meaning. In our case, the shortest and highest activated path determines this explanation (see Figure 4(f)).

D. Implementation

The proposed recommendation system is implemented in a prototype called *HARvESTer (Hazard Analysis and Risk assessment dEcision Support Tool)*. We examined different scenarios, generating recommendations for functions, malfunctions and safety goals. First experiments in a safety expert environment led to positive feedback regarding usefulness and showed promising results. Expected recommendations have been found in most cases.

IV. CONCLUSION AND FUTURE WORK

In this paper, we presented a decision support system for hazard analysis and risk assessment which aims at increasing efficiency and more consistent and reliable results. The system has two main capabilities: automated construction of a knowledge base from different information sources and finding related information for deriving recommendations during the HARA steps. Since these recommendations are based on already finished analyses, the experts have fast access to decisions that have been made before and can decide to reuse them. Although our first results are very promising, we see much potential for future research.

Our method focuses on HARAs, but could be easily adapted to other analyses of ISO 26262, or even outside of the safety domain. A challenging idea is the automatic configuration of the spreading algorithm to improve results. User feedback could be a useful addition for the recommendation system such that it could learn which recommendations were actually useful, and which were not. Furthermore, an extensive case study is planned to evaluate the overall approach and its usability as well as the effects of different configurations.

REFERENCES

[1] ISO 26262 - Road vehicles - Functional safety, International Organization for Standardization, Nov. 2011.

[2] C. Maier, A. Schloske, and S. Bothe, "Studie zur Funktionalen Sicherheit in der Automobilbranche [Survey of Functional Safety in the Automotive Domain (ISO 26262)]," Fraunhofer Institute for Manufacturing Engineering and Automation (IPA), Tech. Rep., Mar. 2013.

[3] M. R. Quillian, "Semantic Memory," in Semantic Information Processing, M. Minsky, Ed. MIT Press, 1968, pp. 216–270.

[4] A. M. Collins and E. F. Loftus, "A spreading activation theory of semantic processing," Psychological Review, vol. 82, no. 6, Nov. 1975, pp. 407–428.

[5] J. R. Anderson, "A Spreading Activation Theory of Memory," Journal of Verbal Learning and Verbal Behavior, vol. 22, 1983, pp. 261–295.

[6] F. Crestani, "Application of Spreading Activation Techniques in Information Retrieval," Artificial Intelligence Review, vol. 11, 1997, pp. 453–482.

[7] T. Berners-Lee, J. Hendler, and O. Lassila, "The Semantic Web," Scientific American, vol. 284, no. 5, May 2001, pp. 34–43.

[8] L. Sauermann, A. Bernardi, and A. Dengel, "Overview and Outlook on the Semantic Desktop," in Proceedings of the 1st Workshop on The Semantic Desktop at the ISWC 2005 Conference, ser. CEUR Workshop Proceedings, S. Decker, J. Park, D. Quan, and L. Sauermann, Eds., vol. 175. CEUR-WS, Nov. 2005.

[9] K. Schumacher, M. Sintek, and L. Sauermann, "Combining Fact and Document Retrieval with Spreading Activation for Semantic Desktop Search," in ESWC, ser. Lecture Notes in Computer Science, S. Bechhofer, M. Hauswirth, J. Hoffmann, and M. Koubarakis, Eds., vol. 5021. Springer, 2008, pp. 569–583.

[10] T. Groza, S. Handschuh, K. Moeller, G. Grimnes, L. Sauermann, E. Minack, C. Mesnage, M. Jazayeri, G. Reif, and R. Gudjonsdottir, "The NEPOMUK Project – On the way to the Social Semantic Desktop," in Proceedings of the Third International Conference on Semantic Technologies (I-SEMANTICS 2007), Graz, Austria, 2007, pp. 201–211.

[11] J. M. Álvarez, D. Berrueta, L. Polo, and J. E. Labra, "ONTOSPREAD: A Framework for Supporting the Activation of Concepts in Graph-Based Structures through the Spreading Activation Technique," in Information Systems, E-learning, and Knowledge Management Research, ser. Communications in Computer and Information Science, vol. 278. Springer Berlin Heidelberg, 2013, pp. 454–459.

[12] J. M. Álvarez, L. Polo, W. Jimenez, P. Abella, and J. E. Labra, "Application of the spreading activation technique for recommending concepts of well-known ontologies in medical systems," in Proceedings of the 2nd ACM Conference on Bioinformatics, Computational Biology and Biomedicine - BCB '11, 2011, pp. 626–635.

[13] "KPIT - medini analyze - Functional Safety Tool," 2016, URL: http://www.kpit.com/engineering/products/medini-functional-safety-tool [accessed: 2016-03-11].

[14] "OWL 2 Web Ontology Language. Structural Specification and Functional-Style Syntax (Second Edition)," W3C, W3C Recommendation, Dec. 2012.

[15] H. Bohring and S. Auer, "Mapping XML to OWL Ontologies," in Computer Science Days Leipzig, ser. LNI, K. P. Jantke, K.-P. Fähnrich, and W. S. Wittig, Eds., vol. 72. GI, 2005, pp. 147–156.

[16] I. Bedini, C. Matheus, P. F. Patel-Schneider, A. Boran, and B. Nguyen, "Transforming XML Schema to OWL Using Patterns," in Proceedings of the 5th IEEE International Conference on Semantic Computing, ICSC 2011. IEEE Computer Society, 2011, pp. 102–109.

[17] N. Yahia, S. A. Mokhtar, and A. Ahmed, "Automatic Generation of OWL Ontology from XML Data Source," International Journal of Computer Science Issues, vol. 9, Mar. 2012, pp. 77–83.

[18] "RDF 1.1 Concepts and Abstract Syntax," W3C, W3C Recommendation, Feb. 2014.

[19] "OWL 2 Web Ontology Language. Mapping to RDF Graphs (Second Edition)," W3C, W3C Recommendation, Dec. 2012.

ReSCU: A Trail Recommender Approach to Support Program Code Understanding

Roy Oberhauser
Computer Science Dept.
Aalen University
Aalen, Germany
email: roy.oberhauser@hs-aalen.de

Abstract —**Society is faced with an ever-increasing volume of computer program code that must be developed and maintained, exacerbated by a limited pool of trained human resources. Thus, effective and efficient automated tutor systems or recommenders for program comprehension are imperative. This paper introduces the Recommendation Service for Code Understanding (ReSCU), an approach that utilizes program code as a knowledgebase and automatically recommends a code trail to support effective and efficient human program code comprehension. Initial evaluation results with a prototype and an empirical study with obfuscated program code demonstrates its viability.**

Keywords-recommendation systems; intelligent tutoring systems; knowledge-based systems; program code comprehension; software engineering.

I. INTRODUCTION

The growing utilization of software throughout industry and society entails ever-increasing volumes of (legacy) program code and associated maintenance activity. While the total lines of program code worldwide is unknown, the Year 2000 (Y2K) crisis [1] with global costs of $375-750 billion gave us an indicator of the scale and importance of program comprehension, while a study of 5000 active open source software projects shows code size doubling on average every 14 months [2]. Moreover, the available pool of programmers to develop and maintain code remains limited and is not growing correspondingly. For instance, US bachelor degrees in Computer Science in 2011 were roughly equivalent to that seen in 1986 both in total number (~42,000) and as a percentage of 23 year olds (~1%) [3]. This is exacerbated by high employee turnover rates in the software industry.

Thus, there is resulting pressure on programmers to rapidly come up to speed on existing code or comprehend and maintain legacy code (a type of knowledge) in a cost-effective manner. It thus becomes imperative that programmers be supported with automated tutors and recommenders that efficiently and effectively support program code comprehension. In this space, recommendation systems for software engineering provide information items estimated to be valuable for a software engineering task in a given context [4].

This paper introduces a solution in this space called Recommendation Service for Code Understanding (ReSCU), a knowledge-centric recommendation service and planner for program code comprehension. ReSCU can be viewed as an intelligent tutor system, applying a practical form of granular computing [5] and concepts like knowledge distance. In support of human knowledge comprehension, it automatically recommends knowledge navigation as a Hamiltonian cycle [6] in an unfamiliar knowledge landscape of program code.

The paper is organized as follows: Section II discusses related work. Section III describes the solution concept and then the prototype realization. In Section V, the evaluation is described, which is followed by the conclusion.

II. RELATED WORK

An overview of recommendation systems in software engineering is provided by [4]. In the Eclipse IDE, NavTracks [7] recommends files related to the currently selected files based on their previous navigation patterns. Mylar [8] utilizes a degree-of-interest model in Eclipse to filter our irrelevant files from the File Explorer and other views. The interest value of a selected or edited program element increases, while those of others decrease, whereby the relationship between elements is not considered. In support of developers with maintenance tasks in unfamiliar projects, Hipikat [9] recommends software artifacts relevant to a context based on the source code, email discussions, bug reports, change history, and documentation. The eRose plugin for Eclipse mines past changes in a version control system repository to suggest what is likely also related to this change based on historical similarity [10]. To improve navigation efficiency and enhance comprehension, the FEAT tool uses concern graphs either explicitly created by a programmer [11] or automatically inferred [12] based on navigation pathways utilizing a stochastic model, whereby a programmer confirms or rejects them for the concern graph. With the Eclipse plugin Suade [13], a developer drags-and-drops related fields and methods into a view to specify a context, and Suade utilizes a dependency graph and heuristics to recommend suggestions for further investigation. To support the usage of complex APIs in Eclipse, the Prospector system [14] recommends relevant code snippets by utilizing a search engine in combination with Eclipse Content Assist. Strathcona [15] analyzes structural facts of an incomplete code selection and utilizes heuristic matches to determine the most similar example. The Eclipse plugin FrUiT [16] supports example framework usage via association rule mining of applications that utilize a specific framework.

In contrast, various facets differentiate the ReSCU approach, including independence from any visualization paradigm, generating ordered code trails without necessitating an explicit context or prior history, and that it requires no human expert intervention or confirmation. Furthermore, the approach is unique in applying a conceptual mapping of geographical points of interest (POI) and the traveling salesman problem/planning (TSP) to source code and the generation of code trail planning. The foregoing tools and approaches enhance program comprehension for certain kinds of developer tasks and intentions and can be viewed as complementary.

III. SOLUTION

The ReSCU solution approach focuses on supporting the learning, understanding, and navigation of unfamiliar program source code by programmers in an automated, systematic way, without requiring additional knowledge, historical information, or human expert assistance.

A. Principles

The solution concept includes these principles (P:):

- *P:POI*: program source code locations are identified and viewed as Points-of-Interest (POI) (or knowledge entities), analogous to geographical locations in navigational systems. Each POI is identified by a unique name, such as a fully qualified name (FQN) in the Java programming language consisting of the concatenation of a package name, class name, colon, and method name. A POI can be viewed as a granule or information entity of interest in a knowledge "landscape".
- *P:POIRanking*: To determine the importance of a POI (or knowledge granule) for human comprehension, they are ranked relative to each other. The algorithm *MethodRank* described below exemplifies such a ranking that fulfills this principle.
- *P:POILocality*: POI locality, which can conceptually viewed as knowledge closeness from the perspective of knowledge distance [17], is taken into consideration. This is intended to address the cognitive burden of context switches to a human when viewing program source code, by ordering POIs such that the number of unnecessary switches in a POI visitation order is reduced. The POI Distance calculation described later is an example for applying this principle.
- *P:Timeboxing*: Human comprehension and learning is assumed to be time-limited in the form of a session. Thus, the visitation time for POIs is estimated, and only the subset of priority ordered POIs that can be feasibly visited in the given timebox is selected. This subset will then be reordered to consider locality.
- *P:CodeTrails*: the recommendation service provides code trails as output with a navigation and visitation order recommendation for the POIs, whereby POI locality is taken into account. A mapping of the TSP and related planning algorithms [18] are applied to these granules (the POIs) and the associated knowledge distance between them. While the path suggest may not necessarily be the most optimal path, it provides an efficient path nonetheless through the knowledge landscape (source code).

In ReSCU, POI visitation planning via the generated code trails focuses on invocation relationships rather than class relationships. Not following class relationships can be viewed as supported by an empirical eye-tracking study finding that "software engineers do not seem to follow binary class relationships, such as inheritance and composition" [19].

B. Features

Besides the aforementioned principles, the solution includes the following additional capabilities:

- *User profiles*: user's knowledge level (e.g., familiar vs. unfamiliar) and competency level (junior vs. senior) are taken into consideration.
- *Trail (Re-)planning*: Two modes are supported: *initial trail* mode that generates a trail from scratch, and *refactor trail* mode that dynamically incorporates user actions and re-optimizes the trail based on the visited POI and the session time left. Visited POIs (including deviations) are detected via events and automatically removed from the next suggested trail.
- *Easily integratable:* A REST-based service interface provides distributed local and remote access to the recommender service from various software development tool and integrated development environments (IDEs).

C. Conceptual Architecture

The conceptual architecture is shown in Figure 1 consists of three primary modules: *Database Repository*, *Knowledge Processing*, and *Integration*.

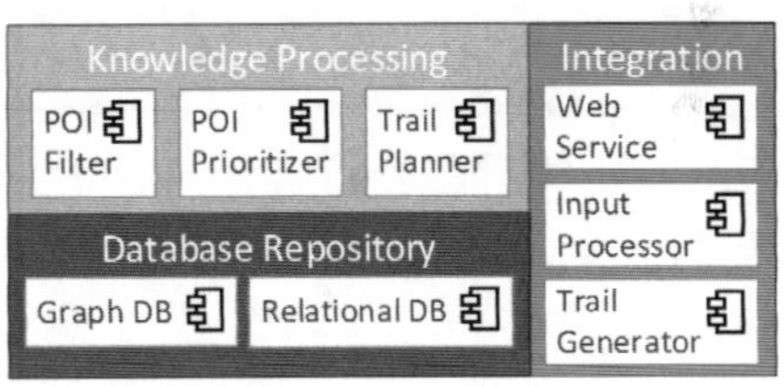

Figure 1. ReSCU solution architecture.

The *Database Repository* module logically groups various databases to retain metadata and knowledge in forms such as a graph database for modeling the source code as a graph of nodes with properties, and a relational/NoSQL database for dealing with non-graph-related knowledge related to source code.

The *Knowledge Processing* module includes components such as a POI Prioritizer for ranking POIs and a Trail Planner for planning the POI visitation time and order.

The *Integration* module includes a Web Service API (application programming interface) for supporting integration with other tools, an input processor to deal with tool events (such as a POI visit) and importing and transforming code information from analysis tools, and a trail generator for generating or transforming a planned trail into a desired format.

D. MethodRank Calculation

With regard to *P:POIRanking*, it is assumed that in general, given no other knowledge source besides the source code and assuming limited learning time, it is more essential for the user to become familiar with the methods of a project that are used frequently throughout the code, rather than ones that are only sparsely utilized. Thus, a variation of the PageRank [20] algorithm call *MethodRank* is used to prioritize the POIs, whereby instead of webpages we map methods and instead of hyperlinks we map invocations. Thus, those methods that have the most references (invocations) in the code set are ranked the highest. While this does not consider runtime invocations (such as loops), it can be an indicator for a method with broader relative utilization and thus likely of greater interest for comprehension.

E. POI Distance Calculation

To address *P:POILocality*, an underlying assumption is that (sub)packages map vertically to (sub)layers and classes serve as a type of horizontal grouping of methods. Thus, the distance between any two POIs (given in (3)) A and B (analogous to geographical distance) is determined by their *vertical* (1) and *horizontal* (2) distance.

$$VerticalDistance = |\ layer(A) - layer(B)\ | \quad (1)$$

$$HorizontalDistance = \begin{cases} 0 & if\ class(A) = class(B) \\ 1 & otherwise \end{cases} \quad (2)$$

$$POIDistance = VerticalDistance + HorizontalDistance \quad (3)$$

For instance, the POIDistance between methods in the same class is 0, between classes in the same package 1, etc. Depending on the implementation, a higher layer may only represent a greater abstraction (e.g., only interfaces) and not necessarily be that far in cognitive "distance". Nevertheless, any sublayers between them should still be cognitively "closer".

F. Hamiltonian POI Visitation Trail

Assuming the principles of proper modularity and hierarchy are applied in a given project, a greater distance between POIs is equivalent to a larger mental jump. Thus, to reduce mental effort, once the distance for all pairs has been calculated, we desire the overall shortest trail that provides the visitation order for all POIs such that each POI is visited exactly once except that the starting point is also the end point, i.e. a Hamiltonian cycle. The calculation problem is equivalent to the well-known TSP.

G. Knowledge Processing

ReSCU knowledge processing stages are shown in Figure 2 and described below.

Figure 2. ReSCU knowledge processing stages.

1) Input Processing: the source code as text files are imported and analyzed. A list of all the POIs in the project as FQNs is determined. The layer of each POI is determined by counting the subpackage depth of its FQN. If the project actually utilizes a layer structure is irrelevant here. This is then used to apply the aforementioned POI distance calculation.

2) POI Filtering: POIs already visited by this user (either in the expected order or out of order) are filtered from the set for the initial planning or replanning.

3) POI Prioritization: the aforementioned MethodRank calculation is used to create an ordered list of POIs.

4) POI Time Planning: the actual POI visitation time is stored per user. Given no prior actual POI visitation time, a default visitation time can be estimated based on a user's profile utilizing a basis time per line of code in seconds, and factors correlated with the size and complexity of the current POI method, the knowledge level (stranger or familiar), and the competency level (junior or senior). Based on the limited session time available, the set of POIs the POI Time Planner component limits the set to an ordered list by priority that is cut off at the point that the cumlative time exceeds the timeboxed session. This reduces the size of the FQN set for locality planning and traversal.

5) POI Locality Planning: from the resulting set, the POIs are then ordered using a planner for a Hamiltonian cycle and a TSP path that takes locality into account, such that those nearby are visited first before jumping to POIs at a further distance.

6) Trail Generation: the recommended trail in the order visitation is generated.

IV. REALIZATION

To support validation of the solution concept and architecture, a prototype was realized in Java. It currently analyzes and generates code trails for Java program code. For simplification, only class methods are considered and method overloading is ignored (a single FQN is used for methods of the same name in trails).

As a Representational State Transfer (REST) service, the *Web Service* component was realized with Restlet and can be run locally, on the team's server, or the cloud in order to easily integrate with various integrated development environments or software engineering environments. The *Database Repository* used H2 as a relational and Neo4J as a graph database. To support flexible integration, the output trail format is XML.

The actual POI visitation time is tracked via navigation events received via the web service, with the table METHODRATING_TIMEONMETHOD storing MethodID, UserID, and visitation time (in seconds). POIs that were already visited (expected or not) are then filtered and removed from the replanned trail.

MethodRank requires a data structure with methods (as FQNs) and their target invocation relationships and counts. For this, static code analysis of a project's methods and invoke relationships is performed using jQAssistant 1.0.0 and the GraphAware Neo4j NodeRank plugin [21]. A Cypher query selects all Method FQNs and their invoked Method FQNs and the result is exported to a CSV file. A separate simplified graph is then created by importing the CSV file into the Static Analysis Program with FQN(Method)->INVOKES->FQN(TargetMethod) relationships in the Neo4J server. GraphAware NodeRank then provides NodeRanks (i.e. MethodRanks) for every node (Method) for the number of invocations with the NodeRank stored in each node's property (Figure 3 shows a partial graph in Neo4J). The result is retrieved via the Neo4J REST API in JSON (example shown in Figure 4). The JSON was parsed, converted to FQNs, and placed in the H2 MethodRank table.

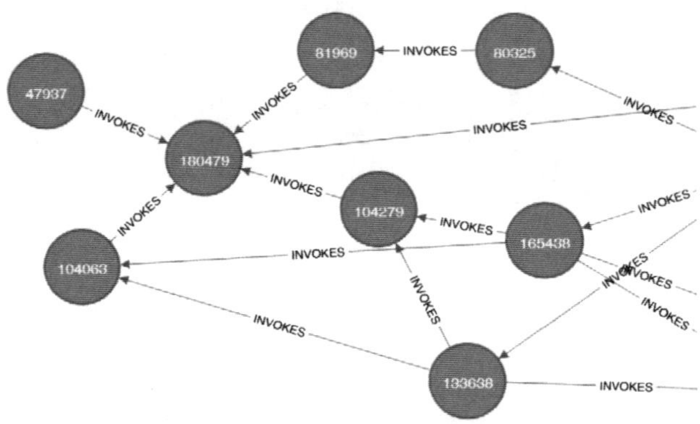

Figure 3. Example partial MethodRank graph in Neo4J.


```
[
  {
    "id": 41,
    "labels": ["STATICANALYSIS",
      "STATIC_de.ba.Class:getString(java.lang.String)"],
    "MethodRank": 504220
  },
  {
    "id": 90,
    "labels": ["STATICANALYSIS",
      "STATIC_de.ba.GlobalSettings:getInstance()"],
    "MethodRank": 335443
  },
  {
    "id": 1801,
    "labels": ["STATICANALYSIS",
      "STATIC_de.ba.package1.Helpers:someHelp()"],
    "MethodRank": 156736
  }
]
```


Figure 4. Example NodeRank request result in JSON.

Users are differentiated by a user ID. The visitation time is adjusted by a factor (default = .5) was used to halve the estimated time if it is a senior engineer, and a factor (.5) also if the user is already familiar with the code. All user sessions are time-boxed (default setting is termination at midnight, but any end time can be set). Once the prioritized POI list is calculated, POIs are selected in priority order to be included in the trail until the accumulated expected visitation times exceed remaining session time. The Hamiltonian path calculation is then applied on this subset.

To order the POI trail according to POI locality, the *Trail Planner* component integrated OptaPlanner, specifically optimizing the trail with regard to the TSP. For sufficient IDE interaction responsiveness during trail generation, the OptaPlanner solving time was explicitly limited to a maximum of 5 seconds to likely provide sufficient time for at least a solution to be found (depending on the project size, session time, and computation hardware) but not necessarily an optimum (absolute shortest path).

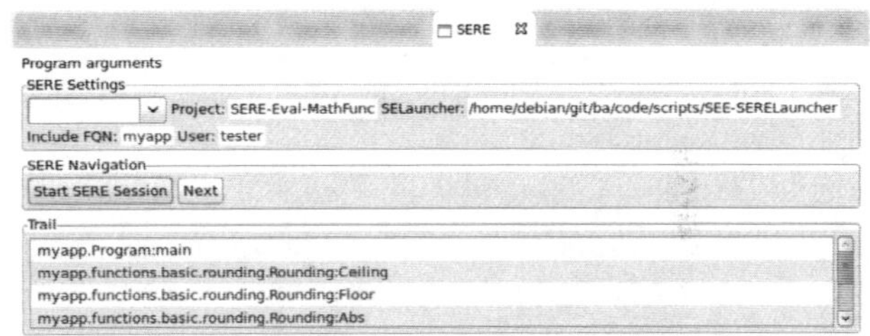

Figure 5. Eclipse client plugin that utilizes the ReSCU service.

To demonstrate REST-based integration of ReSCU with an IDE tool, an Eclipse IDE client (SERE) was developed, shown in Figure 5. The upper part shows the current project, the middle part is used for starting and navigating a session, and the bottom displays the upcoming trail locations (methods). Double-clicking causes the method to be shown in the Eclipse source view.

V. EVALUATION

The focus of our initial evaluation was to a) validate that the solution principles, conceptual architecture, and processing work in harmony when applied to program code as knowledge. Having converted code into a knowledge representation of granules with properties and relationships, determine if it, as a tutor, automatically generates a realistic knowledge-based navigation recommendation for a time-boxed session, and b) empirically validate the effectiveness and efficiency of the automatically generated code trails (i.e., as an automated tutor) in navigating and understanding unfamiliar program code (i.e., unfamiliar presented knowledge). For that, obfuscation was utilized to limit any intuitive mental model creation or semantic ordering so that ReSCU's effectiveness and efficiency for knowledge navigation could be assessed.

The prototype ran in a VirtualBox (Debian 8 x86, single CPU, 1.7GB RAM) VM running on a Windows 10 x64 host with a T9400 CPU@2.5GHz and 4GB RAM. A project consisting of 15 POIs was used as shown in Figure 6a.

A. Code Trail Generation Validation

For the original code (the source for the structure in Figure 6a), a code trail was generated as shown in Figure 7 with a session timebox much larger than the cumulative estimated visitation time for the entire trail (46 minutes and 4 seconds). Thus, no POI was time-filtered.

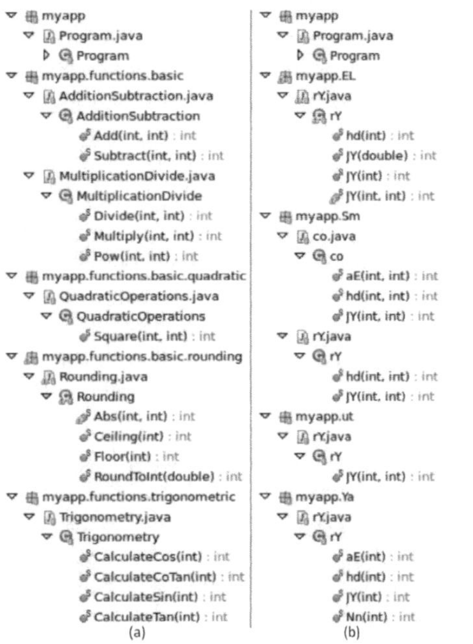

Figure 6. Project structure a) original b) obfuscated.

```
myapp.Program:main
myapp.f.basic.rounding.Rounding:Ceiling
myapp.f.basic.rounding.Rounding:Floor
myapp.f.basic.rounding.Rounding:Abs
myapp.f.basic.rounding.Rounding:RoundToInt
myapp.f.basic.quadratic.QuadraticOps:Square
myapp.f.trigonometric.Trigonometry:CalculateTan
myapp.f.trigonometric.Trigonometry:CalculateCos
myapp.f.trigonometric.Trigonometry:CalculateSin
myapp.f.trigonometric.Trigonometry:CalculateCoTan
myapp.f.basic.MultiplicationDivide:Divide
myapp.f.basic.MultiplicationDivide:Multiply
myapp.f.basic.MultiplicationDivide:Pow
myapp.f.basic.AdditionSubtraction:Add
myapp.f.basic.AdditionSubtraction:Subtract
```

Figure 7. Code trail generated without limiting session timebox.

```
myapp.Program:main
myapp.f.trigonometric.Trigonometry:CalculateCos
myapp.f.trigonometric.Trigonometry:CalculateSin
myapp.f.trigonometric.Trigonometry:CalculateCoTan
myapp.f.basic.MultiplicationDivide:Divide
myapp.f.basic.MultiplicationDivide:Multiply
myapp.f.basic.MultiplicationDivide:Pow
myapp.f.basic.AdditionSubtraction:Add
myapp.f.basic.AdditionSubtraction:Subtract
```

Figure 8. Code trail generated with limited session timebox.

When the session timebox was limited to 30 minutes, lower ranked POIs with fewer invocations were removed from the set and the code trail replanned preserving locality as exhibited in Figure 8.

B. Empirical Structural Code Analysis Study

Obfuscation transforms or destroys the original software structure and semantics and negatively impacts the efficiency of attacks while reducing the gap between a novice and skilled attacker [22]. Although obfuscation is usually used to avoid code from being understood by an attacker, we apply it here to explicitly remove the semantic and structural points of reference in order to determine how well ReSCU supports a programmer navigating unfamiliar code.

Code identifiers (as in Figure 9) were obfuscated with ProGuard utilizing random dictionaries containing strings of two character length generated by Random.org. Obfuscated .class files were decompiled to source code files with Java's decompiler (as in Figure 10).

Using the convenience sampling technique, two users experienced with Java and the Eclipse IDE were asked to sketch a model of the program code using only the classic Eclipse IDE without ReSCU and then, after a new obfuscation, with ReSCU.

```
package myapp.func.trigonometric;
...
public class Trigonometry {
    ...
    public static int calculateTan (int x) {
      int numeratorSin = calculateSin(x);
      int denominatorCos = calculateCos(x);
      return multiplicationDivide.divide(
        numeratorSin , denominatorCos);
    }
}
```

Figure 9. Example original project source code snippet.

```
package myapp.Ya;
...
public class rY {
  ...
  public static int aE(int paramInt) {
    int i = JY(paramInt);
    int j = hd(paramInt);
    return co.hd(i, j);
  }
}
```

Figure 10. Example obfuscated project source code snippet.

User1 took 15:30 and User2 11:20 minutes to produce the diagrams transposed in Figure 11a and Figure 11b respectively (italic names were added afterwards to show mappings). A number of structural errors exist in the diagrams.

Repeating it with a fresh obfuscation and with ReSCU, User1 needed 8:20 and User2 7:30 minutes to produce the diagrams transposed in Figure 12a and Figure 12b respectively (italic names were added afterwards to show mappings).

We observed that the diagrams created by users using ReSCU code trail guidance exhibited an order based on locality (which ReSCU preserves) and had fewer errors. This limited empirical study showed improved effectiveness and efficiency in helping navigate unfamiliar program code. Future work will study a larger pool of subjects and projects.

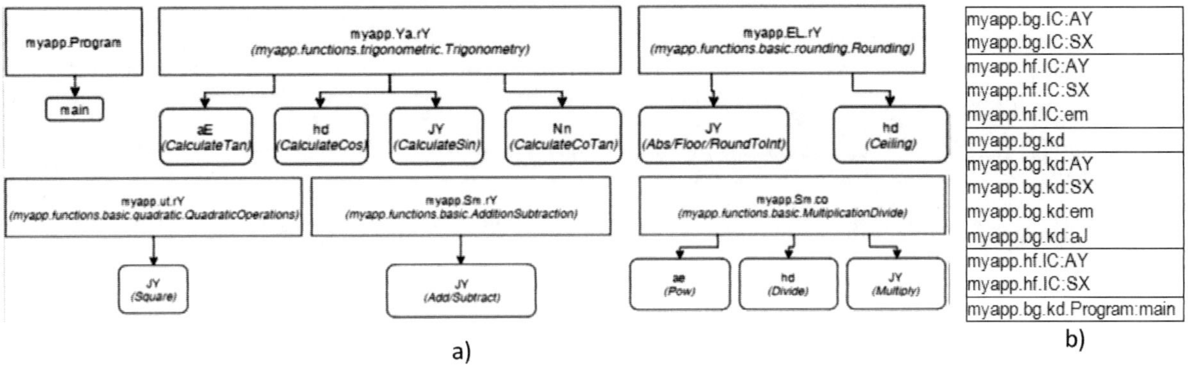

Figure 11. Transposed structure created without ReSCU by a) User1 b) User2.

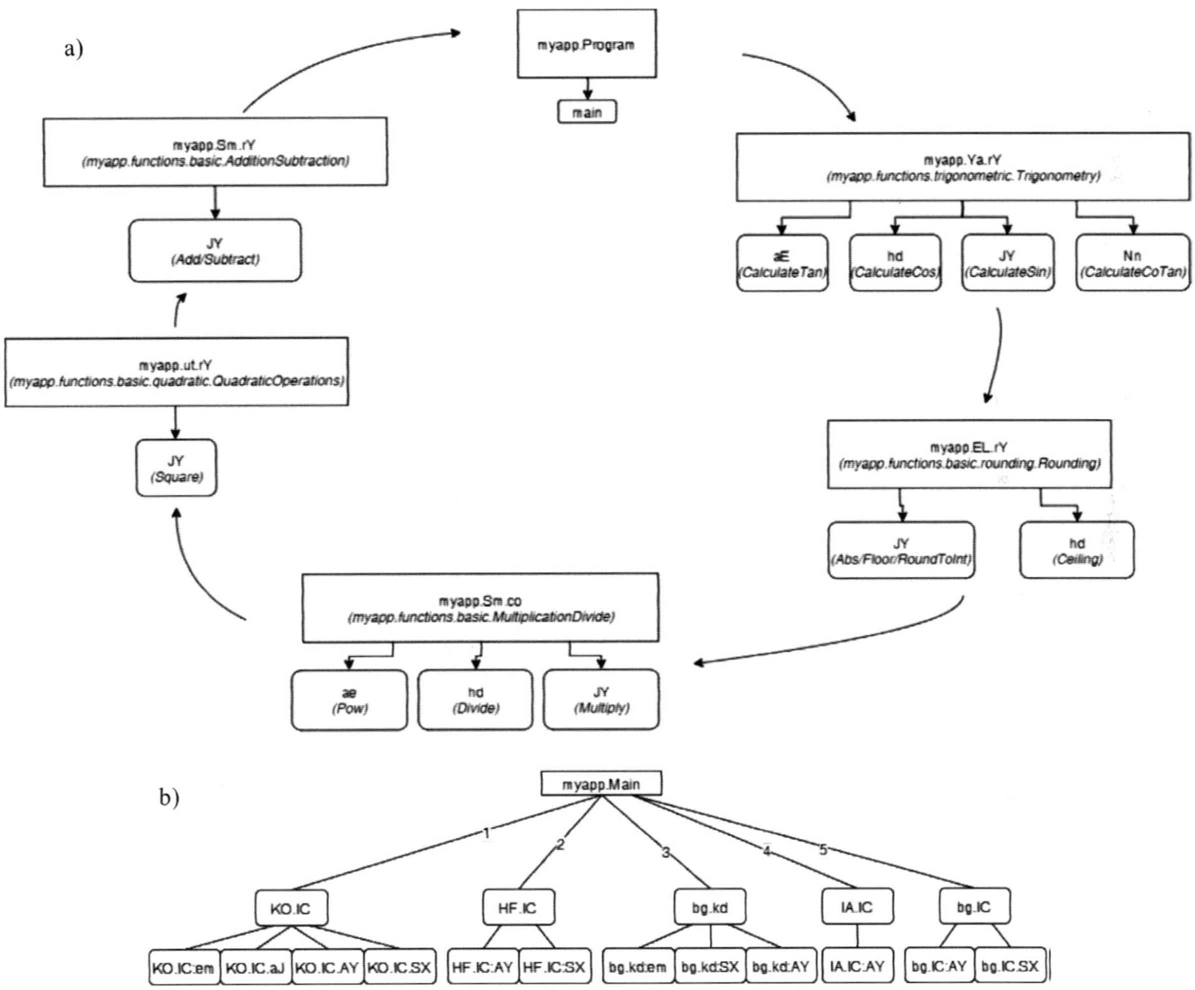

Figure 12. Transposed structure created when using ReSCU by a) User1 b) User2.

VI. Conclusion and Future Work

As an automated tutor and recommender system in the program code comprehension space, ReSCU applies a conceptual mapping of geographical POIs to code locations, considers the locality or knowledge closeness of such granules, and applies TSP to an unfamiliar knowledge landscape consisting of program code. It incorporates MethodRanking as a variant of PageRanking and granular distance in the form of POI locality. Furthermore, it recommends a knowledge navigation order by generating a code trail as a Hamiltonian cycle. The evaluation based on a prototype and limited empirical study applied to obfuscated code indicated effectiveness and efficiency benefits for the ReSCU solution approach.

Future work includes a comprehensive empirical study, utilization in larger scale code projects, support for additional programming languages, and the integration with visualization paradigms. Application of the elaborated ReSCU solution principles to other domains beyond software engineering could provide beneficial knowledge navigation guidance and recommendations in form of a trail for other unfamiliar knowledge landscapes.

Acknowledgment

The author thanks Claudius Eisele for his assistance with the realization, evaluation, and diagrams.

References

[1] L. Kappelman, "Some strategic Y2K blessings," Software, IEEE, 17(2), 2000, pp. 42-46.

[2] Deshpande and D. Riehle. "The total growth of open source". In: IFIP International Federation for Information Processing. Vol. 275. 2008, pp. 197–209

[3] Schmidt, http://benschmidt.org/Degrees/ 2016.01.26

[4] M. P. Robillard, W. Maalej, R. J. Walker, and T. Zimmermann, Recommendation Systems in Software Engineering. Springer, 2014.

[5] Bargiela and W. Pedrycz, Granular computing: an introduction. Springer Science & Business Media, vol. 717, 2012.

[6] M. S. Rahman and M. Kaykobad, "On Hamiltonian cycles and Hamiltonian paths," Information Processing Letters, 94(1), 2005, pp. 37-41.

[7] J. Singer, R. Elves, and M.-A. Storey, "NavTracks: Supporting Navigation in Software Maintenance," Proc. Int'l Conf. on Software Maintenance, 2005, pp. 325–334.

[8] M. Kersten and G. Murphy, "Mylar: A degree-of-interest model for IDEs," Proc. 4th international conf. on aspect-oriented software development, ACM, 2005, pp. 159-168.

[9] D. Cubranic G.C. Murphy, J. Singer, and K. S. Booth, "Hipikat: A project memory for software development," Software Eng., IEEE Trans. on, 31(6), 2005, pp. 446-465.

[10] T. Zimmermann, A. Zeller, P. Weissgerber, and S. Diehl, "Mining version histories to guide software changes," Software Eng., IEEE Trans. on, 31(6), 2005, pp. 429-445.

[11] M. P. Robillard and G. Murphy, "FEAT: A tool for locating, describing, and analyzing concerns in source code," Proc. 25th Int'l Conf. on Software Eng., IEEE, 2003, pp. 822–823.

[12] M. P. Robillard and G. Murphy, "Automatically Inferring Concern Code from Program Investigation Activities," Proc. 18th Int'l Conf. Autom. SW Eng., IEEE, 2003, pp. 225-234.

[13] M. P. Robillard, "Topology Analysis of Software Dependencies," ACM Trans. Software Eng. and Methodology, vol. 17, no. 4, article no. 18, 2008.

[14] D. Mandelin, L. Xu, R. Bodik, and D. Kimelman, "Mining Jungloids: Helping to Navigate the API Jungle," Proceedings of PLDI, Chicago, IL, 2005, pp. 48–61.

[15] R. Holmes, R. J. Walker, and G. C. Murphy, "Approximate structural context matching: An approach to recommend relevant examples," IEEE Transactions on Software Engineering 32(12), 2006, pp. 952–970.

[16] M. Bruch, T. Schaefer, and M. Mezini, "Fruit: IDE support for framework understanding," Proc. 2006 OOPSLA workshop on eclipse technology eXchange, eclipse '06, ACM, 2006, pp. 55–59.

[17] Y. Qian, J. Liang, C. Dang, F. Wang, and W. Xu, "Knowledge distance in information systems," J. of Systems Science and Systems Engineering, 16(4), 2007, pp. 434-449.

[18] E. L. Lawler, The traveling salesman problem: a guided tour of combinatorial optimization. Wiley, 1985.

[19] Y. G. Guéhéneuc, "TAUPE: towards understanding program comprehension," Proc. 2006 conf. Center for Adv. Studies on Collaborative research (CASCON '06) IBM Corp., 2006.

[20] L. Page, S. Brin, R. Motwani, and T. Winograd, "The PageRank citation ranking: bringing order to the Web," In:World Wide Web Internet And Web Information Systems 54.1999-66, 1998, pp. 1–17.

[21] https://github.com/graphaware/neo4j-noderank [2016.03.18]

[22] M. Ceccato et al. "The effectiveness of source code obfuscation: An experimental assessment," In: IEEE Int'l Conference on Program Comprehension, 2009, pp. 178–187.

Knowledge Discovery from Social Media Data: A Case of Public Twitter Data for SMEs

Christopher Adetunji, Leslie Carr
Web Science Institute
School of Electronics and Computer Science
University of Southampton
Southampton, England
Email: {ca6g14, lac}@soton.ac.uk

Abstract—**Making sense of social media data is increasingly becoming a subject of concern to corporate organisations. It is therefore, no coincidence that the subject of Knowledge Identification and Discovery is currently receiving a huge attention within industry and academia. Research has shown that there is an enormous wealth of actionable knowledge to be gained from social media data for organisations' strategic competitive advantage. However, this opportunity is not being harnessed by Small and Medium-sized Enterprises (SMEs) as much as it is by larger enterprises. This is due, in part, to a misconception that social media is not that relevant to SMEs as much as it is to larger corporations. This paper presents a qualitative exploratory study, which attempts to show that social media can be mined for organisational knowledge that is relevant to the strategic competitive advantage of SMEs. A case of a medium-sized enterprise, which is previously without a significant social media presence, is explored with regards to how public Twitter data is exploited to discover actionable knowledge that propels the enterprise's strategic competitive advantage.**

Keywords—social-media; data; twitter; SME; knowledge.

I. Introduction

Beyond their use for building relationships, connections, and/or marketing leads, social media present an opportunity for Small and Medium-sized Enterprises (SMEs) — just as they do for large corporate enterprises — to exploit the wealth of intrinsic insights embedded in the mass of social data publicly available, for their strategic competitive advantage. Yet, due to a perceived lack of relevance of social media to certain types of industry/sector, SMEs are often disinclined to adopting social media [1]. This work presents a case of a medium-sized enterprise for which social media is perceived as not relevant. Since the organisation is without a huge social media presence, this work utilises public Twitter data, which are mined for relevant insights, and the knowledge gained are actioned for strategic competitive advantage. The pieces of knowledge extracted are explored with a discussion on their actionability as well as other valuable insights potentially embedded in such public social data.

Background

Social media has been adopted by organisations to support both the individual and corporate Knowledge Management processes [2]. It forms a social machine that facilitates human interactions on the Web [3], enabling people to create new knowledge by sharing and synthesising knowledge from various sources. This is aided by the technological platforms upon which social media tools are built, which facilitate the cognitive processes previously performed by people [4][5]. Essentially, *social media* includes tools and software platforms that enable humans to participate in the social process of content and knowledge generation, collaboration and knowledge sharing. Social media trends began with the rise of so-called Web 2.0 [6], in which sites became sophisticated apps and content-management platforms designed to facilitate the creation and sharing of user-generated data and content [7]. These platforms include social sharing and networking tools like Facebook, Twitter, blogs, wikis and forums [8][9][10]. In addition, [3, p.2] identifies mySpace, Ushahidi, Galaxy Zoo, reCaptcha and Wikipedia as social software exemplars of social machines.

With their support for contributions and knowledge sharing from across a wide range of avenues (e.g., tweeting via Short Messaging Services (SMS) or smart phone apps), social media tools enhance knowledge sharing within the organisation in their capacity for fostering discussions over documents and thereby enabling organisations to build social environment or communities of practice necessary for facilitating the sharing of tacit knowledge [11][12, p.26]. This has impacted the strictly-controlled world of corporate Information Technology (IT) services, creating an agenda of Enterprise Mobility that is implemented by employee-owned devices adapted for company use, a concept commonly referred to as Bring Your Own Device (BYOD); and/or company-owned devices that support personal use, also commonly referred to as Company-Owned Personally-Enabled (COPE). Consequently, an enormous amount of rapid and varied data is being produced by social applications embedded in the workplace, potentially available for organisations' insight using techniques of big data analytics such as text analysis of unstructured data sources and massively parallel processing (MPP) to analyse streaming data for informed decision and better results [13][12]. This work utilises text analysis techniques to make sense of the unstructured social media data harvested through Twitter's Streaming API.

As a social micro-blogging utility, Twitter creates increased interest in organisations with regards to growth, features and potential benefits to the organisation [14]. For example, apart from its significant role in the US Elections of 2008 [15], [6] also alluded to Dell's claim that its use of Twitter has generated $1 million in incremental revenue due to sales alerts. Meanwhile, [16] describes Twitter as 'a glorified piece of valuable infrastructure that enables rapid and easy communication' and, unlike Facebook or LinkedIn, its asymmetric relationship model of 'following' allows one to keep up with the tweets of any other user without the need for the other user to reciprocate. This facilitates a lateral flow of knowledge that is powered by the intrinsic motivation of individual employees within the organisation. Moreover, the consumerisation and proliferation of mobile devices like smart phones has driven the popularity of social media and enabled the adoption of Web 2.0 affordances, especially the deployment of micro-blogging, to the business environment. This offers powerful opportunities to distribute 'tacit knowledge' and 'best practices' within an enterprise [15].

An increasing number of large enterprises have already been able to tap into the benefits of Twitter as a micro-blogging platform. According to a Gartner report referenced in [15], leading-edge companies are investigating the potential of micro-blogging to enhance other social media and channels, and, as mentioned above, Dell recounts its use of Twitter as a leverage for increased revenue gains while the electoral success of Barack Obama as president in the US General elections of 2008 is largely credited to the use of Twitter by the Democratic Party [15]. Also, Ford Motors and Zappos [17] are a few examples of large enterprises already exploiting social media. How could this trend be beneficial to Small and Medium sized enterprises even where the social applications may not be hugely embedded in the work place? This work presents how a medium-sized enterprise was able to tap into the wealth of Twitter data for its operational and strategic insights.

II. Case Study Methodology

The role of Small and Medium-sized Enterprises within an Economy is so crucial that the World Bank commits hugely to the development of the sector as a significant part of its efforts in promoting employment and economic growth [18]. *Liaise Loddon* is a medium-sized enterprise with about 220 employees, providing residential social care for adults with autism and learning disabilities in Hampshire, United Kingdom. As typical in this sector, operational procedures result in an enormous amount of documentation arising from daily diaries, incident/activity reports and several other reporting in compliance with regulatory requirements, analytical purposes and decision making. Although the company has recently deployed an enterprise mobility suite of mobile devices and applications to replace the existing paper-based documentation system, this experiment explores how this enterprise mobility agenda could be hardened with knowledge sharing and knowledge extraction from the mass of social data freely available on Twitter, for example, in such a way as it supports the organisation at the second level of organisational change, which highlights the people dimension of a socio-technical system [19, p.35-38]. This work utilises simple textual analysis techniques to make sense of the unstructured social media data harvested through Twitter's Streaming API. This is a practical approach that is replicable with a cost of next to nothing.

Ordinarily, Liaise Loddon's operations do not require social media marketing, neither does it appear like the company could benefit from its employees' conversations and knowledge sharing over social blogging platform like Twitter. As such, this organisation, just like many other small and medium-sized enterprises (SMEs), does not have a huge following on Twitter, neither does it have any such enterprise micro-blogging platform that generates sufficient data from which employees' conversations could be mined for insights. Yet, in a bid to stay abreast of — and respond quickly to — issues surrounding its area of specialism, this work harvested, from global public tweets, for *Autism*, and its variants like 'ASD' and 'disability', which are categorical keywords that tend to define aspects of its business domain.

III. Data Gathering and Filtering

For the experiment, a week's worth of tweets are harvested (from 30th April to 6th May, 2015) with a toital of 149,501 from the Twitter streaming API and, using textual analysis technique, extraneous elements are filtered out in order to reduce the data. In data mining, one solution to the challenges of handling vast volumes of data is to reduce the data for mining [20].

TABLE I: 3.5% OF TWEETS WITH LOCATION ENABLED

		Percentage (%)
No. of Tweets without Country Value	144246	96.5
No. Tweets with Country Value	5255	**3.5**
Total No. of Tweets	**149501**	100

This dataset is a microcosm of the global public tweets that feature the categorical keywords of interest as mentioned above. In reducing the data, we also need to remove tweets that are not in English language. For example, the French word 'autisme', which is the same as 'autism' in English, may have had the letter 'e' mistakenly omitted by a person tweeting in French and this would have resulted in the French tweet being harvested. As a way of delimiting the scope of the study, tweets that are not in English language are filtered out. Also, the abbreviation, 'ASD', would not always represent our intended use neither would it always represent *Autistic Syndrome Disorder* even in the English language.

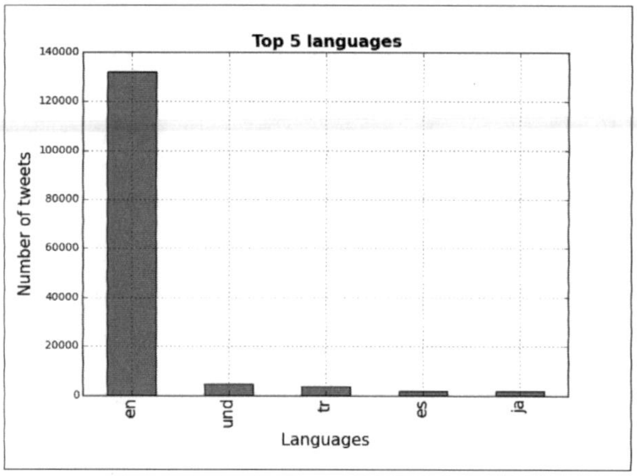

Figure. 1: The Top 5 Languages of Tweets Polled

In essence, those tweets containing the polled keywords are filtered out where they are deemed to be out of context. Moreover, we could only determine the country for about 3.5% of tweets in the harvested Twitter data, as indicated in Table I. This is due to Twitter users not updating their profile with

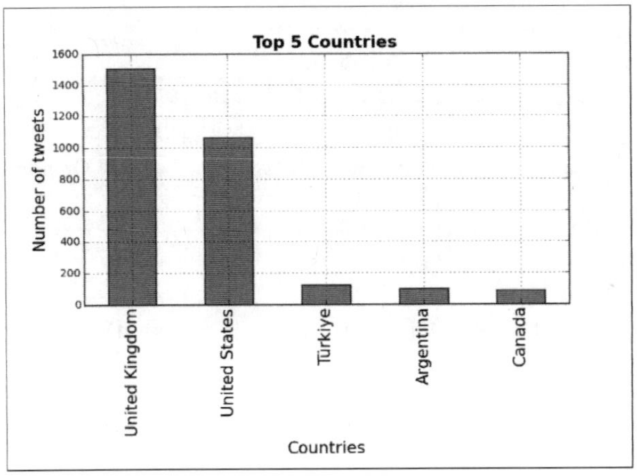

Figure. 2: The Top 5 Countries of Tweets Polled

their locations as well as some imperfection with Twitter's geolocation algorithm [21].

Therefore, to begin making sense of this data, we concentrate on the top 5 languages and top 5 countries as presented in Figures 1 and 2 respectively, out of which the experiment was narrowed to tweets in English language and from the United Kingdom. *(Please note the following expanded abbreviations as used in Figure 1: en, English; und, Undecided; tr, Traditional Chinese; es, Spain; ja, Japan.)*

TABLE II: CONTENT CLASSIFICATION OF TWEET DATA

Contents	*No. of Tweets (Including RTs)*
Impact of Technology on Disability	15
Information Gathering	10
Political Opinions (#votecameronout)	132
Social Welfare Benefits	327
Living with Autism	989
Total Tweets	**1473**

As indicated in Figure 2, there are 1,473 tweets emanating from the United Kingdom. Using regular expressions, the tweets are classified according to the contents as indicated in Table II.

IV. Findings and Knowledge extracted from the Data

Despite the data collection being based on domain-specific keywords of interest to this paper's case study, the research is an exploratory study in which there was not a preconceived idea of the insights/knowledge inherent in the data. Out of an enormous amount of data, only a handful may contain the valuable and actionable knowledge that propels an organisation towards strategic competitive advantage [20, p.5]. As such, the bulk of the contents as seen in Table II, are largely re-tweets (RT) of the original messages and so, may be regarded as extraneous amplification of the original tweets. Therefore, this section describes the categories observed in the data and the next section follows with a discussion on the value and actionability of the knowledge so discovered:

1) **Impact of Technology on Disability**

> *"RT @BILD_tweets: Helping to unlock the secrets of autism - a project using innovative technology aims to change how we address autism http:..."*

The above tweet provides an insight into a project using innovative technology to change how we address *autism*. As this paper's case study organisation is in the business of autism support and also currently implementing mobile technologies to enhance its operational performance, it is worth exploring this piece of insight further.

Figure. 3: Original Tweet with Link to Project on Innovative Technology

Although the link to the actual URL of the story about the project is missing from the tweet, we can easily follow up with the original source of the tweet, as the above is a RT (Re-Tweet) of @BILD_tweets, which is the Twitter handle for BILD (British Institute of Learning Disabilities). BILD actually tweeted that piece of content on the 29th of April, which is a day before our data capture began, as can be seen in Figure 3. This explains why the original tweet was not captured in our twitter streaming data capture of 30th April to 6th May. From this original tweet, we have been able to extract the URL link (bit.ly/1JRNhV0) to the story about the project on innovative technology. This is about the National Autism Project, which "aims to create a more strategic approach to addressing the challenges of the condition". This project highlights the impact of iPads, picture dictionaries and interactive schedules on the improvements of communication and vocabulary of autistic people. Strategic competitive advantage requires an alignment/tagging along with this project. Below are samples of other tweets related to this content of Technology's impact on disability while its pertinence, as an actionable piece of knowledge, is discussed further in Section V:

> *"tech reducing the impact of disability - or are the latest gadgets too pricey? Watch @SkyNewsSwipe at 2130 http://t.co/iHtX1spOqQ"*

> *"Technology limits impact of disability but is it affordable? @TwitterUser_GT http://t.co/Az3nJejO32"*

2) **Information Gathering**

"@TwitterUser @BBCNewsUS @BBCWorld Please direct me to this research, the thing about vaccines causing autism was admitted to be a fraud."

The first tweet about vaccines causing autism in this category is a request for information. Just as an enterprise micro-blogging tool could be used within the organisational social network, public micro-blogging tools like Twitter provide the platform to quickly seek information, knowledge and/or ideas from a heterogeneous audience defying the constraints of space, time and location. Thus, the above tweet was almost instantly replied to by the one below:

"@TwitterUser Here's the original study that said that vaccines cause autism, from a respected, peer-reviewed journal: http://t.co/cmVVKpLQgh"

Even though the original study is from a 'respected, peer-reviewed journal', as claimed by the sender of the above tweet, we know from the link provided that the publication of the research has been retracted as shown in Figure 6. The ability for anyone to search, gather and distribute information seamlessly in this manner provides an interesting dimension of social media as "relatively inexpensive and widely accessible electronic tools that enable anyone to publish and access information..."[22].
Meanwhile, the following two tweets provide link to further information that could help drive home the knowledge that the research study in question has actually been rebuffed:

"RT @TwitterUser: @SB277FF vaccines do not cause autism. They don't. But if they did, what would you prefer? Autism or incurable smallpox/po"

""RT @BILD_tweets: There is 'no link between MMR and autism', major study concludes. http://t.co/Re9L8fPfGV via the @guardian #autism""

In as much as Twitter allows for an almost spontaneous expression of opinions by anyone, it offers a good platform for healthy debate on topical issues from which knowledge could be mined, as exemplified by the question of preference between autism and incurable smallpox posed by one of the tweets above.

Moreover, the following tweet with a URL link to *Learning Disability Census* is an example in knowledge discovery (of an official census and regional data on Learning Disabilities), which when actioned in conjunction with the enterprise resource planning, could have an impact on the company's strategic planning:

"RT @dmarsden49: Learning disability census with regional stats is out. Check http://t.co/Ja3tk7ZRDZ"

RT @mmaher70: 5 more years of the Tories we will lose\nSocial Care\nNHS\nHuman Rights\nWorkers Rights\nUnions\nDisability support\n#VoteCameronOut
RT @mmaher70: 5 more years of the Tories we will lose\nSocial Care\nNHS\nHuman Rights\nWorkers Rights\nUnions\nDisability support\n#VoteCameronOut
RT @mmaher70: 5 more years of the Tories we will lose\nSocial Care\nNHS\nHuman Rights\nWorkers Rights\nUnions\nDisability support\n#VoteCameronOut
RT @mmaher70: 5 more years of the Tories we will lose\nSocial Care\nNHS\nHuman Rights\nWorkers Rights\nUnions\nDisability support\n#VoteCameronOut
RT @mmaher70: 5 more years of the Tories we will lose\nSocial Care\nNHS\nHuman Rights\nWorkers Rights\nUnions\nDisability support\n#VoteCameronOut
RT @mmaher70: 5 more years of the Tories we will lose\nSocial Care\nNHS\nHuman Rights\nWorkers Rights\nUnions\nDisability support\n#VoteCameronOut
RT @mmaher70: 5 more years of the Tories we will lose\nSocial Care\nNHS\nHuman Rights\nWorkers Rights\nUnions\nDisability support\n#VoteCameronOut
RT @mmaher70: 5 more years of the Tories we will lose\nSocial Care\nNHS\nHuman Rights\nWorkers Rights\nUnions\nDisability support\n#VoteCameronOut
RT @mmaher70: 5 more years of the Tories we will lose\nSocial Care\nNHS\nHuman Rights\nWorkers Rights\nUnions\nDisability support\n#VoteCameronOut
RT @mmaher70: 5 more years of the Tories we will lose\nSocial Care\nNHS\nHuman Rights\nWorkers Rights\nUnions\nDisability support\n#VoteCameronOut

Figure. 4: The Proliferated Re-tweets of Political Opinion

3) **Political Opinions (#votecameronout)**

The role of public opinion cannot be over-emphasised insofar as it shapes and is shaped by government policies. A recent and relevant example is the UK tax credits row [23], which has seen the planned tax credit cuts, at the time of writing this report, suspended by government because the scheme proved unpopular to the public and thus defeated in the House of Commons. Social media, especially Twitter, provides a means of capturing and measuring the sentiments and opinions of the electorate.
It is therefore, no coincidence that political opinions that have been expressed, are included in the Twitter data gathered over *autism* and *disability* keywords:

"#votecameronout Because he wants to get rid of Human Rights Act which will affect: Maternity Rights; Workers rights; Disability Rights"

"For the harassment of people struggling on sick & disability benefits... #VoteCameronOut"

"5 more years of the Tories we will lose Social Care, NHS, Human Rights, Workers Rights, Unions, Disability support. #VoteCameronOut"

Using the hashtag #votecameronout in the run up to the UK General Elections of 2015, the above tweets represent an active campaign against the then incumbent Tory-led government in which David Cameron is Prime Minister. It is interesting to note that the bulk (129) of the political tweets in this experiment's Twitter data are a proliferated re-tweets (RT) of the above 3 original tweets as exemplified in Figure 4. The correlation between public sentiments on social media and elections results and/or on government policies, is another growing area of interest in social media research. In politics meanwhile, it is not uncommon for opponents to whip up public sentiments by whatever means possible. Social Welfare issues are quintessentially core, and often politicised, concerns in the UK. A parallel category of tweets in this work is that of social welfare benefits, which is described in the next section. Although this research's data-set is based, as stated earlier, on categorical keywords that define the business of the case study organisation, the infiltrated political opinions cannot be ignored in as much as these are public opinions that shape political trends which potentially impacts on businesses in terms of government policies. Akin to this is the category on

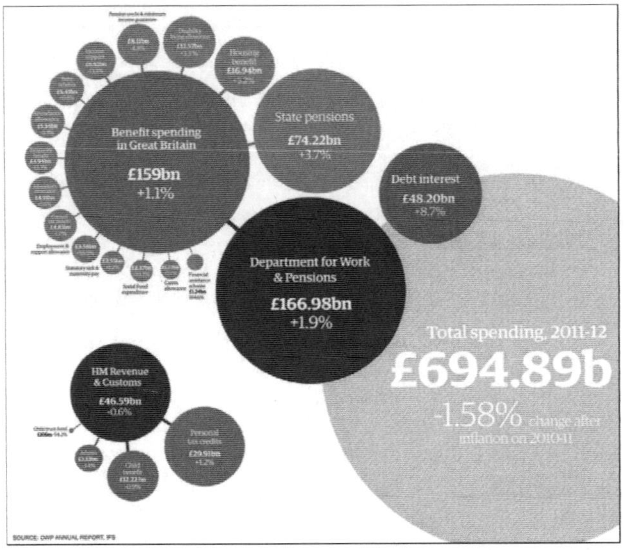

Figure. 5: Public Spending on Benefits in the UK

social welfare benefits, described in the next section.

4) **Social Welfare Benefits**
Social Welfare simply implies the "Well being of the entire society" [24], which promotes inclusivity for the disabled, the sick, the elderly/pensioner, the unemployed and even the low income earners. As this is the hallmark of an egalitarian society, the UK government renders financial assistance to these categories of people in form of a range of Social Welfare Benefit payments. Figure 5 provides an insight into public spending on social welfare benefits in the UK. [25]. As indicated in the preceding section, social welfare issues affect the fabrics of the society and any proposed significant cut in social welfare benefits is a natural invitation for public dissent. This category of tweets from this work represents genuine sentiments and opinion of those expressing them, without political motivations like the preceding category:

> *"Uproar at thought of @Conservatives cutting child benefits if elected - I wish there was same media outrage over disability cuts #GE2015"*

> *"@George_Osborne If only I could live until pensionable age. You've reduced my disability benefit well below living standards!"*

> *"39 yo woman killed herself after Department Work and Pensions threats to cut off disability benefits http://t.co/TkVQF2UYki..."*

Again, the above are a few samples of sentiments and opinions about *Child Benefits* and *Disability Benefits*, which provide an initial understanding to the unassuming, that social welfare benefits are not a one-size-fits-all affair but are multifarious (see Figure 5), with some being exclusively non- means tested (e.g, Child Benefit). These tweets provide some insights into public sentiments towards government policies. Since any of such social welfare benefit cuts would directly and/or indirectly impact the service users and providers of social care, it can be inferred that the case study organisation would also share these public sentiments.

5) **Living with Autism**

Autism is defined as a *life-long neurodevelopmental condition interfering with the person's ability to communicate and relate to others* [26]. How can this definition be juxtaposed with one of the myths surrounding autism [27, item 8] that *autistic people do not interact*? This myth is however, dispelled by the tweet below, which is a re-tweet of an original tweet by an actual autistic blogger who attempts to use his blog posts to connect with the general public:

> *"@matt_diangelo RT? It would be truly amazing if u could view my blog about living with Autism&OCD. Would mean a lot-http://t.co/JCGBBZz8fJ"*

This category constitutes the bulk of the Twitter data for this work as it contains multiple unique re-tweet of the same tweet over 900 times (see Table II. This is an indication of the public interest/curiosity and positive sentiment towards the subject of autism in general, and towards the autistic blogger in particular. Despite the National Health Service (NHS)'s attempts at educating the general public by diffusing some of the myth surrounding the subject of *Autism* [28], among several *Autism Awareness* initiatives, the story of autism as told by an autistic person appears to garner more public support and understanding .
Measuring public opinion and sentiments through social media impact, reach and networks is another interesting research area in social media research towards which this work can potentially be extended.

V. Actionability of Knowledge Extracted

The real essence of knowledge is its actionability, especially when it contributes to the advancement of a proposed undertaking [29]. Each of the knowledge items discovered from the tweet data, as highlighted above, is capable of providing significant insights that would inform decision making, which impacts company's proposed undertakings at one point or the other. However, the first item, *Impact of Technology on Disability*, (No.1) is more pertinent to the enterprise mobility agenda by which the company deploys mobile application and devices to its operations. For example, one of the shortened URL above (http://t.co/Az3nJejO32) leads us to a Sky News supplement on *'How Tech is Helping with Struggle of Disability'*. To aspire to a leadership position in the health and social care sector, the case study organisation cannot afford to be oblivious to such reports as this, which could potentially shape the industry trends and direction. This knowledge, coupled with the insights gained from the use of iPads and pictorial dictionary mentioned in the *'Project on Innovative Technology'* resulted in an official resolution by the company to extend the use of mobile devices to its service users as well, and not only to help staff in operational performances. It is worth noting that, although the piece of actionable knowledge regarding the impact of technology on disability was on the news prior to the extraction of data for this work, it was neither known nor acted upon by the company until the above decision was driven through a presentation made by the authors of this paper.

Meanwhile, without a preconceived agenda, this work has been able to discover actionable knowledge and strategic insights from Twitter. As discussed, these are, that the use of technology being embarked upon by the organisation is not misguided; that the widespread belief that MMR vaccines cause autism has been debunked; and the regional distribution of autism through the *Learning Disability Census* about autism; among others.

Apart from the above insights, there are more valuable insights that an organisation could derive from these kinds of public social data. These include:

1) *Expertise location:*
The micro-blogging, hash-tagging and re-tweeting affordances of Twitter places its contents in the public space, as opposed to emails or local files, which are prone to privacy concerns. According to [10], "the diversity of both the content type and the user associations with contents is an indication that expertise information derived from social media data can be of great value". [10] further assert that social media that reside behind a firewall (e.g., *Yammer* — a corporate Twitter clone [30]), is typically used by employees to discuss internal topics, and hence reflects the organisation's unique vocabulary and areas of interest. This enables the organisation to find people (or employees) who are knowledgeable in a given topic.

2) *Public Opinion and Sentiments:*
Public opinion about the organisation's image, product or services can make the difference between success and failure for the organisation. Knowing the sentiments of the public would help the organisation in responding in such a way that would ginger or maintain favourable public opinion. Businesses have made efforts to find out customers' sentiments and opinions, often expressed in free text, towards company's products and services [31]. Twitter enables expressions in free text, which is why the bulk of Twitter data is textual. [12] cited a real world example of a client who introduced a different kind of environmentally friendly packaging for one of its staple brands. Customer sentiment was somewhat negative to the new packaging, and some months later, after tracking customer's feedback and comments, the company discovered an unnerving amount of discontent around the change and therefore moved to a different kind of eco-friendly packaging. They therefore, hypothesise that, "*if you dont have some kind of micro-blog oriented customer sentiment pulse-taking going on at your company, you're likely losing customers to another company that does.*"

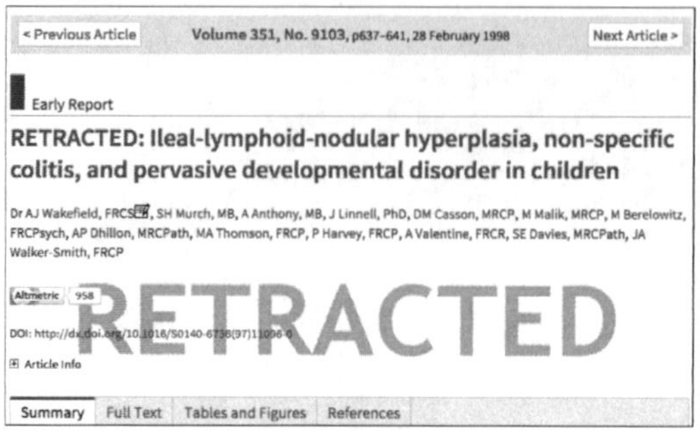
< Previous Article | Volume 351, No. 9103, p637-641, 28 February 1998 | Next Article >

Early Report

RETRACTED: Ileal-lymphoid-nodular hyperplasia, non-specific colitis, and pervasive developmental disorder in children

Dr AJ Wakefield, FRCS, SH Murch, MB, A Anthony, MB, J Linnell, PhD, DM Casson, MRCP, M Malik, MRCP, M Berelowitz, FRCPsych, AP Dhillon, MRCPath, MA Thomson, FRCP, P Harvey, FRCP, A Valentine, FRCR, SE Davies, MRCPath, JA Walker-Smith, FRCP

Altmetric 958

RETRACTED

DOI: http://dx.doi.org/10.1016/S0140-6736(97)11096-0

Article Info

Summary | Full Text | Tables and Figures | References

Figure. 6: Retracted Study Linking Vaccine to Autism

VI. Conclusion

This paper has attempted to explore the viability of social media as rich data sources from which SMEs — like large enterprises — can discover knowledge and insights for their strategic competitive advantage. The paper presented Twitter as a prolific data source of all social media and examined the case of a medium-sized enterprise for which public Twitter data was explored and exploited for valuable insights without a preconceived idea of the insights/knowledge inherent in the data. The paper further examined the contents of the social data with regards to the actionability of the pieces of knowledge so discovered, which helped in demonstrating that out of an enormous amount of data, only a handful may contain the valuable and actionable knowledge that propels an organisation towards strategic competitive advantage. In view of this, this paper posits that small and medium sized enterprises are not precluded from using social media data to augment their corporate knowledge assets through knowledge discovery, whether or not they have a huge presence or following on social media. The paper concludes therefore, that any enterprise of any size can explore and exploit public social data to its organisational advantage whether or not they are players in the social media sphere. Meanwhile, the structure of the connections and relationships within a social network like Twitter can be visualised to provide further depth and insights to the pieces of knowledge discovered from the network. This work can be extended to cover these terrains in future studies.

References

[1] N. Michaelidou, N. T. Siamagka, and G. Christodoulides, "Usage, barriers and measurement of social media marketing: An exploratory investigation of small and medium B2B brands," *Industrial Marketing Management*, vol. 40, no. 7, Oct. 2011, pp. 1153–1159. [Online]. Available: http://www.sciencedirect.com/science/article/pii/S0019850111001374 [Last Accessed 01 March 2016].

[2] L. Razmerita, K. Kirchner, and T. Nabeth, "Social Media in Organizations: Leveraging Personal and Collective Knowledge Processes," *Journal of Organizational Computing and Electronic Commerce*, vol. 24, no. 1, Jan. 2014, pp. 74–93.

[3] P. R. Smart and N. R. Shadbolt, "Social Machines," in *Encyclopedia of Information Science and Technology*, M. Khosrow-Pour, Ed. Pennsylvania: IGI Global, Aug. 2014.

[4] M. Sigala and K. Chalkiti, "Knowledge management, social media and employee creativity," *International Journal of Hospitality Management*, vol. 45, 2015, pp. 44–58. [Online]. Available: http://linkinghub.elsevier.com/retrieve/pii/S027843191400173X [Last Accessed 02 March 2016].

[5] L. Carr and S. Harnad, "Offloading cognition onto the Web," *IEEE Intelligent Systems*, Jan 2011. [Online]. Available: http:

//eprints.soton.ac.uk/271030/1/lesdoc2.pdf [Last Accessed 02 March 2016].

[6] A. M. Kaplan and M. Haenlein, "Users of the world, unite! The challenges and opportunities of Social Media," *Business Horizons*, vol. 53, no. 1, 2010, pp. 59–68.

[7] M. Kleek and K. O'Hara, "The Future of Social is Personal: The Potential of the Personal Data Store," 2014. [Online]. Available: http://eprints.soton.ac.uk/363518/1/pds.pdf [Last Accessed 02 March 2016].

[8] D. P. Ford and R. M. Mason, "A Multilevel Perspective of Tensions Between Knowledge Management and Social Media," *Journal of Organizational Computing and Electronic Commerce*, vol. 23, no. 1-2, Jan. 2013, pp. 7–33.

[9] A. P. McAfee, "Enterprise 2 . 0 : The Dawn of Emergent Collaboration," *MIT Sloan Management Review*, vol. 47, no. 3, 2006, pp. 21–28.

[10] I. Guy, U. Avraham, D. Carmel, S. Ur, M. Jacovi, and I. Ronen, "Mining expertise and interests from social media," *Proceedings of the 22nd international conference on World Wide Web*, 2013, pp. 515–526.

[11] T. H. Davenport and L. Prusak, *Working Knowledge: How Organizations Manage what They Know, Part 247*. Boston: Harvard Business Press, 1998.

[12] P. Zikopoulos, C. Eaton, D. DeRoos, T. Deutsch, and G. Lapis, *Understanding Big Data: Analytics for Enterprise Class Hadoop and Streaming Data*, S. Sit, Ed. New York: McGraw Hill, 2012.

[13] J. Lamont, "Big data has big implications for knowledge management," *KMWorld*, vol. 21, no. 4, 2012. [Online]. Available: http://www.kmworld.com/Articles/Editorial/Features/Big-data-has-big-implications-for-knowledge-\\management-81440.aspx [Last Accessed 02 March 2016].

[14] M. Bulearca and S. Bulearca, "Twitter: a Viable Marketing Tool for SMEs?" *Global Business and Management Research: An International Journal*, vol. 2, no. 4, 2010. [Online]. Available: http://www.gbmr.ioksp.com/pdf/BulearcaandBulearca,2010.pdf [Last Accessed 02 March 2016].

[15] M. Böhringer and A. Richter, "Adopting social software to the intranet: a case study on enterprise microblogging," in *Proceedings of the 9th Mensch & ...*, 2009, pp. 1–10. [Online]. Available: http://www.kooperationssysteme.de/docs/pubs/BoehringerRichter2009-M&C-Enterprise%20Microblogging.pdf [Last Accessed 02 March 2016].

[16] M. A. Russell, *Mining the Social Web, 2nd Edition - O'Reilly Media*. O'Reilly Media, 2013.

[17] A. Porterfield, "9 Companies Doing Social Media Right and Why," 2011. [Online]. Available: http://www.socialmediaexaminer.com/9-companies-doing-social-media-right-and-why/ [Last Accessed 02 March 2016].

[18] M. Ayyagari, T. Beck, and A. Demirguc-Kunt, "Small and Medium Enterprises Across the Globe," *Small Business Economics*, vol. 29, no. 4, 2007, pp. 415–434.

[19] G. Piccoli, *Information Systems for Managers: Texts & Cases*. Hoboken: John Wiley & Sons, 2008.

[20] T. W. Liao and E. Triantaphyllou, *Recent Advances in Data Mining of Enterprise Data: Algorithms and Applications*. World Scientific Publishing Company Pte Limited, 2008.

[21] M. Graham, S. A. Hale, and D. Gaffney, "Where in the World Are You? Geolocation and Language Identification in Twitter," *The Professional Geographer*, vol. 66, no. 4, May 2014, pp. 568–578.

[22] D. Murthy, *Twitter: Social Communication in the Twitter Age*. Cambridge: Polity Press, 2013.

[23] "Tax Credits Row What Will Happen Now After Government Defeat?" 2015. [Online]. Available: https://uk.news.yahoo.com/tax-credits-row-happen-now-100031983.html [Last Accessed 29 February 2016].

[24] "What is social welfare? definition and meaning." [Online]. Available: http://www.businessdictionary.com/definition/social-welfare.html [Last Accessed 03 March 2016].

[25] S. Rogers, "UK welfare spending: how much does each benefit really cost?" 2013. [Online]. Available: http://www.theguardian.com/news/datablog/2013/jan/08/uk-benefit-welfare-spending [Last Accessed 30 April 2016].

[26] M. Elsabbagh *et al.*, "Global prevalence of autism and other pervasive developmental disorders." *Autism research : official journal of the International Society for Autism Research*, vol. 5, no. 3, Jun. 2012, pp. 160–79.

[27] J. Baldock, "World Autism Awareness Day 2015: 16 autism myths debunked," Apr. 2015. [Online]. Available: http://metro.co.uk/2015/04/02/autism-sixteen-myths-debunked-5123051/ [Last Accessed 03 March 2016].

[28] N. Choices, "Autism spectrum disorder - NHS Choices." [Online]. Available: http://www.nhs.uk/Conditions/Autistic-spectrum-disorder/Pages/Introduction.aspx [Last Accessed 03 March 2016].

[29] R. Cross and L. Sproull, "More Than an Answer: Information Relationships for Actionable Knowledge," *Organization Science*, vol. 15, no. 4, Aug. 2004, pp. 446–462.

[30] J. Zhang, Y. Qu, J. Cody, and Y. Wu, "A case study of micro-blogging in the enterprise," in *Proceedings of the 28th international conference on Human factors in computing systems - CHI '10*. New York, USA: ACM Press, apr 2010, p. 123.

[31] C. Lin and Y. He, "Joint sentiment/topic model for sentiment analysis," in *Proceeding of the 18th ACM conference on Information and knowledge management - CIKM '09*. New York, USA: ACM Press, Nov. 2009, p. 375.

Semantic Network Skeletons - A Tool to Analyze Spreading Activation Effects

Kerstin Hartig and Thomas Karbe

Institute for Software Engineering - TU Berlin
10587 Berlin, Germany
Email: {kerstin.hartig, thomas.karbe}@tu-berlin.de

Abstract—**Spreading Activation algorithms are a well-known tool to determine relevance of nodes in a semantic network. Although often used, the configuration of a spreading activation algorithm is usually very problem-specific, and experience-driven. There are practically no guidelines or tools to help with the task. In this paper, we present semantic network skeletons, which are essentially a structural summary of a semantic network. We show how to derive the skeleton from a given semantic network, and how to derive conclusions about good configurations from it. Our results are then demonstrated in a case study from the automotive domain.**

Keywords–Spreading Activation; Information Retrieval; Semantic Network; Advisory System.

I. INTRODUCTION

Spreading Activation algorithms are a long-known tool to determine relevance of nodes in a semantic network. Originally from psychology, they have been used in many other application areas, such as databases, artificial intelligence, biology, and information retrieval [1].

All spreading activation algorithms follow a basic pattern: chunks of activation are spread pulsewise from nodes to neighbor nodes, which marks those nodes as being relevant to a certain degree. However, practically, each known implementation differs in many details, such as the amount and distribution of activation. Whether a specific configuration for such an algorithm is good or bad depends largely on two factors: the problem to be solved by spreading, and the structure of the underlying semantic network. Although there are many working examples of such algorithms, until now there are almost no guidelines on how to achieve a good configuration.

In this paper, we aim to gain insights on spreading configurations by analyzing the structure of the semantic network. In many cases a semantic network consists of many thousands of nodes and edges, and is therefore hard to comprehend. We present a tool called *semantic network skeleton* that summarizes basic structural information of a semantic network and, thus, focuses on a few essential pieces of information.

In Section II, we will give a short summary about semantic networks and spreading activation. In Section III, we will introduce semantic network skeletons formally and visually, followed by a description of the necessary steps to retrieve skeletons from a semantic network in Section IV. Now, that we have network skeletons available, we can use them to analyze the underlying semantic network and to derive spreading effects for different configuration decisions. In Section V, this skeleton analysis for preconfiguration optimization will be presented. Section VI is dedicated to a case study on an advisory systems in the automotive domain. We finish the paper with conclusions and an outlook on future research potentials regarding semantic network skeletons.

II. BASICS AND RELATED WORK

We apply spreading activation as semantic search technique on semantic networks. Therefore, we shed some light on both concepts.

A. Semantic Network

Historically, the term semantic network had its origin in the fields of psychology and psycholinguistics. Here, a semantic network was defined as an explanatory model of human knowledge representation [2][3]. In such a network, concepts are represented by nodes and the associations between concepts as links. Generally, a semantic network is a graphic notation for representing knowledge with nodes and arcs [4][5]. Notations range from purely graphical to definitions in formal logic.

Technically, among others semantic networks can be described by RDF and RDF Schema (RDFS). The RDF data model [5] is defined to be a set of RDF triples whereas each triple consists of a subject, a predicate and an object. The elements can be Internationalized Resource Identifiers (IRI), blank nodes, or datatyped literals. Each triple can be read as a statement representing the underlying knowledge. A set of triples forms an RDF Graph, which can be visualized as directed graph, where the nodes represent subject and object and a directed edge represents the predicate [5].

According to the RDF Specification [5], resources such as IRI and literals carry a particular meaning whereas blank nodes stand for anything. Therefore, statements containing blank nodes denote the existence of something with the statements predicate. In contrast, statements without blank nodes mean the relationship between concrete resources holds.

For the rest of this paper, we use the terms RDF and semantic network interchangeably.

B. Spreading Activation

Spreading activation, like semantic networks, has a historical psychology and psycholinguistic background. It was used as a theoretical model to explain semantic memory search and semantic preparation or priming [2][3][6].

Over the years, spreading activation evolved into a highly configurable semantic search algorithm and found its application in different fields. In a comprehensive survey, Crestani examined different approaches to the use and application of spreading activation techniques, especially in associative information retrieval [1]. Spreading Activation is capable of both identifying and ranking the relevant environment in a semantic network.

The processing of spreading activation is usually defined as a sequence of one or more iterations, so-called pulses. Each node in a network has an activation value that describes its current relevance in the search. In each pulse, activated nodes spread their activation over the network towards associated concepts, and thus mark semantically related nodes [1]. If a termination condition is met, the algorithm will stop. Each pulse consists of different phases in which the activation values are computed by individually configured activation functions. Additional constraints control the activation. Fan-out constraints limit the spreading of highly connected nodes because a broad semantic meaning may weaken the results. Path constraints privilege certain paths or parts of them. Distance constraints reduce activation of distant nodes, because distant nodes are considered to be less associated to each other. There are many other configuration details such as decays, thresholds, and spreading directions.

A challenge, mentioned in spreading activation related research is the tuning of the parameters, e.g., values associated with the different constraints as well as weighting or activation functions [7]. For evaluation of the prototype WebSCSA (Web Search by Constrained Spreading Activation) in [7], values and spreading activation settings are identified experimentally, empirically, or partly manually according to the experiments requirements. Álvarez et al. developed a framework for the application and configuration of spreading activation over RDF Graphs [8]. They state that a deep knowledge of the domain and the semantic network is necessary and domain-specific customization configuration is needed. It is a known fact that spreading activation configuration has a huge impact on the quality of the spreading results. Currently, there exists no systematic approach for the determination of proper configuration settings. Moreover, not even guidelines for the appropriate configuration are available to potential users. There is a lack of systematic analyses of the impact and interaction of different settings and parameters. The semantic network skeleton presented in this paper aims at facilitating such analyses in order to gain helpful insights and support appropriate configurations.

III. SEMANTIC NETWORK SKELETON

As stated before, proper configuration of a spreading activation algorithm is a challenging task. One important influencing factor for a good configuration is the structure of the underlying semantic network. Often however, semantic networks tend to be very large, and therefore hard to comprehend.

In this paper, we propose a tool called *semantic network skeleton*, which is supposed to summarize the structure of a semantic network. Therefore, using a skeleton shall make it easier to comprehend their structural properties and draw conclusions for configurations.

A. Skeleton Introduction

A skeleton of a semantic network is a directed graph that has been derived from a semantic network. We will call the semantic network from which the skeleton has been derived the *source (network)*.

Generally spoken, the skeleton shall represent the semantic structure of the source. Therefore, similar nodes and edges are grouped and represented by single node representatives and edge representatives in the skeleton. Thus, the skeleton hides all the parts of the source which are similar, and it makes the structural differences in the network more explicit.

Often, a semantic network contains also nodes and edges that carry little semantic value and therefore should be ignored by a spreading activation algorithm. An example are blank nodes, which by definition carry no specific meaning. Therefore, before creating a skeleton from a source, one first has to define the *semantic carrying* set of nodes and edges. This choice is very problem-specific, and therefore cannot be generalized. We call the semantic carrying subnetwork of the source the *spread graph*.

Since the skeleton is based on the spread graph, it represents only semantic carrying nodes and edges. The skeleton usually contains three types of node representatives: those classes, instances, and literals. Since the relationships between instance node representatives carry the most structural information about the semantic network, we call this part the *skeleton core*.

B. Types of Semantic Network Skeletons

We distinguish between two types of skeletons regarding their completeness and detail level: the maximum and the effective skeleton of a network.

A *maximum skeleton* contains all potential nodes and relations of the source. It is comparable with a UML class diagram in the sense that it shows everything that is theoretically possible in that network. However, it does not transport any information about the actual usage of classes/instances in the source network. Therefore, the maximum skeleton might contain nodes and relationships that have never been instantiated in the source.

An *effective skeleton* represents the structure of a specific instance of a semantic network. Therefore, it contains only nodes and relations that are actually part of the source network. This means, that a class that is part of an RDF schema, but that has not been instantiated in a concrete instance of that RDF schema would have a node representation in the maximum skeleton, but not in the effective skeleton.

Comparing maximum and effective skeletons, we find advantages and disadvantages for both of them: The maximum skeleton is the more generalized skeleton version, and therefore it applies to many different network instances of the same RDF schema. However, its generality also means, that it carries less specific information about each single instance, and therefore, conclusions drawn from a maximum skeleton are weaker than those drawn from an effective skeleton. The effective skeleton is specific to one instance of a semantic network. Thus, it cannot be reused for other instances, but it results in more precise conclusions.

C. Annotations

While the skeleton structure helps to understand the basic structure of the source network better, a detailed analysis often requires more information: It might be useful to know, how many node or edges are subsumed by a node or edge representative in the skeleton; The average number of incoming or outgoing edges for all represented nodes could indicate a certain spreading behaviour; Maybe there are 10.000 edges of the same type subsumed by one edge representative, but actually they all originate in only 10 different nodes. To capture such (often numerical) information, skeletons can be enhanced by annotations. Typically, there are four types of annotations: those, that describe node or edge representatives and those that describe the source or target of an edge representative.

Since effective and maximum skeletons carry different information, this also applies to annotations on them. While annotations on an effective skeleton refer to a concrete network instance of an RDF Schema (e.g., the concrete count of instances of a node type), annotations on a maximum skeleton describe potential values. Thus, an instance count could have the value $*$, meaning that any number of instances is possible.

D. Syntax

Let L be a set of labels. A Semantic Network Skeleton S is defined by

$$S = (N, E, s, t, l),$$

where

- N is a non-empty set of *node representatives*,
- E is a set of *edge representatives*,
- $s : E \rightarrow N$ is the *source map*,
- $t : E \rightarrow N$ is the *target map*, and
- $l : N \times E \rightarrow L$ is the labelling.

The node and edge representatives each represent a set of nodes/edges of the same type from the original semantic network. Each edge representative $e \in E$ has a source node representative $s(e)$ and a target node representative $t(e)$. Furthermore, all node and edge representatives have a label $l(n)/l(e)$ assigned.

Given a semantic network skeleton $S = (N, E, s, t, l)$, and let $n_1, n_2 \in N$, $e \in E$, $s(e) = n_1$, and $t(e) = n_2$. Then the triple

$$T = (n_1, e, n_2)$$

is called a *skeleton triple* of S. A skeleton triple represents all corresponding RDF triples of the source network.

It is often useful to annotate statistical values to node or edge representatives, or sources/targets of edge representatives. For a skeleton S the *skeleton annotation* A_S is defined as

$$A_S = (A_n, A_e, A_s, A_t),$$

where

- $A_n : K \times N \rightarrow V$ is the *node annotation*,
- $A_e : K \times E \rightarrow V$ is the *edge annotation*,
- $A_s : K \times E \rightarrow V$ is the *edge source annotation*, and
- $A_t : K \times E \rightarrow V$ is the *edge target annotation*.

Here, K stands for a set of *annotation keys*, and V stands for a set of *annotation values*.

E. Graphical notation

The graphical notation for the skeleton corresponds to the graphical notation of RDF Graphs. In Figure 1, the proposed graphical notation is depicted. A node representative $n \in N$ is represented by a circle with its label $l(n)$ denoted over the circle. An edge representative $e \in E$ is represented by an unidirectional arrow with its label $l(n)$ denoted next to the arrow center. An arrow must connect two circles, with the arrow start connecting to the circle that represents the source and the tip of the arrow connecting to the circle that represents the target. Annotations are denoted in the circles, or near the start, middle, or end of the arrow, depending on their annotation type (node, edge, edge source, or edge target annotation).

F. Formal notation of graphical example

A skeleton $S = (N, E, s, t, l)$ that contains among others the node and edge representatives depicted in Figure 1 would be formally denoted by

- the labels *Function, Malfunction, hasMalfunction* $\in L$,
- two nodes $n_1, n_2 \in N$ with $l(n_1) =$ *Function*, and $l(n_2) =$ *Malfunction*,

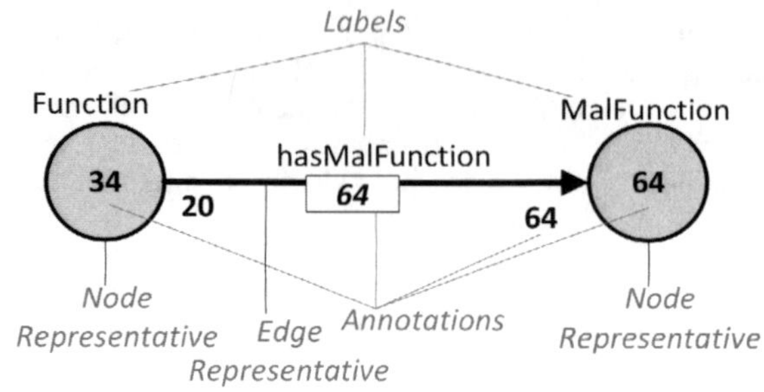

Figure 1. Graphical notation for skeletons.

- an edge $e \in E$ with $l(e) =$ *hasMalfunction*, $s(e) = n_1$, and $t(e) = n_2$.

Additionally, the skeleton annotation $A_S = (A_n, A_e, A_s, A_t)$ would contain the following mappings:

- $A_n(node\_count, n_1) = 34$,
- $A_n(node\_count, n_2) = 64$,
- $A_e(edge\_count, e) = 64$,
- $A_s(src\_rep, e) = 20$, and
- $A_t(tgt\_rep, e) = 64$.

Here, $node\_count$ and $edge\_count$ are the numbers of nodes/edges that have been subsumed by a node/edge representative. The source and target annotations src_rep and tgt_rep are the number of represented nodes, that are part of represented RDF triples. Thus, 20 of the 34 nodes represented by n_1 are connected to nodes represented by n_2 via an edge represented by e.

IV. SKELETON RETRIEVAL

Semantic network structures are as diverse as their potential applications and user-specific design decisions. Generally, semantic networks of all kinds can be subject to skeleton retrieval. However, transformation rules must guarantee that the semantic definition described in Section III-A holds.

In this paper, we focus on retrieving skeletons from semantic networks based on RDF and RDF Schema, more specifically, we utilize the RDF statements from the corresponding RDF Graph. Technically, different approaches are possible from successively parsing RDF Statements to utilizing query languages such as SPARQL [9]. A comprehensive technical description of potential transformations would go beyond the scope of this paper. Therefore, we rather offer an abstract method focusing on semantic compliance.

A. Creating Effective Skeletons

For retrieving the effective node and edge representatives from the spread graph, we apply the following abstract method.

1) Find all resources that are RDF classes. Each class becomes a node representative in the skeleton.
2) For each class find all its instances. All instances of one class are subsumed by one node representative.
3) Find all literals. They are subsumed by one node representative in the skeleton.
4) For each statement, add an edge representative (if not yet existent) for the predicate between the node representative of the statements subject and the node representative of the statements object in the skeleton.

Additionally, during the skeleton retrieval process, the desired annotation values can be computed.

We propose to subsume all literals by one node representative in the skeleton. In RDF, the literals of the class rdfs:Literal contain literal values such as strings and integers. A literal consists of a lexical form, which is a string with the content, a datatype IRI, and optionally a language tag. It is of course possible to further distinguish dependent on datatype or even analysing value equality instead of term equality. However, the content string of the lexical form seems to be most important and sufficient for the application.

B. Creating Maximum Skeletons

For creating a maximum skeleton, we apply the following method to retrieve node and edge representatives from a spread graph.

1) Find all resources that are RDF classes. Each class becomes a node representative in the skeleton. Additionally a node representative for instances of this class must be created. For resources that are classes themselves and subclasses of another class all properties must be propagated from its superclass.
2) Find all properties and their scope (range, domain). For each property add (if not existent yet) an edge representative from the node representative for the instances of the specified domain to the node representative for the instances of the specified range. For each subproperty p_1 of a property p_2 edge representatives must be created between all node representatives connected via p_2.

Again, required annotation values can be computed during the skeleton retrieval process.

V. SKELETON ANALYSIS FOR PRECONFIGURATION OPTIMIZATION

Structural network properties as well as spreading activation constraints and configuration settings affect spreading activation results. Each particular network property and spreading activation setting may have a particular effect. In combination they even have mutual effects. Knowledge about effects and their causes allows for pre-configuration analyses in order to optimize the settings to retrieve the desired effects.

Therefore, in this section, we present some basic skeleton pre-configuration analysis. First, we examine network properties as well as node and edge properties, that can be derived from skeleton annotation analysis. Furthermore, we introduce two potential effects. The analysis can easily be extended and deepened by attaching other useful annotations to the skeleton, developing different metrics and measures.

A. Network Properties - Distance Analysis

Due to its abstraction from a very complex background, the skeleton view gives a clear overview about potential spreading routes through the network. Routes between specific nodes are of special interest. For example, spreading allows for searching for specific node types initiated from some starting node(s). Thus, the *distance* between representatives of starting and search goal nodes denotes the minimal number of spreading pulses required to at least arrive at and possibly distribute any activation to search goal nodes and, therefore, show relevance between both nodes. In distance analysis, the distance between interesting pairs of node representatives can be calculated. Usually, consideration of the environment semantically contributes to the results and is wanted because a straight route may neglect additional useful relationships. Therefore, in order to gain a proper recommendation result, we propose balancing the pulse step configuration based on the distance. Moreover, the *diameter* of the skeleton (maximum path length between any pair of node representatives) stands for the minimal number of spreading pulses necessary to at least spread the entire source represented by this skeleton. With this knowledge, it is possible to prearrange an appropriate spreading pulse count, which may decrease efforts made for a well-spread solution graph.

B. Node and Edge Properties

The presented semantic network skeleton allows for extensible annotation options for customized analyses. Annotations presented in this paper aim at analyzing how and where nodes and edges are connected. The provided statistical information can be utilized for calculation measures describing the state of specific zones in the network, e.g., the zone around a specific node representative or the zone of a skeleton triple.

Common basic annotations are those presented in Section III-F, e.g., $node\_count$. From those, one can derive further more advanced annotations, of which we will present some of the most useful ones. The presented annotations mostly relate to a specific skeleton triple, but usually a global version is possible, too.

For a skeleton triple $T = (n_1, e, n_2)$, the *branching probability* of a node representative n_1 denotes the probability that a represented node of n_1 connects with any represented node of n_2 in the underlying network.

$$b_{prob}(n_1) = \frac{A_s(src\_rep, e)}{A_n(node\_count, n_1)} \tag{1}$$

The *effective average degree* $deg_{eff}(n_1)$ of a node representative n_1 is the average number of edges to which each represented node of n_1 is connected to.

For a skeleton triple T, the *branching ratio* of a node representative n_1 denotes the average number of edges each represented node of n_1 connects with any represented node of n_2 in the underlying network.

$$b(n_1) = \frac{A_e(edge\_count, e)}{A_n(node\_count, n_1)} \tag{2}$$

Node representatives with high branching ratios can be considered to be *high connectors*, which means their represented nodes are highly connected to neighbor nodes in the source network. In contrast, node representatives with low branching ratios can be considered to be *low connectors*, which means their represented nodes are sparsely connected to neighbor nodes in the source network. Branching ratio 1 indicates a *simple connector*. It means that averagely one edge per represented node connects with a neighbor.

C. Potential Effects of Network Properties on the Spreading Result

Spreading Activation effects result from the impact of configuration settings on network properties. An effect describes a behavior specific nodes or edges have while spreading, with respect to the given input.

Two important effects for pre-configuration analysis are the *distributor effect* and the *sink effect*. If a node generously spreads activation to a number of neighbor nodes above average the node operates as a *distributor*. If a node does not (or only sparsely) spread activation to neighbor nodes the node operates as a *sink* (one-way street).

The distributor and sink effects correlate with connectivity information as well as configuration settings such as fan-out constraints and activation thresholds. As an example, a high connector can operate as a distributor and spread activation values via many connected edges. Assuming restrictive fan-out constraints in combination with a low threshold, a high connector may also operate as a sink because the high branching values affect potential distribution disadvantageously and the threshold may be unmanageable.

VI. CASE STUDY

The research of this paper contributes to the enhancement of recent research on an advisory system for decision-making support for hazard and risk analysis in the automotive domain, called *HARvESTer (Hazard Analysis and Risk assessment dEcision Support Tool)*. This advisory system will be utilized for first experiments with the skeleton presented in this paper. Below, the advisory system will be introduced as well as its skeleton creation and subsequent analyses.

A. Recommendation and Advisory System for Decision-making Support for Hazard and Risk Analysis

Since 2011, automotive companies have to adhere to the functional safety standard ISO 26262 [10]. One important safety activity described in the standard is the hazard analysis and risk assessment (HARA), which is strongly expert-driven, and therefore expensive, time consuming, and dependent from the individual experts opinion. In this analysis, experts examine the system under consideration with respect to its functions, possible malfunctions, and the consequences of those malfunctions in different situations. The result of the analysis is a certain safety level and safety goals to reduce the risk introduced by the new system to an acceptable level. According to [11], the experience of experts is still the main means to conduct a proper HARA. Without automation and tool support, a HARA becomes expensive and its results can become inconsistent with results of earlier analyses conducted by other experts.

Therefore, the advisory system automatically combines finished HARA projects and supporting information in a knowledge base and searches it for useful recommendations during a new HARA. Useful recommendations are found by applying spreading activation on the spread graph of the knowledge base. The algorithm determines the most relevant nodes for a specific user query with predefined starting nodes and a search goal, e.g., finding possible hazards for a specific function.

In our preliminary case study, we examined a spread graph of this advisory system. This network is based on RDF Graph and consists of more than 118.000 edges (representing 45 predicates) and more than 48.000 nodes. It contains data from more than 150 HARA projects. A part of this spread graph is depicted in Figure 2. Basically, some functions, malfunctions, hazards, and safety goals are shown. Our expectation is, that the hazard originating from the unintentional closing of the sun roof, i.e., *contusion of body parts*, may also be relevant for the function *close boot lid*, as well as the associated safety goal. For the recommendation query *Show safety goal recommendations for Ins_Function_2*, we expect the special semantic relevance to be detected.

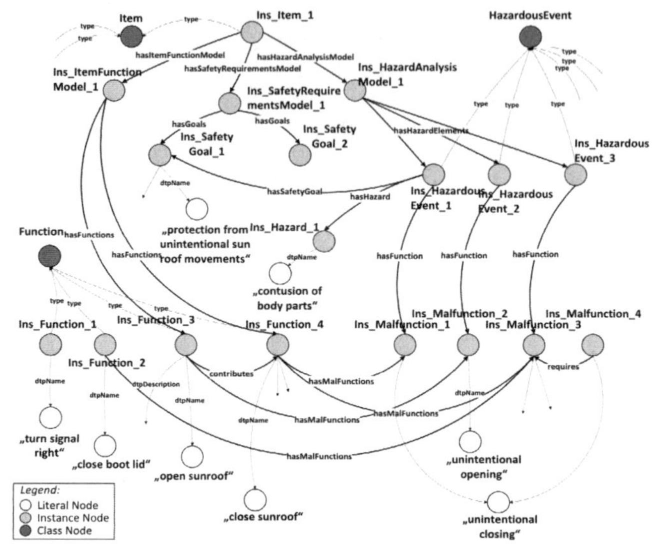

Figure 2. HARA Spread Graph - Extract from the Semantic Network.

B. Effective Skeleton of HARA Spread Graph

The spread graph shown partly in Figure 2 is the input for the skeleton creation process. Since the spread graph is an instance of a network model with concrete data, it does not necessarily contain all potential relations between each pair of nodes. Therefore, we retrieve an effective skeleton of the spread graph. Figure 3 depicts the effective skeleton of the HARA spread graph used for the presented advisory system. The used annotations in this skeleton are those described in Section III-F. The semantic center of the skeleton is the *skeleton core* which only contains representatives of instance nodes.

The effective skeleton of the network only consists of 37 node representatives and 94 edges. The maximum skeleton of the network only consists of 37 node representatives and 103 edges. The difference originates from the fact that in the concrete spread graph not all specified relationships are used at least once.

C. Analysis

Analyses are performed on the effective skeleton in Figure 3.

1) Distance Analysis: The diameter of the skeleton core in the example is 4. The diameter informs us about the necessary spreading steps for reaching each node representative at least once.

For the earlier mentioned query, we would start spreading at some node represented by $Ins\_Function$ and search for goal nodes represented by $Ins\_SafetyGoal$. The distance between those two node representatives is 3, which means that we have to spread for at least 3 pulses before any activation can reach the goal node. However, for more meaningful activation values, the influence of the other node representatives on the result is interesting, too. Therefore, a good spreading configuration ensures, that the activation values reached all node representative in the skeleton (6 pulses) before reaching the goal node representative (again 6 pulses). Altogether 12 pulses are therefore necessary. Of course, other spreading parameters could heavily influence the number of meaningful pulses, but at least the diameter provides some first insights.

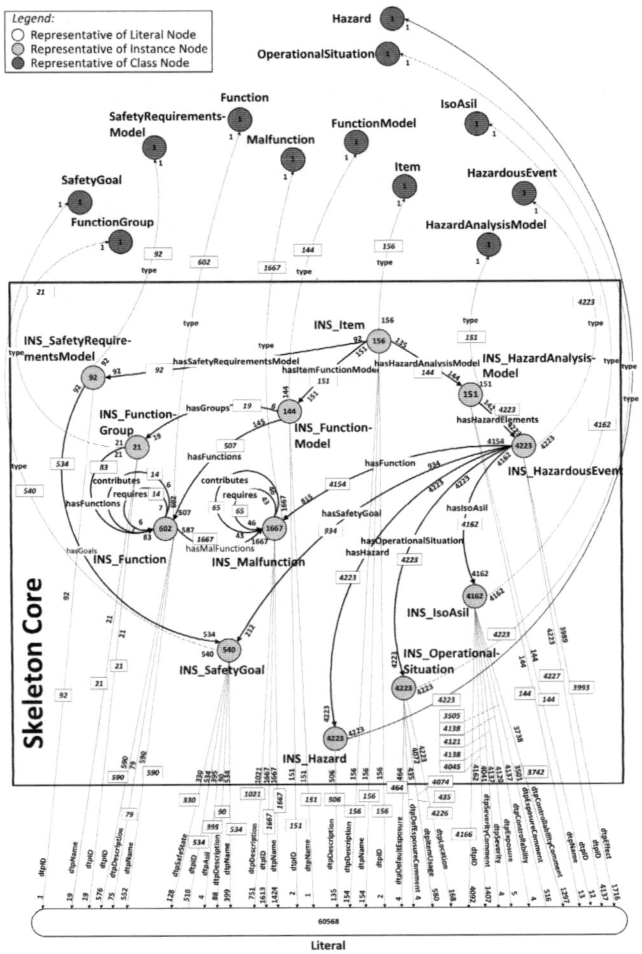

Figure 3. Skeleton of HARA Semantic Network.

2) Connectivity Analysis: We distinguish between high and low connector nodes. Low and high connector nodes are characterized by a high and low branching ratio, respectively. A high connector triple would be T_1*=(HazardousEvent, type, INS_HazardousEvent)* with a branching ratio of 4223, whereas T_2*=(INS_HazardousEvent, hasIsoAsil, INS_IsoAsil)* is a simple and low connector with a branching ratio of 1.

With T_1 being such a high connector, any configuration with a strong fan-out constraint would make it a sink, meaning that it would distribute almost no activation. In combination with an activation threshold, T_1 would probably distribute no activation at all. Since a sink does not contribute to the overall spreading result, such a configuration would make T_1 meaningless (except as a search goal).

VII. CONCLUSION AND FUTURE WORK

In this paper, we introduced semantic network skeletons as a new tool for analyzing semantic network properties and spreading activation configuration settings on semantic networks. The skeleton syntax was presented formally and visually. Furthermore, we described how a skeleton can be retrieved from a semantic network based on RDF Graph and explained analyses on network, node, and edge properties. Additionally, we described two effects observable while performing spreading activation and how skeleton analyses may support effect detection. We then presented our results in a case study on an advisory system for hazard analysis and risk assessment in the automotive domain and showed analyses on a real skeleton in order to optimize pre-configuration.

In this paper, only selected analyses were introduced. In future, description of more effects and their correlation with network properties and configuration settings can improve analysis results. Especially, new metric, measure, and ratio definitions can be helpful. A long term goal may be self-configured spreading activation, independently performing spreading activation without manual configuration. A short term goal is providing extensive guidelines for optimally configuring the spreading algorithm with respect to a given network. We furthermore plan on extended case studies experimenting with preconfigured spreading activation. Lastly, potential spreading activation micro-simulation can be examined. Skeletons can be valuable beyond utilization in the context of spreading activation. The compressed and summarized character of network skeletons might be useful for cognate disciplines also dealing with large semantic networks.

REFERENCES

[1] F. Crestani, "Application of Spreading Activation Techniques in Information Retrieval," Artificial Intelligence Review, vol. 11, 1997, pp. 453–482.

[2] M. R. Quillian, "Semantic Memory," in Semantic Information Processing, M. Minsky, Ed. MIT Press, 1968, pp. 216–270.

[3] A. M. Collins and E. F. Loftus, "A spreading activation theory of semantic processing," Psychological Review, vol. 82, no. 6, Nov. 1975, pp. 407–428.

[4] J. F. Sowa, Principles of Semantic Networks: Exploration in the Representation of Knowledge, J. F. Sowa and A. Borgida, Eds. Morgan Kaufmann, Jan. 1991.

[5] "RDF 1.1 Concepts and Abstract Syntax," W3C, W3C Recommendation, Feb. 2014.

[6] J. R. Anderson, "A Spreading Activation Theory of Memory," Journal of Verbal Learning and Verbal Behavior, vol. 22, 1983, pp. 261–295.

[7] F. Crestani and P. L. Lee, "Searching the web by constrained spreading activation," Information Processing and Management, vol. 36, no. 4, 2000, pp. 585–605.

[8] J. M. Álvarez, D. Berrueta, L. Polo, and J. E. Labra, "ONTOSPREAD: A Framework for Supporting the Activation of Concepts in Graph-Based Structures through the Spreading Activation Technique," in Information Systems, E-learning, and Knowledge Management Research, ser. Communications in Computer and Information Science, vol. 278. Springer Berlin Heidelberg, 2013, pp. 454–459.

[9] "SPARQL 1.1 Query Language," W3C, W3C Recommendation, Mar. 2013.

[10] ISO 26262 - Road vehicles - Functional safety, International Organization for Standardization, Nov. 2011.

[11] C. Maier, A. Schloske, and S. Bothe, "Studie zur Funktionalen Sicherheit in der Automobilbranche [Survey of Functional Safety in the Automotive Domain (ISO 26262)]," Fraunhofer Institute for Manufacturing Engineering and Automation (IPA), Tech. Rep., Mar. 2013.

AUTHOR INDEX

International Academy, Research,
and Industry Association (IARIA)
412 Derby Way
Wilmington, DE 19810

ISBN 978-1-5108-2313-6

CURRAN ASSOCIATES INC.
proceedings.com

Nineteenth International Conference on Emerging Security Information, Systems and Technologies (SECURWARE 2025)

Held at NetWare 2025

Barcelona, Spain
26-30 October 2025

IARIA